BUILD IT. FIX IT. OWN IT.

A BEGINNER'S GUIDE TO BUILDING AND UPGRADING A PC

Paul McFedries

que® 800 East 96th Street,
Indianapolis, Indiana 46240

Build It. Fix It. Own It. A Beginner's Guide to Building and Upgrading a PC

Copyright © 2008 by Que Publishing

All rights reserved. No part of this book shall be reproduced, stored in a retrieval system, or transmitted by any means, electronic, mechanical, photocopying, recording, or otherwise, without written permission from the publisher. No patent liability is assumed with respect to the use of the information contained herein. Although every precaution has been taken in the preparation of this book, the publisher and author assume no responsibility for errors or omissions. Nor is any liability assumed for damages resulting from the use of the information contained herein.

ISBN-13: 978-0-7897-3827-1
ISBN-10: 0-7897-3827-9

Library of Congress Cataloging-in-Publication Data:

McFedries, Paul.

  Build it, fix it, own it : a beginner's guide to building and upgrading a PC / Paul McFedries. — 1st ed.

    p. cm.

  ISBN 0-7897-3827-9

  1. Microcomputers—Design and construction—Amateurs' manuals. 2. Microcomputers—Upgrading—Amateurs' manuals. 3. Microcomputers—Maintenance and repair—Amateurs' manuals. I. Title.

  TK9969.M44 2008

  621.39'160288—dc22

                                2008014897

Printed in the United States of America

Third Printing: February 2009

Trademarks

All terms mentioned in this book that are known to be trademarks or service marks have been appropriately capitalized. Que Publishing cannot attest to the accuracy of this information. Use of a term in this book should not be regarded as affecting the validity of any trademark or service mark.

Warning and Disclaimer

Bulk Sales

Que Publishing offers excellent discounts on this book when ordered in quantity for bulk purchases or special sales. For more information, please contact

U.S. Corporate and Government Sales
1-800-382-3419
corpsales@pearsontechgroup.com

For sales outside the United States, please contact

International Sales
international@pearson.com

This Book Is Safari Enabled

The Safari® Enabled icon on the cover of your favorite technology book means the book is available through Safari Bookshelf. When you buy this book, you get free access to the online edition for 45 days.

Safari Bookshelf is an electronic reference library that lets you easily search thousands of technical books, find code samples, download chapters, and access technical information whenever and wherever you need it.

To gain 45-day Safari Enabled access to this book:

- Go to http://www.informit.com/onlineedition
- Complete the brief registration form.
- Enter the coupon code VJDU-65TC-SJE7-IXCN-PWLE.

If you have difficulty registering on Safari Bookshelf or accessing the online edition, please email customer-service@safaribooksonline.com.

Associate Publisher
Greg Wiegand

Acquisitions Editor
Rick Kughen

Development Editor
Rick Kughen

Managing Editor
Patrick Kanouse

Senior Project Editor
Tonya Simpson

Copy Editor
Megan Wade

Indexer
Ken Johnson

Proofreader
Linda Seifert

Technical Editor
Terri Stratton

Publishing Coordinator
Cindy Teeters

Book Designer
Anne Jones

Photography
Karen Hammond

Contents at a Glance

Table of Contents

Part II: PC Building and Upgrading Projects

About the Author

Paul McFedries is a full-time technical writer and passionate computer tinkerer. He is the author of more than 70 computer books that have sold more than three million copies worldwide. His recent titles include the Sams Publishing books *Windows Vista Unleashed* and *Windows Home Server Unleashed* and the Que Publishing books *Networking with Windows Vista*; *Formulas and Functions with Microsoft Excel 2007*; *Tricks of the Microsoft Office 2007 Gurus*; and *Microsoft Access 2007 Forms, Reports, and Queries*. Paul also is the proprietor of Word Spy (www.wordspy.com), a website devoted to tracking new words and phrases as they enter the English language.

Dedication

For Karen

Acknowledgments

In this book you learn that with a bit of know-how, a modicum of patience, and perhaps a screwdriver or two, anyone can build a computer from scratch all by themselves. This makes building a computer a *lot* different from publishing a book. Oh, sure, I *wrote* this book all by myself, but the finished product you're reading now was a group effort, no doubt about it. For proof, go back a bit and read the credits page, which lists everyone who had a finger in this particular publishing pie, and I thank them all for doing such a good job on this book. Some of those people I worked with directly, so I'd like to take a second to thank them personally. **Rick "Two Hats" Kughen** was both the book's acquisitions editor and its development editor, and I'm mighty glad on both counts because this book was a hoot to write, and Rick's editorial direction and suggestions were right on the money and made this book many notches better than it would have been otherwise. **Tonya Simpson** was the book's amazingly competent and organized project editor. **Megan Wade** was the book's copy editor, and besides dotting my i's and crossing my t's, Megan gave the book a consistent style and tone, which requires concentration, confidence, and an eagle eye. **Terri Stratton** was the book's technical editor, and I continue to be amazed at just how much Terri knows about almost all aspects of computing. Her experience and insights were very much welcome in this book. Finally, I'd be sorely remiss if I didn't also single out **Karen Hammond**, who took the wonderful photographs you see throughout this book.

We Want to Hear from You!

As the reader of this book, *you* are our most important critic and commentator. We value your opinion and want to know what we're doing right, what we could do better, what areas you'd like to see us publish in, and any other words of wisdom you're willing to pass our way.

As an associate publisher for Que Publishing, I welcome your comments. You can email or write me directly to let me know what you did or didn't like about this book—as well as what we can do to make our books better.

Please note that I cannot help you with technical problems related to the topic of this book. We do have a User Services group, however, where I will forward specific technical questions related to the book.

When you write, please be sure to include this book's title and author as well as your name, email address, and phone number. I will carefully review your comments and share them with the author and editors who worked on the book.

Email: feedback@quepublishing.com

Mail: Greg Wiegand
        Associate Publisher
        Que Publishing
        800 East 96th Street
        Indianapolis, IN 46240 USA

Reader Services

Visit our website and register this book at informit.com/register for convenient access to any updates, downloads, or errata that might be available for this book.

Introduction

*Man is a shrewd inventor, and is ever
taking the hint of a new machine from
his own structure, adapting some secret
of his own anatomy in iron, wood, and
leather, to some required function in the
work of the world.*

—Ralph Waldo Emerson, *English
    Traits*

*As technology advances, it reverses the
characteristics of every situation again
and again. The age of automation is
going to be the age of "do it yourself."*

—Marshall McLuhan

*Home-made, home-made! But aren't
we all?*

—Elizabeth Bishop, *Crusoe in England*

The 1950s were a hobbyist's paradise with magazines such as *Mechanix Illustrated* and *Popular Mechanics* showing the do-it-yourselfer how to build a go-kart for the kids and how to soup up his lawnmower with an actual motor! Fifty years later, we're now firmly entrenched in what some people are calling the age of tech DIY, where geeks of all persuasions—and both sexes—engage in various forms of digital tinkering and hardware hacking.

One of the main thrusts of this hobbyist renaissance is that it's better to make something yourself than to buy it. When you purchase something, you're really only renting it until its inevitable obsolescence. However, if you make it yourself, you own it and you can delay (often for a very long time) obsolescence by upgrading and repairing the device.

Unfortunately, building most digital devices isn't easy for the beginner because it requires soldering skills, working with complex tools such as multimeters, and knowing the difference between a resistor and a capacitor. However, there's one digital device that doesn't require any of these skills or knowledge, and so can be built by any curious and motivated beginner, a PC:

- All the parts you need—the case, power supply, motherboard, processor, memory, hard drive, expansion cards, and peripherals—are readily available online or from big-box retailers or electronics stores.

- All the tools you need—really not much more than a screwdriver or two, a pair of needle-nose pliers, and perhaps a nut driver—are part of most people's toolkits or can be easily obtained.

- All the techniques you need—inserting chips and cards, connecting cables, and tightening screws—are simple and straightforward.

Add to this the simple fact that building your own computer is much better than buying one because the machine you end up with is *exactly* the one you want, not some faceless machine designed for the masses and loaded with tons of crapware you never asked for and don't want. Besides, building your own PC is both educational and just plain fun, so it's no wonder that so many people nowadays are going (or would like to go) the build-it-yourself route.

Build It. Fix It. Own It!

Welcome, then, to *Built It. Fix It. Own It.*, the book that will be your guide on this build-it-yourself path. This book will show you everything you need to know to build a computer or upgrade an existing one. Even if you've never looked inside a computer and wouldn't know a motherboard from an expansion board or a CPU from a GPU, this book will give you the know-how and confidence to build a computer with your bare hands.

To that end, the first part of the book takes you through the various PC parts: from the case, motherboard, and power supply, to the processor, memory, hard drive, video card, sound card, and networking hardware. In each case, you learn how the hardware works, what it does, what types of hardware are available, and what to look for when buying the hardware. The first part of the book also includes a chapter full of tips, techniques, and cautionary tales for purchasing PC parts (see Chapter 7), a chapter that runs through all the basic skills you need to build and upgrade a PC (Chapter 8), and a chapter on how to scavenge parts from on old PC (see Chapter 9).

The second part of the book takes you through a series of projects. The first five chapters show you how to build five different types of PC: a basic business PC; a home theater PC; a high-performance PC; a killer gaming PC; and a budget PC. Another chapter shows you how to upgrade an old PC and you then learn how to put together a network that uses both wired and wireless connections. The final chapter in Part II explains how to maintain a PC, from cleaning the components to updating the motherboard BIOS and device drivers to basic hard drive maintenance.

Who Should Read This Book?

This book is aimed at budding computer hobbyists who want to try their hand at building a PC from scratch and at upgrading an old PC to get more life or performance out of it. This book should also appeal to people who have tried other books in the same field, only to find them too intimidating, too simplistic, or too cutesy.

To that end, this book includes the following features:

- Buyer's guides that enable you to make smart and informed choices when purchasing hardware
- Easy-to-follow explanations of key concepts for new users
- In-depth coverage of all topics for more experienced users
- Extensive use of clear and detailed photos to illustrate hardware and all building and upgrading techniques
- Tips, tricks, and shortcuts to make building and upgrading a PC easier and faster
- Real-world projects you can relate to
- A friendly and lightly humorous tone that I hope will help you feel at home with the subject and keep boredom at bay

Conventions Used in This Book

To make your life easier, this book includes various features and conventions that help you get the most out of this book and out of building a PC:

Steps	Throughout the book, I've broken many building, upgrading, and repairing tasks into easy-to-follow step-by-step procedures.
Things you type	Whenever I suggest that you type something, what you type appears in a **bold monospace** font.
Filenames, folder names, and code	These things appear in a `monospace` font.
Commands	Commands and their syntax use the `monospace` font, too. Command placeholders (which stand for what you actually type) appear in an *`italic monospace`* font.
Pull-down menu commands	I use the following style for all application menu commands: *Menu, Command*, where *Menu* is the name of the menu you pull down and *Command* is the name of the command you select. Here's an example: File, Open. This means you pull down the File menu and select the Open command.

This book also uses the following boxes to draw your attention to important (or merely interesting) information:

note The Note box presents asides that give you more information about the current topic. These tidbits provide extra insights that offer a better understanding of the task.

caution The all-important Caution box tells you about potential accidents waiting to happen. There are always ways to mess things up when you're working with computers. These boxes help you avoid those traps and pitfalls.

tip The Tip box tells you about methods that are easier, faster, or more efficient than the standard methods.

I

Getting to Know Your PC

The Barebones: The Motherboard, Case, and Power Supply

"Begin at the beginning," the King said gravely, "and go on till you come to the end: then stop."

—Lewis Carroll, *Alice's Adventures in Wonderland*

One of the things that you learn in this book is that, although building your own PC isn't difficult, the level of difficultly is directly related to how methodical you approach everything. This is particularly true when you're just starting out because—in the electronic equivalent of dotting your i's and crossing your t's—there are lots of little connections to be made, and missing out on just one or two can make all the difference between ending up with a working PC or a boat anchor.

So, in the spirit of methodicalness (yes, it's a word), in this chapter we begin at the beginning with the three most fundamental components of any computer: the motherboard to which everything else connects; the computer case, which holds everything together; and the power supply, which makes everything go. This chapter introduces you to these components, shows you why they are important, and gives you pointers on purchasing them for your PC-building projects.

Mobo Mojo: Understanding the Motherboard

The motherboard is a large printed circuit board that sits inside the computer case and performs a number of functions crucial to the functioning of the PC. In fact, I'm not exaggerating even a little when I say that the motherboard—it's also called the *mainboard* or the *mobo*—will be the single most important component in any computer you build. The motherboard you choose will determine, among other things, the processor you can use, the memory (how much and what type), the video card type, the hard drive type, and even the computer case.

What does the motherboard do? Lots of things, really, but most of them can be broken down into four main areas:

- **Supporting electronics**—The motherboard implements tons of electronics that serve to support many of the computer's basic functions. For example, all motherboards come with a number of *controllers*, chips that control hardware such as memory, hard drives, and keyboards.

- **Data pathways**—The motherboard implements the pathways, called *buses*, that your computer uses to transfer data.

- **Integrated peripherals**—All motherboards come with a collection of integrated devices. The most common of these are an integrated video card, integrated sound card, and integrated network card. Having these devices built right in to the motherboard saves money (because you don't have to purchase these components separately) and time (because you don't have to install these components). However, sometimes these components aren't of the highest quality, so many system builders opt for separate devices anyway.

- **Connectors galore**—The motherboard is the main connection point

> **note** The *processor*—also called the *central processing unit* or *CPU*—is the computer's most important and most powerful chip. You learn all about it in Chapter 2, "The Brains: The Central Processing Unit."

for almost everything that goes inside your PC. You use the motherboard to connect internal components such as the processor, memory, hard drives, CD or DVD drives, expansion cards, and power supply, as well as external components such as the keyboard, mouse, USB devices, and FireWire (IEEE 1394) devices.

note An *expansion card* (also sometimes called an *expansion board*, an *interface card*, an *adapter card*, or simply an *adapter*) is a circuit board that plugs into a slot on the motherboard. (See "Understanding Expansion Slot Types" later in this chapter). You learn about video and audio cards in Chapter 5, "Eyes to See and Ears to Hear: Video and Audio Hardware"; you learn about network cards in Chapter 6, "Getting Connected: Networking Hardware."

The motherboard also contains the *chipset*, which is the set of chips that control all the communication that goes on between components on the motherboard. Most chipsets are divided into two main chips: the northbridge and the southbridge. The *northbridge* (also sometimes called the *memory controller hub*) controls the lightning-speed communications between the processor, the memory, and the graphics expansion card (a separate card, not the integrated video). The pathway along which the northbridge communicates with the processor is called the *front-side bus* (FSB); the pathway that the northbridge uses to communicate with memory is called the *memory bus*. The *southbridge* (also sometimes called the *I/O controller hub*) handles communications between the slower input/output devices such as the hard drives, USB devices, and other types of expansion cards.

A Tour of a Typical Motherboard

To make good decisions about which type of motherboard to buy, and to know how your other PC components connect to the motherboard (and, of course, to claim Alpha Geek status the next time computers come up in a cocktail party conversation), you need to get familiar with the lay of the motherboard land. Fortunately, you don't need to know what all the typical motherboard's hundreds of components do—just the most common ones. Figure 1.1 points out these common features.

note Just so you know, the motherboard shown here is a DFI Infinity 975X/G. I should also mention that although this board is a fairly typical example of the species, the boards you deal with will likely come with a different set of features. For example, older boards might not have an IEEE 1394 header, whereas newer boards might not have a floppy drive or IDE header.

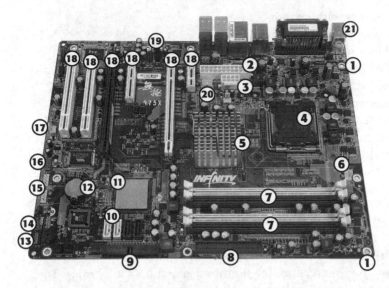

1. Mounting Holes
2. Main Power Connector
3. 12V Power Connector
4. Processor Socket
5. Northbridge
6. Processor Fan Header
7. Memory Sockets
8. IDE Connector
9. Floppy Drive Connector
10. Serial ATA Connectors
11. Southbridge
12. Battery
13. Speaker Header
14. Front Panel Header
15. USB Headers
16. IEEE-1394 Header
17. Front Chassis Fan Header
18. Expansion Slots
19. Front Panel Audio Header
20. Rear Chassis Fan Header
21. Back Panel Ports

FIGURE 1.1

Common features of a typical motherboard.

If the sheer number of features in Figure 1.1 seems a tad daunting at this point, don't sweat it. Most of the features are simple to explain, and the more complex ones I'll take you through in the next few chapters. For now, here's a summary of the features pointed out in Figure 1.1:

Mounting holes	These are the holes through which you'll screw the motherboard to the case mounting points.
Main power connector	Your power supply comes with a main power cable that connects here to give power to the rest of the motherboard and the devices attached to it.
12V power connector	Your power supply comes with a 12-volt power cable that connects here to give juice to the processor.
Processor socket	This is where you insert the processor.
Northbridge	This is the northbridge part of the motherboard's chipset. It's shown here with a heatsink in place to keep the chip from overheating.

→ To learn what a heatsink does, **see** "Keeping It Cool: Fans and Heatsinks," **p. 56**.

Processor fan header	This is the power connector for a fan that you attach to the processor to keep it cool.
Memory sockets	You use these sockets to insert memory modules.
IDE connector	This is where you insert the data cable from an Integrated Drive Electronics (IDE) hard drive or CD/DVD drive. Some older motherboards will have both a Primary and a Secondary IDE connector, although this newer board includes just a single connector.
Floppy drive connector	This is where you insert the data cable from a floppy disk drive (if you decide to add one to your system).
Serial ATA connectors	You use each of these connectors to insert the data cable from a Serial Advanced Technology Attachment (SATA) hard drive.

➜ For information on IDE and SATA, **see** "The Hard Drive Interface and Throughput," **p. 82**.

Southbridge	This is the southbridge part of the motherboard's chipset. It's shown here with a heatsink in place to keep the chip from overheating.
Battery	This battery maintains power to the onboard clock so the system can keep track of the current time even when the power is off. The battery also maintains system setup data, such as the system password.
Speaker header	This connector is for the case speaker.
Front panel header	This connector is used for front panel features such as the power button, reset button, and hard drive activity light.
USB headers	These are connectors for internal USB devices, or for any USB slots that appear on the front panel of the computer case.

IEEE 1394 header	This is the connector for an IEEE 1394 (FireWire) slot that might appear on the front panel of the computer case.
Front chassis fan header	This is the connector for a fan that you attach to the front of the computer case. See "Going with the Flow: Case Fans," later in this chapter.
Expansion slots	You use these slots to insert expansion cards such as a video card or wireless networking card.
Audio header	These are connectors for any audio ports that appear on the front panel of the computer case.
Rear chassis fan header	This is the connector for a fan that you attach to the rear of the computer case.
Back panel ports	These are the built-in ports you use to connect external devices to the motherboard. These ports stick out through a special plate that comes with the motherboard and that you attach to the back of the computer case.

The number of back panel ports you see depends on the motherboard: larger and more expensive motherboards offer more ports than smaller and cheaper boards. Figure 1.2 shows the ports that come with a high-end board.

Table 1.1 gives you a summary of the various ports pointed out in Figure 1.2, as well as a few other ports offered on some motherboards.

note Internal USB devices? Sure. For example, Logic Supply (www.logicsupply.com) offers a product called a USB Header Adapter, which you insert into a USB header. You can then plug a USB flash drive into the adapter and set up Windows Vista to use this drive for its ReadyBoost feature (which improves performance by writing frequently used bits of data to the flash drive). This way, you get the improved performance of ReadyBoost without having to give up an external USB slot.

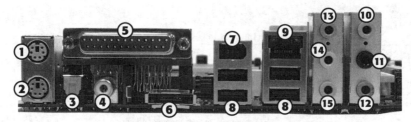

1. Mouse
2. Keyboard
3. Optical S/PDIF
4. Coaxial S/PDIF
5. Printer
6. eSATA
7. IEEE 1394
8. USB

9. Network
10. Center/Subwoofer
11. Rear Speaker
12. Side Speaker
13. Line In
14. Line Out
15. Mic In

FIGURE 1.2

Different motherboards offer different collections of back panel ports.

Table 1.1	Back Panel Ports Found on Many Motherboards	
Port	**Color**	**Use This Port to Connect**
Mouse	Green	A PS/2 mouse
Keyboard	Purple	A PS/2 keyboard
Optical S/PDIF	Gray	A digital audio device that supports digital optical audio port
Coaxial S/PDIF	Orange	A digital audio device that supports digital coaxial audio
Parallel	Burgundy	A printer
eSATA	Black	An external SATA device (such as a hard drive)
IEEE 1394	Gray	Any IEEE 1394 (FireWire) device
USB	Black	Any USB device
Network	Black	A network device such as a switch, router, or broadband modem
Center/Subwoofer	Orange	The center/subwoofer speaker in a surround-sound 5.1-channel or 7.1-channel audio configuration
Rear Speaker	Black	The rear speakers in a surround-sound 4-channel, 5.1-channel, or 7.1-channel audio configuration
Side Speaker	Gray	The side speakers in a surround-sound 7.1-channel audio configuration
Line In	Light Blue	An audio device such as a digital audio tape player or CD player
Line Out	Lime Green	Headphones, 2-channel speakers, or the front speakers in a surround-sound 4-channel, 5.1-channel, or 7.1-channel audio configuration

Continues

Table 1.1   Continued

Port	Color	Use This Port to Connect
Mic In	Pink	A microphone
Serial	Teal	(Not shown) A modem
VGA	Dark Blue	(Not shown) A monitor via its VGA connector
DVI	White	(Not shown) A monitor via its DVI connector
Composite Video	Yellow	(Not shown) A TV set via its composite video connector
S-Video	Black	(Not shown) A TV set via its S-Video connector
Game	Gold	(Not shown) A game controller (joystick)
Wireless	Gold	(Not shown) A wireless networking antenna

Understanding Expansion Slot Types

Back in Figure 1.1, I pointed out the various expansion slots on the typical motherboard. All mobos come with at least one expansion slot, and most come with four to six slots. These slots are an important part of the motherboard because they enable you to upgrade your system by inserting expansion cards. For example, if your motherboard comes with integrated video capabilities but you want to use your homebrew system to play games or edit video, then you need to insert a more powerful graphics card. Other common expansion cards add or upgrade your system's sound, enable you to watch and record TV signals, give you faster wired or wireless networking, or add more USB or IEEE 1394 ports.

As you might have noticed in Figure 1.1, not all expansions slots have the same configuration. There have been a number of slot standards over the years and, just to add more complication to our lives, each standard uses a different type of slot. So it's important to understand that if you want to add an expansion card to your system, that card must use a connector that fits one of your motherboard slots. That's the bad news. The good news is that these days you only have to worry about four slot types, although in the list that follows I've thrown in a fifth type just for the heck of it:

PCI   PCI (Peripheral Connect Interface) has been the standard expansion slot type for at least 10 years. Most motherboards come with several PCI slots, as shown in Figure 1.3. Almost all expansion cards come in a PCI version.

PCI Express x16	Regular PCI is quite slow (the PCI bus speed is typically 33MHz) and is in fact too slow for intensive graphics work. To remedy this, PCI Express (also called PCIe or PCI-X) was created a few years ago. PCI Express is much faster than PCI, with a bus speed of 5,000MHz. Most decent mobos now come with at least one PCI Express x16 slot (see Figure 1.4). The *x16* designation tells you the width of the PCI Express bus: 16 bits.
PCI Express x4	This version PCI Express uses a bus width of just 4 bits. Some motherboards come with one or two PCI Express x4 slots (see Figure 1.3).
PCI Express x1	This version of PCI Express uses a bus width of just 1 bit. Most motherboards now come with at least a couple of PCI Express x1 slots (see Figure 1.3).

1. PCI Slots
2. PCI Express x1 Slot
3. PCI Express x4 Slot
4. PCI Express x16 Slots

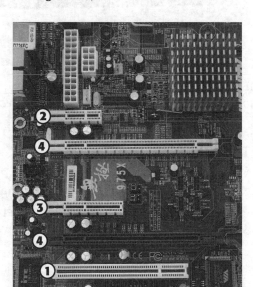

FIGURE 1.3

Most modern mobos offer a selection of PCI and PCI Express expansion slots.

AGP

AGP (Accelerated Graphics Port) is an older standard for graphics expansion cards. It has now been almost completely replaced by PCI Express, but a few low-end motherboards still come with AGP slots (see Figure 1.4).

AGP Slot

FIGURE 1.4

Older and cheaper mainboards offer an AGP slot instead of PCI Express.

Sizing Up Motherboard Form Factors

The motherboard might be the most complex (by far) of the components that you'll use when building your PC, but fortunately that complexity doesn't extend to the motherboard *form factors*, which tell you the size and general feature set in each motherboard. There are actually many form factors, but first-time system builders need only worry about three of them: ATX, microATX, and Mini-ITX. Figure 1.5 shows these three types side by side.

note A new PCI Express standard is just starting to appear: PCI Express 2.0. This new standard offers double the bandwidth of PCI Express and is backward compatible with PCI Express devices (which means you'll be able to insert PCI Express expansion cards in PCI Express 2.0 slots). Expect to see motherboards with PCI Express slots in 2008, although probably only at the high end of the market.

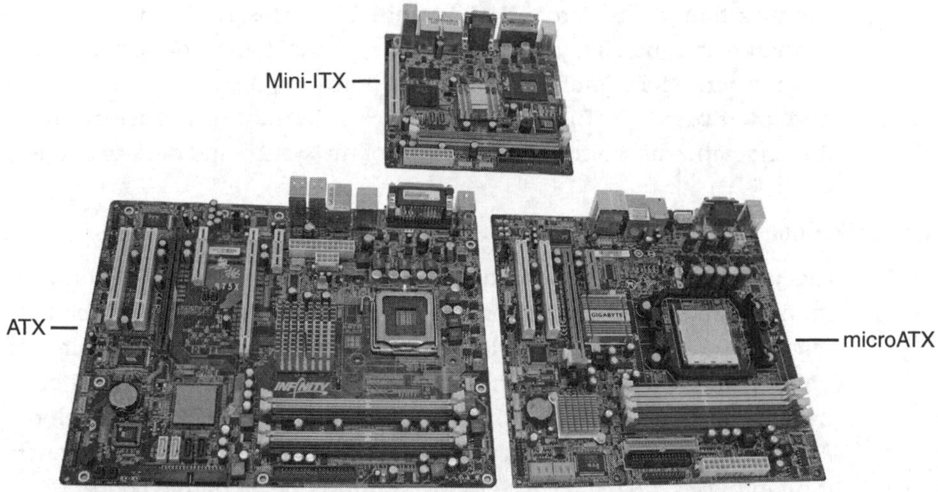

Mini-ITX —

ATX —

— microATX

FIGURE 1.5

Comparing the ATX, microATX, and Mini-ITX motherboard form factors.

ATX: The Standard

The ATX (advanced technology extended) form factor is the current motherboard standard. It measures 12 inches wide and 9.6 inches deep (if you're on the metric system, that's 305mm wide and 244mm deep), which makes it the biggest of the three form factors.

That size is the main benefit of using an ATX board because it means you get two advantages compared to the smaller microATX and Mini-ITX boards:

- You get more of everything: more memory slots, more expansion slots, more drive connectors, and a larger selection of back panel ports.

- You get extra room to work with and configure your system. The larger layout of an ATX motherboard makes inserting components easier and there's less chance of one component not fitting because another component is in the way.

However, using the ATX form factor does have some downsides. For one thing, ATX motherboards are the most expensive, so they're not always the best choice if you're on a budget. Perhaps more importantly for a first-time builder, ATX boards are more

note With motherboard dimensions, when I say "deep" I mean as measured from the top of the board to the bottom, and when I say "top" I mean the side that appears topmost when you orient the motherboard with the back panel ports on the left.

1

complex than their microATX and Mini-ITX cousins, so they take longer to configure and there's a greater chance to miss a connection or make the wrong connection. Finally, ATX motherboards require either a full-tower or mid-tower case (see "That's About the Size of It: Case Form Factors" later in this chapter), which also adds to the cost of the system and the size of the system.

microATX: Good for First-Timers

Given the (admittedly minor) negatives associated with the ATX form factor, many beginning PC builders opt for a microATX mobo the first time out. The microATX (also sometimes called mATX) form factor measures 9.6 inches wide and 9.6 inches deep (for the metrically inclined, that's 244mm wide and 244mm deep). In other words, a microATX board has the same depth as an ATX board, but it's 2.4 inches narrower. That might not sound like much, but it often makes a big difference in the features offered on the board:

- Most microATX boards offer only two memory slots instead of four (or even six) on ATX boards.

- A typical microATX board offers only two or three expansion slots, although on most newer microATX boards you get one PCI Express x16 slot.

The relatively small number of expansion slots is offset by the fact that most microATX motherboards come with integrated video, audio, and networking. In other words, if you just want to build a very basic system that doesn't cost a lot of money, microATX is the perfect choice because not only is the motherboard itself going to be cheaper, but you also don't have to fork out any extra cash for graphics, sound, and networking. It's the faster way to go, too, because not having to install or configure these three components means that building your system will take that much less time.

caution Yes, going with integrated video, audio, and networking is cheaper and easier, but just remember that on most microATX mobos these components are not usually of the highest quality. They're fine for simple systems, but the low-end video means you won't be able to play certain games or run Windows Vista's Aero interface; low-end audio means you won't get Dolby digital sound; and low-end networking means your network connection might be limited to 100Mbps. Fortunately, we're starting to see microATX motherboards that come with better graphics, Dolby sound, and gigabit networking, so shop around.

Mini-ITX: The Small Form Factor Choice

If you're looking to build a PC that's as unobtrusive as possible or that will fit into a very small space, check out the Mini-ITX form factor, which measures a mere 6.7 inches (170mm) on all four sides. The small size of Mini-ITX motherboards makes them the perfect choice for building a so-called *small form factor (SFF)* PC, which is a computer with a drastically smaller footprint than a traditional PC. Of course, the smaller size means you get far fewer features than even a microATX motherboard:

- Many Mini-ITX boards offer only one memory slot (although some come with two).

- Most Mini-ITX boards offer only one PCI expansion slot (but boards are available with either two PCI slots or one PCI slot and one PCI Express x16 slot).

Still, upgradeability and expandability are really beside the point with these motherboards (particularly because all Mini-ITX boards come with integrated video, audio, and networking). You get a Mini-ITX motherboard because you want to create a small system, period.

You might be wondering whether there are any motherboard form factors even smaller than the Mini-ITX. Why, yes, there are. The Nano-ITX form factor measures 4.7 inches (120mm) on all sides, and the impossibly small Pico-ITX form factor is jaw-droppingly small at just 3.9 inches (100mm) wide and 2.8 inches (72mm) deep. Figure 1.6 shows examples of the Mini-ITX, Nano-ITX, and Pico-ITX form factors.

FIGURE 1.6

The Mini-ITX, Nano-ITX, and the cute-as-a-button Pico-ITX motherboard form factors.

Buying a Motherboard

The inherent complexity of motherboards makes them one of the more diffi-cult PC components to purchase, particularly if you're new to the PC construc-tion game. It doesn't help that most motherboards come with head-scratching names such as GA-P35C-DS3R and NF650iSLIT-A. (Fortunately, some mother-board makers are breaking away from these geek-friendly names. For exam-ple, ASUS has mobos with names such as Striker Extreme and Commando.) The best advice I can give you is to stick with the larger motherboard manu-facturers because they almost always use quality parts and construction tech-niques and offer good support. Here's a list of motherboard manufacturers I recommend:

Abit (www.abit.com)

ASUS (www.asus.com)

Biostar (www.biostar.com.tw)

DFI (www.dfi.com.tw)

ECS (www.ecs.com.tw)

EVGA (www.evga.com)

Foxconn (www.foxconn.com)

Gigabyte (www.giga-byte.com)

Intel (www.intel.com)

MSI (www.msi.com.tw)

XFX (www.xfxforce.com)

Here are a few points to bear in mind when purchasing a motherboard:

- **Determine your system needs**—If you want maximum expandabil-ity and don't mind paying a little extra, choose an ATX motherboard; for a smaller, less-expensive, and easier-to-build system, choose a microATX board; for an SFF PC, choose a Mini-ITX board.

- **Get the right processor socket**—If you want to use an Intel Celeron, Pentium Dual Core, Core 2 Duo, Core 2 Quad, or Core 2 Extreme processor, get a Socket 775 motherboard. If you want to use an AMD Sempron, Athlon 64, Athlon 64 X2, or Athlon 64 FX processor, in most cases you need a Socket AM2 motherboard, although some Athlon 64 FX processors require a Socket F motherboard. (Again, see Chapter 2 to learn what all the processor designations mean.)

- **Look for a well-documented board**—All motherboards document the board's features with text printed on the circuit board's surface.

1

That's a good thing, but some motherboard manufacturers make the text impossibly small to read. A well-designed board labels (and color-codes) each connector clearly, which makes life much easier when it comes time to build your system.

- **Check the motherboard's processor and memory support—** Before buying any motherboard, go to the manufacturer's website and find the page that details the board's specifications. This page will tell you exactly which processors you can use with the board and exactly what types and speed of memory you can use.

- **Look for motherboard/processor bundles**—Some retailers will sell you a motherboard and processor together for a cheaper price than the two components would cost if you purchased them separately. This not only saves you money, but also guarantees that you get a processor that works with your motherboard.

- **Check the feature set on microATX boards**—Before buying a microATX board, examine the board's specs to see exactly what you're getting. A bargain board might offer only a couple of PCI slots and low-end integrated video, audio, and networking. For a few dollars more, you may be able to get a board that has more slots (including a PCI Express slot) and better integrated peripherals.

The Case Is Your Base

The computer case's job is to act as a kind of high-tech house for the rest of your PC pieces. In this chapter—indeed, throughout this book—I ignore peripheral doodads such as the keyboard, mouse, and monitor. So, with the exception of some of the external network knickknacks that I talk about in Chapter 16, "Putting Together a Network," every bit of hardware you learn about in this book will find itself inserted into some cozy nook inside the case. As you'll see, the case you choose needs to be compatible with some of the other components you select, and it needs to be the right size for your needs and for the space where it will reside in your home or office. Besides these necessary-but-dull considerations, the case you choose should also have a look that suits your style, from the straight edges and one-color finish of a buttoned-down business PC to the curvilinear, multihued colors of a gaming PC.

In this section, you learn all the basic case parts, you find out about case form factors and designs, and you get a buyer's guide for purchasing a case.

Buttons, Bezels, and Bays: A Case Parts List

Computer cases seem like simple affairs, but there are actually quite a few bits and pieces you need to understand. Let's start with what's on the outside:

Power button	This button turns on the computer's power if it's currently off, or it turns off the power if the machine is currently on. With some operating systems, you can configure the power button to make the computer enter sleep mode.
Reset button	This button shuts off the computer briefly and then turns it back on. Note that many cases don't come with a Reset button these days.
Activity lights	These LEDs glow when the computer's power is turned on and when the hard drive is active.
Readout	Some of the fancier cases come with a readout that tells you things like the internal temperature of the case.
Front ports	These are ports for things like a headphone, a microphone, one or more USB devices, and a FireWire device. These are usually more convenient to use than the computer's rear ports.
Front panel	This is a door that swings open to reveal the case's external drive bays (which I discuss in a second), so you can insert a disc into a DVD drive or insert a memory card into a card reader.
Front bezel	This is an access panel that comprises the front of the case (and includes the front panel). You remove the front bezel to insert a device into or remove a device from an external drive bay.
Side panel	This is an access panel the comprises the side of the case. You remove the side panel to access the inside of the case. (Many cases have panels on both sides for easier installation of things such as power supplies.)
Lock	Some cases come with a lock so no one else can open up your case and mess with your machine.

Window	This is a plastic insert that enables you and your friends to see inside the computer. Some case fans (discussed later in the "Going with the Flow: Case Fans" section) come with lights to illuminate the inside of the case.
I/O plate	This is where the motherboard's input/output (I/O) shield appears. This contains the motherboard's ports for the monitor, mouse, keyboard, USB devices, network cable, and so on.
Slot covers	You remove these covers when you attach a circuit board such as a video card to the motherboard. The circuit board's ports (such as a video card's monitor port) are exposed through the slot.
Power supply bay	This is where the external portion of the power supply unit appears.
Carry handles	Some cases come with handles to make them easier to lug from one place to another.

Figures 1.7, 1.8, and 1.9 point out many of these parts.

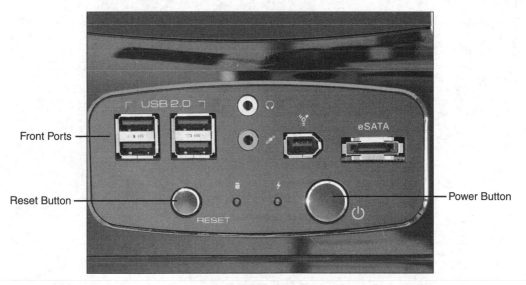

FIGURE 1.7

Buttons and ports on the front of a computer case.

Front Bezel —

— Front Panel

FIGURE 1.8

The front panel and front bezel of a computer case.

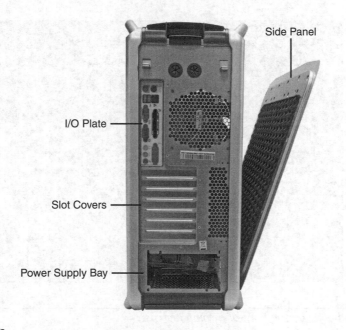

Side Panel

I/O Plate —

Slot Covers —

Power Supply Bay —

FIGURE 1.9

The side panel (open) and carrying handles of a computer case.

Here's a summary of some of the key features you'll find inside most computer cases:

Motherboard mounting panel	This takes up most of one side of the case's innards, and it's where you attach the motherboard (technically, the mounting points on which the motherboard sits). Some cases use a removable mounting tray, which is slick because it allows you to remove the tray and mount the motherboard without fumbling around inside the case.
5.25-inch drive bays	These are slots into which you install 5.25-inch-wide devices such as a CD or DVD drive or memory card reader. The fronts of these devices are exposed (via the case's front panel) to enable you to insert discs or memory cards.
3.5-inch drive bays	These are slots into which you install 3.5-inch-wide devices. One or more of these slots might be exposed to give you front-panel access to devices such as a floppy disk drive or tape drive. However, most of these slots are enclosed within the case and are used to install hard drives.
Fans	Most cases come with at least one and as many as four fan mounts, to which you attach cooling fans to keep cool air circulating within the case. See "Going with the Flow: Case Fans," later in this chapter.
Cables	These connect various case features to the motherboard. For example, the power switch has a cable that connects it to the power connector on the motherboard.
Soundproofing	Some larger cases come with soundproofing material on the sides to reduce noise from the fans and power supply.

Figures 1.10 and 1.11 point out many of these features.

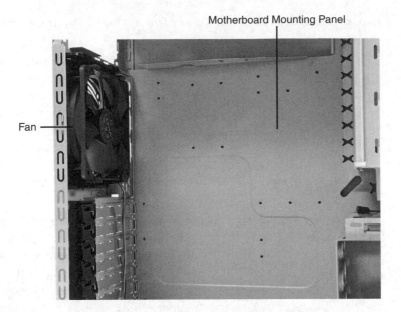

Motherboard Mounting Panel

Fan

FIGURE 1.10

The motherboard mounting panel and a fan inside a computer case.

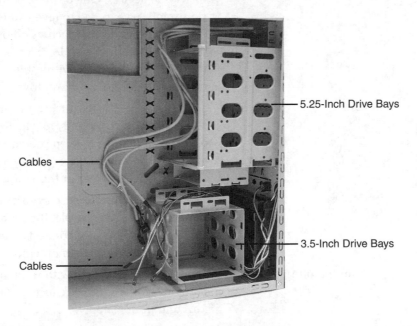

5.25-Inch Drive Bays

Cables

3.5-Inch Drive Bays

Cables

FIGURE 1.11

Drive bays and cables inside a computer case.

That's About the Size of It: Case Form Factors

The case form factor refers to the overall shape and size of the case, and it runs the gamut from behemoth full-tower cases to teensy mini-ITX cases. In general, the bigger the case, the more room you have inside to add devices. However, the bigger the case, the heavier the resulting computer, the more room it takes up, and the harder it is to move.

There are many form factors, but I'll keep things simple and discuss just the five most common:

Full tower   This is the big boy of the case world (see Figure 1.12). Full-tower cases are huge, and that size gives you tons of room for expansion: typically, four or five 5.25-inch drive bays and five or six 3.5-inch drive bays. You also have lots of room to work inside the case, so installing parts such as the motherboard, power supply, hard drives, and expansion cards is easy because they don't overlap each other as they often do in smaller cases. However, these cases are always very heavy, take up a lot of room under your desk, and are often noisy because they require extra fans for cooling.

Mid tower   This is the most common case form factor because it gives you a good trade-off between size and convenience. That is, a standard mid-tower case is big enough to allow for expansion in the future (typically, three or four 5.25-inch bays and three or four 3.5-inch bays) and to offer an internal work area that's not too cramped; it's also small enough that you won't break your back moving it (see Figure 1.12). Mid-tower cases also can accept the most common power supply and motherboard types, so you have lots of flexibility when designing or upgrading a system.

Micro tower   This form factor is great if you don't have much room. Typically only about 9 inches high (see Figure 1.13), micro-tower cases are as cute as a button and as light as a feather. On the downside, you don't get much room for expansion (typically, just two 5.25-inch bays and two 3.5-inch bays) and working inside a micro-tower case requires patience and a steady hand. Note, too, that only a smaller motherboard—usually either microATX or Mini-ITX—will fit inside this form factor.

Mini-ITX

This is the smallest form factor that's still relatively common (see Figure 1.13). Mini-ITX cases are usually no more than a few inches high, so they're small enough to fit almost anywhere. They almost always use external power supplies, so that frees up a bit more room

note I mentioned the small form factor PC earlier in this chapter, and I associated the SFF PC with a Mini-ITX motherboard. So you might think that only Mini-ITX cases qualify for the SFF label, but in practice that's not true. If you hear people talking about an SFF PC, they're quite often talking about a computer in a micro-tower case.

inside the case. However, you still don't get much room. After you add the Mini-ITX motherboard, you usually have a room for only a slimline optical drive (the type you see in notebook computers), a 2.5-inch hard drive, and perhaps a couple of circuit boards. All this means there's little room to grow with this form factor, but it's possible to build powerful little machines that are not much bigger than a dictionary.

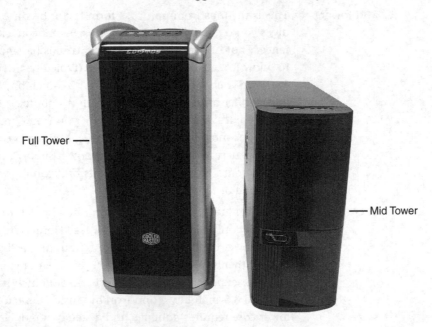

Full Tower

Mid Tower

FIGURE 1.12

The full-tower and mid-tower form factors.

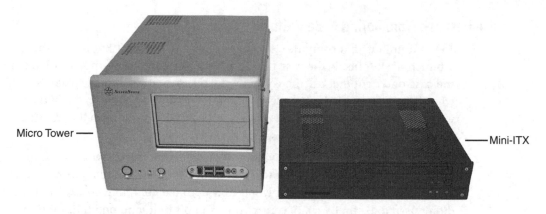

Micro Tower —   — Mini-ITX

FIGURE 1.13

The micro-tower and Mini-ITX form factors.

HTPC
This form factor stands for home theater PC, and in terms of overall dimensions it's very close to a mid-tower case. However, an HTPC case is designed to lie on its side (somewhat like the old desktop computers that were once common). Most importantly, however, a typical HTPC doesn't look like a computer at all. Instead, as you can see in Figure 1.14, it looks more like a receiver or other home theater component. The idea is to build a computer to use as the hub of your home theater system, and by using this type of case, it will blend in with your existing audio and video components.

FIGURE 1.14

An HTPC case helps your computer blend in with the rest of your home theater components.

Case Designs: From Boring to Beautiful

To the uninitiated, a computer is a single device. They don't know that there's a bunch of stuff inside the case that forms the *real* computer—they just look at the case and treat *that* as "the computer." This isn't surprising because it's what those of us who don't understand much about, say, toasters or TV do with those devices. I don't know diddley about what goes on inside a toaster, so to me "the toaster" is what I see from the outside.

And just as you when you're buying a toaster you might base your decision on how the toaster looks and how it will fit in with your kitchen decor, so too might you use the same criteria when considering a computer case. Things didn't used to be that way, of course. It wasn't all that long ago that all (non-Apple) PC cases looked exactly the same: beige boxes with sharp corners. Yawn.

Nowadays, however, case designs have become positively beautiful. Yes, you can still get a basic box if that's all you want. However, it's now possible to add frills such as side window so you can peer inside; illuminated case fans to make things glow; decals to add flames and other finishing touches; and refreshingly curved surfaces that can make your PC so good-looking that you won't want to hide it under your desk. Figure 1.15 compares a basic box case and a more adventuresome case with lots of nice touches.

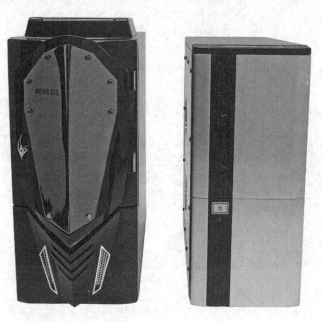

FIGURE 1.15

Case styles range from the basic box to curvilinear creations that'll have passersby doing double-takes.

Going with the Flow: Case Fans

Modern computers generate heat—lots and lots of heat. The biggest culprit is the processor, but your typical high-end graphics card can also raise the temperature in a hurry. You normally keep these components cool by adding devices such as heatsinks and fans to dissipate the heat (more on this in Chapter 2).

➔ To learn about processor cooling, **see** "Keeping It Cool: Fans and Heatsinks," **p. 56**.

However, moving that heat away from the processor or graphics card just lets it build up inside the case, which doesn't do the rest of your PC's components much good. To avoid this heat build-up, almost all cases come with at least a couple of mounts for fans, and some cases come with three or more. The two main fan types are as follows:

note The fan mounts in your case usually accept only fans of a certain width. The most common widths are 80mm and 120mm (which you might also see written as 8cm and 12cm), although some cases use widths such as 60mm and 90mm. Before purchasing fans, check the case specifications to see which size fans to buy. Another important fan spec to check is the noise level, expressed in decibels (dBA); values under 30dBA are quiet. Finally, also check the fan's *airflow*, which tells you how much air the fan moves, expressed in cubic feet per minute (CFM); values of 70 CFM or more are good.

Intake fan   This type of fan usually mounts on the front of the case, and its job is to bring air into the case. This helps cool the case because the air from outside the case is almost always cooler than the air inside the case.

Exhaust fan   This type of fan usually mounts on the rear of the case, and its job is to send air out of the case. This helps keep the case cool by getting rid of whatever hot air has built up inside the case.

The intake and exhaust fans work together to flow air through the case, thus keeping the PC's internal temperature relatively steady. Many high-end cases come with fans preinstalled, but on most cases you need to purchase the case fans separately. Figure 1.16 shows a couple of typical case fans.

tip If your case has a side panel window, crank up the cool factor by purchasing fans that come with LEDs that light up the interior of the case.

FIGURE 1.16

Add fans to your case to keep things cool.

Buying a Case

Buying a computer case involves making a few decisions about what you want in a case. Some of these decisions will be practical (how many drive bays do I need?), and some will be more aesthetic (do I want a side window?). However, unlike most electronic components, you don't need to spend lots of money to get a case that will get the job done—particularly if you're on a budget. Yes, you can spend $750 and up to get a case that nearly qualifies as a work of art, but you can also fork out just $75 and get a no-frills case that will still do a good job housing the rest of your PC.

There are a lot of case manufacturers out there, most of whom make good cases. To help you narrow the field a bit, here's a list of manufacturers I recommend:

Antec (www.antec.com)

Apevia (www.apevia.com)

Coolermaster (www.coolermaster.com)

Lian-Li (www.lian-li.com)

NZXT (www.nzxt.com)

Thermaltake (www.thermaltake.com)

note Let me give you an idea about just how crucial case fans are to the overall operation and health of your system. I once built a computer that would power up fine, but then it would shut right back down again after about 15 or 20 seconds. I triple-checked the connections, regreased the processor's heatsink, you name it. Nothing solved the problem. Then I decided to check the case fans. Sure enough, I'd installed the fan in the back of the case backward. This was supposed to be the exhaust fan, but now it was acting as another intake fan. Hot air had no way to escape the case, so things quickly got so hot that the processor shut down the system automatically. When I reversed the back fan so that it would act as an exhaust fan, the system booted normally!

Silverstone (www.silverstonetek.com)

Ultra (www.ultraproducts.com)

Zalman (www.zalman.com)

Here are a few points to bear in mind when purchasing a case:

- **Match your motherboard**—The most important thing a case must do is hold your PC's motherboard. Therefore, before buying any case, check the specifications to ensure that the case supports the type of motherboard you're using.

- **Give yourself room to maneuver**—As a general rule, the smaller the case, the harder it is to build and upgrade a PC. That's because, by design, small cases cram everything more closely together to make things fit. That gives you more internal options (for example, more drive bays), but it also means that things start to overlap. For example, a large graphics card might sit over the motherboard hard drive connectors, so the only way to connect or disconnect a hard drive cable is to remove the graphics card. Therefore, I always recommend that beginning PC builders get at least a mid-tower case so they have extra room to work. If you want lots of room, though, get a full-tower.

- **Look for a tool-free design**—Old-time cases had screws everywhere: the side panels, the drive bays, the slot covers, you name it. In many modern cases, however, all these components come with special connectors that enable you to open the case, add a DVD drive or hard drive, or install a circuit board without using tools.

- **Keep it simple**—Case bells and whistles such as several front panel connectors and LED readouts are fun, but each one of those components must be connected to the motherboard. This can complicate the installation and create a real mess of cables inside the computer. By all means, get a case with some front connectors for the convenience, but keep them to a minimum to keep your installation as simple as possible.

- **Watch out for sharp edges**—If you're perusing cases in a store, always check the case corners and edges for burrs and other sharp metal pieces. Cheaper cases always have these nasty bits, and inevitably blood will flow if you buy such a case.

- **Get your power supply separately**—Many cases come with the power supply preinstalled. That saves you a step, but sometimes the power supply unit isn't of the highest quality. In general, you're better off buying the power supply separately, as described in the next section.

1

Power to the PC: The Power Supply Unit

I know what you're probably thinking at this point: "Power supply? Dude, what can you possibly have to say about the power supply? It's just a box." Au contraire, mon frére. You can easily make a case that the power supply (sometimes called the PSU, short for *power supply unit*) is one of the three most important components in any system (the other two being the motherboard and the processor). Why? Because without the power supply, your PC—no matter how lovingly handcrafted—is nothing but an oversized paperweight. Almost every aspect of your PC requires a direct current (DC) source, and that source is the power supply. However, it isn't enough that the PSU doles out the watts to the motherboard and everything connected to it. The PSU must also supply that electrical power smoothly and efficiently, and a failure to do this (a symptom of many a cheap PSU) is often the cause of system glitches and crashes that are otherwise inexplicable. Low-end power supplies are also prone to simply dying, which at best shuts down your PC, but at worst can damage other components.

In short, skimping on the power supply for your computer is really just asking for glitches, crashes, and other bad things to happen. Of all the components you choose for your custom PC, the power supply should be the one on which you spend a few extra bucks to get a high-quality unit.

Getting to Know the Power Supply

From the standpoint of a first-time PC builder, power supplies are relatively simple affairs that don't require tons of research or know-how. However, there are a few things you need to know to make the right choice when deciding on which power supply to get for your system:

Form factor

Like motherboards and cases, power supplies also come in different form factors that specify the dimensions of the power supply unit, as well as the types of motherboard power connections the unit supports. By far the most common is the ATX form factor (see Figure 1.17), which fits all ATX cases and most microATX cases. The EPS form factor is the same size as the ATX but uses different connectors, as described in the next item.

FIGURE 1.17

A typical ATX form factor power supply.

Power connectors   These are the main power connectors that supply power to the motherboard and the 12V power connector that supplies power to the processor. The three different combinations you might come across are as follows:

ATX 1.3   This older version of the ATX form factor uses a 20-pin main connector and a 4-pin 12V connector.

ATX 2.2   This more recent version of the ATX form factor uses a 24-pin main connector and a 4-pin 12V connector (see Figure 1.18).

EPS   This form factor uses a 24-pin main connector and an 8-pin 12V connector (called EPS12V; see Figure 1.19).

Other connectors   A good power supply comes with a variety of wires so you can provide power to different types of components. Most power supplies come with wires for CD and DVD drives, older hard drives, and floppy drives. Most units should also have wires for SATA hard drives and for direct connections to high-end graphics cards.

24-Pin Main
Connector

4-Pin 12V
Connector

FIGURE 1.18

The ATX 2.2 form factor uses a 24-pin main connector and a 4-pin 12V connector.

8-Pin 12V
Connector

24-Pin Main
Connector

FIGURE 1.19

The EPS form factor uses a 24-pin main connector and an 8-pin 12V connector.

Watts

Perhaps the most important consideration with any power supply is the maximum number of watts the unit can handle. All your system's components—from the motherboard to the processor to the expansion cards to the drives—require a certain number of watts of power to function. Add up those watts and you get the total wattage of your PC; your power supply's maximum wattage must exceed that value. Of course, I don't expect you to actually add up the watts required by all your components! Instead, here are some general guidelines based on system type:

System	Recommended Wattage
Budget PC	300W
Basic Business PC	400W
Home Theater PC	400W
High Performance PC	500W
Gaming PC	600W

Buying a Power Supply

By far the best advice I can give you about buying a power supply is this: buy a brand name. You might pay a few more dollars, but you'll be assured of getting a power supply that uses quality parts; is at least relatively quiet; and provides solid, smooth power to all your components. Here's a list of power supply manufacturers I recommend:

Antec (www.antec.com)

Coolermaster (www.coolermaster.com)

Corsair (www.corsair.com)

Enermax (www.enermax.com)

FSP (www.fsp-group.com)

PC Power & Cooling (www.pcpower.com)

Thermaltake (www.thermaltake.com)

Seasonic (www.seasonic.com)

Silverstone (www.silverstonetek.com)

Ultra (www.ultraproducts.com)

Zalman (www.zalman.com)

Here are a few points to bear in mind when purchasing a power supply:

■ **Match the form factor to your motherboard**—When you're buying a power supply, make sure it comes with either 8-pin or 4-pin connector wires, as required by your motherboard.

■ **Look for detachable connectors**—For maximum flexibility when matching up your power supply with any motherboard, look for a unit that comes with detachable connectors. The most common such connector is a 24-pin main power connector with 4 of the pins detachable, which enables you to use the unit with a motherboard that has a 20-pin main connector. (This is often called a 20+4 connector and is shown in Figure 1.18.) Similarly, you can also get 8-pin EPS12V connectors where 4 of the pins are detachable, which enables you to use the unit with a motherboard

> **tip** Are you out of luck if your power supply has 4-pin wires but your motherboard has an 8-pin connector? Not at all. You can purchase a power cable adapter that converts the power supply's 4-pin ATX12V connector to an 8-pin EPS12V connector. (In addition, some adapters work the other way around, converting an 8-pin EPS12V connector to a 4-pin ATX12V connector.)

that has a 4-pin 12V power connector. (This is often called a 4+4 connector.)

■ **Look for a modular design**—A modular power supply is one that lets you use only the cables you need. The main and 12V cables are hard-wired, but all the other cables are optional and you just plug in the ones you need (see Figure 1.20). This reduces cable clutter and improves airflow through the case.

FIGURE 1.20

A modular power supply (left) lets you use only the power cables you need, whereas a regular power supply (right) comes with all its cables hard-wired.

■ **Make sure the power supply has the connectors you need—** Check the connectors that come with the unit to ensure that it has everything you need for your devices, particularly SATA drives and graphics expansion cards that require a power connection.

■ **Get a unit with high electrical efficiency—***Electrical efficiency* measures the percentage of the AC that comes into the power supply and is converted into DC power. For example, a power supply that's only 50% efficient would convert 100 W of AC into 50 W of DC. Ideally, your power supply should be at least 80% efficient.

From Here

■ To learn about heatsinks and processor cooling, **see** "Keeping It Cool: Fans and Heatsinks," **p. 56**.

■ For information on IDE and SATA, **see** "The Hard Drive Interface and Throughput," **p. 82**.

■ For more general information on buying parts for your home-built system, **see** Chapter 7, "Buying PC Parts," **p. 171**.

■ For instructions on removing a power supply from an old PC, **see** "Releasing the Power Supply," **p. 234**.

■ To learn how to take out a motherboard from an old PC, **see** "Removing the Motherboard," **p. 237**.

■ To learn how to insert an expansion card, **see** "Installing an Expansion Card," **p. 211**.

The Brains: The Central Processing Unit

I have a theory about the human mind. A brain is a lot like a computer. It will only take so many facts, and then it will go on overload and blow up.

—Erma Bombeck

nthropomorphic metaphors that compare computers to the human body have an unfortunate tendency to be stretched beyond the breaking point. However, it is reasonable to compare two of Chapter 1's subjects—the computer case and the motherboard—to parts of the body. Specifically, the case is like the body's skin and skeleton because it holds everything, and the motherboard is like the spinal cord because most things are attached to it either directly or indirectly.

2

Which brings us to this chapter and its topic, the *central processing unit*, also known as the *CPU*, the *microprocessor*, or simply the *processor*. What body part extends our metaphor to the CPU? I know you know the answer already, but bear with me a second as I justify taking the metaphor this far. As you might know, the spinal cord acts as a conduit for signals that other body parts send to the brain and for signals the brain sends to other body parts. The spinal cord itself doesn't process these signals in any way; all the processing goes on inside the brain. The motherboard, too, doesn't process any of the electrical signals that ride along its data buses, which is yet another reason the spinal cord is a good motherboard metaphor. But just as the spinal cord relays signals to and from the brain, so too does the motherboard relay signals to and from the processor. So it will come as no surprise by now that the brain forms the third part of our metaphor because (at least at the level we're dealing with here) it's a good analogue to the processor.

With a few exceptions, no matter what happens on your computer, the CPU has a hand in it somehow. Press a key or your keyboard, for example, and the signal goes through the motherboard's keyboard port to the processor, which then passes along the keypress to the operating system. Similarly, if a program you're using needs to send data to a network location, it hands off that data to the operating system, which sends it to the CPU, which then routes the data to the motherboard for transmission via the network card. The only major exception to the CPU's micromanaging is with most of today's graphics cards, which usually have a dedicated graphics processing unit (GPU) that handles much of the graphics chores so the CPU can work on other things.

The CPU will obviously play a very important role in the system you build, so you need to think carefully about which processor you use. This chapter tells you everything you need to know.

Intel or AMD?

From the point of view of a first-time (or, indeed, a tenth-time) system builder, the CPU world is a duopoly, with just two colossi bestriding the market: Intel and AMD. Yes, VIA is a player in the mini-ITX market, but it's small potatoes compared to Intel and AMD, and of these, Intel is by far the bigger. So, which one should you choose when picking out a processor for your home-built rig? The short answer is that it really doesn't matter even a tiny bit. Both Intel and AMD are world-class CPU designers and manufacturers, and almost any CPU you choose from either company will be a high-quality product and will serve you well whatever you do with your computer.

Having said all that, it's possible to differentiate the two CPU giants a little bit by resorting to some gross generalizations (one of my favorite things to do):

■ AMD generally competes on price, so for processors that offer low- and mid-range performance and features, an AMD processor will be cheaper than an equivalent Intel processor.

■ Intel generally competes on performance, so if you want to get the most out of your computer, Intel processors that offer higher-end performance and features are the way to go.

Of course, all this might have changed by the time you read this. For example, the next generation of AMD processors (not yet available as I write this) are said to have features that will enable AMD to once again compete with Intel on the high end. Similarly, AMD's competitive pricing has forced Intel to reduce its own prices, and further reductions could mean that Intel's low- and mid-range processors could become just as good a bargain as AMD's generally are.

Okay, have I hedged enough bets for you? The bottom line is that choosing a CPU really comes down to two things:

■ Buy a processor that matches your motherboard. As I mentioned in Chapter 1, "The Barebones: The Motherboard, Case, and Power Supply," all mobos are designed to work with a limited set of CPUs. In particular, every motherboard accepts only either an Intel CPU or an AMD CPU. So first and foremost, get a CPU that's compatible with your motherboard.

■ Buy the processor with the best features you can afford. What features am I talking about? Ah, that's the subject of the next section, so read on....

Clocks, Cores, and More: Understanding CPU Specs

If you're shopping around for a CPU, you might come across a description similar to this:

Intel Core 2 Duo E6750 2.66GHz LGA775

1333MHz FSB 4MB L2 cache Conroe 65nm

This shockingly unintelligible bit of prose is actually jam-packed with information about the processor, but it's couched in a form of "CPU speak" that could warm the cockles of only the geekiest of hearts. Fortunately, you need to understand only some of this when buying a CPU. However, I'm going to explain all of it just so you have an idea of what the retailers or the online reviewers are nattering on about when they talk this way. The previous description can be broken down into 10 discrete components, most of which I discuss in more detail in the sections that follow:

Intel	This, clearly, is the company name.
Core 2	This is the broad brand name under which the processor exists within Intel. This is usually called the processor's *family* (see the next section, "The Processor Family").
Duo	This tells you that the CPU has two *cores*, a term I explain a bit later (see "The Processor Cores" later in this chapter).
E6750	This is the name of the processor (see "The Processor Name" later in this chapter).
2.66GHz	This is the processor's clock speed (see "The Processor Clock Speed" later in this chapter).
LGA775	This is the motherboard socket the processor fits into (see "The Processor Socket" later in this chapter).
1333MHz FSB	This is the speed of the front-side bus (see "The Processor Bus Speed" later in this chapter).
4MB L2 cache	This is the size of the CPU's L2 cache (see "The Processor Front-Side Bus Speed" later in this chapter).
Conroe	This is the type of core the processor uses (see "The Processor Core Type" later in this chapter).
65nm	This is the CPU manufacturing process (see "The Processor Manufacturing Process" later in this chapter).

The Processor Family

The processor's family name is kind of an umbrella term that encompasses a series of related processors that use the same underlying architecture. For example, Intel's Core 2 processors all use the second generation of the Core architecture, which includes features such as Advanced Smart Cache, Smart Memory Access, and Intelligent Power Capability. Fortunately, you don't need to understand even word one about any of this, and I'm certainly not going to pad this chapter with descriptions of these features. All you need to know is that both Intel and AMD have a set of processor families from which you can choose, and that generally speaking these families can be divided (very roughly) into low-, mid-, and high-end ranges, as shown in Table 2.1.

Table 2.1   The Low-, Mid-, and High-Range Processor Families

Range	Families	Description
Low	Intel Celeron, AMD Sempron 64	These are inexpensive CPUs (generally around $50–$60) that offer fewer features and lower performance than other processor families (see Figure 2.1).
Mid	Intel Pentium Dual Core, AMD Athlon 64 X2	These are mid-priced CPUs (generally around $100–$200) that offer extra features and better performance than the low-range processor families (see Figure 2.2).
High	Intel Core 2, AMD Athlon 64 FX	These are expensive CPUs (generally $200–$1,000) that offer more features and better performance than other processor families (see Figure 2.3) .

FIGURE 2.1

The Intel Celeron and AMD Sempron 64 represent the low-range processors.

2

FIGURE 2.2

The Intel Pentium Dual Core and AMD Athlon 64 X2 represent the mid-range processors.

FIGURE 2.3

The Intel Core 2 and AMD Athlon 64 FX represent the high-range processors.

The Processor Cores

The processor *core* (short for *execution core*) refers to the actual processing unit that performs all the tasks a CPU is asked to handle. Until recently, the terms *core* and *processor* were equivalent because all CPUs contained just one core. In early 2005, however, Intel changed everything by introducing the Pentium D and the Pentium Extreme Edition, both of which somehow managed to shoehorn *two* cores into a single chip. Older CPUs were now described as *single core*, and these newfangled processors were described as *dual core*.

> **note** The divisions outlined in Table 2.1 are very general, perhaps ridiculously so. For example, you'll see a bit later in the section "The Processor Market: What's Available" that you can get some Intel Core 2 CPUs for around $120–$130. Similarly, the performance of some midrange Pentium Dual Core processors is pretty close to or even better than the performance of some high-range Intel Core 2 processors.

Does dual core mean twice the performance? Well, yes and no:

- Yes, because the processor can now divide tasks *between applications* among the cores (a process Intel calls HyperThreading). So if you're, say, compressing a large file, the processor can hand off that task to one core, and the other core is free to handle tasks from other programs.

- No, because the processor usually can't divide tasks *within an application* among the cores. For example, if you're compressing a large file, you won't be able to do anything else with that program until that task is complete. Note that it *is* possible to program individual applications to take advantage of two cores, and we're starting to see more of this as dual-core processors become mainstream.

Intel's current dual-core families are the Pentium Dual Core and the Core 2 Duo; for AMD, the dual-core families are Athlon 64 X2 and Athlon 64 FX.

In early 2007, Intel introduced the first *quad-core* processor: yup, *four* cores stuffed into a single chip. This gives you even better performance than a dual-core CPU, although not twice the performance. Again, because most systems and programs aren't optimized to take advantage of quad core, performance gains over dual core are only on the order of 10%–20%, depending on the task. Intel's current quad-core families are the Core 2 Quad and Core 2 Extreme.

> **note** You might sometimes see the Athlon 64 FX family referred to a "quad core." This actually means that the retailer is selling a *pair* of Athlon 64 FX processors, and you need to insert them on a special motherboard that has two CPU sockets. This effectively gives you four cores, albeit with two chips.

2

The Processor Name

Each CPU is given a name (sometimes called the *model number*), and that name tells you a bit about the processor's features.

Let's start with Intel's processor names, which for all of its dual- and quad-core CPUs take the form of a letter or two followed by four digits. The four general names you'll see most often are

Ennnn   This name refers to the Core 2 Duo family's dual-core processors (for example, E4300).

Xnnnn   This name refers to the Core 2 Extreme family's dual-core processors (for example X6800).

Qnnnn   This name refers to the Core 2 Quad family's quad-core processors (for example, Q6600).

QXnnnn   This name refers to the Core 2 Extreme family's quad-core processors (for example, QX6850).

The numbers themselves don't meaning anything per se, except as follows:

- The first number stays the same for processors that use the same core type (see the section "The Processor Core Type" later in this chapter).

- The next three numbers get higher as better features are added to each chip.

For example, consider the E4000 series processors. They all use the Allendale CPU core, and they all use the same bus speed and L2 cache size. What's different is the clock speed:

CPU Name	Clock Speed
E4300	1.8GHz
E4400	2.0GHz
E4500	2.2GHz

In other cases, a higher number might mean a bigger L2 cache or a faster bus speed.

For AMD, the model numbers are simpler, but a bit weird. The weirdness stems from a few years ago when AMD abandoned using CPU speed as part of its model numbers. It did that because the new (at the time) Athlon XP processor could generate the same performance as a Pentium 4 (Intel's top-of-the-line CPU at the time) while running at a slower clock speed! For example, an Athlon XP running at 1.67GHz would give the same performance as a Pentium 4 running at 2.0GHz. So AMD took out the CPU speed from the model number and substituted it with a number that indicates the processor's relative capability compared to the Pentium 4. So, for example, if you see 3200 in the name of an AMD processor, it means the chip gives performance equivalent to a Pentium 4 running at 3.2GHz (3200MHz).

The Processor Clock Speed

The *clock speed* is a measure of how fast the process operates internally. With each "tick" (which is called a *cycle*) on the clock, the processor performs an operation; therefore, the more ticks per second, the faster the processor, and the better performance your computer will have. Note that clock speeds are now measured in gigahertz (GHz), where 1GHz is one billion cycles per second. That's fast! Current processor clock speeds range from 1.6GHz in low-end CPUs to 3.2GHz in some high-end chips.

note AMD model numbers are complicated by the fact that the same model number is often used with chips that have different configurations. For example, an Athlon 64 X2 with the model number 3600+ can refer to a chip with a 1.9GHz clock speed, 1MB L2 cache, and Windsor CPU core that uses socket AM2, while another can refer to a chip with a 2.0GHz clock speed, 512KB L2 cache, and Manchester core that uses socket 939. The performance of both chips is equivalent to a 3.6GHz Pentium 4, so they both get the same 3600+ model number. Confusing!

The Processor Socket

The processor *socket* refers to the type of motherboard connector required by the processor:

- Almost all mainstream Intel processors use a socket named LGA775 (or just 775).
- Almost all mainstream AMD processors use a socket named AM2, although a few still use older sockets named 754 and 939. Some high-end AMD processors use socket F (also called 1207 FX).

The good news is that you don't need to know anything about the inner workings of sockets. However, there's one absolutely crucial bit of information you must tape to your cat's forehead so you won't forget:

The socket on your motherboard *must* match the socket type supported by the CPU.

caution Don't read *too* much into CPU clock speeds. Yes, if everything else is the same, a 2.2GHz processor will be a bit faster than a 2.0GHz processor. However, other factors are at play when it comes to CPU performance, including the bus speed and size of the cache.

Each socket has a particular number of connection points arranged in a particular pattern, and this combination produces a unique connector. That uniqueness means you simply can't plug in a CPU designed for a different socket, or you could damage the processor, the motherboard, or both.

How the processor connects to the motherboard depends on the socket. For example, a socket 775 CPU has copper pads on the bottom that match up with pins on the motherboard socket, as shown in Figure 2.4. A socket AM2 processor is the opposite, with pins on the bottom of the chip and corresponding holes in the motherboard socket, as shown in Figure 2.5.

Copper pads on the CPU match...

...the pins on the motherboard socket.

FIGURE 2.4

The copper pads on the bottom of a socket 775 CPU match the pins on the motherboard socket.

The Processor Bus Speed

The *system bus* is the motherboard data pathway that connects the processor and the northbridge. This makes it by far the most important data path in the computer because all data must at some point travel along this bus. On Intel machines, the system bus is called the *front-side bus (FSB)*, while on AMD machines it's called the *HyperTransport (HT) bus*.

→   To learn about the northbridge chipset, **see** "Mobo Mojo: Understanding the Motherboard," **p. 8**.

The tiny pins on the CPU match...

...the holes on the motherboard socket.

FIGURE 2.5

The pins on the bottom of a socket AM2 CPU match the holes on the motherboard socket.

Not surprisingly, the faster you can transfer data, the faster your computer performs. This means a CPU with a higher system bus speed will outperform one with a lower bus speed (assuming other performance features such as the clock speed and cache size are equal). Bus speed is measured in *megahertz (MHz)*, or millions of cycles per second. Current bus speed ranges are from 800MHz to 1333MHz for Intel's FSB and from 800MHz to 1000MHz for AMD's HT bus.

The Processor L2 Cache Size

One of the main jobs a CPU performs is to transfer data to and from storage areas such as the hard drive and system memory. The time it takes for the processor to

note As I write this, most AMD processors operate their HT buses at 1000MHz. However, you might see some retailers list the bus speed as 2000MHz. This is a bit of a misnomer, but technically it's accurate—sort of. The deal is that the HT bus actually performs *two* data transfers with each clock cycle. So, even though the bus is running at 1000MHz, it's actually performing twice that number of transfers per second. AMD measures this using the metric *mega-transfers per second* (millions of transfers per second), or MT/sec. Thus, saying the HT bus runs at 1000MHz is the same as saying it runs at 2000MT/sec.

retrieve data from either area isn't significant for data that's required only every now and then. However, processors are constantly dealing with the same data over and over. In that case, having to request that data from memory or the hard drive every time is inefficient.

To get a sense of what I mean, imagine that when you're preparing a meal and using a knife to chop vegetables, you put the knife away after every cut and then grab it again for the next cut. You'd be lucky to eat one meal a week! The solution is to hang onto the knife until you've finished chopping one vegetable, put the knife off to the side while you bring the next veggie onto the cutting board, grab the handy knife, and off you go again.

The processor does something similar, although with less tasty results. All processors have a couple of on-chip memory areas they use to store frequently accessed bits of data. These are called *memory caches*, and all CPUs have at least two: the L1 cache and the L2 cache. The L1 cache is tiny and doesn't affect CPU performance significantly, so you can ignore it. The bigger deal is the L2 cache, which does have an impact on system performance. Generally speaking (and as usual, assuming the other CPU features are equal), the bigger the L2 cache, the better the performance.

L2 cache sizes are measured in *kilobytes (KB)* or, more often, *megabytes (MB)*. The L2 cache on current Intel processors ranges in size from 512KB to 8MB, while AMD L2 cache sizes range from 128KB to 2MB.

The Processor Manufacturing Process

The earliest PC processors (such as Intel's 4004) contained just 1,000 transistors. Today's Intel Core 2 processors pack a whopping 291 *million* transistors into a much smaller space, and forthcoming Intel CPUs will up the number of transistors to an amazing 820 million. How does Intel (and AMD) cram more transistors into its chips? It does it by improving the chip *manufacturing process* (also called the *fabrication process*). This refers not only to how the transistors themselves are built, but also to the on-chip pathways that connect the transistors. By making these components smaller, the manufacturer can squeeze more transistors onto the chip.

The CPU process is known by the width of the pathways that connect the transistors, and these widths are becoming vanishingly small. For example, most modern Intel

note A *transistor* is a semiconductor device that's the most basic component in the integrated circuits that make up most electronic devices. Transistors amplify and control the current running through the circuit.

processors use pathways that are a mere 65 nanometers (nm) wide. You could put 1,000 of these paths side-by-side and the resulting bundle would be only as thick as a human hair! Other common process widths you see today are 90nm and 1.3 microns (130nm).

note Intel's next-generation processors, to be released in early 2008, will use a 45nm process to get 410 million transistors on a dual-core CPU and 820 million transistors on a quad-core processor.

The Processor Core Type

The final processor spec is the core type, which is a codename that refers to a combination of CPU process and CPU family. So, for example, the Intel Core 2 Duo chips that use the 65nm process go by the codename *Conroe*, and the Intel Core 2 Quad chips that use the 65nm process go by the codename *Kentsfield*. These names are essentially meaningless for a first-time builder, so feel free to ignore them. However, you might want to bear in mind that the codenames of Intel's next-generation processors, if only because you'll be hearing them constantly:

note Processors are following the seemingly inevitable trend known as *Moore's Law*, which tells us that the number of transistors on an integrated circuit will double every two years. The Moore behind this law is Gordon E. Moore, a co-founder of Intel, and he first formulated his idea back in 1965, although in his original formulation he thought the number of chip components would double every year:

The complexity for minimum component costs has increased at a rate of roughly a factor of two per year.

Penryn   This is the overall codename for all cores that use the new 45nm process.

Wolfdale   This is the codename for the dual-core Penryn CPU.

Yorkfield   This is the codename for the quad-core Penryn CPU.

The Processor Market: What's Available

To give you some idea what to expect when you're shopping around, Table 2.2 lists the Intel and AMD processors you're mostly likely to find, and for each CPU the table shows you the number of cores, the processor speed, the socket required, the system bus speed, and the size of the L2 cache. I've also included an average price, but bear in mind that this price was current in late 2007 as I write this, so you'll almost certainly see different (hopefully lower) prices when you shop.

note All of Intel's processor codenames are based on the names of rivers.

Table 2.2   Specifications for Various Intel and AMD CPUs

Processor	Cores	Speed	Socket	Bus Speed	L2 Cache	Price
Intel						
Celeron 420	1	1.6GHz	775	800MHz	512KB	$45
Celeron 430	1	1.8GHz	775	800MHz	512KB	$50
Celeron 440	1	2.0GHz	775	800MHz	512KB	$65
Celeron E1200	2	1.6GHz	775	800MHz	512KB	$60
Pentium Dual Core E2140	2	1.6GHz	775	800MHz	1MB	$70
Pentium Dual Core E2160	2	1.8GHz	775	800MHz	1MB	$80
Pentium Dual Core E2180	2	2.0GHz	775	800MHz	1MB	$90
Core 2 Duo E4300	2	1.8GHz	775	800MHz	2MB	$130
Core 2 Duo E4400	2	2.0GHz	775	800MHz	2MB	$120
Core 2 Duo E4500	2	2.2GHz	775	800MHz	2MB	$130
Core 2 Duo E4600	2	2.4GHz	775	800MHz	2MB	$160
Core 2 Duo E6300	2	1.86GHz	775	1066MHz	2MB	$170
Core 2 Duo E6320	2	1.86GHz	775	1066MHz	4MB	$180
Core 2 Duo E6400	2	2.4GHz	775	1066MHz	2MB	$160
Core 2 Duo E6420	2	2.13GHz	775	1066MHz	4MB	$210
Core 2 Duo E6540	2	2.4GHz	775	1066MHz	4MB	$160
Core 2 Duo E6550	2	2.33GHz	775	1333MHz	4MB	$160
Core 2 Duo E6600	2	2.4GHz	775	1066MHz	4MB	$240
Core 2 Duo E6700	2	2.67GHz	775	1066MHz	4MB	$320
Core 2 Duo E6750	2	2.66GHz	775	1333MHz	4MB	$190
Core 2 Duo E6850	2	3.0GHz	775	1333MHz	4MB	$280
Core 2 Quad Q6600	4	2.4GHz	775	1066MHz	8MB	$280
Core 2 Quad Q6700	4	2.66GHz	775	1066MHz	8MB	$540
Core 2 Extreme X6800	2	2.93GHz	775	1066MHz	4MB	$985
Core 2 Extreme QX6700	4	2.66GHz	775	1066MHz	8MB	$950
Core 2 Extreme QX6800	4	2.93GHz	775	1066MHz	8MB	$999
Core 2 Extreme QX6850	4	3.0GHz	775	1333MHz	8MB	$1,030
Core 2 Extreme QX9650	4	3.0GHz	775	1333MHz	12MB	$1,300

Table 2.2   Continued

Processor	Cores	Speed	Socket	Bus Speed	L2 Cache	Price
AMD						
Sempron 64 2600+	1	1.6Ghz	754	800MHz	128KB	$40
Sempron 64 3200+	1	1.8Ghz	AM2	800MHz	128KB	$40
Sempron 64 3400+	1	1.8Ghz	AM2	800MHz	256KB	$40
Athlon 64 X2 3600+	2	1.9GHz	AM2/939	1000MHz	1MB	$50
Athlon 64 X2 3800+	2	2.0GHz	AM2/939	1000MHz	1MB	$60
Athlon 64 X2 4000+	2	2.0GHz	AM2/939	1000MHz	2MB	$65
Athlon 64 X2 4200+	2	2.2GHz	AM2/939	1000MHz	2MB	$70
Athlon 64 X2 4400+	2	2.3GHz	AM2/939	1000MHz	1MB	$85
Athlon 64 X2 4600+	2	2.4GHz	AM2/939	1000MHz	1MB	$90
Athlon 64 X2 4800+	2	2.5GHz	AM2/939	1000MHz	2MB	$99
Athlon 64 X2 5000+	2	2.6GHz	AM2	1000MHz	1MB	$115
Athlon 64 X2 5200+	2	2.7GHz	AM2	1000MHz	1MB	$120
Athlon 64 X2 5400+	2	2.8GHz	AM2	1000MHz	1MB	$125
Athlon 64 X2 5600+	2	2.8GHz	AM2	1000MHz	2MB	$140
Athlon 64 X2 6000+	2	3.0GHz	AM2	1000MHz	2MB	$160
Athlon 64 X2 6400+	2	3.2GHz	AM2	1000MHz	2MB	$175
Athlon 64 FX-62	2	2.8GHz	AM2	1000MHz	2MB	$170
Athlon 64 FX-70	2	2.6Ghz	F	1000MHz	2MB	$320
Athlon 64 FX-72	2	2.8Ghz	F	1000MHz	2MB	$280
Athlon 64 FX-74	2	3.0GHz	F	1000MHz	2MB	$300

Note that there are some real bargains in Table 2.1:

- **Athlon 64 X2 4000+**—A 2.0GHz dual-core CPU with a 2MB L2 cache for a mere $65 on average.
- **Athlon 64 X2 5600+**—A 2.8GHz dual-core CPU with a 2MB L2 cache for an average price of $140.
- **Intel Core 2 Duo E6550**—At about $160, this is the cheapest 1333MHz front-side bus processor available.
- **Intel Core 2 Duo E6750**—A 2.66GHz dual-core CPU with a 1333MHz front-side bus for only about $190.

- **Athlon 64 X2 6400+**—The fastest processor (at 3.2GHz) available, and for only $210.

- **Intel Core 2 Quad Q6600**—A quad-core CPU for just $280, a mere $70 per core (plus 2MB of cache per core and a 1066MHz bus) .

Keeping It Cool: Fans and Heatsinks

Processors consume a *ton* of electricity, more than any other component in the system (with the possible exception of some high-end video expansion cards, which have their own processors built-in). Processor manufacturers speak of a CPU's *thermal design power* (*TDP*), which is, roughly speaking, the amount of power (measured in watts) a processor requires under maximum load. Some mobile CPUs designed for notebooks might have a TDP of only about 10 watts (W). Desktop CPUs typically require several times that. For example, most Intel Core 2 Duo processors require 65W, and their Core 2 Extreme cousins require a whopping 130W. (AMD's numbers are similar, with most Athlon 64 X2 processors requiring either 65W or 89W and Athlon 64 FX processors requiring 125W.)

Intel and AMD take these numbers seriously and have taken steps in recent years to reduce power consumption in their CPUs. For example, the Core 2 Duo's 65W TDP is a far sight better than the 95W–130W TDPs that were typical of the previous Pentium D and Pentium Extreme Edition CPUs.

No matter how much power a CPU requires, some of that power is converted to heat—*lots* of heat. For example, each time a transistor handles a pulse of electric current, the transistor gives off a tiny amount of heat. One transistor's heat output is insignificant, but put tens or

tip How do you compare one processor with another using Table 2.1? It's not easy, to be sure. The ideal way to compare would be to give each CPU a performance score and divide that score into the CPU's price. The result would be a price/performance ratio, where the lower the score, the more processing bang you get for your buck. That sounds like a lot of work, and it is. Fortunately, someone has already done all the work for you. The great Internet site Tom's Hardware (http://www.tomshardware.com/) has a CPU chart that calculates the price/performance ratio for all current CPUs. To load the chart, navigate to the site, click the CPU category, click the CPU Charts link, and then select Price/Performance Index in the Choose Benchmark list.

tip For a complete list of CPUs and their respective TDP values, see Chris Hare's Processor Electrical Specifications page at http://users.erols.com/chare/elec.htm.

hundreds of millions of transistors together (as in any modern CPU) and heat becomes a problem. In fact, we've reached the point now where it's impossible to operate a modern CPU without some kind of cooling equipment attached because it would simply overheat and either shut itself down or destroy itself.

To prevent this, most processors now require some form of *forced-air cooling*, which is a system that consists of two parts:

Heatsink   This is a metal component (made of copper, aluminum, or some other highly conductive material) that literally sits on top of the processor. Technically, it sits on top of the processor's *integrated heat spreader (IHS)*, a piece of copper glued on top of the processor to help dissipate heat away from the cores. The heat generated by the processor conducts into the heatsink, which keeps the processor relatively cool.

Fan   The heat transferred to the heatsink has to go somewhere, and that's the job of the fan attached to the heatsink. The fan pulls air up from the heatsink into a collection of fins attached to the heatsink, and from there the heat dissipates into the computer case. The case's natural airflow created by the

note By the time you read this, both Intel and AMD will have released their next-generation processors. For Intel, the new Penryn Wolfdale CPUs include the Core 2 Duo E8000 series running at speeds from 2.6GHz to 3.2GHz, with 6MB L2 caches and 1333MHz front-side bus speeds. You'll also see several Penryn Yorkfield processors in the Core 2 Quad Q9000 series running at speeds from 2.5GHz to 2.8GHz, with 6MB and 12MB L2 caches and 1333MHz front-side bus speeds. The new Core 2 Extreme QX9000 series will feature CPUs running at speeds from 3.0GHz to 3.2GHz, with 12MB L2 caches and 1333MHz and 1600MHz front-side bus speeds. Even more exciting is yet another new generation of Intel processors, expected by the end of 2008 or early 2009. Code-named Nehalem, these CPUs will have as many as *eight* cores and will feature QuickPath, Intel's long-awaited replacement for the front-side bus, which will offer much faster transfer rates between the processor, RAM, and northbridge.

For AMD, the next generation is called Phenom (pronounced *FEE-nom*), and you'll see three basic versions: the dual-core CPUs will be named Phenom X2; the quad-core processors will be called Phenom X4; and the high-end quad-core CPUs will be named Phenom FX.

2

intake and exhaust fans (refer to Chapter 1) moves the hot air away from the heatsink and eventually out of the case.

→ To learn more about case fans and airflow, **see** "Going with the Flow: Case Fans," **p. 31**.

LIQUID COOLING

Forced-air cooling is by far the most common method for keeping a processor's temperature steady under load, but it's not the only one. One system that's becoming more popular is *liquid cooling*, which operates much like the cooling system in a car. A pump circulates liquid through a series of pipes attached to the motherboard. One pipe leads to a *waterblock*, a metal (usually copper or aluminum) reservoir that sits on top of the CPU and draws heat away from the processor into the water. From there, the heated water flows into a radiator, which uses fans to cool the water and return it to the pump to start the cycle over again. Liquid cooling is effective, but it's also very complex to implement, so I don't cover it in this book.

Heatsinks come in many styles and shapes, as you can see in Figure 2.6.

FIGURE 2.6

All modern CPUs require a heatsink and fan to keep cool.

Here are a few notes to bear in mind when deciding on which heatsink to buy for your CPU:

- **Decide whether you need a third-party heatsink**—Many CPUs either come with their own heatsink (and fan) or offer a heatsink as an option. These stock coolers do the job, but they don't tend to be as good as third-party coolers (that is, they don't keep the processor as cool), and the fans tend to be loud. If you're working on a strict budget, stick with the stock heatsink/fan. Otherwise, you're almost always better off with a third-party cooling system, although note that you're voiding your CPU warranty if you do so.

- **Buy from a reputable heatsink manufacturer**—A few companies specialize in PC cooling products, and you're better off dealing with these companies to ensure quality products that do the job. Here's a list of heatsink manufacturers I recommend:

    AeroCool (www.aerocool.com)

    Coolermaster (www.coolermaster.com)

    Thermalright (www.thermalright.com)

    Thermaltake (www.thermaltake.com)

    Silverstone (www.silverstonetek.com)

    Scythe (www.scythe-usa.com)

    Zalman (www.zalman.com)

- **Make sure the heatsink fits your CPU socket**—Most heatsinks work with a variety of processor sockets, such as AM2 and LGA775. However, some of them work with only a particular socket, so check compatibility with your motherboard.

- **Watch the heatsink height**—Some heatsinks are incredibly tall (140mm–5.6 inches or more). This helps dissipate heat, but it can also make the heatsink a tight, or impossible, fit for some cases, particularly anything smaller than an ATX case. Many case manufacturers list the maximum heatsink height, so check the website.

- **Check the noise level**—The better heatsinks come with quiet fans that don't add much to the overall noise level of your system. Check the heatsink's fan specs and make sure the noise level doesn't exceed 30dBA (and is, ideally, much less than that) at maximum RPMs.

- **Buy some thermal compound**—Earlier I said that the heatsink sits directly on top of the processor (or, really, the IHS). To improve the conduction from the process to the heatsink, you need to apply a little

2

thermal compound to one of the surfaces. Thermal compound is a thick substance with a glue-like consistency that contains metal particles to enhance its conductivity. Most new processors come with the thermal compound already applied to the stock heatsink; third-party CPU coolers usually come with enough thermal compound for a one-time installation. However, if you think

caution When applying thermal compound, be sure not to overdo it or when you install the cooler on the processor the extra compound will squeeze out onto the motherboard, causing who knows how many problems. You just need to apply a thin, even layer to either the processor's IHS or to the cooler's heatsink.

you might need to reuse a processor in a different project later, having your own tube of thermal compound is a necessity (see Figure 2.7).

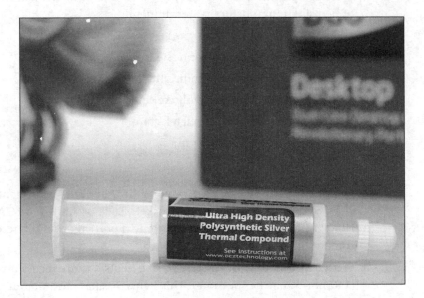

FIGURE 2.7
You improve conductivity between the CPU's heat spreader and the heatsink by applying thermal compound to one of the surfaces.

Buying a CPU

I mentioned earlier that on most levels, particularly when you're just getting started with the PC-building business, there really isn't much to choose from between Intel and AMD. Both are world-class companies that make uniformly excellent products, so you really can't go wrong whichever you choose. So your choice of a processor comes down to other considerations, the most important of which I've listed here:

note In late 2007, Intel announced that it would be phasing out its single-core Celeron processors and releasing the first dual-core Celerons early in 2008 and, sure enough, the first dual core Celerons began appearing in January 2008. AMD is also scheduled to phase out the single-core Sempron and replace it with a dual-core version. So by the time you read this, don't be surprised if there are no single-core CPUs around.

- **Match your motherboard**—Your motherboard includes a particular socket type, and that socket fits only a limited collection of CPUs. So first and foremost, your choice of processor must be one that will fit your motherboard socket.

- **Assess your needs**—Everyone's talking about dual-core processors, but you don't need two cores if all you'll be doing is surfing the web and sending and receiving email. You can get single-core processors for around $40–$45, and they'll do you just fine. Of course, you need spend only another $20–$30 to move up to dual-core, so consider an entry-level dual-core CPU unless your budget's particularly tight. On the other side of the spectrum, if you're into high-end 3D gaming, then you have no choice but to head for quad-core territory and get the best processor you can afford.

- **Look for price anomalies**—If you examine the table of processors I laid out earlier (see "The Processor Market: What's Available"), you see the odd price anomaly where a particular CPU is priced significantly less than similar processors. For example, the Intel Core 2 Quad Q6700 sells for an average of $540, but the very similar (and only slightly slower) Core 2 Quad Q6600 sells for just $280 on average. This is a rather extreme case, but you can often find these kinds of bargains if you do your homework.

- **Shop around**—The processor is a relatively expensive component, and in the mid-range and high-range you'll often find that one online retailer is selling the same CPU for $100 more than another. Don't assume that prices are the same wherever you shop.

- **Look for motherboard/processor bundles**—Many retailers bundle a motherboard and a processor together and sell the package for less than the products would sell for if purchased individually. This not only saves you cash, but it also ensures that you match the motherboard and CPU.

■ **Pass on the stock heatsink**—Unless you're on a strict budget, buy the CPU without the stock heatsink and fan (most online retailers offer CPUs with and without heatsinks). You'll save a bit of money this way, and you can put that cash toward buying a quality heatsink, as described in the previous section.

From Here

■ To learn about the northbridge chipset, **see** "Mobo Mojo: Understanding the Motherboard," **p. 8**.

■ To learn more about case fans and airflow, **see** "Going with the Flow: Case Fans," **p. 31**.

■ A really fast processor won't do you much good if you don't have an adequate amount of system memory. To learn why, see Chapter 3, "The Work Area: Memory," **p. 63**.

■ To learn how to remove a processor from an old PC, **see** "Prying Out a CPU," **p. 230**.

■ If you need a CPU for business computing, **see** "Picking Out a CPU for the Basic Business PC," **p. 246**.

■ If the processor will go inside a home theater PC, **see** "Picking Out a CPU for the Home Theater PC," **p. 284**.

■ If you're building a system to maximize performance, **see** "Picking Out a CPU for the High-Performance PC," **p. 329**.

■ If you want tips on how to pick out the best processor for gaming, **see** "Picking Out a CPU for the Killer Gaming PC," **p. 376**.

■ If you're choosing a processor on a budget, **see** "Picking Out a CPU for the Budget PC," **p. 418**.

The Work Area: Memory

"Living backwards!" Alice repeated in great astonishment. "I never heard of such a thing!"

"—but there's one great advantage in it, that one's memory works both ways."

"I'm sure MINE only works one way." Alice remarked. *"I can't remember things before they happen."*

"It's a poor sort of memory that only works backwards," the Queen remarked.

—Lewis Carroll, *Through the Looking Glass*

A s you might be starting to appreciate by now, the performance of your homebrew computer depends on many different but interrelated factors. These include (but most definitely aren't limited to) the processor's clock speed, the size of the processor's L2 cache, the speed of the motherboard data bus, and (as you see in this chapter) the amount of memory installed. In the computing world before Windows, memory wasn't all that important in the sense that there wasn't much you could do about it. Your computer had a maximum memory size of 1MB, and only 640KB of that was available to DOS and whatever programs you were running.

As processor technology improved, the amount of potential RAM in a system increased by several orders of magnitude, to the point where it was possible (at least in theory) to have several *gigabytes* of RAM in a system. Suddenly RAM had become a crucial part of the overall configuration of a computer because the more RAM you could stuff inside, the better the computer's performance. These days, as we approach the RAM limit in most mainstream PCs, we face new and harder decisions about not only how much RAM to add to our systems, but also what type of RAM. This chapter will help you make those decisions for your home-built computer.

What Is RAM?

As you'll see, your computer's *random access memory (RAM)* is just an innocuous collection of chips on a special module you plug in to the system's motherboard. But although these chips might not look like much, they perform some pretty important tasks.

Their basic purpose in life is to be used as a work area for your programs and data. These things normally slumber peacefully on your hard disk, but when you need them, the operating system rouses everyone from their spacious beds and herds the program code and data into the relatively cramped confines of memory. From there, different bits of code and data are swapped in and out of memory, as needed. Why not just work with everything from the hard disk itself? One word: *speed*. Even the highest of high-tech hard drives is a tortoise compared to the blazing memory chips.

Entire books can be (and, indeed, have been) written about the relationship between your computer and its memory. What it all boils down to, though, is quite simple: The more memory you have, the happier your computer (and the operating system and programs you run on it) will be.

This all sounds well and good, but a fundamental problem underlies everything. Most hard disks can store dozens or even hundreds of gigabytes of data, but the memory capacity of a typical computer is limited to a measly few gigabytes.

Picture it this way: Think of your computer as a carpenter's workshop divided into two areas—a storage space for your tools and materials (the hard disk) and a work area where you actually use these things (memory). The problem is that your computer's "work space" is much smaller than its "storage space." For a carpenter, a small work space limits the number of tools and the amount of wood that can be used at any one time. For a computer, it limits the number of programs and data files you can load.

Why not simply have as much RAM as you have hard disk space? The problem there is that, although there's no theoretical reason hard drives can't keep increasing their capacities (other than certain laws of physics, which might come into play in 10 or 15 years), the amount of RAM you can put into your computer has a maximum that can't be exceeded on most systems. That maximum value is 4GB, which is far smaller than any modern hard disk.

To see how that number was arrived at, you need to look at the physical characteristics of the processor. Specifically, processors work with memory chips via *address lines*, which are (more or less) physical connections between the processor and the individual locations in the memory chips, each of which stores a single byte of data. Each address line carries a single bit of a memory address, so the total amount of memory—the *address space*—any processor can work with is limited by the number of address lines. If you had only a single address line, for example, you could address only two memory locations (addresses 1 and 0; see the following sidebar for details), two lines could address four locations, and so on.

UNDERSTANDING ADDRESS-LINE STATES

Each address line can take on only one of two states: high current or low current (on or off). These two states are represented inside the processor by 1 and 0, respectively. Computers have to store all their data using this binary number system. In the simplest case (one address line), you have two memory locations. If you send a low current through the line, you get the byte stored at location 0. A high current refers to memory location 1. In a two-line situation (call them lines A and B), you have four possibilities: both lines low (memory location 00), line A low and line B high (01), line A high and line B low (10), and both lines high (11).

The original IBM PC used Intel's 8088 processor, which had 20 address lines. This might seem like a lot (it sure did back then), but it gives you an address space of only 1,048,576 bytes (2 to the power of 20)—or a mere 1MB. (Hence, the 1MB limitation I mentioned earlier.) By contrast, the 80286 processor with its 24 address lines could access up to 16MB (2 to the power of 24) and the 80386 processor had an address space of 4GB (2 to the power of 32), thanks to its 32 address lines.

We now have processors that support 64 address lines, but that doesn't matter so much at the moment because most operating systems and most motherboards support only 32-bit addresses. (Most, but not all: There are 64-bit versions of Windows XP and Windows Vista.) For now, then, we're stuck at 4GB. (For more on this, particularly as it relates to Windows, see "Windows and RAM: The 4GB Conundrum," later in this chapter.)

Combining Memory Chips Into Memory Modules

It used to be that you would plug memory chips directly into the motherboard, a time-consuming process because you typically had to deal with a few dozen sockets! Then there were the maintenance headaches because, inevitably, the chips would come loose or even fall out of their sockets!

This was not a good situation, to say the least, but luckily some bright spark hit upon an ingenious idea: Solder a bunch of chips, say 8 or even 16, to a single circuit board. This brilliant invention meant that not only did you have fewer memory "pieces" to worry about (from several dozen to just several), but you no longer had to worry about chips coming loose because they were soldered into place.

This invention is called a *memory module* (or sometime a *memory stick*), and the first ones were called single inline memory modules (SIMMs), a term I talk more about later (see "The Memory Module Configuration and Pins"). Figure 3.1 shows a typical memory module.

Memory Chips

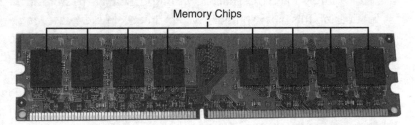

FIGURE 3.1
Modern-day memory comes in the form of a memory module, where the individual memory chips are soldered into place.

DDR, DIMM, and More: Understanding Memory Specs

If you go online to your favorite computer parts retailer and click the Memory section, you might see a bunch of listings for memory modules that look something like this:

Corsair XMS TWINX2048-3200C2 PC-3200 DDR400 Dual Channel

1GB CL2.5-3-3-6 184-Pin DIMM

This raises computer prose to new heights of unintelligibility, but there's actually quite a bit of useful data packed ever so obscurely into just a few seemingly random characters. You need to understand only a bit of this geekspeak to buy memory modules for your system, but I'll trudge through all the terms anyway, just so you know what you're up against. This description breaks down into a dozen discrete components, most of which I discuss in more detail in the sections that follow:

Corsair	This is the name of the company that manufactures the module.
XMS	This is the name of the family of memory products that the module falls within in the company's hierarchy.
TWINX2048-3200C2	This is the module's model number.
PC-3200	This is a code that specifies the type of memory standard used by the module.
DDR	This tells you the memory type, which in this case is double data rate (DDR) memory.
400	This is the effective speed of the memory chips, in MHz.
Dual Channel	This tells you that the module supports dual channel mode.
1GB	This is the capacity, the amount of RAM contained in the memory module.
CL2.5-3-3-6	This tells you the latency and timings of the memory chips used in the module.
184-Pin	This is the number of pins the memory module uses.
DIMM	This tells you that the module uses a dual inline memory module (DIMM) configuration.

The Memory Module Standard

All memory modules adhere to a particular standard that specifies certain things such as the speed of the memory chips and the configuration of the module pins. The standard is indicated by a code number that takes one of the following three forms:

PC-*nnnn*	The PC part tells you that the module's chips use the double data rate (DDR) memory type (see the next section, "The Memory Type and Speed"), and the *nnnn*

	part is a number that tells you the theoretical bandwidth of the memory.
PC2-*nnnn*	The PC2 part tells you that the module's chips support the DDR2 memory type, and the *nnnn* part tells you the theoretical bandwidth of the memory.
PC3-*nnnn*	The PC3 part tells you that the module's chips support the DDR3 memory type, and the *nnnn* part tells you the theoretical bandwidth of the memory.

Let's take a closer look at the theoretical bandwidth of the memory module, which is a measure of the amount of data that can pass through the module per second under ideal conditions. It's measured in megabytes per second (MBps) and, generally speaking, the higher the value, the better the memory's performance.

For example, PC-3200 implies a theoretical bandwidth of 3200MBps. To calculate theoretical bandwidth, you first multiply the base chip speed (see the next section, "The Memory Type and Speed") by 2 to get the effective clock speed (this is thanks to DDR, as explained in the next section). You then multiply the effective clock speed by 8 (because the memory path is 64 bits wide and there are 8 bits in each byte). So a 200MHz chip has an effective clock speed of 400MHz and, therefore, a theoretical bandwidth of 3200MBps; thus, it's called PC-3200 memory.

The Memory Type and Speed

Modern memory uses *synchronous dynamic RAM (SDRAM)*, which is a type of RAM that contains an internal clock that enables it to run in synch with the motherboard clock. The memory's *clock speed* is the number of ticks (or *cycles*) per second, measured in megahertz (MHz), or millions of cycles per second.

SDRAM was originally *single data rate (SDR)* memory, which meant it transferred data with each clock cycle (that is, each time the clock ticked). All modern memory uses *double data rate (DDR)* memory, which means it transfers data at the beginning and the end of each clock cycle. (DDR memory is said to be *double-pumped*.) The name of each DDR memory chip type is DDR-*nnn*, where *nnn* is the effective clock speed of the chip. For example, DDR memory with a clock speed of 200MHz is called DDR-400 because the effective clock speed is 400MHz. The effective speeds of DDR memory chips range from 200MHz (DDR-200) to 600MHz (DDR-600).

note Most motherboards support several memory standards. For example, a board might support PC2-4200, PC2-5300, and PC2-6400.

Currently, the most common memory chip type is DDR2 SDRAM, which uses faster clock speeds than DDR. The effective clock speeds of DDR2 memory chips range from 400MHz (DDR2-400) to 1250MHz (DDR2-1250).

The high end of the memory module market is currently occupied by DDR3 chips, which boast even faster clock speeds than DDR2. Currently, the effective clock speeds of DDR3 memory chips range from 800MHz (DDR3-800) to 1866MHz (DDR3-1866). It's expected that we'll see DDR3 chips with effective speeds of 2000MHz (DDR3-2000) in 2008.

tip If you're upgrading an existing system, how do you know which type of memory it uses? One way is to access the system's BIOS utility, which usually tells you the type of memory the system uses. Alternatively, if you know the motherboard model number, you can look it up on the manufacturer's website and access the board's specifications. If you purchased the system rather than building it, go to the computer manufacturer's website and look up the model number. If all else fails, you can open the case and remove a current memory module to see whether it displays the memory type.

Dual Channel Mode

On all motherboards, the data exchange between the CPU and memory is handled by a chip called the *memory controller*. A regular motherboard has a single pathway—called the *memory channel*—between the RAM and the memory controller, and that path is 64 bits wide. However, many newer mobos come with two 64-bit memory channels between the RAM and the memory controller. If you have two memory modules installed, the system can transfer data using both channels, which doubles the memory bandwidth. This is called *dual channel mode*. For example, you saw earlier that PC-3200 memory provides a theoretical bandwidth of 3200MBps using a single 64-bit channel. In dual channel mode, that same PC-3200 RAM offers a maximum of 6400MBps.

Most motherboards that support dual channel mode come with color-coded memory module sockets, such as two yellow sockets and two red sockets. The idea is that sockets that are the same color are the ones that create the dual channel. So, for example, if you insert two modules in, say, the yellow sockets, then those modules will operate in dual channel mode; if, instead, you put one module in a yellow socket and another in a red socket, then both modules would operate in single channel mode. (If your motherboard's RAM sockets aren't color-coded, they

caution To ensure best results when working in dual channel mode, the two memory modules you use should be exactly the same—not just the same type of memory, but the same module from the same company, right down to the model number.

should at least be labeled. For example, it's common to label one pair as Channel A with one socket numbered 0 and the other 1 and to label the other pair as Channel B with sockets numbered 0 and 1. In this case, you enable dual channel mode with two modules by placing them in the two sockets that are numbered 0.)

The Memory Module Capacity

The capacity value you see in a memory module description just tells you how much RAM the module contains. All modules come in one of the following five capacities: 128MB, 256MB, 512MB, 1GB, and 2GB. If you're not sure of the capacity of a module, most have a sticker on the side that tells you, as shown in Figure 3.2.

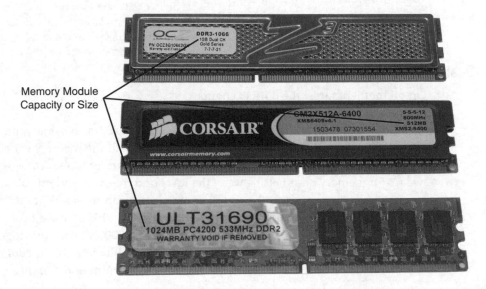

Memory Module
Capacity or Size

FIGURE 3.2

Most RAM modules come with a sticker that tells you the module's capacity, as well as other data such as the memory type.

The Memory Latency and Timings

In computing circles, *latency* refers to the delay that one component experiences between the time it makes some sort of request of a second component and the time the other component answers that request. In the RAM game, the CPU is always much faster than the memory, so the processor often has to wait while data is either read from memory or written to memory—a phenomenon known as *memory latency* or *RAM latency*. When you see a description for a memory module, it often displays one or more numbers that quantify the latency of the memory:

- If you see only one number, it's a value called the *CAS latency* (or *CL*; here, CAS stands for Column Address Strobe, but it's not something you need to worry about). This is the value, in clock cycles, of the delay between when the CPU requests data and when the data is ready. This is the most important number, and the lower the CAS latency, the faster the memory performs.

- If you see four numbers, these numbers are usually separated by dashes, such as CL2.5-3-3-6 or CL4-4-4-12. The first number is the CAS latency, and the other three numbers are the values, in clock cycles, that the memory takes to perform certain tasks; these are called the *memory timings*. The specifics of these timings are extremely arcane. Just understand that the lower the values, the faster the memory's performance.

The Memory Module Configuration and Pins

The configuration of the memory module tells you the overall layout of the module and how the memory chips are placed on the module. The three kinds you should know about are as follows:

SIMM   Short for *single inline memory module*, a SIMM has contacts on both sides of the module, but those contacts are redundant, so it really has only a single set of contacts. The memory channel on a SIMM is 32 bits wide. SIMMs are now largely obsolete.

DIMM   Short for *dual inline memory module*, a DIMM has a separate set of contacts on both sides of the module. This enables a DIMM to support a memory channel of 64 bits. DIMMs are by far the most common memory module.

SODIMM   Short for *small outline DIMM*, a SODIMM is a smaller, cuter version of a DIMM designed for use in notebooks and small form factor PCs that use Mini-ITX, Nano-ITX, and Pico-ITX motherboards.

The memory module's pins are its connection points to the motherboard. That is, when you insert a memory module into a motherboard socket, it's the module's pins that you're inserting. Figure 3.3 shows a close-up of the pins on a memory module.

FIGURE 3.3

The pins are the memory module's connection points to the motherboard.

Most DDR DIMM memory modules come in a 184-pin configuration, and most DDR2 and DDR3 DIMM modules come in a 240-pin configuration. DDR and DDR2 SODIMM modules usually come in a 200-pin configuration (although you also see 72-, 100-, and 144-pin configurations). Figure 3.4 shows these three types of modules.

DDR2 SODIMM (200 Pins)

DDR DIMM (184 Pins)

DDR2 DIMM (240 Pins)

FIGURE 3.4

The three main types of memory module configurations.

Notice that each of the memory modules shown in Figure 3.4 has a notch in the pin area. This notch matches a corresponding ridge inside the motherboard's memory socket, as shown in Figure 3.5. This prevents you from installing the module the wrong way around. Also, because the different module configurations have their notches in different places, it also prevents you from installing the wrong type of memory.

> **note** DDR2 and DDR3 memory modules have the same number of pins (240), but the notch is in a different place. This prevents you from accidentally inserting a DDR3 module in a DDR2 slot (and vice versa).

The notch on the module...

...matches the ridge inside the memory socket.

FIGURE 3.5

The memory module's notch lines up with the DIMM socket ridge to ensure correct installation.

Windows and RAM: The 4GB Conundrum

Most versions of Windows Vista and XP are 32-bit operating systems. That "32-bitness" means these systems can address a maximum of 4GB RAM (because 2 raised to the power of 32 is 4,294,967,296 bytes, which is the same as 4GB). However, if you install 4GB on your motherboard and then check the amount of system memory, you might see only 3,198MB (3.12GB), as shown in Figure 3.6.

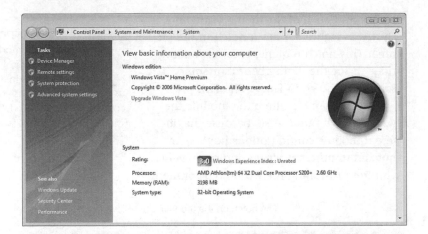

FIGURE 3.6
On a system with 4GB of physical RAM installed, Windows shows only 3,198MB.

What's going on here? The problem is that some devices require a chunk of system memory to operate. For example, the memory on the video card must be mapped to an area in system memory. To allow for this, 32-bit versions of Windows set aside a chunk of the 4GB address space for devices. This means the maximum amount of RAM available to your programs will always be 3.12GB, and it could be even less if you have a lot of devices that require system memory or devices that require a lot of memory (again, some video cards fall into this category).

> **note** To see the amount of memory installed using Vista, select Start and then either right-click Computer and then click Properties, or type **sys-tem** in the Search box and then click System in the search results. To see the amount of memory installed in XP, select Start, right-click My Computer, and then click Properties. In the System Properties dialog box, look for the RAM value in the General tab.

> **note** If you have 3GB physical RAM installed, 32-bit Windows gives you all 3GB. Why doesn't it lop off some of that RAM for the system devices? Because Windows always reserves the area from 3.12GB to 4GB for system devices, no matter how much physical memory is installed. If no physical RAM is present, Windows uses *virtual memory*, instead.

VIRTUAL MEMORY

Regardless of how much RAM is actually installed on your system, Windows operates as though it has the entire 4GB address space to deal with. In reality, Windows uses up the physical RAM first, and then, if more memory is needed, it uses hard disk locations as though they were memory locations. This is called *virtual memory*.

To understand how this process works, you need to know the processors look at memory in 4KB chunks called *pages*. The processor divides the entire address space into the 4KB pages and assigns pages as necessary. When you begin running programs and opening documents, the processor assigns pages that correspond to physical RAM. The processor uses a *page table* to keep track of which piece of data is in which page, which process the page belongs to, whether the data has changed, and so on.

The key is that the pages can be moved to a different location simply by changing the appropriate entry in the page table. In particular, pages can be moved *outside* physical memory and stored temporarily in a special file on the hard disk. This file—it's called a *swap file* or a *paging file*—is set up to emulate physical memory. If you open enough programs or data files so physical memory is exhausted, the swap file is brought into play to augment memory storage.

In the carpenter analogy, the swap file is like a nearby tool shed that holds tools and materials the carpenter might need soon. This method is faster than returning these items to the main storage area.

This means you have two choices when deciding how much memory to buy:

- Limit your RAM purchase to 3GB because a 4th gigabyte is mostly wasted.
- Upgrade your system to support RAM greater than 4GB.

You might be wondering how you upgrade past 4GB when 32-bit Windows can address a maximum of only 4GB. The answer is that you must leave 32-bit versions of Windows behind and opt for a version that supports 64-bit addressing: Windows Vista 64-Bit (Ultimate, Enterprise, Business, Home Premium, or Home Basic) or Windows XP Professional x64 Edition. In theory, 64-bit systems can support 2 to the power of 64 address lines, which is a whopping 18,446,744,073,709,551,616 bytes, or 16 exabytes (about 17 billion gigabytes). That's a staggering number, but we're nowhere near to reaching it, for several reasons:

- Windows Vista Home Basic 64-Bit supports a maximum of 8GB physical RAM.
- Windows Vista Home Premium 64-Bit supports a maximum of 16GB physical RAM.
- Windows Vista Ultimate, Enterprise, and Business 64-Bit support a maximum of 128GB physical RAM.
- XP Pro x64 supports a maximum of 128GB of physical RAM.

Even more limiting, most motherboards don't support more than 8GB RAM installed, so that's really the practical maximum you can install for the foreseeable future. Bear in mind, too, that you need a few other hardware features to make the move past the 4GB barrier:

- The motherboard's chipset must support more than 4GB of address space (this is guaranteed if the motherboard supports installing up to 8GB physical RAM).
- The processor must support 64-bit instructions. This includes all Intel Core 2 processors and all AMD Athlon 64 processors.
- The motherboard's BIOS must support *memory remapping*, which remaps the addresses used by devices from the 3.12GB to 4GB region to a region above 4GB. This feature is usually turned off even in boards that support it, so you need to access the motherboard's BIOS program and turn on memory remapping.

Buying Memory

Buying RAM isn't nearly as complex as buying many of the other components that will make up your homebrew PC. Yes, you can obsess on obscure factors such as latency and timings (plus many other memory features I mercifully spared from you in this chapter), but when you're just starting out there are only a few things you need to worry about. Before I talk about those things, I should mention that, as with the motherboard and processor, quality counts when it comes to RAM modules, so always buy from a major memory manufacturer. Here are a few I recommend:

Corsair (www.corsair.com)

Crucial Technology (www.crucial.com)

G.SKILL (www.gskill.com)

Kingston Technology
(www.kingston.com)

Mushkin (www.mushkin.com)

OCZ Technology
(www.ocztechnology.com)

Patriot (www.patriotmem.com)

> **tip** Crucial Technology offers a handy Memory Advisor tool that enables you to look up a motherboard or computer (by manufacturer, product line, and model) and find out the exact memory you can use. See www.crucial.com.

Here are some pointers to think about before purchasing memory for your system:

- **Match your motherboard**—The memory you buy should match the memory supported by your motherboard. Check your motherboard specs (use the box if you still have it, the product manual, or the manufacturer's website) and determine the exact type of memory you need. Don't worry if you have to use a faster module than what your board supports because the module will still operate fine at the slower speed.

- **Don't exceed you motherboard's capacity**—All motherboards have a maximum RAM capacity, so you shouldn't try to install more RAM than the board can handle. This max is often 8GB, so in most cases you won't have to worry about it.

- **Match your RAM to your needs**—512MB is the minimum amount of RAM required by Windows Vista, and you should consider that a bare minimum. (Note that Windows XP's minimum RAM needs are a mere 64MB.) RAM isn't very expensive these days, so unless you're on a very tight budget, get 1GB RAM for everyday computing needs. If you'll be working with big files, move up to 1.5GB or 2GB. Gamers will want to go right up to 3GB.

- **Get at most 3GB for 32-bit Windows**—As I explained earlier (refer to "Windows and RAM: The 4GB Conundrum"), 32-bit versions of Windows don't give your applications much more than 3GB to work with, even though those versions of Windows support up to 4GB RAM. Therefore, save yourself a bit of money and install only a maximum of 3GB.

- **Buy matching pairs for dual channel mode**—If your motherboard supports dual channel mode, buy your memory modules in pairs (sometimes called *kits*). That way, you're ensured that you're using identical modules in the dual channel configuration, which will prevent problems.

- **Get a heat spreader**—Most memory modules now come with built-in attachments called *heat spreaders* that act like heatsinks to wick heat

3

away from the module. The heat spreader is a metal plate that sits over the memory chips. Some modules use quite elaborate heat spreaders, such as the one shown in Figure 3.7. Heat spreaders keep the memory chips cool, which is always a good idea, so look for modules that come with heat spreaders.

FIGURE 3.7

Some high-end memory modules come with built-in heat spreaders to keep the memory chips cool.

From Here

- To learn how to insert memory modules in motherboard RAM sockets, **see** "Installing Memory Modules," **p. 205**.
- To learn how to remove memory modules from an old PC, **see** "Pulling Out Memory Modules," **p. 232**.
- If you're putting together a PC for business, **see** "How Much Memory Does the Basic Business PC Need?," **p. 248**.
- If you're building a home theater PC, **see** "How Much Memory Does the Home Theater PC Need?," **p. 286**.
- If you're constructing a PC for maximum performance, **see** "How Much Memory Does the High-Performance PC Need?," **p. 331**.
- If you're building a gaming PC, **see** "How Much Memory Does the Killer Gaming PC Need?," **p. 378**.
- If you're putting together a PC on a budget, **see** "How Much Memory Does the Budget PC Need?," **p. 419**.

Hard Drives and Other Storage Devices

Data expands to fill the space available for storage.

—Parkinson's Law of Data

When I bought my first computer back in the mid-80s, its storage features were limited to a single 5.25-inch floppy drive. Yup, there was no hard drive in sight. If I wanted to run a program, I'd insert its disk into the floppy drive and run it from there. If I wanted to save some data, I'd have to remove the program disk, swap in a data disk, save my work, and then reinsert the program disk. (A couple of years later I "upgraded" to a system with *two* floppy drives. I still didn't have a hard drive, but at least I no longer had to swap disks. Bliss!)

More than 20 years later, it's hard to even imagine trying to use a computer that way, particularly because we currently have an embarrassment of riches in the storage world, not only because capacity is as cheap as it has ever been, but also because we have a wide variety of formats to choose from.

That's good news for you because it means you have lots of choices for the storage component of your custom PC. This chapter shows you what's available and gives you pointers on how to make the smartest buys for your PC.

Drive Time: How a Hard Drive Works

Hard drives are an amazing combination of speed and precision, and their inner workings are fascinating. However, I'll save all that for another book because all we're interested in here is those hard drive principles that relate to building your PC. To that end, this section gives you a basic primer on how hard drives get the job done.

In simplest terms, a hard drive consists of three main parts:

■ A rotating disk or platter (often more than one, but we'll ignore that complication here) that is divided into concentric areas called *tracks*.

■ A *read/write head* that floats just above the surface of the platter and performs the actual reading of data to and writing of data from the disk.

■ An actuator arm on which the read/write head moves back and forth. The arm itself is controlled by a highly precise motor.

Figure 4.1 points out these hard drive parts.

FIGURE 4.1

The main parts of a typical hard drive.

Here's the basic procedure the hard drive follows when it needs to write data to the disk:

1. The processor locates a free storage location (called a *sector*) on the disk and passes this information (as well as the data to be written) to the hard drive.

2. The hard drive's actuator arm moves the read/write head over the track that contains the free sector. The time it takes the hard drive to do this is called the *seek time*.

3. The hard drive rotates the disk so that the free sector is directly under the read/write head. The time is takes for the hard drive to do this is called the *latency* (or sometimes the *rotational latency*).

4. The writing mechanism on the read/write head writes the data to the free sector. The time it takes the hard drive to do this is called the *write time*.

Reading data from the disk is similar:

1. The processor determines which sector on the disk contains the required data and passes this information to the hard drive.

2. The hard drive's actuator arm moves the read/write head over the track that contains the sector to be read.

3. The hard drive rotates the disk so the sector to be read is directly under the read/write head.

4. The reading mechanism on the read/write head reads the data from the sector. The time it takes the hard drive to do this is called the *read time*.

As you'll see a bit later, measurements such as the seek time and latency are measured in milliseconds (ms; thousandths of a second), which makes even the cheapest hard drive a near-miracle of engineering.

> **note** Native Command Queuing (NCQ) is a relatively new hard-disk technology aimed at solving a long-standing hard-disk performance problem. Requests for hard-drive data are stored in the memory controller and handled in sequence by the disk's onboard controller. Unfortunately, whenever the controller processes requests for data that is stored in areas far away from each other, it causes a significant performance hit. For example, suppose that request 1 is for data stored near the start of the disk, request 2 is for data near the end of the disk, and request 3 is again for data near the start of the disk. In a typical hard disk, the read/write heads must travel from the start of the disk to the end and then back again, processing each request in the order it was received. With NCQ, the controller reorders the requests so that the 1 and 3, which are close to each other, are carried out first, and only then is the distant request 2 carried out.

4

Capacity, Cache, and More: Understanding Hard Drive Specs

Hard drives are relatively simple devices, at least from the point of view of buying them. However, in your hard drive shopping excursions, you might still come across descriptions that look something like this:

Seagate Barracuda 7200.10 ST3250410AS SATA-300 3.0Gb/s

3.5-inch Internal 250GB 7200RPM 16MB Cache 8.5ms

As is so often the case, these descriptions are pure gobbledygook if you're not used to seeing them. The good news is that not only is it possible to translate this apparently foreign language without much fuss, but you'll also see that the translation itself offers tons of useful information that will help you make an informed choice. Here's a quick summary of what each item in the previous description represents, and the sections that follow expand on most of them:

Seagate	This is the name of the hard drive manufacturer.
Barracuda	This is the manufacturer's hard drive product line.
7200.10 ST3250410AS	This is the hard drive's model number.
SATA-300	This is the hard drive's interface.
3.0Gbps	This is the hard drive's throughput.
3.5-inch Internal	This is the hard drive's form factor.
250GB	This is the capacity of the hard drive.
7200RPM	This is the speed or spin rate of the hard drive.
16MB Cache	This is the size of the hard drive's data cache.
8.5ms	This is the hard drive's average seek time.

The Hard Drive Interface and Throughput

The hard drive *interface* refers to the method by which the drive connects to the motherboard, and the *throughput* (sometimes called the *data transfer rate* or the *bandwidth*) is a measure of how much data the drive can transfer per second. A number of interfaces are available, but the five you'll come upon most often when shopping for a hard drive are PATA, SATA, USB, IEEE 1394, and eSATA.

The PATA Interface

The Parallel Advanced Technology Attachment (PATA) interface is also known as Integrated Device Electronics (IDE) interface and is the old hard drive standard that's slowly being phased out in favor of SATA (which I discuss in the next section). However, most (although not all) motherboards can work with PATA hard drives, so you can always repurpose an old drive to use for backups.

> **tip** See your hard drive documentation to learn which jumpers control the master/slave configurations. The docs might be available online if you no longer have them. If you don't have any documentation, many drives print a jumper diagram on the label. If you don't have that either, you can usually place a jumper on the far left pins for a master configuration and remove the jumper entirely for a slave configuration.

Before going on, I should note that to differentiate this older drive standard from the newer SATA standard, I'm using the term *PATA* here. However, most retailers (indeed, most people) instead use the term *ATA* for the older technology and *SATA* for the newer technology. This isn't strictly accurate (both PATA and SATA are part of the ATA standard), but there you go.

The two main PATA standards you'll see are

PATA/100   This is also called ATA-6, ATA/100, or Ultra-ATA/100. In all cases, the "100" part tells you the throughput, which in this case means 100MBps.

PATA/130   This is also called ATA-7, ATA/133, or Ultra-ATA/133. Here, the "133" tells you that the throughput for this standard is 133MBps.

The back of a PATA hard drive has three sections, pointed out in Figure 4.2.

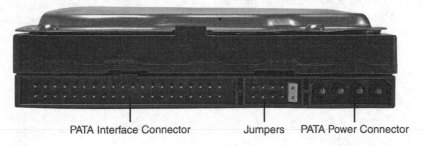

PATA Interface Connector   Jumpers   PATA Power Connector

FIGURE 4.2

The back of a PATA drive holds a couple of connectors and some jumpers.

The PATA interface connector accepts a 40-pin PATA interface cable, shown in Figure 4.3, and the other side of that cable connects to a corresponding 40-pin connector on the motherboard, as shown in Figure 4.4. The PATA power connector accepts a 4-pin power cable, shown in Figure 4.3, and that cable comes from the computer's power supply. The jumpers are mostly used to determine whether the drive is the *master* (the first or only drive on the PATA cable) or a *slave* (the second drive on a PATA cable).

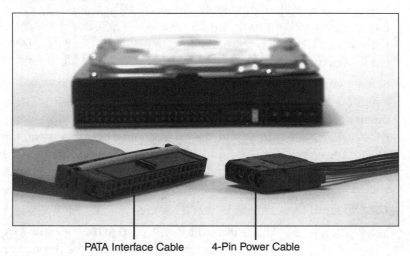

PATA Interface Cable   4-Pin Power Cable

FIGURE 4.3

A PATA interface cable connects the drive to the motherboard, and the PATA power cable connects the drive to the power supply.

While we're on the subject of PATA cables, note that most of them use the flat "ribbon" style shown in Figure 4.5. Unfortunately, these wide cables impede airflow through the case by trapping or blocking air. Whenever possible, swap ribbon cables with rounded cables, also shown in Figure 4.5, which greatly improve case airflow.

caution Some people caution against using rounded cables because they believe there's a greater chance of interference since the data lines are closer together. I've never experienced any problems using these cables, but it's something to keep in mind.

Motherboard PATA Connector

FIGURE 4.4

All motherboards come with at least one PATA interface connector.

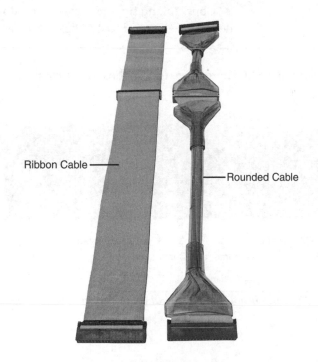

Ribbon Cable

Rounded Cable

FIGURE 4.5

Replace PATA ribbon cables with rounded cables to improve case airflow.

The SATA Interface

The Serial Advanced Technology Attachment (SATA) interface is the current gold standard for PCs, and it's the only standard you should really consider for the internal hard drive (or drives) on your homebuilt system. Why? Two reasons: SATA drives cost about the same as the equivalent PATA drive, but the SATA drive will be significantly faster. How much faster? Anywhere from 1.5 times to 3 times faster! To see why, consider the two SATA standards you'll encounter:

SATA/150   This is also called SATA 1. The "150" part tells you the throughput, which in this case means 150MBps. You might also see a SATA/150 drive's throughput listed as 1.5Gbps. Technically, that's the rate at which the hard drive transfers data, but some of that is overhead, so the actual rate is closer to 1.2Gbps, which is the same as 150MBps (because there are 8 bits in a byte).

SATA/300   This is also called SATA 2. The "300" part tells you the throughput, which in this case means 300MBps. Again, you sometimes see a SATA/300 drive's throughput listed as 3.0Gbps. Taking signaling overhead into account, the actual rate is closer to 2.4Gbps, which is the same as 300MBps.

The back of a SATA hard drive usually has four sections, pointed out in Figure 4.6.

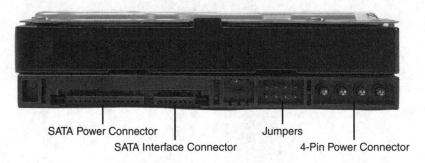

SATA Power Connector

SATA Interface Connector

Jumpers

4-Pin Power Connector

FIGURE 4.6

The back of a SATA drive usually holds several connectors and some jumpers.

The SATA interface connector accepts a 7-pin SATA interface cable, shown in Figure 4.7, and the other side of that cable connects to a corresponding 7-pin connector on the motherboard, as shown in Figure 4.8. The SATA power connector accepts a 15-pin power cable, shown in Figure 4.7, and that cable comes from the computer's power supply. (Many SATA drives also include a legacy 4-pin power connector, just in case your power supply doesn't come with either a SATA power cable or a 4-pin-to-15-pin power adapter.) The jumpers are mostly used to limit a SATA/300 drive to 1.5Gbps throughput, which enables you to use the drive on a motherboard that supports only a 1.5Gbps transfer rate.

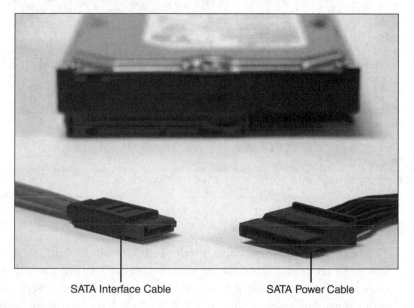

SATA Interface Cable   SATA Power Cable

FIGURE 4.7

A SATA interface cable connects the drive to the motherboard, and the SATA power cable connects the drive to the power supply.

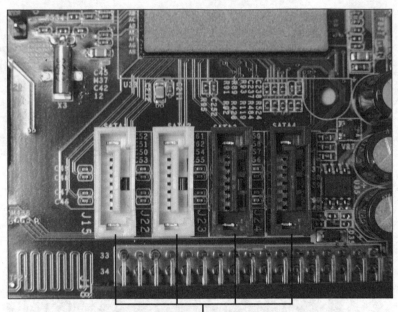

Motherboard SATA Connectors

FIGURE 4.8

All motherboards come with two or more SATA interface connectors.

External Drive Interfaces

The PATA and SATA hard drive interfaces are for internal drives. If your case has room for only a small number of internal drives, then the only way to augment your local storage is to add one or more external drives. Note, too, that external drives also offer portability, which lets you attach the drive to another system, take important files with you, and so on. For external drives, you have three more choices:

USB 2.0   These external drives attach to a USB 2.0 port, either a motherboard connector on the back of the computer or a case connector on the front of the computer (see Figure 4.9). Make sure you get USB 2.0, which offers a transfer rate of 480Mbps (60MBps), compared to a mere 12Mbps (1.5MBps) for USB 1.1.

eSATA   This is an external version of SATA (that's what the *e* stands for), and these drives attach to an eSATA connector, which could be a motherboard connector on the back of the computer, a case connector on the front of the computer (see Figure 4.8), or a connector on an expansion card. Other than the fact that it sits outside your PC, an eSATA drive is the same as an internal SATA/300 drive, which means you still get the 300MBps throughput.

IEEE 1394   These external drives attach to an IEEE-1394 (also called FireWire) connector, which could be a motherboard connector on the back of the computer, a case connector on the front of the computer (see Figure 4.8), or a connector on an expansion card. You can get either IEEE 1394a (FireWire 400), which offers 400Mbps data throughput, or IEEE 1394b (FireWire 800), which offers 800Mbps data throughput.

For maximum flexibility, consider an external drive that offers two or more of these interfaces. For example, it's now fairly common to see external drives that offer both a USB 2.0 port and an eSATA port, as shown in Figure 4.10.

USB 2.0 Connectors

eSATA Connector

IEEE-1394 Connector

FIGURE 4.9

Some high-end cases offer front-panel connectors for all three external hard drive interfaces.

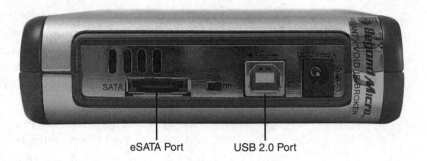

eSATA Port   USB 2.0 Port

FIGURE 4.10

Some external hard drives come with both USB 2.0 and eSATA ports.

The Hard Drive Form Factor

The hard drive *form factor* refers to the dimensions of the drive—and more specifically to the approximate width of the drive. By far the most common hard drive form factor is 3.5 inches (the actual width is closer to 4 inches). Almost every case you buy will have hard drive bays that support 3.5-inch drives. The other common hard drive form factor is 2.5 inches (the actual width is closer to 2.75 inches), which is most often present in notebook drives. However, if you're building a mini-ITX system, there's a good chance your case drive bays will require 2.5-inch drives. Figure 4.11 shows a 3.5-inch and a 2.5-inch hard drive for comparison.

3.5-Inch Hard Drive   2.5-Inch Hard Drive

FIGURE 4.11

The two most common hard drive form factors are 3.5-inch and 2.5-inch.

The Hard Drive Capacity

The hard drive *capacity* is a measure of the amount of data the drive can store. This is always measured in gigabytes these days, and it's getting hard to find a hard drive smaller than 80GB. Even 200GB hard drives can be found for around $50, and prices are falling fast. So storage is becoming more affordable, but we're also storing more. We're ripping and downloading audio CDs and

DVDs, recording TV shows, making digital video movies, and taking digital camera images by the thousands. So how do you know how much storage you need?

One way to get some idea is to examine your storage needs, particularly for media. To help you calculate this, here's how much a gigabyte will store for various types of media:

- 68 minutes of VHS-quality video
- 17 minutes of DVD-quality video
- Less than 3 minutes of HDTV-quality video
- 18 hours of MP3 music (ripped at 128Kbps)
- 7 hours of MP3 music (ripped at 320Kbps)
- 600 digital photos (6 megapixels, JPG format)
- 55 digital photos (6 megapixels, BMP format)

> **note** Keep your eyes peeled on the new *solid-state* hard drives (SSDs) that are starting to appear. These 2.5-inch drives are made from solid-state semiconductors, which means they have no moving parts. As a result, SSDs are faster than HDDs, last longer, use less power, weigh less, and are completely silent. The downside is price. This is still bleeding-edge technology, so expect to pay $300–$400 for a 32GB SSD. Prices are dropping fast, however, so I'm sure it won't be long before SSDs become a viable alternative to regular drives.

The Hard Drive Speed

The hard drive *speed* is a measure of how fast the drive's internal platters spin, measured in revolutions per minute (rpm). In general, the higher the rpm value, the better the drive's performance. Most PATA and SATA hard drives spin at 7200rpm, although some older drives spin at 5400rpm. You should avoid these older drives because the performance hit is substantial, and they're not that much cheaper than the equivalent 7200rpm drive. If money is no object, SATA drives are available that spin at 10000rpm, which offers a substantial performance boost.

The Hard Drive Cache

The hard drive *cache* refers to a RAM memory area embedded in the hard drive. This memory is used as a holding place for frequently used bits of data. If the CPU finds the data it needs in the hard drive cache, it saves time because it can load that data directly into memory instead of asking the hard drive to fetch it from the disk. The bigger the hard drive cache, the more data it can hold, so the more likely the CPU is to find the data it needs, and thus the better the overall performance of the hard drive.

Inexpensive hard drives usually come with just a 2MB cache, whereas most mainstream drives come with either an 8MB or a 16MB cache. Some high-end drives come with a whopping 32MB cache.

The Hard Drive Seek Time

When I explained the workings of a typical hard drive earlier (see "Drive Time: How a Hard Drive Works"), you learned that the four measures of hard disk read/write performance are the seek time, the latency, the write time, and the read time. In all cases, the lower the time, the faster the drive's performance.

Of these, the seek time is the most important—or, at least, it's the one that's most often quoted in hard drive ads and descriptions. The seek time is usually an average because sometimes the read/write head has to travel a relatively long distance along the arm and sometimes a relatively short distance. The seek time, similar to the latency, write, and read time, is measured in milliseconds. For a low-end drive, the average seek time is usually 12ms or higher; for a mainstream drive, the average seek time is usually around 10ms; and for a high-end drive, the average seek time is usually under 9ms. (For comparison, note that most of the 10000rpm drives on the market now boast average seek times around 4.6ms, which is blazingly fast.)

Buying a Hard Drive

Purchasing a hard drive for your homebuilt system doesn't have to be a complex exercise. In fact, you can make a smart hard drive choice by paying attention to just three numbers:

Cost/GB   This is the cost per gigabyte, which you calculate by dividing the price of the hard drive by its storage capacity. Here are some examples:

Price	Capacity	Cost/GB
$35.99	80GB	$0.45
$54.99	200GB	$0.27
$119.99	500GB	$0.24
$199.99	750GB	$0.27
$299.99	1,000GB	$0.30

As you can see, the low end and the high end cost more per gigabyte and the sweet spot is right in the middle with (in this case) the 500GB drive. Note that, from a cost/GB perspective, there's not a lot of difference between the

200GB, 500GB, and 750GB drives. So, if you have only minimal storage needs on your system, get the 200GB drive; if you need a bigger drive to store lots of media, get the 750GB drive.

Cache
The size of the hard drive cache can make a big difference in performance. So, if you're looking at two drives that are more or less the same in other respects (particularly cost/GB), choose the one that has the bigger cache.

Seek time
As you've learned, the lower the average seek time, the faster the drive. So, again, if the other factors are about equal, get the drive that has the lower seek time.

Building a hard drive that's fast, solid, reliable, quiet, and cool is a tall order, which might be why there aren't a large number of hard disk manufacturers—and of those manufacturers, only a few produce top-quality drives. In fact, I recommend only the following three hard drive companies:

Hitachi (www.hitachigst.com)

Seagate (www.seagate.com)

Western Digital (www.westerndigital.com)

Here are a few other points to think about when making your hard drive purchase:

- **For a new drive, choose SATA/300**—These days, there's no point in looking at PATA/100, PATA/133, or SATA/150 drives. SATA/300 drives give you by far the best performance, and the prices are basically the same. Need I say more?

- **Match your motherboard's data transfer rate**—The only time you might want to get a SATA/150 drive is if your motherboard supports only 1.5Gbps data transfers. However, a better idea is to get a SATA/300 hard drive with a jumper that enables the drive to operate at 1.5Gbps. That way, if you later get a mobo that supports 3Gbps, you need only adjust the drive's jumper to get the full benefit of SATA/300.

- **One drive or two**—Whether you opt for one hard drive or two really depends on your budget. The advantage to having two drives is that you can put the operating system (and perhaps your applications) on one drive and your data on another. That way, if the operating system crashes, you can reformat the drive and reinstall the operating system, and all the while your precious data will remain intact. A common setup is to use a relatively small hard drive for the operating system (say, 80GB or 100GB) and a larger hard drive for the data.

■ **Stick with 7200 RPM for now—**
Unless you want a machine that
has the highest performance possible, it's best to avoid 10000rpm
drives for now, and stick with
7200rpm drives. They're cheaper
and quieter, and their performance
is more than adequate for almost
all uses.

> **note** Alternatively, you can
> put everything on
> one drive and use the second
> drive to hold a *drive image*, which
> is an exact copy of the drive. Windows Vista's Complete PC Backup
> feature can create drive images,
> as can third-party utilities such as
> Norton Ghost
> (www.symantec.com) and Acronis
> True Image (www.acronis.com).
> For details on running Vista's
> Complete PC Backup, see "Creating a System Image Backup" in
> Chapter 17, "Maintaining Your
> Computer Hardware."

Disc Driving: Choosing an Optical Drive

Any homebrew system worth its chips
should have an *optical drive*, a catchall term
that includes every type of CD and DVD drive, as well as the latest Blu-ray
and HD DVD drives. The *optical* part tells you that these drives use light—
specifically, a semiconductor laser—to read data from and write data to the
disc. (For example, the *Blu* in Blu-ray comes from the fact that it uses laser
light with a wavelength in the blue section of the spectrum.) Among many
other uses, adding an optical drive enables your system to play audio CD,
DVD movies, high-definition video (you need a Blu-Ray or HD DVD drive for
that), install programs and device drivers, store data, and make backups.

The next few sections tell you a bit more about optical drives, which will help
you decide which kind to buy for the system you're building.

The Data's the Things: Optical Disc Capacities

All the discs you use with optical drives have a specific capacity, and that
capacity determines the type of content that can go on the disc (for example,
most movies can fit on a DVD, but the capacity of a CD is too small). If you
have a drive that can write data to a disc, the capacity also tells you the maximum amount of data you can store on the disc. Table 4.1 lists the maximum
capacities for the major disc types.

Table 4.1   Maximum Capacities for Various Optical Discs

Disc	Capacity
CD	700MB
Single-layer DVD	4.7GB
Double-layer DVD	8.5GB
Single-layer HD DVD	15GB
Dual-layer HD DVD	30GB
Single-layer Blu-ray	25GB
Dual-layer Blu-ray	50GB

A Tour of Optical Drive Types

Here's a quick look at the types of optical drives you're likely to come across when shopping for a drive:

CD-ROM drive   This stands for *compact disc read-only memory*. A CD-ROM drive is one in which you insert a CD-ROM disc that might contain data, software, or music. The *ROM* part of the drive name means that your computer can only read the disc's contents; it can't change the contents.

CD-R drive   This stands for *compact disc-recordable*. A CD-R drive allows you to record, or *burn*, data to a CD-R disc. Keep in mind that you can record data to the CD-R disc only once. After that, you can't change the disc's contents. CD-R drives can also read data from previously recorded CD-R discs, as well as from CD-ROM discs.

CD-RW drive   This stands for *compact disc-rewritable*. A CD-RW drive allows you to record data to a CD-RW disc. You can add data to and erase data from a CD-RW disc as often as you want. CD-RW drives can also read data from CD-R and CD-ROM discs.

note The phrase *dual layer* means that the optical drive writes data on both sides of the disc. Note that the drive must support dual-layer recording to do this.

DVD-ROM drive	This stands for *digital versatile disc-read-only memory.* A DVD-ROM drive allows you to use a DVD-ROM disc, which might contain data or software. The *ROM* part of the drive name means your computer can only read the disc's contents; you cannot change the contents. All DVD drives can also read all CD-ROM, CD-R, and CD-RW discs.

> **note** After the DVD-R format was released, a group called the DVD+RW Alliance released the DVD+R format, which is a bit more robust than the earlier format. The two formats aren't compatible, unfortunately, but you shouldn't have to choose between the two. Almost all drives support DVD±R, a hybrid format that supports both DVD-R and DVD+R.

DVD-R, DVD+R, or DVD±R drive	This stands for *digital versatile disc-recordable.* A DVD-R, DVD+R, or DVD±R drive allows you to record data once to a DVD-R, DVD+R, or DVD±R disc. The ± symbol means the drive supports both the DVD-R and DVD+R formats. DVD-R, DVD+R, and DVD±R drives can read data from previously recorded DVD-R, DVD+R, or DVD±R discs, as well as from DVD-ROM discs.
DVD-RW, DVD+RW, or DVD±RW drive	This stands for *digital versatile disc-rewritable.* A DVD-RW, DVD+RW, or DVD±RW drive allows you to record data to a DVD-RW, DVD+RW, or DVD±RW disc. You can add data to and erase data from the disc as often as you want.
BD-ROM	This stands for *Blu-ray disk-read-only memory.* A BD-ROM drive allows you to use a Blue-ray disc, which might contain data or high-definition video. The *ROM* part of the drive name means your computer can only read the disc's contents; you cannot change the contents. All Blu-ray drives can also read all CD and DVD discs.
BD-R	This stands for *Blu-ray disc-recordable.* A BD-R drive allows you to record data once to a BD-R disc. BD-R drives can read data from previously recorded BD-R discs, as well as from Blu-ray discs.

BD-RE

This stands for *Blu-ray disc-recordable erasable*. A BD-RE drive allows you to record data to a BD-RE disc. You can add data to and erase data from the disc as often as you want.

> **note** If the optical drive supports dual-layer recording, you'll see *DL* added to the supported formats. For example, if a DVD±RW drive supports dual-layer recording, you'll see the format listed as DVD±RW DL.

HD DVD-ROM

This stands for *high-definition digital versatile disc-read-only memory*. An HD DVD-ROM drive allows you to use an HD DVD disc, which might contain data or high-definition video. The *ROM* part of the drive name means your computer can only read the disc's contents; you cannot change the contents. All HD DVD drives can also read all CD and DVD discs.

HD DVD-R

This stands for *high-definition digital versatile disc-recordable*. An HD DVD-R drive allows you to record data once to an HD DVD-R disc. HD DVD-R drives can read data from previously recorded HD DVD-R discs, as well as from HD DVD discs.

HD DVD-RW

This stands for *high-definition digital versatile disc-rewritable*. An HD DVD-RW drive allows you to record data to an HD DVD-RW disc. You can add data to and erase data from the disc as often as you want.

Speed Is All: Understanding Optical Drive Speeds

Besides the supported formats, probably the most important consideration when purchasing an optical drive is the speed at which it operates. Optical drive performance is generally measured by how fast it is in three categories:

Write speed

This determines how fast a recordable drive (CD-R, DVD-R, DVD+R, DVD±R, BD-R, or HD DVD-R) records data.

Rewrite speed

This determines how fast a rewritable drive (CD-RW, DVD-RW, DVD+RW, or DVD±RW, BD-RE, or HD DVD-RW) rewrites data.

Read speed

This determines how fast the drive reads a disc's contents.

In all cases, the speed is measured relative to a baseline amount, which is the audio CD rate of 150KBps. This is designated as 1x, and all optical drive speeds are a multiple of this. For example, a read speed of 52x means the drive reads data 52 times faster than a music CD player.

Note that you sometimes see the drive speed shown like this:

```
DVD+RW  16X8X18
```

You interpret the numbers as *writeXrewriteXread*, so in this example the write speed is 16x, the rewrite speed is 8x, and the read speed is 18x.

The following observations are generally true regarding optical drive speeds:

- CD drives are faster than DVD drives, which are faster than Blu-ray or HD DVD drives.
- Read speeds are faster than write speeds, and write speeds are faster than rewrite speeds.
- ROM drive read speeds are faster than burner read speeds.

Buying an Optical Drive

Optical drives are one of the least expensive components you'll add to your system. For example, if you all you want to do is rip and burn audio CDs, you can buy a super-fast CD-RW drive (I'm talking about 52x write speed, 32x rewrite speed, and 52x read speed) for under $20! Even DVD±RW drives with write speeds of 20x can be had for under $30.

There's lots of competition in this market, which is why prices are low and features are high. Quite a few manufacturers operate in the optical drive market, but here are the ones I've had good dealings with:

LG Electronics (www.lge.com)

Lite-On (www.liteonit.com)

Pioneer (www.pioneerelectronics.com)

Philips (www.philips.com)

Plextor (www.plextor.com)

Samsung (www.samsung.com)

Sony (www.sony.com)

Here are a few other pointers and notes to consider when buying an optical drive for your custom system:

- **Check the cache size**—All optical drives come with an onboard memory cache for storing bits of frequently used data. This improves performance because it's many times faster for the processor to retrieve the data it needs from the cache than from the disc. The bigger the cache, the better the performance. On burners, the cache also helps to keep the burning process running smoothly by feeding a constant supply of data to the drive. Most drives nowadays come with a 2MB cache, but some drives have a 4MB cache.

- **Check the access time**—The average time it takes the optical drive to access data on the disc is called the *access time*, and it's measured in milliseconds. The lower the access time, the faster the drive.

- **Check out SATA optical drives**—It used to be that optical drives came with only an ATA interface, but SATA drives started showing up a while back. Unfortunately, those drives were plagued with all kinds of problems, and the interface never took off. I'm happy to report that the manufacturers have fixed the problems, and SATA/150 optical drives are becoming quite popular. The higher bandwidth improves performance, and the SATA connector and power cables are easier to use than the larger ATA and legacy power cables.

- **Consider buying two drives**—Earlier I mentioned that the read speeds of ROM drives are faster than the reader speeds of burners. Given that, a popular system configuration is to add both a ROM drive and a burner, such as a DVD-ROM drive and a DVD±RW drive. This way, you can use the DVD-ROM drive when you need read-only performance (such as when you're installing a program or accessing data on a disc), and you can use the DVD±RW drive when you need to burn data to a disc.

- **Blu-ray or HD DVD**—As I write this in early 2008, the format war between Blu-ray and HD DVD is all but over. Toshiba, the main company behind the HD DVD format, announced on February 19, 2008 that it would no longer sell HD DVD players. The death blows to the HD DVD format came first in January 2008 when Warner Bros. announced it would ship its high-def movies exclusively in the Blu-Ray format, and then earlier in February 2008 when Wal-Mart announced it would sell only Blu-Ray discs. So if you want to play HD discs in your custom PC, go for a Blu-ray drive.

4

More Storage Devices

Most PCs don't require more than a hard drive and an optical drive (two of each is becoming a common system configuration). However, for the sake of storage completeness, here are three other storage devices to consider:

Memory card reader   If you use various types of memory cards—CompactFlash, Secure Digital, MultiMediaCard, Memory Stick, and so on—you should consider adding an internal memory card reader to your system. Your best bet is to get a USB reader, most of which insert into an external 3.5-inch drive bay inside your computer and connect to one of your motherboard's USB headers. Figure 4.12 shows an example.

FIGURE 4.12

An internal memory card reader is a must if you use multiple memory card formats.

Tape drive   For many years, tape drives were *the* backup option. Of course, this was a time when the alternative was to back up to 1.44MB floppy disks, and most sane people would rather have had a tax audit or root canal. That was also a time when hard drives were too expensive to use as backup media. That has all changed in recent years, and tape drives have become far less popular because they're both slow and expensive. So if you're looking for a good backup solution, spend your money on a second (or third) hard drive and take a pass on the tape drive.

Floppy drive

Most motherboards come with a floppy disk connector, but that doesn't mean you should use one. There's nothing a floppy drive can do that a flash drive or memory card can't do better and faster. All a floppy drive does is use up an external drive bay, add an extra ribbon cable to mess up the airflow in the case, and drain a bit of power. It's time to retire the floppy once and for all and move on with our lives.

From Here

■ To learn how to remove a hard drive from an old PC, **see** "Taking Out a Hard Drive," **p. 228**.

■ If you're putting together a PC for business, **see** "Storage Options for the Basic Business PC," **p. 249**.

■ If you're building a home theater PC, **see** "Storage Options for the Home Theater PC," **p. 286**.

■ If you're constructing a PC for maximum performance, **see** "Storage Options for the High-Performance PC," **p. 333**.

■ If you're building a gaming PC, **see** "Storage Options for the Killer Gaming PC," **p. 373**.

■ If you're putting together a PC on a budget, **see** "Storage Options for the Budget PC," **p. 420**.

■ For the details on running Vista's Complete PC Backup, **see** "Creating a System Image Backup," **p. 520**.

4

Eyes to See and Ears to Hear: Video and Audio Hardware

Nature has given us two ears, two eyes, and but one tongue—to the end that we should hear and see more than we speak.

—Socrates

Many computers are designed to run in *headless* mode, which means the computer isn't connected to a keyboard, mouse, monitor, or speakers. In fact, these "appliances" (as they're sometimes called) often don't come with any video or audio capabilities at all, a configuration that is truly (albeit still figuratively) headless: no eyes and no ears.

A headless configuration is fine for machines you don't interact with directly, such as Windows Home Server boxes that you access remotely via a program called the Windows Home Server Console. That's unlikely to be the setup of your home-built computer, which will almost certainly be connected to a monitor and a pair (or more) of speakers. To make those connections, you need the appropriate hardware inside the computer: a video card to send graphics data to the monitor and a sound card to send audio data to the speakers (as well as to receive data from input devices such as microphones and external audio equipment).

This chapter prepares you for this portion of the building process by giving you some background on both video and sound cards and by giving you a few tips and pointers that will help you pick out the media hardware that's best suited to your needs.

Assessing Your Video Card Needs

The *video card* (sometimes called a *video adapter*) is a system component that usually comes in the form of a circuit board that plugs into a bus slot inside the computer. (Therefore, the video card is also called a *graphics board*, a *graphics card*, and a *graphics adapter*. Note, too, that some video cards are part of the computer's motherboard.)

The video card's job is to enable software to display text or an image on the monitor. How images appear on your monitor is a function of two measurements: the color depth and resolution.

The *color depth* is a measure of the number of colors available to display images on the screen. In general, the greater the number of colors, the sharper your screen image appear—and the more processing power required to display those colors. Color depth is usually expressed in either bits or total colors. For example, a 4-bit display can handle up to 16 colors (because 2 to the power of 4 equals 16). Table 5.1 lists the bit values for the most common color depths.

Table 5.1   Bit Values for Some Standard Color Depths

Bits	Colors
4	16
8	256
15	32,268
16	65,536
24	16,777,216
32	16,777,216

The *resolution* is a measure of the density of the pixels used to display the screen image. The pixels are arranged in a row-and-column format, so the resolution is expressed as *rows × columns*, where *rows* is the number of pixel rows and *columns* is the number of pixel columns. For example, a 1024 × 768 resolution means screen images are displayed using 1,024 rows of pixels and 768 columns of pixels. The higher the resolution, the sharper your images appear. Individual screen items—such as icons and dialog boxes—also get smaller at higher resolutions because these items tend to have a fixed height and width, expressed in pixels. For example, a dialog box that's 320 pixels wide appears half as wide as the screen at 640 × 480. However, it appears to be only one quarter of the screen width at 1280 × 1,024 (a common resolution for medium-size monitors).

> **note** The 32-bit color depth yields the same number of colors as the 24-bit depth because the extra 8 bits are used for an alpha channel, which can hold transparency information.

> **note** On some systems, the color depth value isn't listed as a specific number of bits or colors. Instead, the color depth is listed as either "Medium" or "Thousands", both of which refer to the 16-bit, 65,536-color depth, or as "Highest" or "Millions", both of which refer to the 32-bit, 16,777,216-color depth.

The key thing to bear in mind about all this is that there's usually a trade-off between color depth and resolution, and that trade-off is based on the memory installed on the video card. That is, depending on how much video memory is installed on the card, you might have to trade off higher color depth with lower resolution, or vice versa.

Why does the amount of video memory matter? Earlier I mentioned that each screen image is stored in a frame buffer. The size of that buffer is a function of the total number of pixels used in the resolution and the number of bits required to "light" each pixel. For example, a resolution of 800 × 600 means there are a total of 480,000 pixels. If each pixel uses a color depth of 16 bits, then a total a 7,680,000 bits is required to hold the entire screen image, which is equivalent to about 937KB. If you bump up the resolution to 1280 × 1024 and use a 32-bit color depth, the total number of bits involved leaps to 41,943,040, which is about 5.1MB. However, most video cards support a feature called *triple buffering*,

> **note** A *pixel* is a tiny element that displays the individual dots that make up the screen image (*pixel* is short for "picture element"). Each pixel consists of three components—red, green, and blue—and these are manipulated to produce a specific color.

5

where the card implements two frame buffers for 2D rendering—one for the current screen and one for the next screen image to be displayed—and a third buffer for 3D data (this is called the *Z buffer*). This effectively triples the memory required. In the 1280 × 1024 32-bit example, the total amount of memory needed is 15.3MB. If you have an older video card graphics adapter with just 8MB of video memory, you won't be able to select the 1280 × 1024 resolution unless you drop the color depth down to 16 bits (bringing the memory requirement down to about 7.6MB).

In general, you use the following formula to calculate the number of bytes required to display a screen:

*rows * columns * bits * 3 / 8*

rows	The number of rows in the resolution
columns	The number of columns in the resolution
bits	The number of bits in the color depth

Divide the result by 1,048,576 to get the number of megabytes.

Table 5.2 lists the most common resolutions (I've also included the name of the corresponding display standard) and color depth values and calculates the amount of memory.

Table 5.2   Translating Resolution and Color Depth into Memory Required

Standard	Resolution	Color Depth	Memory
VGA	640 × 480	16 bits	1.8MB
VGA	640 × 480	32 bits	3.6MB
SVGA	800 × 600	16 bits	2.7MB
SVGA	800 × 600	32 bits	5.4B
XGA	1024 × 768	16 bits	4.5MB
XGA	1024 × 768	32 bits	9MB
WXGA	1280 × 800	16 bits	6MB
WXGA	1280 × 800	32 bits	12MB
SXGA	1280 × 1024	16 bits	7.5MB
SXGA	1280 × 1024	32 bits	15MB
WXGA+	1440 × 900	16 bits	7.5MB
WXGA+	1440 × 900	32 bits	15MB
UXGA	1600 × 1200	16 bits	10.8MB
UXGA	1600 × 1200	32 bits	21.6MB

Table 5.2	Continued		
Standard	Resolution	Color Depth	Memory
HDTV	1920 × 1080	16 bits	12MB
HDTV	1920 × 1080	32 bits	24MB
QXGA	2048 × 1536	16 bits	18MB
QXGA	2048 × 1536	32 bits	36MB
QSXGA	2560 × 2048	16 bits	30MB
QSXGA	2560 × 2048	32 bits	60MB

Finally, I should mention that the memory requirements shown in Table 5.2 still don't account for all the memory used by a typical video card. For example, all cards require a bit of extra memory to perform *antialiasing* (a rendering techniques that smoothes jagged lines and other unwanted artifacts).

GPU, GDDR, SLI, and More: Understanding Video Card Specs

Like most PC components, video cards come encrusted with acronyms, jargon, and specs galore. When shopping for a video card, you therefore might come across a description that looks similar to the following:

XFX PVT73EYARG GeForce 7300GT 533MHz 512MB GDDR2,

PCI Express x16, SLI Ready, DVI, VGA, HDTV

The good news is that there's quite a bit of useful information in this description, and not an ounce of marketing fluff. Of course, you need a translator to figure out the useful stuff. Here's a quick summary of what each item in this description represents, and the sections that follow expand on many of them:

XFX	This is the name of the video card manufacturer.
PVT73EYARG	This is the manufacturer's model number for the video card.
GeForce 7300GT	This is the name of the graphics processing unit (GPU) chipset.
533MHz	This is the speed of the memory clock.
512MB	This is the amount of graphics memory on the card.

GDDR2   This is the type of graphics memory on the card.

PCI Express x16   This is the interface slot type used by the card.
                      Refer to Chapter 1, "The Barebones: The
                      Motherboard, Case, and Power Supply," to learn
                      about motherboard slot types.

→   For a rundown on motherboard slot types, **see** "Understanding Expansion Slot Types," **p. 14**.

SLI Ready   This tells you that you can combine this video card
                      with a second video card using the SLI dual-GPU
                      technology.

DVI   This tells you that the card comes with a DVI
                      connector.

VGA   This tells you that the card comes with a VGA
                      connector.

HDTV   This tells you that the card comes with an HDTV
                      connector.

The GPU Chipset

The heart and soul of any modern video card is the graphics processing unit
(GPU). This is a dedicated microprocessor that has been optimized to work
with graphical operations. This enables the chip to render 2D and 3D graphics
at blazing speeds and saves the CPU from having to perform these operations.
The GPU is part of a larger graphics chipset that also includes the video memory and bus interface. The GPU and graphics chipset fully determine the capabilities of the video card.

At the moment, two GPU/chipset manufacturers dominate the market:

■ **ATI**—This company (recently purchased by the CPU manufacturer
AMD) offers several chipset lines, including the Radeon and FireGL,
with the Radeon chipset being the best choice for your home-built PC.
Current offerings are the Radeon X1000 series and the Radeon HD
2000 and HD 3000 series. In the ATI naming scheme, the second digit
tells you the targeted market segment. If the number is from 0 to 4, the
chipset is aimed at the budget or low-end market (for example, the
Radeon X1050 or HD 2400); if the number is from 5 to 7, the chipset is
targeted at the mainstream or mid-range market (for example, the
Radeon X1550 or HD 2600); if the number is from 8 or 9, the chipset is
aimed at the enthusiast or high-end market (for example, the Radeon
X1950 or HD 2900).

- **NVIDIA**—This company currently offers the GeForce and Quadro chipset lines, with the GeForce chipset being the best choice for a custom PC. Current offerings are the GeForce 6 series, GeForce 7 series, and GeForce 8 series. (The GeForce 9 series should be available by the time you read this.) The higher the series number, the more advanced the chipset technology (and the higher the price). Within each series, the higher the number, the more features the chipset offers. For example, the GeForce 7300 chipset is for the low-end market; the GeForce 7600 chipset is for the mid-range market; and the GeForce 7900 is for the high-end market.

It's important to differentiate between the chipset manufacturer and the video card manufacturer. The chipset manufacturers sell their chips to other companies, and those companies add the chips to their video cards. This is why you can easily see a number of different video cards using the same chipset. For example, all the following video cards use NVIDIA's GeForce 8800GTS chipset:

EVGA 320-P2-N815-A3 GeForce 8800GTS

XFX PVT80GGHD4 GeForce 8800GTS

BFG Tech BFGR88320GTSOC2E GeForce 8800GTS

Foxconn FV-N88SMBD2-ONOC GeForce 8800GTS

Finally, note that (just to keep us on our toes) ATI also makes its own video cards.

Video Memory

All video cards come with their own set of memory chips, and a big part of the high performance of modern video cards is that they have easy and fast access to onboard memory rather than relying on a slower pipeline to the system memory. When you're examining the specs of video cards, you'll often come across four memory-related numbers:

- **Memory size**—You saw earlier that the amount of video memory on a card is crucial in determining the resolution and color depth. However, modern video cards use memory for many chores other than frame buffering, so the same is true for a video card as it is for a motherboard: the more memory, the better the performance.

- **Memory type**—In Chapter 3, "The Work Area: Memory," you learned about the various system memory types, and you particularly learned about double data rate (DDR) memory, which transfers data at the beginning and the end of each clock cycle, and DDR2 memory, which offers higher clock speeds than DDR. DDR2 is also a common video memory technology (although it's called GDDR2, where the *G* stands for graphics), although the need for video RAM speed has caused chipset manufacturers to push the envelope a bit in recent years. These days the most common video memory type is GDDR3, which offers higher clock speeds than GDDR2; GDDR4 cards are also available that offer still higher speeds.

➔   For the specifics on DDR system memory, **see** "The Memory Type and Speed," **p. 68**.

- ■ **Memory clock speed**—The speed of the memory clock affects performance in that the faster the clock, the more data the card can process. GDDR2 memory usually offers clock speeds in the 350MHz–700MHz range; for GDDR3, the usual range is 500MHz–800MHz; for GDDR4, the range is 800MHz–1GHz.

- ■ **Memory interface width**—This value tells you the width of the data pathway between the GPU and the video memory, in bits. The wider the path, the better the performance. Lower-end cards use a 64-bit path (some even go as low as 32 bits); mid-range video cards use a 128-bit path; and high-end cards use a 256-bit path. Some video cards now even use 320-bit or 384-bit paths.

Dual-GPU Support

You learned in Chapter 2, "The Brains: The Central Processing Unit," that dual-core processors improve performance because the processing load can be balanced between the two cores. If that works for a CPU, you might be thinking that the same idea could work for a GPU. Sure enough, now technologies are available that enable dual-GPU support. However, instead of two GPUs on a single card, these technologies require two separate video cards that are then bridged to enable both cards to render a single screen in tandem. Both ATI and NVIDIA offer dual-GPU chipsets:

- ■ **ATI CrossFire**—ATI's dual-GPU technology is called *CrossFire*. To use it, you need a motherboard with a CrossFire-compatible chipset and two free PCI Express slots that are designed for CrossFire, as well as two CrossFire-capable video cards from the same Radeon chipset family (for example, two Radeon X1950 cards from any manufacturer). To learn more about CrossFire-compatible equipment, see http://ati.amd.com/technology/crossfire/.

■ **NVIDIA SLI**—NVIDIA's dual-GPU technology is called *scalable link interface (SLI)*. To use it, you need a motherboard with an SLI-compatible chipset and two free PCI Express slots designed for SLI, as well as two SLI-capable video cards that use the same NVIDIA chipset (for example, two GeForce 8800 GTS cards from any manufacturer). To learn more about SLI-compatible equipment, see http://sg.slizone.com/.

Why use two video cards? This is mostly the province of the high-end gaming crowd, because doubling the graphics muscle means that you can play the top games on a big screen and still get stunning visuals and smooth motion. However, some folks also opt for two video cards because they want to connect three or four monitors to their computer. On my own system, for example, I have two video cards combined using a CrossFire bridge and three monitors on the go. Sweet!

Figure 5.1 shows a motherboard with two CrossFire-capable video cards attached with a CrossFire bridge. (Note that a proper CrossFire connection uses two bridges instead of the one shown here. In Chapter 12, see Figure 12.35 for an example.)

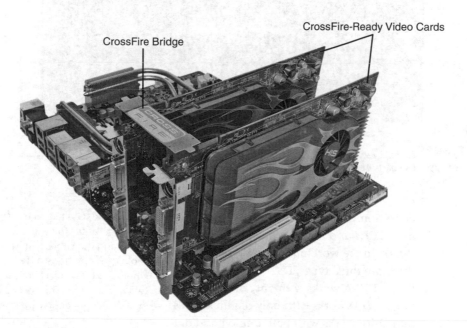

FIGURE 5.1

Two CrossFire video cards in a CrossFire-compatible motherboard, attached with a CrossFire bridge.

Video Card Connectors

Your video card has to direct its output to something, and what that something will be is determined by the connectors that appear on the card's bracket. There are a number of different connectors, but three are by far the most common on desktop PCs: VGA, DVI, and S-Video/HDTV. (With high-def TVs all the rage now, you're also starting to see HDMI connectors on some video cards.)

The VGA connector—also called the D-Sub connector—is a blue, 15-pin port you use to connect to CRT monitors and to the analog input ports on LCD monitors. Figure 5.2 shows a VGA connector.

> **caution** Running two high-powered graphics cards in your system can burn up the watts in a hurry, so make sure your power supply unit (PSU) is up to the challenge. Some PSUs are certified to work with SLI or CrossFire setups, which means they have enough watts to handle two video cards and have two power connectors for video cards that require direct connections to the PSU.

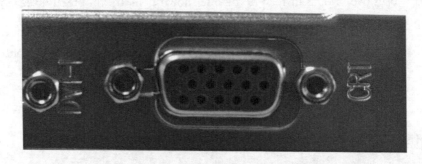

FIGURE 5.2

You use a VGA port for connections to analog CRT and LCD monitors.

Digital Visual Interface (DVI) is a high-definition video connector available on most LCDs and on most older digital TVs. When you're working with DVI, note that there are three types: DVI-A, DVI-D, and DVI-I. DVI-A works with only analog signals; DVI-D works with only digital signals; and DVI-I works with both analog and digital and is shown in Figure 5.3. Unfortunately, each type of DVI uses a

> **note** DVI uses a transmitter to send information along the cable. A single-link cable uses one transmitter, whereas a dual-link cable uses two transmitters. This means that dual-link connections are faster and offer a better signal quality than single-click connections.

slightly different pin arrangement (see Figure 5.4), so when you're matching your monitor, DVI cable, and video card, you need to ensure that they all use the same DVI connectors. Just to confuse matters, DVI-D and DVI-I connectors also come in *single-link* and *dual-link* configurations. In this case, make sure you get dual-link; it will also work with single-link, though. Here's a summary of the five available connection types:

> **tip**
> A dual-link DVI connector can plug into a single-link DVI port. Unfortunately, the reverse isn't true—that is, you can't plug a single-link DVI connector into a dual-link DVI port. Note, too, that a DVI-D connector can plug into a DVI-I port, but a DVI-I connector won't fit into a DVI-D port.

DVI-A	This connector consists of one 4-pin grouping, one 8-pin grouping, a single flat pin.
DVI-D Single-Link	This connector consists of two 9-pin groupings and a single flat pin.
DVI-D Dual-Link	This connector consists of one 24-pin grouping (three rows of 8 pins) and a single flat pin.
DVI-I Single-Link	This connector consists of two 9-pin groupings and a single flat pin surrounded by 4 pins.
DVI-I Dual-Link	This connector consists of one 24-pin grouping (three rows of 8 pins) and a single flat pin surrounded by 4 pins.

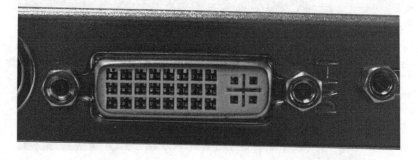

FIGURE 5.3

You use a DVI port for digital connections to LCD monitors and some TVs.

The S-Video connector is the output port you use to connect your PC to a TV that has a corresponding S-Video input port (see Figure 5.5).

1. DVI-A

2. DVI-D Single-Link
3. DVI-D Dual-Link

4. DVI-I Single-Link
5. DVI-I Dual-Link

FIGURE 5.4
Different types of DVI connectors have different pin arrangements.

FIGURE 5.5
You use an S-Video port for connections to a TV.

Note, too, that many modern video cards come with adapters that enable you to make higher-quality connections to an HDTV. For example, some cards come with a separate HDTV adapter or cable that plugs into the S-Video port and offers component video ports (red, green, and blue connectors) for connection to your HDTV's component input ports (see Figure 5.6). Similarly, some cards offer a DVI-to-HDMI adapter. High-Definition Multimedia Interface (HDMI) is currently the gold standard for displaying digital video signals, and it's now relatively common to find an HDMI connector on a digital TV.

> **tip**
>
> AMD's 690G chipset includes HDMI support, so motherboards based on that chipset come with an HDMI port, either integrated into the board itself (so the HDMI port appears with the other back panel connectors) or as part of a separate expansion card.

FIGURE 5.6
Many video cards come with an HDTV adapter that plugs into the S-Video connector and offers component video ports for connecting to a TV.

If you want to watch or record TV on your PC, you need a separate TV tuner card, which comes with a cable TV connector, as shown in Figure 5.7.

FIGURE 5.7
To watch or record TV, you need a TV tuner card with a cable TV connector.

Buying a Video Card

The NVIDIA and ATI chipsets are both excellent products, and because almost all video cards come with one or the other, it's hard to go wrong when choosing a card manufacturer. In general, it's better to stick with larger companies because you're more likely to get better technical support and better driver support. Here are my recommended video card manufacturers:

ASUS (www.asus.com)

ATI (www.ati.com)

BFG (www.bfgtech.com)

EVGA (www.evga.com)

Gigabyte (www.giga-byte.com)

HIS (www.hisdigital.com)

MSI (www.msicomputer.com)

PNY (www.pny.com)

Sapphire (www.sapphiretech.com)

XFX (www.xfxforce.com)

Here are a few other points to think about when making your video card purchase:

- **Decide whether you need a separate video card**—If you don't have any extra cash or bus slots, and your video needs aren't extravagant, you can probably get away with using a motherboard that has an integrated video adapter. Today's built-in video cards are much higher quality than they used to be, so most offer decent-looking screen images. The only major downside to using integrated video is that the adapter doesn't have its own memory supply, so it must use some of the PC's system memory instead. This can slow down overall system performance, unless you put a lot of memory into your PC.

- **Go with PCI Express**—Unless your motherboard either doesn't have any PCI Express slots (unlikely, these days) or has no free PCI Express slots available, be sure to get a video card that uses PCI Express because this bus type is much faster than AGP and PCI.

- **Buy as much memory as you can afford**—Today's graphical systems (particularly Windows Vista) require lots of video memory, and they'll use any memory your video card carries. Therefore, load up your video card with as much memory as you can afford. 128MB should be the minimum these days, but you won't regret getting 256MB, 512MB, or even more.

- **Watch out for "fat" video cards**—Some video cards come with huge fans or heatsinks that make the cards extremely wide. So wide, in

fact, that they hang over the adjacent bus slot, essentially rendering
that slot useless. If your motherboard has only a limited number of
bus slots, avoid fat video cards so
you don't give up a slot.

■ **Decide whether you need
multiple-monitor support**—Even

> **caution** Some video
> cards offer
> two connectors but support only
> one monitor connection at a
> time. Check the video card specs
> to ensure that the card supports
> multiple monitors.

if you're using a nice 20- or even 22-inch LCD monitor, if you use your
computer a lot, you probably find yourself constantly Alt+Tabbing
from one of your many open windows to another. A single monitor—
even a big one—just doesn't have the necessary real estate to show
more than a couple of windows at once. The solution to this problem
that also happens to be a sure-fire way to boost productivity is to add a
second monitor to your setup. Doubling your monitors effectively doubles your desktop (at least horizontally) and enables you to keep more
windows in view. To do the dual-monitor thing, you either need to
install two video cards or, much better, install a single video card that
has two output ports: either one VGA and one DVI or two DVI (as
shown in Figure 5.8).

FIGURE 5.8

*To extend your desktop onto another monitor, you need a video card with dual output ports
and support for connecting two monitors simultaneously.*

■ **Decide whether you need DirectX 10 support**—The current gold
standard in high-end gaming is DirectX 10, which offers stunningly
realistic graphics and shading. It also requires a powerhouse of a
graphics card, so if you want to run DirectX 10 games on your custom
PC, be sure to check the video card specs to ensure that the board
implements the DirectX 10 standard.

■ **Decide whether you need high-definition video support**—Most
modern video cards come with enough processing power and onboard
memory to handle not only whatever day-to-day computing you'll perform on your PC, but also most media tasks. The exception is the video

playback of high-definition video, which requires a video card that supports H.264 acceleration and *High-Bandwidth Digital Content Protection (HDCP)* .

■ **Get a separate TV tuner card**—If you want to watch and capture TV via the digital media hub, you need a TV tuner device. Some video cards have TV tuners built in, but you can also purchase standalone TV tuners either as internal adapter cards or external boxes. In general, standalone TV tuners give you a better signal and are less flaky overall than all-in-one cards that try to do both graphics and TV, so I recommend getting a separate device. Be sure to match the TV tuner device to the type of signal you receive. For example, if your signal arrives via a digital or an analog TV cable, you need a digital or an analog cable connector; similarly, *over-the-air (OTA)* broadcast signals require the appropriate type of antenna to capture the signal.

■ **Decide whether you want to run Windows Vista's Aero interface**—If you'll be installing Windows Vista on your homebrew machine, you might want to take advantage of Vista's new Aero interface, which offers beautiful interface chrome and interesting transparency effects. To run Aero, you need a video card that has at least 128MB video RAM and supports both the DirectX 9 and Pixel Shader 2.0 standards.

Bits, Channels, and More: Understanding Sound Card Specs

The first thing you need to know about a sound card is that there's a really good chance you don't need one! Actually, to be more accurate I should say that there's probably a good change you don't need a *separate* sound card. All modern motherboards have some kind of integrated sound capability, and many come with high-end sound features that are good enough for all but professional audio jockeys and the most rabid gamers. So when I talk about sound cards specs in this section, bear in mind that these specs apply both to standalone sound cards and to motherboard integrated sound chips.

If you're shopping for a sound card, you might come across an ad or a description that looks something like this:

Creative Labs Sound Blaster Audigy2 ZS 192KHz

24-bit 7.1 DTS Dolby Digital S/PDIF

A motherboard description might show a subset of these specs. In any case, here's a quick look at what each part of this description means (and the sections that follow expand on the most important of them):

Creative Labs	This is the name of the sound card manufacturer.
Sound Blaster	This is the name of the overall family to which the sound card belongs.
Audigy2 ZS	This is the name of the sound card.
192KHz	This is the maximum sample frequency supported by the sound card.
24-bit	This is the maximum sample depth supported by the sound card.
7.1	This is the maximum number of channels supported by the sound card.
DTS	This tells you that the sound card supports DTS surround sound.
Dolby Digital	This tells you that the sound card supports Dolby Digital surround sound.
S/PDIF	This tells you that the sound card includes a *Sony/Philips Digital Interface Format (S/PDIF)* digital audio connector.

The Sampling Frequency

When an object such as a violin string or speaker diaphragm vibrates or moves back and forth, it alternately compresses and decompresses the air molecules around it. This alternating compression and decompression sets up a vibration in the air molecules that propagates outward from the source as a wave. This is called a *sound wave*. When the sound wave reaches your ear, it sets up a corresponding vibration in your eardrum, and you hear the sound created by the object.

Each sound wave has two basic properties:

- **Frequency**—This determines the pitch of the sound. It's a measure of the rate at which the sound wave's vibrations are produced. The higher the frequency, the higher the pitch. Frequency is measured in cycles per second, or *hertz (Hz)*, where one cycle is a vibration back and forth.

- **Intensity**—This is a measure of the loudness of the sound (that is, the strength of the vibration). It's determined by the *amplitude* of the sound wave. The greater the amplitude, the greater the motion of the sound wave's molecules and the greater the impact on your eardrum. Amplitude is measured in *decibels (db)*.

5

Figure 5.9 shows part of a waveform for a typical sound. The amplitude is found by taking the midpoint of the wave (which is set to 0) and measuring the distance to a positive or negative peak. Because the period from one peak to the next is defined as a cycle, the frequency is given by the number of peaks that occur per second.

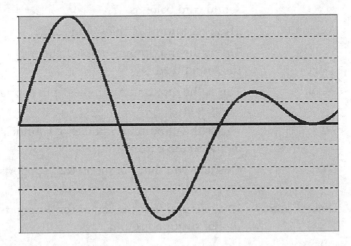

FIGURE 5.9

An analog waveform for a sound.

One of the major determinants of digital audio quality is the rate at which the sound card samples the analog data. The more samples taken per second—that is, the higher the *sampling frequency*—the more accurately the digitized data will represent the original sound waveform.

To see how this works, consider the chart shown in Figure 5.10. This is a graph of digitized data sampled from the analog waveform shown earlier in Figure 5.9. Each column represents an amplitude value sampled from the analog wave at a given moment. In this case, the sampling frequency is very low, so the "shape" of the digitized waveform only approximates the analog wave, and much data is lost.

To improve the quality and fidelity of the digitized waveform, you need to use a higher sampling frequency. For example, the chart shown in Figure 5.11 shows the resulting digital waveform with a sampling frequency four times greater than the one shown in Figure 5.10. As you can see, the waveform is a much more accurate representation of the original analog wave.

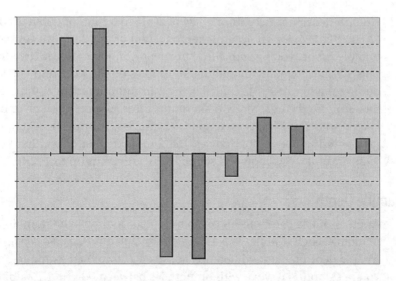

FIGURE 5.10

A digitized waveform generated by a low sampling frequency.

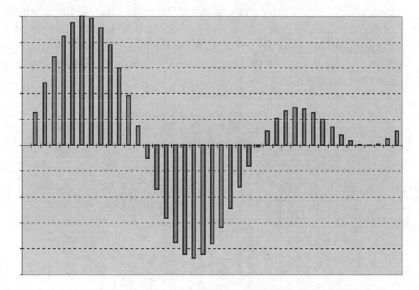

FIGURE 5.11

To improve the sound quality of the digitized waveform, you need to increase the sampling frequency.

So, which sampling frequency is best? The general rule of thumb is that, for the most faithful reproduction of analog sound, your sampling frequency should be roughly twice the highest sound frequency you want to reproduce, plus another 10% for good measure.

5

Human hearing ranges from a low of 20Hz to a high of about 20KHz (20,000Hz). So, for an accurate reproduction of anything within the human audible range, you'd sample at a frequency of about 44KHz (two times 20KHz plus 10%). CD-quality digital audio samples at 44.1KHz, and DVD-quality audio samples at 48KHz, which is the minimum frequency supported by most modern sound cards. Many good sound cards support 96KHz sampling, which is used with some high-resolution DVD movies. For the DVD-Audio format used with high-definition movies, the sample frequency is either 96KHz or 192KHz, and a few high-end sound cards sample at up to 192KHz.

The Sample Depth

Another major determinant of digital audio quality is the number of bits used to digitize each sample. This is sometimes called the *sample depth*. To see why sample depth makes a difference, consider a simplified example. Suppose you're sampling a wave with amplitudes between 0db and 100db. If you had only a 2-bit sample depth, you'd have only four discrete levels with which to assign amplitudes. If you used, say, 25db, 50db, 75db, and 100db, all the sampled values would have to be adjusted (by rounding up, for example) to one of these values. Figure 5.12 shows the result. The smooth line shows the original amplitudes, and the columns show the assigned sample values, given a 2-bit sample depth. As you can see, much data is lost by having to adjust to the discrete levels.

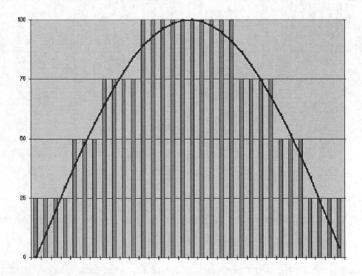

FIGURE 5.12
The lower the sample depth, the more information that gets lost during sampling.

Fortunately, there is no such thing as 2-bit sampling. Instead, older sound cards supported two levels of sample depth: 8-bit and 16-bit, while almost all newer sound cards support 24-bit sampling. The 8-bit sample depth might sound like a lot, but it means that the digitized amplitude values must be shoehorned into just 256 possible levels, which is a far cry from the infinite number of levels in the original analog waveform. With 16-bit sampling, 65,536 discrete levels are available, but when you jump to 24-bit samples, the number of discrete levels rises to a whopping 16,777,216, which makes a huge difference in sound quality.

> **note** Another way to look at sample depth is to consider a ruler. The accuracy with which you can measure something with a ruler depends on the number of divisions. A ruler with only quarter-inch divisions won't provide as exact a measurement as a ruler with sixteenth-inch divisions. In audio, an 8-bit sample depth is like a ruler with 256 divisions per sample; a 16-bit sample depth is like a ruler with 65,536 divisions per sample; and a 24-bit sample depth is like a ruler with 16,777,216 divisions per sample.

The Number of Channels

The final consideration for digital audio quality is the number of channels you want to store. In the old days you only had a choice of mono (one channel) or stereo (two channels), where the latter required a sound card that supported two channels as well as a PC with two speakers attached to the card.

Nowadays, mono-only sound cards are nonexistent and stereo-only cards are almost obsolete. In their place, most modern sound cards support some form of *surround sound* using either Dolby Digital or Digital Theater Systems (DTS), and some cards support both technologies.

The number of surround-sound channels is shown in sound card specs using the *n*.1 format, where *n* is the number of speakers and the 1 represents a subwoofer. (A *subwoofer* is a separate amplifier that helps play low-frequency [bass] sounds, giving the audio a deeper, richer sound.) The most common configurations are 5.1 (sometimes called 6-channel) and 7.1 (sometimes called 8-channel).

> **note** In the discussion that follows, I assume your system will connect to two or more analog speakers. If you have digital speakers, you use different connections, as described in the next section, "Sound Card Connectors."

5

A 5.1 surround-sound configuration consists of five speakers and a subwoofer, arranged as follows:

> **note** Some sound cards support 7.1 surround sound but come with only three analog output ports. How does that work? On such cards, the Rear Speaker and Center/Subwoofer ports usually do double-duty. For example, the Rear Speaker port might also supply the side left channel and the Center/Subwoofer port might also supply the side right channel.

- **Front speakers**—These are two speakers positioned to the left and right of the monitor (or TV). You connect these speakers using the Line Out or Front Speaker port on the sound card, which is usually a lime green color.

- **Rear speakers**—These are two speakers positioned behind and to the left and right of the listener. You connect these speakers using the Rear Speaker port on the sound card, which is usually black.

- **Center/subwoofer**—The center speaker is positioned in the middle behind the display, and the subwoofer is positioned on the ground, usually in the closest corner. You use the Center/Subwoofer port on the sound card, which is usually orange.

A 7.1 surround-sound configuration uses the same setup as the 5.1 configuration, but adds two more speakers:

- **Side speakers**—These are two speakers positioned to the left and right of the listener. You connect these speakers using the Side Speaker port on the sound card, which is usually gray.

Sound Card Connectors

Although I touched on some sound card ports in the previous section, here's a summary of the various types of ports you're likely to come across in your sound card travels (I'm ignoring peripheral ports such as joystick connectors and IEEE-1394 connectors that appear on some cards):

Line Out   This is the main output port on all sound cards. It's a stereo mini jack connector usually colored lime green. You use it to connect headphones, 2-channel analog speakers, or the front analog speakers in a surround-sound 5.1-channel or 7.1-channel audio setup.

Rear Speaker	This is a secondary output port on some sound cards. It's a stereo mini jack connector usually colored black. You use it to connect the rear analog speakers in a surround-sound 5.1-channel or 7.1-channel audio configuration.
Center/Subwoofer	This is a secondary output port on some sound cards. It's a stereo mini jack connector usually colored orange. You use it to connect the center analog speaker and subwoofer in a surround-sound 5.1-channel or 7.1-channel audio setup.
Side Speaker	This is a secondary output port on some sound cards. It's a stereo mini jack connector usually colored gray. You use it to connect the side analog speakers in a surround-sound 7.1-channel audio configuration.
Optical S/PDIF Out	This is a digital output port on some card cards. It's an optical connector that uses the S/PDIF; the sound card connector is labeled S/PDIF Out or Digital Out. You use it to output audio to a digital audio device that has a digital optical (also called TOSLink) audio input port.
Optical S/PDIF In	This is a digital input port on some card cards. It's an optical connector that uses S/PDIF; the sound card connector is labeled S/PDIF In or Digital In. You use it to input audio from a digital audio device that has a digital optical audio output port.
Coaxial S/PDIF	This is a digital output port on some card cards. It's an RCA jack that uses S/PDIF; the sound card connector is labeled S/PDIF Out or Coaxial Out. You use it to output audio to a digital audio device that supports digital coaxial audio.

note You can purchase adapters that convert one type of audio output to another type of audio input. For example, you can get an adapter that enables you to connect a single-channel stereo mini jack on the sound card with a digital (coaxial or optical) input on the audio device.

5

Line In	This is an input port on some sound cards. It's a stereo mini jack connector usually colored blue. You use it to connect an audio device such as a digital audio tape player or CD player.
Mic In	This is an input port on some sound cards. It's a stereo mini jack connector usually colored pink. You use it to connect a microphone.

Figure 5.13 points out these ports on a typical (albeit high-end) sound card.

1. Mic In
2. Line In
3. Line Out
4. Side Speaker
5. Center/Subwoofer
6. Rear Speaker
7. Optical S/PDIF In
8. Optical S/PDIF Out
9. Coaxial S/PDIF Out

FIGURE 5.13

The ports on a high-end sound card.

Buying a Sound Card

The sound card market is thoroughly dominated by Creative Labs and its highly regarded Sound Blaster family of audio products. That isn't to say you should only consider Creative Lab's products, however. There are many other sound card companies out there, but they tend to offer only a limited number of cards. Still, the biggest issue with all sound cards is driver support, so it pays to stick with the major players. Here are my recommendations:

Auzentech	(www.auzentech.com)
Creative Labs	(www.creative.com)
HT Omega	(www.htomega.com)
M_AUDIO	(www.m-audio.com)
Turtle Beach	(www.turtlebeach.com)

Here are some pointers to think about when deciding on a sound card for your homebuilt system:

- **Decide whether you need a separate sound card**—I mentioned earlier that's it's becoming more common to see decent video integrated into modern motherboards. However, decent audio has been a motherboard feature for a while now. Even low-end boards often come with audio chipsets that boast 5.1-channel (usually called 6-channel in motherboard specs) sound, and mid-range mobos routinely come with 7.1 (8-channel) analog audio and connectors for digital audio output. Either way, this audio support is more than good enough for almost all PC applications, including most games. You really only need a separate sound card if your motherboard doesn't have the audio connectors you require (such as S/PDIF) or if you need a sound card's advanced features to get the most out of high-end gaming or audio applications. The downside to using integrated audio is that the chip offloads much of the sound processing to the CPU, which can slow down overall system performance if you do a lot of audio work.

- **Determine whether your motherboard comes with a sound card**—Some higher-end motherboards come with a separate sound card rather than integrated audio. For example, the ASUS Striker Extreme board comes with digital S/PDIF audio integrated, but analog 7.1 audio is handled via a separate sound card (see Figure 5.14).

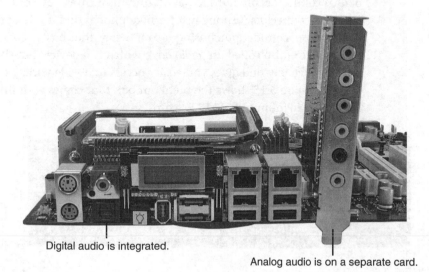

Digital audio is integrated.

Analog audio is on a separate card.

FIGURE 5.14

Some motherboards, such as the ASUS Striker Extreme shown here, come with a separate sound card.

- **Playback features**—To play sounds on your system, check out the card's specs. It should support at least the highest levels of digitized sound you plan to use. For example, if all you want to do is play CDs, the card's DAC should support CD-quality audio: sampling frequencies up to 44.1KHz, 16-bit sample depth, and stereo. If you want to play DVDs, then you might need 48KHz sampling, or possibly even 96KHz sampling. For high-definition audio, you might need a card that supports 192KHz sampling.

- **Decide whether you need 3D audio**—If you're a hardcore gamer, you might want to invest in a sound card that offers *3D audio* (also called *3D spatial imaging* or *positional audio*). This feature means that sounds are located in 3D space. For example, if you're playing a game and an explosion happens in front of you, 3D audio ensures that the sound comes through the center speaker (the one directly in front of you in a 5.1 or 7.1 surround-sound configuration). Similarly, the sound of a car passing on the left would start in the left rear speaker, travel to the left side speaker (in a 7.1 setup), and continue to the left front speaker. 3D audio costs a bit more, but it can add a lot to a high-end game. Note that Creative Labs' 3D audio technology Environmental Audio Extensions (EAX) is currently the gold standard.

- **Get a breakout box for easier access**—If you plan on attaching many devices to your PC's sound system, the sound card (or motherboard) connectors are hard to get at, and most cases have only rudimentary connectors (usually just for headphones and a microphone). In that case, consider purchasing a sound card that has a separate *breakout box* (also called an *audio bay*), which is a device that slips into a front drive bay and gives you easier access to a wide variety of connectors. Figure 5.15 shows the breakout box that comes with the Sound Blaster X-FI Platinum FATAL1TY card.

FIGURE 5.15
Some sound cards come with a breakout box that offers front-of-the-case access to a large collection of audio connectors.

■ **Check device driver support**—Make sure the card comes with drivers for whatever operating system you plan on installing on your custom PC. Although the OS might comes with its own sound card drivers, you're usually better off with the latest drivers from the manufacturer.

From Here

■ For a rundown on motherboard slot types, **see** "Understanding Expansion Slot Types," **p. 14**.

■ For the specifics on DDR system memory, **see** "The Memory Type and Speed," **p. 68**.

■ To learn how to install a sound card, **see** "Installing an Expansion Card," **p. 211**.

■ If you're putting together a PC for business, **see** "Selecting Audio Equipment for the Basic Business PC," **p. 251**.

■ If you're building a home theater PC, **see** "Selecting Audio Equipment for the Home Theater PC," **p. 290**.

■ If you're constructing a PC for maximum performance, **see** "Selecting Audio Equipment for the High-Performance PC," **p. 335**.

■ If you're building a gaming PC, **see** "Selecting Audio Equipment for the Killer Gaming PC," **p. 378**.

■ If you're putting together a PC on a budget, **see** "Selecting Audio Equipment for the Budget PC," **p. 422**.

5

Getting Connected: Networking Hardware

Transport of the mails, transport of the human voice, transport of flickering pictures—in this century, as in others, our highest accomplishments still have the single aim of bringing men together.

—Antoine de Saint Exupèry, *Terre des Hommes*

The PC you build will almost certainly need to include some networking devices. Even if it's the only computer you own, you still need some networking hardware to connect to the Internet, assuming you have a broadband connection. (If you use dial-up, instead, and you don't plan on connecting your PC with other computers, feel free to skip this chapter.) More likely, however, you probably have at least one other computer, and it would be handy if all your machines could see each other and share resources such as folders, printers, and Internet connections. That's what networking is all about, but to get that far requires a hardware investment.

This chapter gives you the information you need to make good networking investments. In the previous chapters I focused on hardware specific to your PC-building project: motherboards, cases, power supplies, processors, memory modules, and so on. In this chapter, I talk about the network devices you can add to your custom PC, but I also expand things a bit and discuss those devices—both wired and wireless—that you'll need to get your network up and running. I show you how to set up a network in the projects section of the book; see Chapter 16, "Putting Together a Network."

Getting Wired: Understanding Ethernet Networks

This chapter covers both wired and wireless networking, so let's start with the wired side, which is also called *ethernet* networking. The specifics of how ethernet works are hideously complex, but fortunately you don't need to know any of it to get your own small network operating successfully. However, it doesn't hurt to have at least a high-level understanding of what's going on when your ethernet devices are hard at work.

All ethernet devices are given a unique identifier called the *Media Access Control (MAC) address*. When data is ready to be sent over the network, ethernet divides the data into small chunks called *frames*, which include part of the data (this is often called the *payload*) and an extra header that includes (among other things) the MAC addresses of the sending and receiving devices. The ethernet device then waits until the network isn't transferring any data (this "wait" is typically measured in milliseconds); then it sends the first frame. This process is then repeated until all the data has been sent. If, along the way, two devices attempt to send data at the same time (resulting in a *collision*), both machines wait for a randomly chosen amount of time (again, we're talking milliseconds here) and then resend their frames.

The medium through which all this data is transferred is the network cable. (For more information, see "The Wired Connection: Network Cables," later in this chapter.) Because of this, and because of the universality of ethernet (it's *the* standard in home and small office networks), the word *ethernet* is, for all intents and purposes, synonymous with wired networking (as opposed to wireless networking, which I talk about a bit later; see "Going Wireless: Understanding Wi-Fi Networks"). In other words, if you hear someone talking about (or see someone writing about) ethernet, rest assured that all that person is really talking (or writing) about is networking that uses cables.

However, that isn't to say that there's only one kind of "networking that uses cables." There are, in fact, a number of ethernet standards, and it's the differences between these standards (and the ways in which these standards are compatible or incompatible) that should form the bulk of your ethernet knowledge. From the point of view of not only your homebuilt PC, but also of your small home or office network, the only significant difference between the standards is the speed at which they transfer data.

10BASE-T

The first commercial ethernet standard, first published more than a quarter of a century ago (so it's pretty much obsolete at this point), was called *10BASE-T*, a name that breaks down as follows:

10	This designates the maximum theoretical data transfer rate of 10 megabits per second (Mbps).
BASE	This is short for *baseband*, which describes a communications medium (in this case, an ethernet cable) that allows only one signal at a time. Compare this with *broadband*, which describes a communications medium that allows multiple simultaneous signals.
T	This tells you that the standard uses twisted-pair cables.

100BASE-T (Fast Ethernet)

Around 1995, a new ethernet standard was introduced: *Fast Ethernet* or *100BASE-T*. As you can tell from the latter, this standard operated at a maximum transmission speed of 100Mbps, making the new devices 10 times faster that 10BASE-T. (To be accurate, the designation *100BASE-T* is an umbrella term for the various implementations of Fast

caution This is as good a time as any to introduce the word *theoretical* into our discussion. The data transfer rate associated with any ethernet standard (indeed, any form of communications) is the rate that would be obtained if conditions were perfect—that is, if there were no noise on the line, no nearby interference, no frame collisions, and so on. So, in the discussion that follows, the speeds I mention are purely theoretical, and it's unlikely you'll ever reach such velocities in practice. However, the comparisons are still useful because the *relative* difference between two standards will still hold in practice. Thus, if the theoretical rate of standard B is 10 times faster than that of standard A, standard B's real-world rate will also be 10 times faster than standard A's real-world rate.

note When you're talking about data communications, a *megabit (Mb)* is equal to one million bits. So, the 10Mbps transmission speed of 10BASE-T means that it can—theoretically, of course—transfer 10 million bits of data per second. Just to confuse matters, if you're talking about memory or data storage, a megabit equals 1,048,576 bits.

6

Ethernet that have appeared, including 100BASE-TX, 100BASE-T2, and 100BASE-T4; of these, only 100BASE-TX survives, so that's now the actual standard underlying the Fast Ethernet moniker.)

Although, like all new technologies, Fast Ethernet was expensive at first, the prices of Fast Ethernet devices quickly fell; by the end of the 1990s Fast Ethernet had become

> **note** In the context of data communications, a *gigabit (Gb)* is equal to one billion bits. As with megabits, if you're talking about memory or data storage, a gigabit equals the more exact value of 1,073,741,824 bits.

the most common implementation of ethernet found in offices and, increasingly, in homes. It helped, too, that most Fast Ethernet devices were *10/100* devices, which means they were also backward compatible with 10BASE-T devices, so you could mix and match the two types in your network. Use of Fast Ethernet remains widespread today, mostly on older networks that haven't yet upgraded to the faster Gigabit Ethernet (discussed next).

1000BASE-T (Gigabit Ethernet)

In 1995, the Institute for Electrical and Electronics Engineers (IEEE), which creates and maintains the ethernet standards (among many other duties), published a new standard technically labeled 802.3ab, but more commonly known as *Gigabit Ethernet* or *1000BASE-T*. This standard boasts an impressive top speed of 1,000Mbps, or 1Gbps, making it 10 times faster than Fast Ethernet.

The prices of Gigabit Ethernet devices have fallen rapidly over the past few years, to the point now where a gigabit-speed network is affordable for almost any home or small office. As with Fast Ethernet, the adoption of Gigabit Ethernet is being helped by the availability of *10/100/1000* devices, which are backward compatible with both 10BASE-T devices and Fast Ethernet devices.

Beyond Gigabit Ethernet

Right now, Gigabit Ethernet is the fastest ethernet standard that's both affordable and readily available. However, it's not the fastest version of Ethernet. That distinction goes to the most recent ethernet standard—*10 Gigabit Ethernet* or *10GBASE-T*—which the IEEE published in 2006. As these names imply, this implementation of ethernet comes with a theoretical transmission speed of 10Gbps, an order of magnitude faster than Gigabit Ethernet. However, as I write this in late 2007, 10GBASE-T devices are extremely rare and extremely expensive. It will likely be a few years before this standard becomes affordable and easy to find.

The need for network speed can never be satisfied, of course, so the folks at the IEEE have started work on an even faster ethernet standard: 100 Gigabit Ethernet, which will ship data at the giddy rate of 100Gbps. It will certainly be quite a few years before this standard is even published, and quite a few years after that before 100 Gigabit Ethernet devices become available.

Learning about Network Interface Cards

The key networking device for your PC project, and the starting point for your ethernet network, is the *network interface card (NIC)*. This device serves as the connection point between some network node and the rest of the network. (A *node* is a device connected to a network. Sample nodes include desktop computers, notebooks, and network devices such as routers and print servers.) As you'll see in the next section, an ethernet NIC connects a node to the network by means of a cable. The back of the NIC contains a port into which you plug the cable.

After the physical connection is established, the NIC works with a device driver to process incoming and outgoing network data. As such, the NIC is the focal point for the computer's network connection, so it plays a big part in the overall performance of that connection. Most NICs sold today—or that come preinstalled in new computers—are either Fast Ethernet or, increasingly, Gigabit Ethernet, and the vast majority are either 10/100 or 10/100/1000 devices you can add seamlessly to your existing network.

Ethernet NICs come in four main varieties:

Motherboard NIC   The components required by a NIC have become so small that most PC manufacturers can now easily place them directly on the computer's motherboard rather than as a standalone card, as was typical for many years. The NIC port appears with the motherboard's other back panel connectors and is almost always labeled in some way, either with text such as LAN or Ethernet (as shown in Figure 6.1) or with some kind of network icon (as shown in Figure 6.2).

6

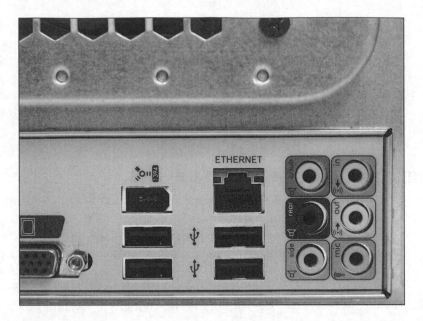

FIGURE 6.1

On some PCs, the motherboard NIC comes with a text label.

Icon for the Ethernet port

FIGURE 6.2

Other PCs label the motherboard NIC with a network icon.

6

Network adapter

If your computer doesn't have a motherboard NIC or if the built-in NIC is only Fast Ethernet and you want to upgrade to Gigabit Ethernet, you need to purchase and attach your own NIC. One common NIC type is an internal adapter card you insert into a free slot on the motherboard. This is usually a PCI slot, but if your computer has a free PCI Express (PCIe) slot, PCIe network adapters are available. Figure 6.3 shows a typical ethernet network adapter.

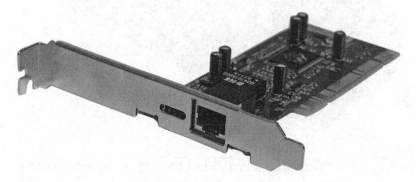

FIGURE 6.3

An ethernet network adapter goes inside the computer and attaches to a free slot on the system bus.

USB NIC

If you don't have any free slots on your motherboard, the alternative is to get an external NIC that you plug into an available USB port. In this case, make sure you get a USB 2.0 NIC to ensure top performance. Figure 6.4 shows an example of a USB-based NIC.

PC Card NIC

Most modern notebook computers come with a built-in ethernet NIC that exposes a port. If your notebook doesn't have a built-in NIC, or if you want to upgrade your notebook to a faster version of ethernet, you have a few options. One possibility (albeit often an expensive one) is to purchase a docking station for the notebook because almost all docking stations come with built-in NICs. Alternatively, because almost all notebooks come with one or more USB ports, you can also attach a USB NIC. Finally, all notebooks come with at least one PC Card (or PCM-CIA) slot, so you can purchase and attach a PC Card (or PCMCIA) ethernet NIC. Figure 6.5 shows an example.

FIGURE 6.4
For easy installation, insert a USB 2.0 NIC into a free USB slot on your computer.

FIGURE 6.5
For a notebook computer, you can insert a PC Card (or PCMCIA) Ethernet NIC.

The Wired Connection: Network Cables

As I mentioned earlier, when it comes to small networks, ethernet networking is synonymous with wired networking, where *wired* means each computer or device is connected to the network by means of a network cable.

The "starting point" (figuratively speaking) for any cable is the network adapter. As I said in the preceding section, every NIC comes with a port into which you insert a network cable, which can be either a twisted-pair cable or a crossover cable.

Twisted-Pair Cable

There are several types of network cable, such as coaxial cable and fiber-optic cable, but virtually all small ethernet networks use twisted-pair cable. It consists of four pairs of twisted copper wires that together form a circuit that can transmit data. The wires are twisted together to reduce interference. This is similar to the cable used in telephone wiring, but network cables are often shielded by a braided metal insulation to further reduce interference problems. This type of cable is called, not surprisingly, *shielded twisted-pair (STP)*. You can use *unshielded twisted-pair (UTP)* cabling, which doesn't have the insulation layer of STP cable. UTP cable is usually cheaper than STP cable, but it does tend to be less reliable than STP.

A twisted-pair cable comes with an RJ-45 jack on each end. (Networking purists cringe if you use the term *RJ-45* to refer to a network cable plug; they insist that the correct term is *8P8C*, which is short for *8 Position 8 Contact*. The rest of us ignore this unwieldy term and stick with RJ-45 or RJ45. The *RJ*, by the way, is short for *registered jack*. Figure 6.6 compares a network cable's RJ-45 jack with the RJ-11 jack used by a telephone cable.

The RJ-45 jack on a network cable plugs into the corresponding RJ-45 port on a NIC or on some other type of network device, such as a switch or router, as shown in Figure 6.7.

Twisted-pair cable is categorized according to the maximum transmission rates supported by various types of cable. With network data, for example, Category 3 (also called Cat 3) cable supports only up to a 16Mbps transmission rate, so it works only with 10BASE-T networks. These days, however, few people purchase anything less than Category 5 (Cat 5) cable, which is rated at 100Mbps and so can handle the transmission rate associated with Fast Ethernet. If you think you're going to move to Gigabit Ethernet at some point, you should get Category 6 (Cat 6) cables, which support 1Gbps throughput. Category 5e cables also support 1Gbps, but Category 6 cables are higher quality.

6

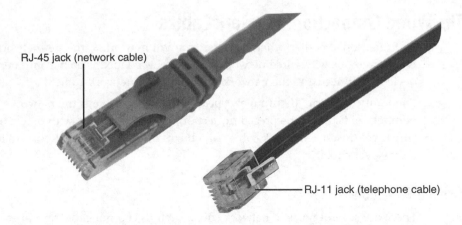

RJ-45 jack (network cable)

RJ-11 jack (telephone cable)

FIGURE 6.6

Network cables come with RJ-45 connectors at each end, which are similar to, but considerably larger than, the RJ-11 connectors used with telephone cables.

FIGURE 6.7

Twisted-pair cables use RJ-45 jacks to plug into the complementary RJ-45 connectors in network switches (as shown here) and in network adapter cards.

Crossover Cable

Plugging one end of an RJ-45 network cable into a computer's NIC is the first step in getting the computer on the network. The second step is clear: Plug in the other end of the network cable. But, plug it in to what, exactly? Your first guess might be to plug the other end of the cable into the NIC of a second computer. Good try, but that won't work.

To understand why, you need to know that each network cable has both a transmit line and a receive line and signals on those lines specify which direction the data is flowing. The NIC's port also has transmit and receive pins, so it can specify or detect the direction of the data flow. For example, suppose you have Computer A and Computer B connected by a network cable. When Computer A wants to send data, the transmit pin on Computer A's NIC is activated, which in turn activates the transmit line on the network cable.

That's fine, but the problem occurs when this signal reaches the NIC port on Computer B. The cable's transmit line will correspond with the transmit pin on the other NIC, so Computer B gets a signal that it should be transmitting data. This won't make sense because Computer B isn't transmitting, so no data goes through.

The solution is to use a special kind of network cable called an *ethernet crossover cable*. This cable reverses the position of the transmit and receive lines. So when Computer A transmits data and activates the transmit pin of its NIC port, the signal goes through the crossover cable's receive line. This in turn activates the receive pin of Computer B's NIC, so the data transfer occurs successfully.

As with regular network cable, crossover cables also come in the same categories—Cat 3, Cat 5, Cat 5e, and Cat 6—so get a cable that corresponds to the ethernet standard supported by your NICs.

IDENTIFYING A CROSSOVER CABLE

From a distance (or, heck, sometimes even up close), crossover cables look identical to regular network cables. To help you identify them, many crossover cables come with a label such as "CROSS" taped to them. If you don't see such a label, I suggest you add your own so you can keep the two types of cable separate. If you didn't do that and now you're not sure which of your cables is a crossover, there's a way to tell. Take the connectors on each end of the cable and place them side by

6

side so you have a good view of the colored wires inside. (A clear plastic covering helps here.) Make sure you hold the connectors with the same orientation (it's usually best to have the plastic tabs facing down). If the layout of the wires is identical on both connectors, then you have a regular network cable. If you see, instead, that two of the wires—specifically, the red and the green—have switched positions, then you have a crossover cable.

A Connection Point for Your Network: The Switch

In the preceding section, you learned you can use an ethernet crossover cable to connect two computers directly via their NIC ports. That's fine if you want to network only two computers, but what if your network consists of three or more computers, or if it also includes other network devices such as a printer or an Xbox gaming console? In these more complex—and decidedly more common—scenarios, direct connections with crossover cables won't work.

To work around the limitations of direct connections, you need some other way to combine multiple computers and devices into a network. Specifically, you need a central connection point each device can use. On simple networks, that connection point is often a *switch*, which is a device with multiple RJ-45 ports. Figure 6.8 shows two switches: a basic 5-port switch and a larger 16-port switch.

FIGURE 6.8

Switches contain multiple RJ-45 ports for connections to computers and other network devices.

The idea here is that each ethernet device on the network connects to a port on the switch using a network cable, as shown in Figure 6.9. The result is a *network segment*, a collection of network devices connected to a single switch. (If this network segment comprises your entire network, you can call it a *switched network*.)

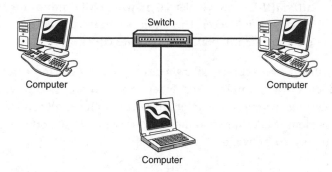

FIGURE 6.9

You can use a switch as the central connection point for your network.

The switch then forwards data from one network node to another. On basic switches such as the type used in homes or small offices, the switch usually reads the MAC address of the destination node in each ethernet frame and sends the frame directly to that device. Most switches maintain a *switching table*, a record of the MAC addresses and network port numbers used by each device on the network. As you use your network, the switch makes note of each new MAC address and adds it to the switching table, which improves overall switch performance.

You can also use a switch to send data across multiple network segments. For example, you might have a network segment in one room or office and a second segment in the room or office next door. Similarly, if your network outgrows your original switch, you might add a second switch to the network instead of upgrading to a switch with more ports. To join the two segments, you have three choices:

■ Many older switches come with a special *uplink* port designed to connect two switches by running a network cable from the uplink port of one switch to the uplink port of the other switch. On some of these switches, a button controls whether the port is used as a regular RJ-45 port or an uplink port.

note The network configuration shown in Figure 6.9—that is, multiple network nodes joined to a central connection point—is called the *star topology*.

- Use an ethernet crossover cable to link two switches by running the cable from any port in the first switch to any port in the second switch.

- Get switches where the ports support *Auto Crossover* (also called *Auto MDI/MDI-X* crossover detection, where MDI stands for *Medium-Dependent Interface*). This enables you to connect two switches without using an uplink port or a crossover cable.

As with NICs and cables, all switches support one or more of the ethernet standards. For example, a Fast Ethernet switch almost always supports 10/100 connections, whereas a Gigabit Ethernet switch usually supports 10/100/1000 connections. Make sure you match your switch to the ethernet standard you're using on your network.

Adding the Internet into the Mix with a Router

You saw in the previous section that a switch forwards ethernet packets according to the device MAC address in the frame header. This works extremely well, and most modern switches are high-performance devices. However, the inherent limitation of a switch becomes obvious when you want to add an Internet connection to your network:

- When you want to request data from a web server, it's impossible to know the MAC address of the remote server computer, so the switch has no way to forward the data request.

- When a web server wants to send data to your computer, it's impossible for the remote machine to know your computer's MAC address, so the switch cannot get to the data to your computer.

In other words, the MAC-address–based forwarding performed by a switch is limited to local area network (LAN) traffic and cannot be used to handle wide area network (WAN) data.

To solve this problem, you need to add a *router* to your network (see Figure 6.10). A router is a device that makes decisions about where to send the network packets it receives. So far, this sounds suspiciously similar to a switch. The major difference is that while a switch uses a MAC-address–based switching table to forward data, a router uses a *routing table* that tracks *IP addresses*, unique addresses assigned to every Internet host and to

> **note** A *wide area network* is a network that covers a wide geographical area. Some corporations use wide area networks, but the Internet is *the* wide area network.

every computer on your network. For example, this is useful when the computers share a high-speed Internet connection because the router ensures that the Internet data goes to the computer that requested it. To make this work, you plug your high-speed modem directly into the special WAN port in the back of the router.

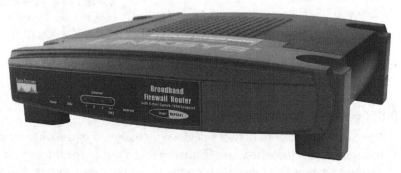

FIGURE 6.10

You add a router to your network when you want to add Internet access.

Understanding IP Addresses

An IP address is a 32-bit value assigned to a computer by a network administrator or, if you've signed up for an Internet account, by your *Internet service provider (ISP)*. As you'll see, these addresses are designed so that every host and router on the Internet or within a network has a unique address. That way, when an application needs to send data to a particular locale, it knows that the destination address it plops into the packet header will ensure that everything ends up where it's supposed to be.

The problem with IP addresses is their "32-bitness." Here's an example:

`11001101110100000111000100000010`

Not very inviting, is it? To make these numbers easier to work with, you use *dotted-decimal notation* (also known in the trade as *dotted-quad notation*). This notation divides the 32 bits of an IP address into four groups of 8 bits each (each of these groups is called a *quad*), converts each group into its decimal equivalent, and then separates these numbers with dots.

Let's look at an example. Here's the previous IP address grouped into four 8-bit quads:

`11001101 11010000 01110001 00000010`

6

Now you convert each quad into its decimal equivalent. When you do, you end up with this:

```
11001101 11010000 01110001 00000010
   205      208      113       2
```

Now you insert dots between each decimal number to get the dotted-decimal form of the address:

```
205.208.113.2
```

> **tip** You can convert a value from binary to decimal using Windows' Calculator. Select Start, All Programs, Accessories, Calculator; then, in the Calculator window, select View, Scientific. Click the Bin (binary) option, use the text box to type the 1s and 0s of the binary value you want to convert, and click the Dec (decimal) option.

The Router and Dynamic IP Addressing

The MAC addresses of network devices are assigned in advance by the device manufacturer. How, then, are IP addresses assigned? For the servers and other remote machines you deal with on the Internet, each network that wants on the Internet must sign up with a domain registrar (such as VeriSign.com or Register.com). In turn, the registrar assigns that network a block of IP addresses the administrator can then dole out to each computer (or, in the case of an ISP, to each customer).

For your own network, however, the IP addresses are assigned as follows:

- Your router is given its own IP address—called the *public IP address*—from the pool of addresses controlled by your ISP. Internet data sent to any computer on your network is first sent to the router's external IP address.

- The computers on your network are assigned IP addresses. In other words, when a computer logs on to the network, it is assigned an IP address from a pool of available addresses. When the computer logs off, the address it was using is returned to the pool. The system that manages this dynamic allocation of addresses is called the *Dynamic Host Configuration Protocol (DHCP)*, and the computers or devices that implement DHCP are called *DHCP servers*. In most home networks, the router acts as a DHCP server.

In most cases, the range of addresses is from 192.168.1.1 to 192.168.1.254. (On some routers, the range is from 192.168.0.1 to 192.168.0.254.) The router itself usually takes the 192.168.1.1 address (this is called its *private IP address*), and the pool of possible addresses is usually some subset of the total range, such as between 192.168.1.100 and 192.168.1.150.

The big advantage of this setup is that your network is never exposed to the Internet. All communication goes through the router's public IP address; so as far as, say, a web or email server is concerned, it's communicating with a device at that address. The router is capable of getting the

> **note** When a device such as a router is set up as the sole connection point between a network and the Internet, that device is called a *gateway*.

correct data to your computer because when you initially request data, it adds your computer's private IP address and the number of the communications port your computer is using and stores this data in a *routing table*. When data comes back from the Internet, the router converts the public destination IP address of the data to the private address of your computer, a process known as *network address translation (NAT)*.

The Router as Firewall

On a small network, the main function of a router is to be used as a gateway between your network and the Internet. Through the magic of NAT, your network cannot be seen from any device attached to the Internet; as far as the Internet is concerned, your network is nothing but a router. (For this reason, an Internet-connected router that performs NAT duties is sometimes called an *edge router*.) NAT, therefore, acts as a kind of simple *firewall*, a technology that prevents unwanted data from reaching a network.

However, most modern routers go one step further and come with separate firewall software. This gives you an interface for controlling and managing the firewall, which mostly means opening and closing specific software ports used by applications. For example, to successfully use a web server on a network, you need to configure the router's firewall to allow incoming connections on port 80.

The Router as Switch

You've seen that a router can act as a gateway device and a firewall device, but there's a third hat worn by most modern routers: a switch device. A typical router has a few RJ-45 ports (usually four; see Figure 6.11); so, as with a dedicated switch, you can create ethernet connections for computers and other devices by running ethernet cable from each device to a router port.

This means that if you have a small ethernet network, you might be able to get away with using just a router as your network's connection point. Figure 6.12 shows this network configuration.

6

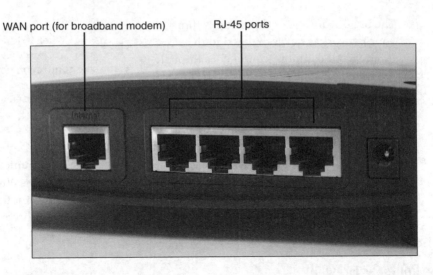

FIGURE 6.11

Most routers have built-in switches, meaning you can use the router's ports to connect devices to your network.

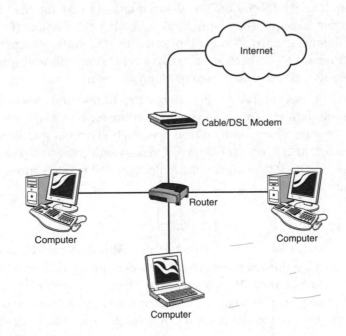

FIGURE 6.12

A small ethernet network can use a single router as both the gateway and the switch.

On the other hand, if your network is larger or if you have a number of other devices you need to connect, your router might not have enough ports. Similarly, you might be upgrading your network to Gigabit Ethernet and your router only comes with Fast Ethernet (or 10/100) ports. In both cases, the easiest solution is to leave your existing router in place and add to the network a dedicated switch that meets your needs. In this scenario, you connect the broadband modem to the router's WAN port, you run a network cable from one of the router's RJ-45 ports to an RJ-45 port on the switch, and you connect your network devices to the switch. Figure 6.13 shows this network configuration.

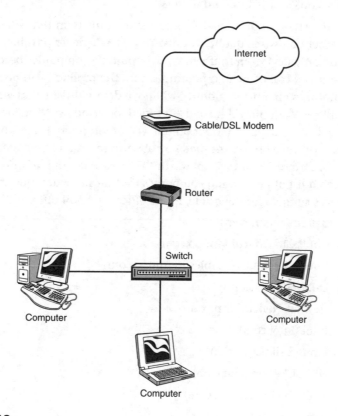

FIGURE 6.13

Larger ethernet networks might require a dedicated switch as the central network connection point.

A Buyer's Guide to Ethernet Hardware

If you're looking to purchase new ethernet hardware, whether you're starting from scratch or looking to upgrade your existing equipment, the buying process is not always easy because you often face a thicket of jargon terms and a list of product specifications that seems to require an advanced degree in electrical engineering to figure out. To make it easier to choose the right ethernet hardware, the next few sections give you a few pointers on what to look for and what to avoid when purchasing the four main hardware types: NICs, cables, switches, and routers.

Before getting to those specific tips, I should mention that when it comes to ethernet hardware, quality counts. That is, whenever possible, you should purchase only devices manufactured by reputable companies because that's the closest you can come to a guarantee that the products will be reliable, will conform to ethernet standards, will have device drivers that work with Windows Vista (they'll have a "Certified for Windows Vista" logo), and will provide good support (either on the web or via phone). Yes, you can save a dollar or three on devices made by obscure manufacturers, but my experience has been that it's simply not worth the grief of buying an inferior product. Here's a list of networking companies that manufacture quality ethernet devices suitable for the home, home office, or small office:

> Belkin (belkin.com)
>
> Cables To Go (cablestogo.com)
>
> Cables Unlimited (cablesunlimited.com)
>
> D-Link (dlink.com)
>
> Hewlett-Packard (hp.com)
>
> Intel (intel.com)
>
> Linksys (linksys.com)
>
> NETGEAR (netgear.com)
>
> TRENDnet (trendnet.com)
>
> Zonet (zonetusa.com)

Purchasing a NIC

Here are a few pointers to bear in mind when shopping for a new NIC:

- **Internal or external**—Because you're building a desktop computer, your first decision is whether to go for an internal adapter card or an external USB device. The USB NIC is obviously much easier to install;

so, if your network uses Fast Ethernet (USB NICs are too slow to support Gigabit Ethernet) and your computer has lots of free USB ports, USB is the way to go.

■ **Get USB 2.0**—If you do go the USB route, check the NIC's specifications carefully to ensure that you're getting a USB 2.0 NIC. USB 1.1 has a maximum data transfer rate of only 12Mbps, so it's useful only for 10BASE-T connections; if your network uses Fast Ethernet, you need USB 2.0, which supports data transfer rates of up to 480Mbps.

■ **Fast Ethernet or Gigabit Ethernet**—Your next major decision is which Ethernet standard to use: Fast Ethernet or Gigabit Ethernet (don't even consider 10BASE-T). Fast Ethernet NICs are cheaper than their Gigabit Ethernet cousins; so, if your budget is tight, go with the former. On the other hand, you're really only looking at spending a few more dollars for a Gigabit Ethernet NIC, and those few measly dollars buy you 10 times the performance.

■ **Check your available bus slots**—Internal NICs insert into a slot on the computer's bus. The most common type of bus is PCI, but some older systems have one or more ISA slots and some newer systems have one or more PCIe slots. Make sure the internal NIC you buy matches your computer's bus, and make sure your computer has at least one slot available to hold the NIC.

■ **Make sure the NIC has drivers that match your operating system**—The NIC requires a device driver configured for a specific operating system. For example, if you'll be installing Vista on your homebuilt PC, you should only purchase a NIC that displays the Certified for Windows Vista logo on the box. This guarantees that the NIC's drivers work with Vista, so the device will install automatically and should work properly right out of the box.

Purchasing Cables

Network cables might seem like the simplest of all networking hardware to purchase, but you do need to consider a few things. Here are a few pointers:

■ **Get the right cable category**—Make sure the cable you buy matches your ethernet standard. If you're setting up a Fast Ethernet network, you need Cat 5 cable; if you're using Gigabit Ethernet, load up on Cat 6 cable (or Cat 5e if you can't find Cat 6).

■ **Shielded or unshielded**—For a small network, STP cable is probably overkill, so in most cases you'll be fine with UTP cable. The exception

6

to this is when you know that the cable will be running near a source of electromagnetic radiation such as an electronic device, a power line, an air conditioner, fluorescent lights, or a motor.

- **Get the right length**—You can reduce cable clutter in your home or office by not purchasing cables that are excessively long. For example, if you know that a computer is 8 feet from the switch or router, don't purchase a 25-foot cable for

note If you're a dedicated do-it-yourselfer, you can create your own custom cable lengths. Most computer retailers sell bulk cable rolls and cable kits that include a stripping tool for removing a section of the cable's plastic covering, a collection of RJ-45 connectors, a crimp tool for attaching a connector the cable, and even a cable tester that tells you whether the new cable works properly.

that computer. Instead, examine the available cable lengths and buy one that's a bit longer than what you need. (A bit of slack on the cable is a good idea because it reduces the pressure on the RJ-45 connectors.) The most typical cable lengths are as follows, in feet: 1, 3, 5, 7, 10, 14, 25, and 50.

- **Mix your colors**—Color might not seem like an important consideration when purchasing cable, but it can actually be extremely handy. The basic idea is that you buy your cables using the widest variety of colors possible: ideally, a different color for each device you'll be connecting to the switch or router. That way, later when you need to, say, swap out of computer's network cable for a new one, you know immediately which cable to disconnect from the switch or router.

- **Go snagless**—All RJ-45 connectors come with a plastic tab that snaps into place when you insert the connector into an RJ-45 port. This prevents the cable from falling out of the port because you need to hold down the plastic tab to remove the connector. Unfortunately, that plastic tab has a nasty habit of snagging on whatever's under your desk when you try to pull out a loose cable. Tugging on the cable usually breaks the plastic tab, which renders the cable useless. To avoid this problem, get cables that have *snagless* connectors, which include a rounded bit of rubber just behind or on either side of the plastic tab. The rubber helps the connector slide over any obstacles, thus preventing the plastic tab from snagging. This extra bit of rubber is called, variously, the *cable boot*, *connector boot*, *mold boot*, or just *boot*.

Purchasing a Switch

The technical specifications for most switches are a maze of impenetrable jargon, acronyms, and abbreviations. People who build massive networks need to know all that minutiae; but for your small network, you need to concern yourself with only four things:

- **How many ports it has**—Purchasing a switch is usually a trade-off between price and the number of ports. That is, the more ports a switch has, the more expensive it usually is. The minimum number of ports you need is, obviously, the same as the number of ethernet devices you'll be connecting to the switch. However, networks do have a habit of growing over time, so it's almost always a good idea to get a switch that has at least a few extra ports. On the other hand, if you think it's extremely unlikely that you'll ever need more than about a half dozen ports or so, don't waste your money buying a 16-port switch.

- **Its port speed**—As the central connection point for your network, the ethernet standard supported by the switch is crucial. For example, even if you have nothing but Gigabit Ethernet cards and Cat 6 cable, it won't matter a bit if your switch's ports operate at only Fast Ethernet speeds. If you want gigabit performance, get a gigabit switch. If you're slowly making your way from Fast Ethernet to Gigabit Ethernet, you can ease the transition by getting a switch that supports 10/100/1000.

- **Whether the switch supports Auto Crossover**—If you think you might expand your network down the road by adding a second switch, make sure the first switch supports Auto Crossover (Auto MDI/MDI-X). This enables you to add a second switch to the network just by running a regular network cable between the two switches.

- **Whether you even need a dedicated switch**—As mentioned earlier, most routers nowadays come with a built-in switch, so you might be able to get away with using the router as your network's central connection point. This is usually the case only with small networks because most routers come with 4-port switches (although 8- and 16-port routers are available).

Purchasing a Router

Most home and small offices now have Internet access via a broadband modem, and sharing that access among the network computers and devices requires a router. Here are a few ideas to keep in mind when you need to purchase a router for your network:

- **Do you need a separate router?**—Some broadband modems come with a built-in router; so, if you need only basic connectivity, you can forego a separate router. The downside to the modem-as-router is that they only rarely include some kind of interface for configuring the router, usually because these are barebones routers without much to configure. Getting the most out of a router almost always means accessing the router's setup program, so I recommend a dedicated router for most small networks.

- **Do you want to use the router as a switch?**—If your network is small, you can save a few bucks by using the router as the network switch. Most modern routers have the capability, but double-check the product specifications to be sure. Check the ethernet standards supported by the router, and get the largest number of ports you can afford.

- **Do you need wireless access?**—If you want to access your network with a wireless connection, your router will also need to include a wireless access point. I discuss this in more detail in the rest of this chapter.

- **Does it have a firewall?**—All routers support NAT for security, but for maximum safety make sure the router comes with a dedicated firewall you can configure. This will help keep out Internet intruders.

- **Do you need VPN?**—If you think you'll need to make secure virtual private network (VPN) connections to your network, get a router that supports VPN.

Going Wireless: Understanding Wi-Fi Networks

You've seen so far that if you want maximum network speed, then ethernet—particularly Gigabit Ethernet—is the only way to connect. However, sometimes a wired connection just isn't practical or even possible. For example, if your switch is in the den, how do you set up a wired connection for the computer in the bedroom next door? One solution is to drill holes in the adjoining walls and then snake a long ethernet cable through the hole. That will work, but holes in the wall are rarely attractive. Even more daunting, how do you connect a computer that's downstairs in the kitchen or even two floors down in the basement? Diehard ethernet types might consider getting special outdoor ethernet cables and poking more holes in the appropriate walls, but at some point the hole-making madness must stop!

A much more convenient solution in all these scenarios is to forego the cables and go wireless. It's not as fast as either Fast Ethernet or Gigabit Ethernet, but if you get the right hardware, it's fast enough, and it means you can easily and quickly connect almost any computer or wireless device to your network. Wireless is also less secure than ethernet (because the signals can broadcast beyond your home or office), but as long as you encrypt the signals and protect the network with a strong password, security isn't a big worry.

Modern wireless networking can be both fast and reliable, but achieving such a state requires a bit of planning and the know-how to purchase the right hardware for your needs. The rest of this chapter tells you everything you need to know.

Wireless devices transmit data and communicate with other devices using *radio frequency (RF)* signals that are beamed from one device to another. Although these radio signals are similar to those used in commercial radio broadcasts, they operate on a different frequency. For example, if you use a wireless keyboard and mouse, you have an RF receiver device plugged into a USB port on your computer (usually). The keyboard and mouse have built-in RF transmitters. When you press a key or move or click the mouse, the transmitter sends the appropriate RF signal, that signal is picked up by the receiver, and the corresponding keystroke or mouse action is passed along to Windows just as though the original device had been connected to the computer directly.

A *radio transceiver* is a device that can act as both a transmitter and a receiver of radio signals. All wireless devices that require two-way communications use a transceiver. In wireless networking—also called *wireless local area network* WLAN)—you still use a NIC, but in this case the NIC comes with a built-in transceiver that enables the NIC to send and receive RF signals. (For more information, see "Learning about Wireless NICs," later in this chapter.) The resulting beam takes the place of the network cable. The wireless NIC communicates with a nearby *wireless access point*, a device that contains a transceiver that enables the device to pass along network signals. (For more details, see "Putting It All Together with a Wireless Access Point," later in this chapter.)

Understanding Wi-Fi

The most common wireless networking technology is *wireless fidelity*, which is almost always shortened to *Wi-Fi* (which rhymes with *hi-fi*); the generic IEEE

caution As with the ethernet standards I discussed earlier, all wireless speeds are theoretical because interference and bandwidth limitations almost always mean that real-world speeds are slower than the optimum speeds.

6

designation for this wireless networking standard is *802.11*. The four main types are 802.11a, 802.11b, 802.11g, and 802.11n—each of which has its own range and speed limits, as you see in the next few sections.

802.11b

The original 802.11 standard was published by the IEEE in 1997, but few people took it seriously because it was hobbled by a maximum transmission rate of just 2Mbps. By 1999, the IEEE had worked out not one but *two* new standards: 802.11a and 802.11b. The 802.11b standard became the more popular of the two, so I discuss it first.

802.11b upped the Wi-Fi data transmission rate to 11Mbps, which is just a bit faster than 10BASE-T, the original ethernet standard, which has a maximum rate of 10Mbps. The indoor range of 802.11b is about 115 feet.

802.11b operates on the 2.4GHz radio frequency, which is an unregulated frequency often used by other consumer products such as microwave ovens, cordless telephones, and baby monitors. This keeps the price of 802.11b hardware low, but it can also cause interference problems when you attempt to access the network near another device that's using the 2.4GHz frequency.

802.11a

The 802.11a standard was released at around the same time as the 802.11b standard. There are two key differences between these standards: 802.11a has a maximum transmission rate of 54Mbps, and it operates using the regulated 5.0GHz radio frequency band. This higher frequency band means 802.11a devices don't have the same interference problems as 802.11b devices, but it also means 802.11a hardware is more expensive, offers a shorter range (about 75 feet), and has trouble penetrating solid surfaces such as walls. So, despite its impressive transmission speed, 802.11a just had too many negative factors against it, and 802.11b won the hearts of consumers and became the first true wireless networking standard.

802.11g

During the battle between 802.11a and 802.11b, it became clear that consumers and small businesses really wanted the best of both worlds. That is, they wanted a WLAN technology that was as fast and as interference free as 802.11a but that had the longer range and cheaper cost of 802.11b. Alas, "the best of both worlds" is a state rarely achieved in the real world. However, the IEEE came close when it introduced the next version of the wireless networking standard in 2003: 802.11g. Like its 802.11a predecessor, 802.11g has a theoretical maximum transmission rate of 54Mbps, and like 802.11b, 802.11g boasts an indoor range of about 115 feet and is cheap to manufacture. That cheapness comes from its use of the 2.4GHz RF band, which means 802.11g devices can suffer from interference from other nearby consumer devices that use the same frequency.

Despite the possibility of interference, 802.11g quickly became the most popular of the Wi-Fi standards, and almost all WLAN devices sold today support 802.11g.

note In the same way that many ethernet devices support multiple standards by offering 10/100 or 10/100/1000 support, so too do many WLAN devices support multiple Wi-Fi standards. Older devices often offer *a/b* support, meaning you can use the device with both 802.11a and 802.11b devices. Newer WLAN devices now often offer *b/g* support, meaning you can use the device with both 802.11b and 802.11g devices. A few devices even offer *a/b/g* support for all three Wi-Fi standards.

802.11n

The IEEE is working on a new wireless standard called 802.11n as this book goes to press, and this amendment is expected to be finalized sometime in 2009. 802.11n implements a technology called *multiple-input multiple-output (MIMO)* that uses multiple transmitters and receivers in each device. This enables multiple data streams on a single device, which will greatly improve WLAN performance. For example, using three transmitters and two receivers (the standard configuration), 802.11n promises a theoretical transmission speed of up to 248Mbps. It's still not Gigabit Ethernet, but 802.11n devices could finally enable us to stream high-quality video over a wireless connection. 802.11n also promises to double the wireless range to about 230 feet.

These are all impressive numbers, to be sure, and even if the real-world results are considerably less, it appears as though 802.11n devices will be about five times faster than 802.11g devices and will offer about twice the range. That's why some manufacturers have jumped the gun and started offering 802.11n Draft 2.0 devices. "Draft 2.0" refers to the second draft of the amendment, which was approved by the IEEE in March 2007. The word on the street is that there are unlikely to be substantive changes to the amendment between the Draft 2.0 version and the final version.

note What does it mean to say that a device is "upgradeable"? Most devices are controlled by *firmware*, programming code embedded in the device, often stored in a special memory chip called an *EPROM*, which is short for erasable programmable read-only memory. The *erasable* part means the firmware can be replaced by a newer version; hence, the device's firmware is upgradeable.

6

Does this mean it's safe to purchase Draft 2.0 devices now? The answer is a resounding *maybe*. Most WLAN manufacturers are saying that their current Draft 2.0 products will be upgradeable; so, if there are changes between now and the final draft, you'll be able to apply a patch to the device to make it conform to the new standard. Trusting that this will be so means taking a bit of a chance on your part, so *caveat emptor*.

tip You can eliminate a bit of the risk associated with 802.11n Draft 2.0 products by purchasing only those that have been certified by the Wi-Fi Alliance, a consortium of Wi-Fi manufacturers. After the Draft 2.0 amendment was approved, the Wi-Fi Alliance began testing Draft 2.0 devices to ensure not only that they conform to the draft specifications, but also that they work well with older 802.11a/b/g devices. See http://www.wi-fi.org for more information.

Understanding Wireless Hot Spots

With Wi-Fi RF signals extending about 115 feet (and stronger signals extend even farther), you won't be surprised to learn that wireless communication is possible over a reasonably long distance. In your home or small office, this means your wireless network is probably available *outside* the building, which is why you need to pay extra attention to wireless security.

However, in some circumstances the relatively long range of a wireless network, or even *extending* the network's range with a special device called a wireless range extender," is an advantage. I'm talking here about the wireless networks that are popping up in cities all across the world: in coffee shops, cafés, restaurants, fast-food outlets, hotels, airports, trains, and even dental offices. Some cities have even started offering universal Wi-Fi access in their downtown areas.

These wireless networks share an Internet connection, so you can connect to the network and then use it to surf the web, check your email, catch up on your RSS feeds, log on to the office network, and more. A public wireless network that shares an Internet connection is called a *wireless hot spot* (or just a *hot spot*). In some cases, the

note Another popular wireless technology is *Bluetooth*, a wireless networking standard that uses RFs to set up a communications link between devices. This is another example of an ad-hoc wireless network. The Bluetooth name comes from Harald Bluetooth, a tenth-century Danish king who united the provinces of Denmark under a single crown, the same way that—theoretically—Bluetooth will unite the world of portable wireless devices under a single standard. Why name a modern technology after an obscure Danish king? Here's a clue: two of the most important companies backing the Bluetooth standard—Ericsson and Nokia—are Scandinavian.

6

establishment offers Internet access free of charge as a perk for doing business with them. However, most hot spots charge a fee to access the network.

Learning About Wireless NICs

A wireless NIC is a transceiver that can both transmit data to the network and receive signals from the network. The rate at which the NIC processes this data and the distance from the network that you can roam depend on the 802.11 standard implemented by the NIC. Almost all wireless NICs sold today (or that come preinstalled in new computers) are 802.11g compliant, and most implement b/g support, meaning the NIC also works seamlessly with 802.11b NICs and devices.

There are four main types of wireless NIC:

Internal card

One common wireless NIC type is an internal adapter card you insert into a free slot on the motherboard's bus. Most computers today use a PCI bus, so you need to get a PCI network adapter. The NIC's backplate usually includes a small post onto which you screw the antenna, either directly or via a longish wire that enables you to position the antenna to avoid interference. Figure 6.14 shows both types.

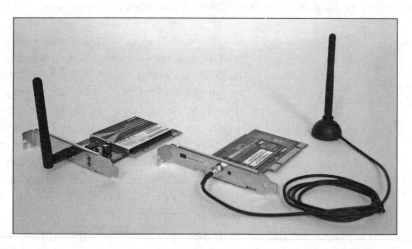

FIGURE 6.14

You insert an internal wireless NIC into a free slot on the system bus inside your computer.

USB

If your motherboard doesn't have any free bus slots, you can still go wireless by attaching an external wireless NIC to an open USB port. As with all USB devices, get a USB 2.0 wireless NIC for optimum performance. USB wireless NICs either attach directly to the USB port or come with a USB cable, as shown in Figure 6.15.

FIGURE 6.15

A USB wireless NIC attaches to a free USB slot on your computer.

PC Card

Almost all notebooks nowadays come with Wi-Fi built in. In some cases, you can enable or disable the built-in wireless NIC by toggling a button (usually labeled Wi-Fi or WLAN). If you want to upgrade your notebook to a faster version of Wi-Fi, you can attach a USB wireless NIC, as long as you have a free USB port. Alternatively, every notebook comes with at least one PC Card (or PCMCIA) slot, so you can purchase and attach a PC Card (or PCMCIA) wireless NIC. Figure 6.16 shows an example.

Motherboard NIC

A few manufacturers are now offering a wireless NIC built directly in to the motherboard, and the post onto which you screw the antenna appears flush with the rest of the back panel connectors, as shown in Figure 6.17.

FIGURE 6.16

You can upgrade your notebook's Wi-Fi capabilities by inserting a PC Card (or PCMCIA) wireless NIC.

FIGURE 6.17

A wireless NIC built in to a motherboard.

Putting It All Together with a Wireless Access Point

If you just want to exchange a bit of data with one or more nearby computers, Windows Vista enables you to set up and connect to an ad-hoc wireless network where the computers themselves manage the connection. A longer-term solution is to set up and connect to an infrastructure wireless network, which requires an extra device called a *wireless access point (AP)*. A wireless AP (Figure 6.18 shows a couple of examples) is a device that receives and transmits signals from wireless computers to form a wireless network, as shown in Figure 6.19.

FIGURE 6.18

Examples of wireless APs.

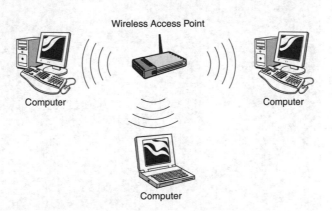

FIGURE 6.19

Add a wireless AP to create an infrastructure wireless network.

For a wireless AP to work properly, it must support an 802.11 standard that's compatible with all your wireless NICs. For example, if all your wireless NICs use 802.11g, your wireless AP must also support 802.11g. Similarly, if your wireless NICs are a mixture of 802.11b and 802.11g, your wireless AP must implement 802.11b/g. Most wireless APs support both 802.11b and 802.11g, and the AP's setup pages usually enable you to choose between support for 802.11b/g or just 802.11g.

These days, standalone wireless AP devices are rare. Instead, most wireless APs are multifunction devices and usually come with some or all of the following features built in:

Switch   Almost all wireless APs also implement an ethernet switch and offer several (usually four) RJ-45 ports. This enables you to mix both wired and wireless connections on your network. As with a standalone ethernet switch, make sure the wireless AP's switch supports an ethernet standard that's compatible with the ethernet NICs you want to use for your wired connections (such as Fast Ethernet, Gigabit Ethernet, or 10/100).

Router   Most wireless APs also come with a built-in router. (Actually, to be accurate, in the vast majority of cases it's the router that's the main device, and it's the wireless AP that's the built-in feature.) This enables you to give your wireless network users access to the Internet (see Figure 6.20) by connecting a broadband modem to the WAN port in the back of the wireless AP.

Firewall   Most wireless APs come with a built-in firewall, which hides your wireless network from the Internet and prevents unwanted packets from reaching your wireless devices.

6

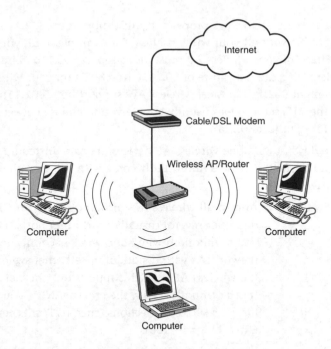

FIGURE 6.20

With a combination wireless AP and router, you can give wireless network users access to the Internet.

Expanding Your Wi-Fi Empire with a Wireless Range Extender

If you find that your wireless AP is not reaching certain areas of your home or office, you can use a *wireless range extender* to boost the signal. Depending on the device and wireless AP, the extender can more than double the normal wireless range. Bear in mind, however, that range extenders are notoriously difficult to incorporate into an existing network. For the best results, use an extender from the same company that makes your wireless AP and make sure the extender is compatible with the AP. (For example, they implement compatible 802.11 standards and support the same wireless security protocols.) Figure 6.21 shows a wireless range extender from Linksys.

FIGURE 6.21

You can use a wireless range extender to boost your wireless signal and extend the range of your network.

A Buyer's Guide to Wireless Networking Hardware

Purchasing wireless hardware is, unfortunately, no easier than buying other types of networking hardware because the acronyms and jargon are just as prevalent. If there's an advantage to outfitting a wireless network, it's that to get started you really need just two types of equipment: wireless NICs for each computer that needs one and a wireless AP to manage the network. The next two sections offer you a few tips and suggestions on what to look for and what to avoid when purchasing devices in these two wireless hardware categories.

Before getting to those tips, I want to reiterate the point I made earlier about quality versus price when it comes to wireless networking devices. There is an inherently finicky quality to Wi-Fi networking because of interference from other devices, humidity, and even the phase of the moon (or so it seems on occasion). Quality wireless devices minimize this flakiness, so on that point alone they're worth the extra few dollars. Of course, wireless devices manufactured by reputable companies are also reliable, conform to the 802.11 standard,

6

come with a wide selection of device drivers, and offer decent support. The following list of companies that manufacture quality wireless networking devices is similar to, but not quite the same as, the list you saw earlier for ethernet devices:

> Belkin (belkin.com)
>
> Buffalo (buffalo.com)
>
> D-Link (dlink.com)
>
> Linksys (linksys.com)
>
> NETGEAR (netgear.com)
>
> TRENDnet (trendnet.com)
>
> USRobotics (usr.com)
>
> Zonet (zonetusa.com)

Purchasing a Wireless NIC

When you need to purchase a wireless NIC or two, here are some things to think about in advance:

- **Internal or external**—You saw earlier that ethernet users face a stark choice: If you want the speed of Gigabit Ethernet, you can get it only in the form of an internal adapter card. You face no such choice in the wireless world because the fastest NICs—those that support 802.11g or even 802.11n Draft 2.0 if you want to take the plunge (more on this next)—are available both as internal cards and as external USB devices. The choice really comes down to whether you have a free USB port. Most computers come with a decent collection of USB ports these days, but more and more devices are coming out in USB form, so it's not unusual for USB ports to fill up.

- **Only get USB 2.0 NICs**—If you want to purchase a USB wireless NIC, make sure it uses the faster USB 2.0 technology, and not USB 1.1. Wireless USB 1.1 NICs are actually hard to find nowadays, but it pays to read the fine print in the specifications, just to be sure.

- **Wireless security**—As you see in Chapter 16, wireless security is a crucial topic, and it's important that all your wireless devices use the same type of security. You get all the details in Chapter 16, but for now you should only consider

note If your computer's USB ports are full, consider purchasing a *USB hub*, a device that offers multiple USB ports (usually three, four, or seven).

purchasing a wireless NIC that offers the strongest possible security. Right now, that means the NIC must support the *Wi-Fi Protected Access (WPA)* security standard, ideally the latest iteration, which is WPA2. At all costs, avoid any wireless NIC that supports only *Wired Equivalent Privacy (WEP)*, an older security scheme that is easily compromised.

■ **802.11b or 802.11g**—This one's a no-brainer: Go with 802.11g, no matter what. If you can even find 802.11b devices (perhaps at a geek's garage sale), they'll be temptingly cheap. However, remember that you get five times the speed with 802.11g, and that extra speed is worth it, believe me.

■ **To 802.11n or not to 802.11n**—As I write this, 80211.n Draft 2.0 devices are still relatively rare, but they should be thick on the ground by the time you read this. Should you take a chance on these products, even though they'll be more expensive than their 802.11g counterparts? My own feeling is that if you have a real need for more wireless speed—for example, if you're itching to stream video over a wireless connection—you should probably jump in. As mentioned earlier, you should ideally stick to devices that have been certified by the Wi-Fi Alliance. Another strategy to consider is purchasing all your 802.11n devices from the same manufacturer, the theory being that devices from the same company should work well together. So, for example, if you want to purchase 802.11n NICs from, say, Linksys, you should also purchase your 802.11n wireless AP from Linksys. The important thing is to ensure that you're getting a Draft 2.0 device. Previous 802.11n products used the "Draft N" moniker, and you want to stay away from those.

■ **Check the claims**—Lots of wireless NICs claim they use fancy new technology to, say, double the data transmission rate or triple the range of standard 802.11g. In some cases, these claims are true. For example, I mentioned earlier that 802.11n uses MIMO technology to improve speed and range, but some companies are incorporating MIMO into 802.11g NICs, too, and those NICs show genuine improvements in speed and range. Other claims might or might not be true. It's best in these cases to do some homework by reading reviews of the NICs to see whether the claims hold up under real-world conditions. Most online retailers solicit reviews from purchasers, online networking sites review the latest NICs, and you can use sites such as Epinions (epinions.com) and ConsumerReview (consumerreview.com) to search for reviews of devices you're considering.

6

Purchasing a Wireless AP

The wireless AP is the most complicated of the wireless products, so not surprisingly the ads and specifications for these devices are riddled with $10 technical terms, acronyms and abbreviations, and a fair dose of marketing hype. Fortunately, you can ignore most of what you read and just concentrate on the following points:

- **Wireless security**—I mentioned in the previous section that you should get only wireless NICs that support WPA security, ideally WPA2. It's important that your wireless AP supports the same security standard. To see why, understand that most new wireless NICs support multiple security standards, usually WEP, WPA, and WPA2. If you purchase an older wireless AP that supports only, say, WEP, *all* your wireless activity will use WEP because the NICs will lower their security to work with the AP. So, again, you should ideally purchase only a wireless AP that supports the WPA2 standard.

- **Get a router**—It's a rare wireless network that doesn't also need to share an Internet connection. If you want your wireless users to be able to access the Internet from anywhere in the house or office, make sure the wireless AP comes with a router (or purchase a router that comes with a built-in wireless AP).

- **Do you need a separate switch**—As mentioned earlier, almost all new wireless APs come with a built-in switch, so you might be able to get away with using the wireless AP as your network's central connection point. This is usually only the case with networks that require just a few wired connections because most wireless APs come with four-port switches (although eight-port APs are available). If your network comes with quite a few devices that require ethernet connectivity, you should consider adding a dedicated switch to the network. Check the ethernet standards supported by the AP ports to ensure that they match the standards used by your ethernet devices, and get the largest number of ports you can afford.

- **Check the 802.11 support**—Because it's the AP's job to manage your network's wireless connections, you must ensure that the AP supports the same 802.11 standards as your wireless devices. For example, if all your wireless devices use 802.11g, you can get a wireless AP that supports only 802.11g. However, if your wireless devices use a mixture of 802.11b and 802.11g, your AP must support both standards. If you get an 802.11n Draft 2.0 wireless AP, make sure it also supports 802.11b and 802.11g because you'll certainly have other devices on your network that use those standards. Look for certification from the Wi-Fi Alliance to ensure that the 802.11n AP correctly implements 802.11b/g.

■ **Make sure it has a firewall**—All wireless APs that have built-in routers support NAT for security, but for maximum safety ensure that the AP comes with a dedicated firewall you can configure.

From Here

■ For the steps involved in adding an expansion card, **see** "Installing an Expansion Card," **p. 211**.

■ If you're putting together a PC for business, **see** "Choosing Networking Hardware for the Basic Business PC," **p. 251**.

■ If you're building a home theater PC, **see** "Choosing Networking Hardware for the Home Theater PC," **p. 290**.

■ If you're constructing a PC for maximum performance, **see** "Choosing Networking Hardware for the High-Performance PC," **p. 336**.

■ If you're building a gaming PC, **see** "Choosing Networking Hardware for the Killer Gaming PC," **p. 379**.

■ If you're putting together a PC on a budget, **see** "Choosing Networking Hardware for the Budget PC," **p. 422**.

■ To learn how to connect all your computers and network hardware, **see** Chapter 16, "Putting Your Network Together," **p. 473**.

6

Buying PC Parts

The buyer needs a hundred eyes; the seller needs but one.

—English proverb

In the first half dozen chapters of the book, I provided you with various "buying guides" for parts such as the motherboard, case, power supply, processor, memory, hard drive, and video card. (See the "From Here" section at the end of this chapter for a list of the page numbers where these guides appear.) My aim in each of those guides was to give you a few pointers to help you get the right part for your PC project. However, savvy builders know that it's not enough to think just about *what* parts you need: you also need to think about *how* you buy those parts. Can you research components online? Which online retailers have what you need? Are all online stores the same? What about things like refurbished parts, open boxes, and extended warranties? My goal in this chapter is to answer all these questions (and quite a few more) so that by the end you'll have all the information you need to purchase parts like a pro.

Researching Parts Online

Sure, we use the Internet to communicate, connect, and have fun, but its main use for most of use is to do research. That's not only because the Web contains a vast amount of information (much of which is actually true!), but also because we can easily search and surf to the information we need. This is a boon to the custom PC builder because it makes it absurdly easy to research components to find the right product at the right price. Whatever part you're looking to add to your homebrew computer, somebody has reviewed it and somebody else is selling it.

To help you get started, the next couple of sections list the best sites for hardware reviews and comparing component prices.

Checking Out Product Reviews

Whether you're looking for a motherboard or memory, a power supply or processor, it's a lead-pipe cinch that someone has reviewed it and posted that review online for all to read. I'm not talking here about little Johnny the budding computer geek proclaiming the latest NVIDIA graphics card to be "Awesome!" on his blog (although, of course, there's no shortage of that kind of thing around). Rather, I'm talking about in-depth, non-partisan reviews by hardware professionals that really put parts to the test and tell you the pros and the cons of each piece of equipment.

Hardware-related sites are a dime a dozen (if that), but a few are really good. Here are my recommendations:

- **AnandTech**—Although this site offers extras such as forums, blogs, product pricing, and hardware news, its heart and its claim to fame is the massive collection of incredibly in-depth reviews (see Figure 7.1). They're often quite technical, but feel free to skim the mumbo-jumbo because there's still plenty of useful information for everyone.

  http://www.anandtech.com/

- **Ars Technica**—The name means "The Art of Technology," and that's an appropriate description of this deep, sprawling site aimed at computer enthusiasts. For system builders, the site includes buyer's guides, technology guides, how-to articles, and lots more.

  http://arstechnica.com/index.ars

tip When you read a review, be sure to note the date it was published. If it was quite a while ago, the review might be talking about an older version of the component.

7

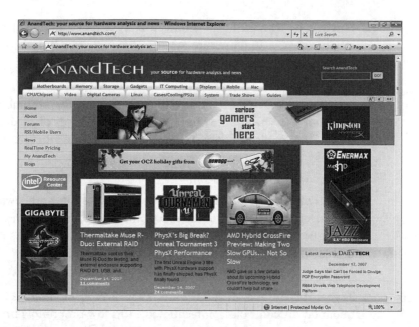

FIGURE 7.1
AnandTech is one of the best sites for hardware product reviews.

■ **CNET**—This massive site has a Reviews section that covers tons of products. Each review is simply laid out with headings such as Pros, Cons, Suitability, Value, and Suggestions. The layout of the site leaves something to be desired, so use the search engine to find what you want.

http://www.cnet.com/

■ **Computer Power User**—This is the online companion site for my favorite computer magazine: *Computer Power User*. The magazine (and therefore the site) is dedicated to custom PC building and modifying, so its chock full of useful product reviews geared to builders. You'll also find how-to articles, forums, chat rooms, and more.

http://www.computerpoweruser.com/

■ **ExtremeTech**—This professional site (it's affiliated with *PC Magazine*) is loaded with in-depth product reviews and recommendations for the products suited to building your own PC.

http://www.extremetech.com/

> **note** To get the most out of the Computer Power User site, you either need to subscribe to the magazine (as I write this, it's $29 for a year, $64 for three years), or you can pay for full access to the site ($17 per year).

7

■ **HardOCP**—This hardware enthusiasts site offers minutely detailed product reviews that are sure to warm the cockles of a geek's heart, but they also offer plenty of good information for the rest of us.

http://www.hardocp.com/

■ **Maximum PC**—This is the web home of the terrific print magazine *Maximum PC*. The website offers reviews of thousands of products in every conceivable category. The reviews aren't particularly exhaustive, but they give you a good overview of each product.

http://www.maximumpc.com/

■ **The Tech Report**—If you want your reviews to tilt more toward the obsessively detailed side of the spectrum, look no further than this site, which has some of the most in-depth reviews on the web. It's not the best-looking website I've ever seen, but the content rules here.

http://www.techreport.com/

■ **Tom's Hardware**—If you want to know everything there is to know about a particular piece of technology, this jaw-droppingly impressive site is the place to go (see Figure 7.2). The reviews and technology articles are a geek's dream, and there's plenty of great information for everyone else, too.

http://www.tomshardware.com/

■ **Newsgroups**—With such good websites at your click and call, it's easy to forget that you can often find really good reviews of products on the Usenet newsgroups, particularly the following:

    alt.comp.hardware

    alt.comp.hardware.pc-homebuilt

    alt.comp.hardware.homebuilt

    comp.sys.ibm.pc.hardware

Access the groups using your favorite newsreader or Google Groups:

http://groups.google.com/

tip Besides checking specific sites for reviews of a particular component, you can also try running a Google search that includes the product name and the word *review*. Be sure to search not only the Web, but also Google Groups.

tip No time to read a long-winded review? No problem! Almost all reviews have a "summary" section at the end that recaps the highlights of the review, including the major pros and cons, the reviewer's kudos and caveats, and whether the reviewer recommends the product.

7

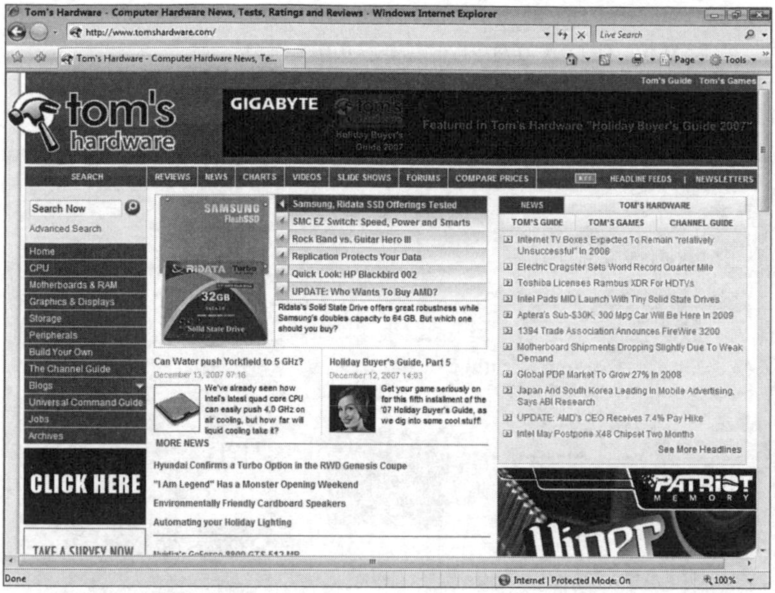

FIGURE 7.2
Tom's Hardware features awesomely in-depth product reviews.

Performing Price Comparisons

After you've read the reviews and know exactly what you want, your next step as a savvy shopper is to find the best price. You could do that by jumping around to various online retailers, searching for your product, and making note of the price each time. However, plenty of sites out there will do all the hard work for you. I'm talking about the web's price comparison sites (sometimes called *shopping portals*), where you select or specify the product you want and the site returns the product listings from a number of online retailers. You can then compare prices with just a few mouse clicks.

Here are some decent shopping portals to check out:

- **Become**—This site shows you not only the prices for each listing, but also the product's rating at each store (1 to 5 stars, based on user reviews).

  http://www.become.com/

- **CNET Shopper.com**—This is the Shopper.com section of the CNET site. Its nicest feature is that for each store returned in the listings, you get the store's rating (1 to 5 stars) and whether the store currently has stock of the item—and if you enter your ZIP Code, the taxes and shipping fees are displayed (see Figure 7.3).

http://shopper.cnet.com/

FIGURE 7.3

CNET's Shopper.com site not only compares prices, but also provides each store's rating, stock, taxes, and shipping costs to your ZIP Code.

- **Google Product Search**—This site (formerly known as Froogle) applies the awesome power of Google's search engine to online products. You search on the name of the product you want, and Google returns product listings from around the web.

  http://www.google.com/products/

- **PriceGrabber.com**—This is one of the most popular shopping portals, and no wonder because, for each product, you get tons of information: price, stock, product details, user reviews and discussions, expert reviews, seller rating, and taxes and shipping for your ZIP Code. What more could you want?

  http://www.pricegrabber.com/

■ **Shopzilla**—This site doesn't have all the bells and whistles that you see with some of the other sites, but it often returns a broader array of listings and has all the basic information you need: price, taxes, shipping, product details, and product reviews.

http://www.shopzilla.com/

■ **Yahoo! Shopping**—Lots of people like this section of Yahoo! because it provides all the standard shopping portal data and gives you full product specifications, user ratings, and the ability to send listings to a mobile phone (perfect if you're doing your shopping offline).

http://shopping.yahoo.com/

Researching Retailers Online

With hundreds of online retailers out there, how can you tell the ecommerce stars from the fly-by-night shysters? The best way is to ask your friends, family, and colleagues who they've used and had good experiences with in the past. Because these are people you trust, you can rely on the information you get.

Besides that, you can also go by the ratings online users have applied to retailers. These are usually stars (usually up to 5 stars, and the more stars the better). Many of the shopping portals in the previous section also include user ratings for each store. For example, Google Product Search (http://www.google.com/products/) also doubles as a retailer ratings service. When you run a product search, the name of the reseller appears below the price and below that are a rating (1 to 5 stars) and the number of user ratings that have produced the result. As you can see in Figure 7.4, you can also sort the results by seller rating, and there are links to restrict the results based on seller rating (for example, to show only the results for sellers with 4 or more stars) .

A site that's dedicated to rating resellers is the appropriately named ResellerRatings.com (see http://www.resellerratings.com/). This site uses a 1-to-10 scale, where the higher the rating, the better the store. You can use the site as a shopping portal, or you can look up an individual store to see its rating. (Usefully, you get two ratings for each store: a lifetime rating and a six-month rating; if the latter is much lower than the former, that's a sign something has gone seriously wrong at the store over the past few months and you might want to shop elsewhere.) There are also interesting lists of the "Highest Rated Stores" (see Figure 7.5) and "Lowest Rated Stores."

7

FIGURE 7.4

You can sort the Google Product Search results by reseller rating.

FIGURE 7.5

ResellerRatings.com is a massive database of online retailer ratings and reviews.

Buying Parts Online

Buying components online isn't the scary proposition it was a few years ago. There are many reliable, reputable, and secure merchants to choose from now, so buying online is no longer a big deal. Even still, it's different from buying at a retail store or via mail order. To ensure the best online transaction possible, here are a few pointers to bear in mind:

> **tip** Some sites offer RSS feeds that alert you to upcoming promotions, which can be an easier way to stay on top of things. If a site doesn't have an RSS feed, look for a mailing list.

- The three most important things to remember when buying online are compare, compare, compare. It's not at all unusual to find one store selling the same part for 10% or even 20% less than other stores, so use the shopping portals I mentioned earlier to get the best price.

- Keep an eye out for special deals. Many online retailers offer promotions on a particular day of the week or when they need to clear out inventory. Troll the sites of your favorite online retailers to watch out for these specials.

- Be wary of a price that seems too good to be true. Yes, some retailers occasionally offer a product as a loss leader: a price that's substantially lower than their competitors as a way of tempting you to buy something and thus establish a relationship with the store. (After you purchase at least one thing from a store, you're more likely to go back, particularly if the experience was a positive one.) However, it's also entirely possible for some of the shadier outfits to offer super-low prices on returned or refurbished parts without telling you what you're getting. Unless you know the store is reputable, assume really low prices are bogus and move on to the next store.

- Following on from that last point, note that a really cheap price might be the *net* price you pay after processing a mail-in rebate. Obviously you'll pay a higher price up front, but some retailers don't tell you that, or they hide the fact in small print somewhere. Also, beware of extra handling charges and other fees that the retailer might try to tack on. Before committing to the sale, always give the invoice a thorough going-over so you know exactly what you're paying.

- Be sure you understand the difference between an original equipment manufacturer (OEM) version and a retail box version of a component. The OEM version of a product is the version that would normally go to a system builder. It's the same part, but minus the extras that come

7

with the retail box version, so it's often much cheaper. At best this just means no-frills packaging, but it can also mean no manual, no device drivers, no extra parts such as hard drive data cables or a CPU cooler, and often a shorter warranty. If you just need the part itself, the OEM version can save you a few shekels, but be sure you know what you're getting.

> **note** The term "OEM" is pretty universal, but some retailers use alternative terminology for specific products. For example, an OEM hard drive is sometimes called a *bare drive*.

- Buy just off the bleeding edge. It's a truism in PC component retailing that the latest-and-greatest parts cost the most. The newest Intel processors come with a hefty price tag that's usually north of $1,000, but the previous generation can often be had for half that, or less. A top-of-the-line (as I write this) 768MB NVIDIA GeForce 8800GTX video card can set you back $500, but the almost-as-good 512MB NVIDIA GeForce 8800GT card can be found online for well under $300.

- Most good online vendors will give you a chance during checkout to enter your ZIP Code or postal code so you can see exactly what your shipping charges will be. Because the cost of shipping can often be extravagant, whenever possible you should find out the cost in advance before completing the sale.

- Some retailers allow you to mail a check or money order and will ship the order when they receive the payment. You should avoid these payment options like the plague because, if something goes wrong (for example, the product never shows up), getting your money back could be a challenge. If you pay by credit card, however, you always have the option of charging back the cost to the vendor.

- If the retailer offers a PayPal option, use it. Currently owned by eBay, PayPal is an online payment service that enables you to buy online without exposing your credit card data to the retailer. You sign up for a PayPal account at http://www.paypal.com/ and provide them with your credit card, debit card, or bank account information. (It's all super-secure and everything is verified before your

> **caution** Watch out for online retailers who charge some kind of extra fee (usually a percentage of the product price) for accepting credit card payments. This is almost always a sign of a shady dealer who's either trying to squeeze an extra few percentage points out of you or is trying to discourage you from using a credit card.

7

account goes online.) When you buy something online with a PayPal-friendly retailer, that retailer tells PayPal the cost of the sale and PayPal charges it to your credit card, debit card, or bank account and then passes along the money to the retailer. The retailer never sees your financial data, so you never have to worry about that data being stolen or accidentally exposed.

> **note** In the unlikely event that the retailer doesn't provide a confirmation email message, either print the screen or capture it to an image: in Windows, press Print Screen and then paste the image into Paint; on your Mac, press Command+Shift+3 to save the screen image to the desktop.

■ When the checkout process is complete, leave the final window open on your desktop so you have access to the order number, final total, tracking information, and other order details. After you get an email confirming the transaction and you've checked the email for accuracy, you can close the web window.

Returning Parts Online

The arrival of a new PC part is often quite exciting, particularly for meaty components such as motherboards and cases. However, that initial excitement occasionally turns to disappointment when your new toy doesn't live up to expectations. It might be defective, incompatible, or just not what you want. Bummer. The good news is that the vast majority of the time you're not stuck with your part because almost all retailers offer returns for either refund or replacement. This is usually a fairly straightforward process, but to ensure a smooth return, there are a few things you need to know; I detail them in this section.

First, when you get your package resist the temptation to tear off the cellophane and dive into the box to eyeball your new bauble. A more deliberate pace should always be the norm when building a custom PC, but it also has ramifications in the returns department:

> **note** With so many vendors offering returns privileges, you should avoid retailers that don't offer them. If a reseller can't stand behind its products by offering returns, then there's no reason you should ever stand in front of them!

■ You run the risk of scattering teensy-but-vital bits to the nether regions of your office. When you return an item, the retailer will check to see whether all the parts are present, and if anything's missing, it might disallow your refund.

■ It's a general rule that hastily liberating the contents of a box means that those contents *never* go back in as neatly, or at all! Your return stands far less chance of being rejected if you pack the contents back into the box exactly the way you found them originally.

■ Don't throw anything away, even if you think you're *really*, *really* sure you're going to keep the component. First, the component might not work, which makes a return mandatory. Second, the component might not work the way you thought it would, and you can assuage your disappointment by sending the sucker back and getting something better. However, that's going to be a lot harder if you've already tossed the manual and other previously nonessential pieces.

■ Open bags and containers as carefully as possible. If you just rip into things, you won't be able to put their components back in if the need for a return arises. This means either you have to leave them loose in the box (which could cause damage to other parts) or you need to improvise a new container (which is just a waste of your precious time).

■ Don't remove any stickers, decals, or barcode labels. Try to keep the components as pristine as possible just in case they need to go back.

■ Try the component as soon as possible. Most retailers offer returns for only a limited time—for refunds, it's sometimes as short as 14 days, but more typically it's 30 days—so give your product a whirl within that timeframe.

■ Check to ensure that you can send your nondefective product back. Many retailers have return exceptions for parts such as processors and memory modules, as well as for special purchases such as open-box items.

note No reputable reseller will charge a restocking fee on an item you're returning for replacement. For refund returns, thumb your nose at any vendor that charges more than a 15% restocking fee. Unfortunately, fees in the 20% to 30% range aren't unheard of, so watch out for them and don't give any business to a company that would charge such an outrageous amount.

■ Check to see whether the retailer charges a restocking fee. This might be something like 15% of the cost, so find out in advance so you're not surprised when an apparently too-small refund comes through on your next credit card statement.

If, after all that, you do have something to return, you need to contact the retailer and ask for a return authorization number—usually called a return merchandise authorization (RMA) number. Most of the larger online retailers enable you to request an RMA number on their sites, usually by accessing your account. Otherwise, you need to contact the retailer's customer service department. After you have authorization, you're ready to make the return:

- Keep a box or three around for use with returns. Retailers often ship components in boxes filled with Styrofoam chips, so I keep a box of those around for safe shipping.

- If the retailer supplies you with a label, be sure to place the label on your box in a visible location. The label usually contains information—such as the retailer's address, the RMA number, and the original invoice number—that can help smooth the returns process.

- If you don't have a special label, write "RMA Number:" on the box, followed by the number the retailer supplied to you for the return. This helps steer the package to the retailer's returns department and helps the returns clerk process the package. If you want, you can also add the original invoice number to the box to help speed up processing.

- When sending back the component, use a traceable method such as registered mail or a courier. This enables you to keep track of the package. It's also a good idea to insure the contents, so you're not on the hook if the package gets lost or damaged.

- Keep an eye peeled on your credit card to look for the refund. (Having online access to your card is particularly handy here.) Most reputable retailers will process the return in just a few business days, and it shouldn't take more than another couple of business days for the credit to show up. If you don't see anything after a couple of weeks, see whether the retailer offers an option for checking the status of your return online. If not, contact the retailer's customer service department to see what the holdup is.

Buying Parts Offline

Should you buy your PC parts from a bricks-and-mortar store such as Best Buy, Circuit City, CompUSA, Costco, Fry's, Future Shop, Staples, or your local electronics store? Here's the simple answer to that question: It depends. Buying in person has its advantages, but it's not without it disadvantages. So the retail route you choose depends on what you need, when you need it, and a host of other factors.

7

Here are the main advantages of buying offline:

- **No shipping charges**—When you buy retail, the only "shipping charge" is the cost of gas for the trip to the store and back. This is particularly advantageous with large items such as computer cases and heavy items such as power supplies, which often generate exorbitant shipping charges when ordered online.

- **Faster**—If you need a part *now*, the only way to get it done (assuming you're not mid-build at 3 a.m.) is to go to a store. Even the fastest online service can only offer overnight delivery (for big bucks, too).

- **Expertise**—In-store sales associates are often quite knowledgeable and can help you make a decision if you're having trouble finding the right part or choosing between two similar components. However, see also my note later about aggressive salesmanship and the commission connection.

- **Easier returns**—If your component isn't right for whatever reason, you can drive it back to the store and get an instant refund or replacement, usually without any hassle. (Although someone will give the package a thorough going-over to ensure it's in returnable condition.) This is much easier than the online rigmarole of getting an RMA number, shipping the component (at your own expense), and waiting for the refund or replacement to show up.

- **Mail-in rebates**—Both online and offline retailers sometimes offer instant rebates that immediately reduce the price of a component. Real-world stores often go one better and also offer a mail-in rebate where you have to send a form and proof-of-purchase to a mailing address and a check comes your way a couple of weeks later.

Here are the main disadvantages of buying offline:

- **Smaller selection**—Due to the inevitable shelf space limitations, even the largest superstore can carry only a limited number of items in any one area. Even mid-size online retailers have access to many times more products.

- **More expensive**—Buying retail is almost always more expensive than buying online, although the big

note Truth be told, mail-in rebates are a way for the retailer to make the product appear cheaper (because they usually show the after-rebate price prominently), and the retailer is counting on people not bothering to follow through on the rebate. Don't fall into their trap: send in those rebates! Also, to make sure the rebate is honored keep copies of the rebate forms and send the rebate via registered mail or some other traceable method.

electronics superstores usually have fairly competitive prices. Not only that, but the retailer will have to charge you sales tax, and chances are an online retailer won't, depending on where you and the retailer are located. (Remember, however, that to compare retail apples with online apples, you also have to factor in the shipping costs that are part of most online orders.)

- **Aggressive salesmanship**—Many electronics retailers put their sales staff on commission, which means the more they sell, the more money they make. That's a very simple recipe for aggressive and often annoying sales come-ons. Ask any overly insistent sales associate whether he's on commission and, if so, be sure to stick to your guns and purchase only what you need. Even better, take your business to a retailer that doesn't use commissioned sales staff.

Buying Non–Shrink-Wrapped Parts

In the same way that as soon as you drive a new car off the dealer's lot its value immediately plummets, as soon as the shrink-wrap comes off a PC component its value drops significantly. That can be good news for you as a consumer because you can often take advantage of this to get a good deal. Here are four possibilities:

- **Display model**—Most bricks-and-mortar stores keep items out for display so consumers can see and touch the item. This is rarely the case for sensitive PC parts such as processors and expansion cards, but it might be true for less-sensitive components such as cases, fans, and routers. If the store has no other stock but the display model, you can often negotiate a discount. (You'll probably have to talk to the manager to get it.)

- **Open-box**—Many online retailers offer 10% or even 20% off *open-box* items, which are usually returns that have had their boxes opened. This is why all retailers want you to be careful when you return something because if it's in good enough shape, they can sell it. All reputable retailers carefully inspect open-box items, so these are safe to buy and you save a few dollars in the process. However, you should check

caution There are two main problems with purchasing a display model. First, there's a good chance it has been handled roughly, so check it over carefully to ensure that it's not damaged. (Just in case, make sure the item is returnable.) Second, if the component has multiple parts, be sure you're getting everything.

7

the item carefully when you get it to ensure that everything's okay. (Although, note that most retailers impose a shorter returns period on open-box items.)

■ **Reconditioned**—These are used items the retailer has cleaned and checked, and where it has repaired or replaced any defective parts. You can often save a substantial amount on reconditioned parts, so they're a good way to go if the budget's tight. Bear in mind, however, that you're almost always getting older technology and the part won't last as long as a new one will.

■ **Used**—This refers to used parts that haven't been reconditioned. Although the low prices of these components are tempting, you should probably avoid them because you can't be sure what you're getting or how long it will last.

From Here

■ For tips on purchasing a motherboard, **see** "Buying a Motherboard," **p. 20**.

■ For information on purchasing a case, **see** "Buying a Case," **p. 32**.

■ For some pointers on purchasing a power supply, **see** "Buying a Power Supply," **p. 37**.

■ For tips on purchasing a processor, **see** "Buying a CPU," **p. 60**.

■ For some things to think about when purchasing memory, **see** "Buying Memory," **p. 76**.

■ For information on purchasing a hard drive, **see** "Buying a Hard Drive," **p. 92**.

■ For some data related to purchasing a CD or DVD drive, **see** "Buying an Optical Drive," **p. 98**.

■ For some points on purchasing a video card, **see** "Buying a Video Card," **p. 115**.

■ For tips on purchasing a sound card, **see** "Buying a Sound Card," **p. 126**.

■ For information on purchasing NICs, cables, and other ethernet hardware, **see** "A Buyer's Guide to Ethernet Hardware," **p. 150**.

■ For pointers on purchasing a wireless NIC and access point, **see** "A Buyer's Guide to Wireless Networking Hardware," **p. 165**.

Basic Skills for PC Building and Upgrading

"Build me straight, O worthy Master!
Stanch and strong, a goodly vessel,
That shall laugh at all disaster,
And with wave and whirlwind wrestle!"
—*Henry Wadsworth Longfellow,* "The Building of the Ship"

Building a PC from scratch and upgrading an existing computer are arts that anybody can master. If you can wield a knife and fork without poking yourself in the eye, then you have the requisite dexterity to perform any PC building or upgrading task. If you can dress yourself in the morning, then you have the needed organizational abilities to coordinate any PC building or upgrading project.

That's not to say that working on the innards of a PC is trivial work—far from it. It's just that installing and configuring components such as a motherboard, processor, and memory module just *seem* like tasks that require an advanced electrical engineering degree. The reality is that PC-building is a craft that falls somewhere in the middle of that spectrum, making it accessible to everyone. Accessible, that is, to everyone who's willing to learn a few basic skills that lie at the heart of the PC maker's craft. Those skills are the subject of this chapter, where you learn about the tools you need; how to set up your work area; how to work safely; and fundamental techniques such as opening the case, connecting cables, and installing memory module and expansion cards.

What Tools Do You Need?

These days, you can almost get away with building a PC from the ground up without requiring *any* tools at all! This is mostly thanks to the so-called "tool-less" designs of many modern computer cases, which enable you to install expansion cards, hard drives, and other internal drive bay components such as optical drives and memory card readers using clips (or variations on the clip theme) instead of screws.

I said *almost* because you'll still need a Phillips-head screwdriver to install the motherboard, the power supply unit, and possibly the CPU cooler. In other words, you can perform probably 99% of all PC building and upgrading chores using just an average Phillips screwdriver (see Figure 8.1)!

FIGURE 8.1

The simplest PC-builder's toolkit: a single Phillips screwdriver!

Of course, if you're anything like me, the tools are almost as much fun as the components themselves, so a single screwdriver doth not a toolkit make. If you're just starting out, one option is to buy a preassembled computer toolkit. For example, Figure 8.2 shows a toolkit that includes almost everything a new builder could want: a couple of Phillips- and flat-head screwdrivers, tweezers, pliers, extra screws, and more.

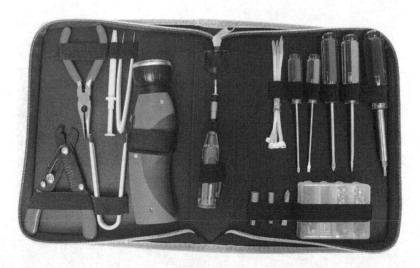

FIGURE 8.2

A preassembled computer toolkit.

The problem with almost all preassembled toolkits is that they're never perfect. For example, the kit shown in Figure 8.2 originally included a cheap soldering iron that's simply not going to be useful for most people. If they'd asked me, I'd have told them to replace the soldering iron with a decent flashlight, which is what I've done in Figure 8.2. So if you want to assemble your own toolkit (which is much more fun, anyway), here are my recommendations, more or less in descending order of importance:

- **Phillips-head screwdrivers**—This is the only essential computer tool. Note that not all Phillips screws are the same size, so I suggest getting several sizes of Phillips heads. At a minimum, get a #2 and a #1, and throw in a #0 if your budget permits it. (The smaller the number, the smaller the head; see Figure 8.3.)

- **Flashlight**—Although your work area should be well-lit (see "Setting Up Your Work Area," later in this chapter), computer cases can have dark areas where it's tough to see what you're doing. A good flashlight can help illuminate these areas.

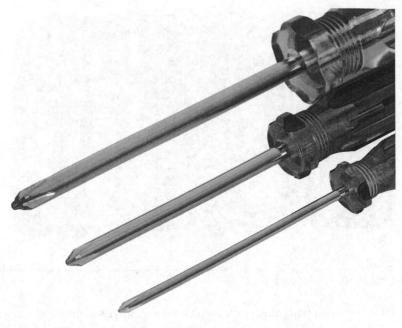

FIGURE 8.3
Several Phillips-head screwdrivers.

■ **Tweezers**—You'll be surprised how often you have to manipulate tiny parts such as motherboard standoffs, jumpers, and screws that have fallen into one nook or another. Trying to maneuver these parts with your fingers is an exercise in frustration. The solution is a good pair of tweezers. I like to keep around both a regular pair of tweezers and a screw grabber, which is often easier to maneuver into tight spots (see Figure 8.4). Instead of tweezers, you can use needle-nose pliers, particularly a pair with a long nose.

■ **Nut driver**—A 3/16-inch (or 5mm) nut driver makes short work of the motherboard standoffs. I also recommend getting a 1/4-inch (or 7mm) nut driver, which is useful for screws that need to be inserted into or removed from tight spaces.

■ **Cable ties**—To improve the air flow in your case, you need to combine cables and move them out of the way. Nylon cable ties make this easy.

■ **Canned air**—A can of compressed air is great for thoroughly cleaning the dust off any component you've scavenged from an old PC.

■ **Spare parts box**—A small plastic box is a handy way to store extra screws, washers, jumpers, and other teensy parts that will get lost in 5 minutes unless you have a place to store them.

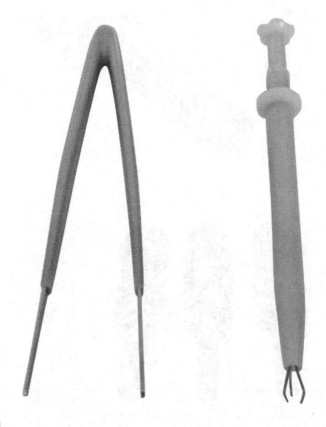

FIGURE 8.4

Regular tweezers and a screw grabber often come in handy when manipulating small objects.

- **Flat-head screwdrivers**—These are also called *slotted screwdrivers* because the screws they work with include a slot across the top. You don't see these screws very often when working with PCs, but they sometimes come in handy with Phillips screws that also include a slot.

- **TORX screwdrivers**—You use these screwdrivers to manipulate tiny screws with star-shaped slots (see Figure 8.5). You'll never need a TORX screwdriver when installing PC components, but they're often used in the components themselves. So, for example, if one day you decide you want to see what the inside of a hard drive looks like, chances are you'll need a TORX screwdriver to remove the cover.

> **caution** The inside of a PC case is no place for a power screwdriver (corded or cordless). The risk of overtightening a screw is just too great with these otherwise-useful tools, so you can easily break your motherboard or some other component. Also, power screwdrivers are bulky beasts that can easily slip off the screw and damage the board circuits.

FIGURE 8.5
Some TORX bits.

What Software Do You Need?

Building a PC is a hardware-based task, but you'll still eventually need some
software to animate the hardware and make it do something useful. At the
very least, you need an install CD or DVD for whatever operating system you
intend to run on your new computer.

Other than that, the only other essential software bits you need are the device
drivers that enable the operating system and your computer's devices to communicate with each other. There are two considerations here:

■ **The motherboard's BIOS**—The basic input/output system (BIOS)
controls everything from the system startup diagnostic tests to the system configuration utility. The BIOS also launches the operating system.
Your motherboard will come with the BIOS code already installed on a

chip. However, most manufacturers regularly update the BIOS code, so you should download the latest version and store it on a floppy disk (if your system has one), USB flash drive, or writable CD.

→   **See** "Updating the Motherboard BIOS," **p. 507.**

- **Other device drivers**—All components that require a device driver, such as a video card and network card, ship with the driver on a CD. After you build your PC and install the operating system, you might need to manually load the device driver if the OS doesn't recognize the device automatically. Again, it's a good idea to download the device's most recent driver and place it on a CD, flash drive, or network share for later use.

> **note** All motherboards come with a utility you can run to update the BIOS. In some cases you must do this using the system configuration program, but some mobos have Windows utilities that can do this. I explain how this works in Chapter 17, "Maintaining Your Computer Hardware."

Finding BIOS programs and device drivers on the World Wide Web is an art in itself. I can't tell you how much of my life I've wasted rooting around manufacturer websites trying to locate a BIOS download or device driver. Most hardware vendor sites seem to be optimized for sales rather than service, so although you can purchase, say, a new printer with just a mouse click or two, downloading a new driver for that printer can take a frustratingly long time. To help you avoid such frustration, here are some tips from my hard-won experience:

- If the manufacturer offers different sites for different locations (such as different countries), always use the company's "home" site. Most mirror sites aren't true mirrors, and (Murphy's Law still being in effect) a mirror site usually is missing the driver you're looking for.

- The temptation when you first enter a site is to use the search feature to find what you want. This works only sporadically for BIOS updates and drivers, and the site search engines almost always return marketing or sales material first.

> **caution** If as part of your build you'll be taking parts from an existing computer, and you don't have any other computers kicking around, don't open up the old PC just yet. Instead, use it to head out on the Web and download all the device drivers and BIOS updates you'll need for the new PC. Copy these to a CD, USB flash drive, or external hard drive so you have access to them when your new machine is built.

8

- Instead of the search engine, look for an area of the site dedicated to downloads. The good sites will have links to areas called Downloads or Drivers, but it's far more common to have to go through a Support or Customer Service area first.

- Don't try to take any shortcuts to where you *think* the BIOS update or driver might be hiding. Trudge through each step the site provides. For example, it's common to have to select an overall driver category, and then a device category, and then a line category, and then the specific model you have. This is tedious, but it almost always gets you where you want to go.

- If the site is particularly ornery, the preceding method might not lead you to your device. In that case, try the search engine. Note that device drivers seem to be particularly poorly indexed, so you might have to try a lot of search text variations. One thing that usually works is searching for the exact filename. How can you possibly know that? A method that often works for me is to use Google (www.google.com) or Google Groups (groups.google.com) or some other web search engine to search for your driver. Chances are someone else has looked for your file and will have the filename (or, if you're really lucky, a direct link to the driver on the manufacturer's site).

- Still no luck finding the file you need? See if the manufacturer has a tech support line (phone or chat) and, if so, tell a support engineer what you're looking for. More often than not, the engineer will be able to tell you the filename you seek, and might even send you the exact URL.

- When you get to the device's download page, be careful which file you choose. Make sure that it's a driver written for your operating system, and make sure that you're not downloading a utility program or some other nondriver file.

- When you finally get to download the file, be sure to save it to your computer—ideally on removable media such as a USB flash drive, CD, or external hard drive—rather than opening it. If you reformat your system or move the device to another computer, you'll be glad you have a local copy of the driver so you don't have to wrestle with the whole download rigmarole all over again.

Setting Up Your Work Area

Building a PC doesn't require a high-tech workshop, but it's not a task you should perform on the living room carpet, either. A proper PC-building area is one that makes the job easier, so here are a few considerations to help you set up the perfect construction zone:

> **tip** A good flashlight helps you illuminate even the murkiest corners of a case, but when it comes time to work in those corners, you almost always need two hands, so you have to put the flashlight down and try to angle it just so, which rarely works. Technology rides to the rescue here, too, by offering hat lights (sometimes called cap lights) that clip to the brim of a hat for hands-free illumination.

- **Lights, lights, and more lights**—When it comes to cobbling together a PC, you simply can't have too much light. Some of the tasks you face take place in dim corners of the case or require you to make fairly precise connections. All this is much easier if you have a lot of light. A bright overhead light is great, but I also suggest a table lamp with some kind of adjustable neck so you can concentrate the light where you need it.

- **You need power!**—Your area must have at least one power outlet nearby. You'll need it during the build to plug in any lamps you use, and you'll need it post-build to connect the power for your power supply and monitor.

- **Get up off the floor**—A hardwood floor or other noncarpeted surface makes a nice even surface, but it's not a comfortable place for most people over a certain age. It's also more of a problem if dogs, cats, children, and other pets (kidding!) come along. It's better to build your new machine on a table or some other surface.

- **Give yourself plenty of elbow room**—Speaking of a table, be sure you use one that has a reasonable amount of room. It should be big enough to hold your case lying flat and still give you plenty of room around the case to hold your tools and parts.

- **A work area of one's own**—The ideal work surface is one you can claim as your own for the duration of your build. That way, you can leave things as they are until you get a chance to resume building. If you use a kitchen table, coffee table, or dining room table, chances are you're going to have to clear out to let others use it at some point, and you run the risk of losing things or just forgetting where you left off.

8

Playing It Safe

We live in a world where concerns for our personal safety have become borderline absurd: An iron-on transfer for a T-shirt comes with a piece of paper that warns, "Do not iron while wearing shirt," and a letter opener has a label that says, "Caution: Safety goggles recommended." I'm hip to this over-the-top concern, so when I tell you that you need to observe a few safety precautions when working inside a PC, remember that I'm coming at this from necessity, not paranoia.

Keeping Yourself Safe

So just how dangerous is it to work inside a PC? The answer depends on the PC's current state:

- **The PC has never been turned on, or has been off for a long time**—This is the safest state because you have to worry about only one thing: cutting or scratching yourself on something sharp. Many PC components are quite sharp. The solder points under most motherboards and expansion cards are nasty little daggers; devices such as power supplies and hard drives often have sharp, metal edges; and the cooling fins on some CPU coolers are razor thin. Handle all PC components carefully to avoid getting a nasty cut or abrasion.

- **The PC has only recently been turned off**—In this state, you still have to worry about sharp objects, but you also have two other things to watch out for:

    Heat—Components such as the processor, power supply, and hard drive work hard while the computer is on and so build up a tremendous amount of heat. Give everything a few minutes to cool down before diving into the case to prevent getting burned.

    Electricity—Most electronic components use capacitors to store electricity, and that voltage often drains out of the capacitors slowly after you turn off the PC and yank out the power cord. Because you're waiting a few minutes to let the PC's components cool down anyway, that's also enough time for most capacitors to drain. The exception is the power supply and its massive capacitors, which can retain life-threatening amounts of voltage for quite a while after you shut off the power. This is a concern only if you're going to open the power supply casing and, because you shouldn't ever do that, it's not a problem.

- **The PC is powered up**—This is the PC at its most dangerous because the components remain sharp (duh), parts such as the processor and power supply can heat up to burn-inducing levels within a few minutes, and electricity is everywhere. Not only that, but a running PC has a fourth danger: spinning fans on the case, CPU cooler, and often the video card, too. The danger here isn't so much that you might stick a finger in a fan (that would be unlikely to cause you much harm), but that you might get something caught in a fan, such as clothing, a bracelet, hair, and so on. Because of all this, the inside of a running PC is definitely a "hands-off" area. Feel free to open the case and look around, but touching things is just asking for trouble.

> **caution** Let me reiterate that when you shut down your computer and are going to open it to work inside, *always* disconnect the power cable. This ensures that the computer has no incoming electricity, so the chances of electrocution are virtually nil.

> **caution** To be safe, open the case before you turn on the computer, and don't close the case until after you shut down the computer. Also, the open case wrecks the airflow inside the PC, so components can run hotter than usual; therefore, don't leave the computer running for an extended time with the case open.

Keeping Your Components Safe

Keeping yourself out of harm's way when working inside a PC is important, obviously, but it's not the only safety concern. Without proper precautions, you can also damage sensitive computer components, which means your PC either might run erratically or might not run at all. It also means you might have wasted good money. Fortunately, it takes only a few sensible precautions to keep your components safe:

- **Discharge static electricity**—If you walk across a carpeted floor, or if your clothes rub together as you walk, your body builds up static electricity, perhaps as much as a few thousand volts! If you were to touch a sensitive component such as a processor or motherboard, the resulting electrical discharge could easily damage or destroy the part. To prevent this, the first thing you should do after you open the PC case is ground yourself by touching the chassis, the power supply unit, or some other metal object. This discharges your static electricity and

8

ensures that you won't damage any of the computer's sensitive electronic components. Ideally, you shouldn't walk around the room until you've finished working inside the PC. If you need to walk away from the computer for a bit—particularly if you're wearing socks on a carpeted surface—be sure to ground yourself again when you're ready to resume working.

tip If you find that you always forget to ground yourself, you can take the matter out of your hands, literally, by using an antistatic wrist strap. This is a device with a wrist strap on one end and a metal clip at the other. You attach the clip to a metal object to ground yourself full-time. However, if you move away from the computer, be sure to check that the clip hasn't fallen off before continuing to work with the PC.

- **Avoid liquids in your work area**—Liquids and computer components definitely don't mix, and spilling almost any amount of liquid on a part could damage the part or render it inoperable. Therefore, keep all liquids well away from your work surface.

tip If you do touch a contact, you can clean it either by using isopropyl alcohol (also called rubbing alcohol) and a cotton swab or with an unused pencil eraser.

- **Don't touch electrical connectors**—Many parts have electrical connectors that serve as conduits for data or power. The natural oils that reside on even the cleanest of hands can reduce the conductivity of these contacts, resulting in the part acting erratically. Therefore, never touch the connectors.

- **Handle all components with care**—This means not only avoiding the contacts, but also leaving components in their electrostatic discharge (ESD) bags (if they come with one) when not being used, carefully removing parts from their packaging to avoid breaking them, handling components with exposed electronics (such as resistors and capacitors) by the edges, setting parts down carefully, and allowing cold parts to heat up to room temperature before using them.

caution After you take a component out of its ESD bag, if you need to put the component back down, don't lay it on the ESD bag because the outside of those bags can draw static electricity! Put the component back inside the bag.

Opening the Computer Case

All PC building, upgrading, and repairing jobs begin with an apparently simple task: opening the computer case, usually by removing a side panel. (If you're facing the case from the front, you almost always remove the left side panel.) Why is this an "apparently" simple task? Because the technology case manufacturers use to secure the side panel isn't universal. That wasn't the case a few years ago. In those days, the vast majority of side panels were attached using two or three screws, and removing the panel was a straightforward matter of removing the screws and sliding or lifting the panel away from the case. Figure 8.6 shows an example.

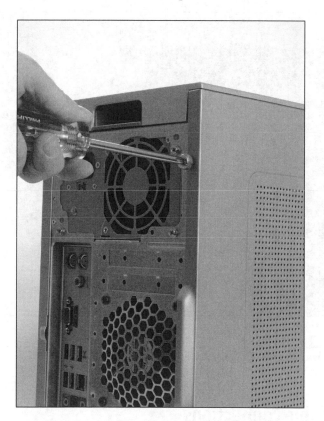

FIGURE 8.6

A case side panel attached with screws.

Those days are long gone. Yes, most cases still connect their side panels with screws, but this method is no longer even remotely universal. Nowadays case manufacturers have come up with an endless variety of ways to attach side panels. The goal in almost all cases is "tool-free access." That is, the older method required the use of a screwdriver, although many cases now use thumb screws. In modern case designs, tools are verboten. Instead, you usually have to press a button or hold down a latch, sometimes while sliding the side panel at the same time!

My favorite case opening mechanism by far is the one that appears on some models of Cooler Master cases. As you can see in Figure 8.7, the back of the case contains a simple lever. Press that lever down, and the side panel slides open as slowly and deliberately as if it were mechanized. Beautiful! To close the side panel, you simply snap it into place. Bliss!

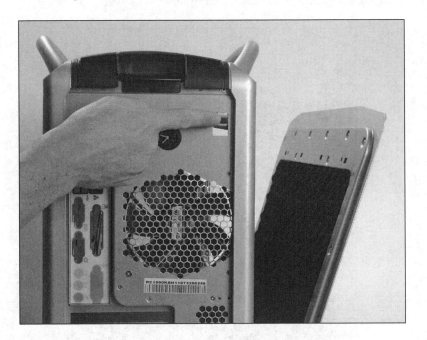

FIGURE 8.7
Some Cooler Master cases open with the press of a simple latch.

Making Cable Connections

Great chunks of your PC-building time will be taken up connecting cables either to provide components with power or to provide a conduit along which the device can send and receive data. There are many cable types, and at first blush you might think this is just the computer industry's way of confusing novice builders. In fact, the opposite is the case: There are so many types because that's the only way to ensure that the connections you make are

8

pretty close to foolproof. In other words, because each cable connector has a unique shape and configuration, it's nearly impossible for you to insert the cable in the wrong port or to insert the cable incorrectly in the right port.

Before going any further with all this, I should establish some terminology:

- **Connector**—This is a generic term for any piece of hardware that enables one thing to connect to another. So, the hardware at the end of a cable is a connector, as is the corresponding hardware on the other device to which you want the cable attached.

- **Male**—This is a connector that has protruding pins. Each pin corresponds to a wire in the cable. A male connector is also called a *header* or *plug*.

- **Female**—This is a connector that has holes, and it's also called a *jack* or *port*.

The key thing here is that on a proper connection, each pin on a male connector maps to a corresponding hole in a female connector. (There are some exceptions to this, such as female connectors with more holes than there are pins on a male connector.)

→   An example of an exception is a male DVI-D connector, which can connect to a female DVI-I port despite having fewer pins; **see** "Video Card Connectors," **p. 112**.

For example, PATA hard drives connect to the motherboard using a 40-pin ribbon cable. In Figure 8.8, you can see that the cable has a 40-hole female connector, the motherboard has a 40-pin male connector, and the holes and pins match up perfectly. However, if you place the same cable beside a floppy drive connector, which uses a 34-pin male connector as shown in Figure 8.9, it's obvious that the two don't match. In other words, it isn't possible to insert an PATA hard drive cable in a floppy drive header, even though they look similar.

So, your first clue when deciding where to insert a cable is to look for a connector that has the corresponding number of pins (or holes). Next, you often have to decide which way to insert the cable connector. As you can see in Figure 8.8, you can either insert the cable as shown or turn the cable 180° and try it that way. The pin configuration is the same both ways, so how do you know which is correct?

In this particular case, you need to look for the notch that appears in the back of the plastic shroud that surrounds the pins. That notch corresponds with a protrusion that appears on one side of the cable connector (you can see it in Figure 8.9). The only way to insert the cable is to match up the protrusion and the notch.

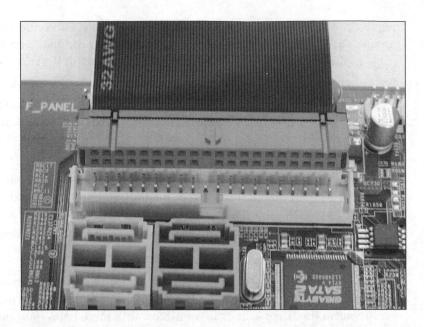

FIGURE 8.8

The holes on an ATA hard drive ribbon cable connector match up perfectly with the pins on the motherboard's ATA cable header.

FIGURE 8.9

The pin configuration on a motherboard's floppy drive header doesn't match the ATA hard drive connector.

Another way system designers help you orient a cable connector correctly is by using a nonsymmetrical pin layout. For example, a motherboard's USB header has nine pins: five in one row and four in another. The case's USB jack has nine holes: five in one row and four in another. As you can see in Figure 8.10, there's only one way to match up the holes and pins, so there's only one way to connect the header and jack.

FIGURE 8.10

The arrangement of the pins on a USB header matches the arrangement of the holes on the USB jack, so there's only one way to make the connection.

A third way system designers ensure that you don't insert a connector incorrectly is to use a nonsymmetrical shape for the connector. For example, the 4-pin Molex power jack is designed to connect to a 4-pin Molex power header on a device. As you can see in Figure 8.11, two of the jack's four corners are rounded, and these match the rounded corners on the header. Again, there's only one way to make the connection.

All this rigmarole of matching the numbers of pins, notches, and connector shapes is a complex business, so there has been a movement of late to reduce the complexity. System designers are accomplishing this by making connectors with a unique shape, period. With such connectors, you don't have to worry about pins or any other physical characteristics of the connector because there's only one kind of matching connector and only one way to insert the cable.

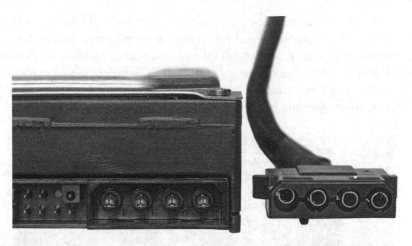

FIGURE 8.11

The rounded corners of the 4-pin Molex power jack match the rounded corners of the 4-pin Molex power header, so there's only one way to make the connection.

A good example is the SATA hard drive data interface. As you can see in Figure 8.12, the unique shape of the cable connector has a corresponding match on the hard drive. There's no danger here of inserting the cable in the wrong device or in the wrong way.

caution I mentioned at the beginning of this section that it's *nearly* impossible to connect a cable incorrectly, either to the wrong device or in the wrong orientation. I said *nearly* because with some connections, where you can reverse the orientation since neither the jack nor the header has an unambiguous method for determining the correct orientation. The biggest culprits here are the case cables for things such as the power LED, power switch, and reset switch. The good news is that inserting these cables backward won't damage the components involved. If the component doesn't work, you simply reverse the connector and move on with your life.

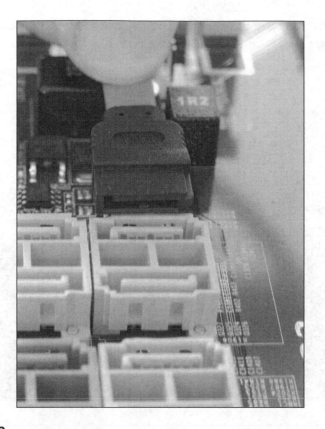

FIGURE 8.12

The unique shape of a SATA hard drive data cable connector matches the corresponding SATA hard drive data header for an unambiguous connection.

Installing Memory Modules

As with cable connections, much work has gone into ensuring that you can't install the wrong type of memory in a motherboard memory socket and that you can't install the correct type with the wrong orientation. In Chapter 3, "The Work Area: Memory," you learned that DDR, DDR2, and DDR3 DIMMs and SODIMMs have different physical characteristics. For example, most DDR DIMMs come in a 184-pin configuration, most DDR2 and DDR3 DIMMs come in a 240-pin configuration, and most SODIMMs come in a 200-pin configuration. So, when you install a DIMM, the first thing to check is that the length of the module's connectors matches the length of the motherboard's memory socket. For example, Figure 8.13 shows a SODIMM beside a DIMM memory socket. As you can see, the module is smaller than the memory socket.

➔   For the details on DIMM and SODIMM configurations, **see** "The Memory Module Configuration and Pins," **p. 71**.

FIGURE 8.13

This SODIMM module is too small to fit into the DIMM memory socket.

The other configuration factor is the notch that appears in the DIMM's connector area. This notch matches a corresponding ridge inside the motherboard's memory socket, and this prevents you from installing the module the wrong way around. Also, because the different module configurations have their notches in different places, it also prevents you from installing the wrong type of memory. For example, although DDR and DDR2 DIMMs are the same size, their notches are in different places. This makes inserting a DDR DIMM in a DDR2 socket impossible, as shown in Figure 8.14.

FIGURE 8.14

The notch on this DDR DIMM doesn't match the ridge in the DDR2 memory socket.

When you're sure you have the correct memory module, here are the steps to follow to install it:

1. If the memory socket's ejector tabs, shown in Figure 8.15, are in the vertical position, open them by pivoting them away from the socket.

2. Orient the DIMM over the motherboard memory socket so that the DIMM's notch lines up with the socket's ridge, as shown in Figure 8.15.

3. On the ends of the socket, you'll see thin vertical channels. Slide the memory module into these channels, as shown in Figure 8.16.

note Although it often doesn't matter which memory socket you use, some motherboards require that you populate the sockets in a particular order. This is usually from the lowest-numbered (or lettered) socket to the highest. The sockets on most boards are numbered either from 0 to 3 or from 1 to 4. So, if you're just inserting one module, use socket 0 (or 1, if that's the lowest). For two modules, use sockets 0 and 1 (or 1 and 2). See your motherboard manual to confirm, particularly if you want to use a dual-channel memory configuration.

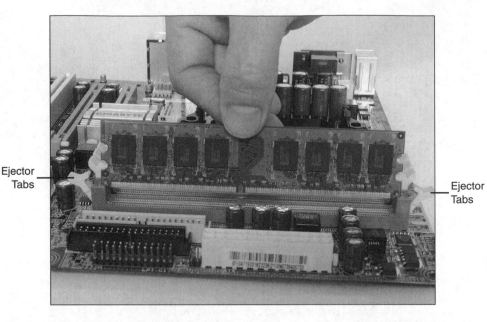

Ejector Tabs

Ejector Tabs

FIGURE 8.15

Line up the DIMM's notch with the socket's ridge.

4. Place your thumbs on the top edge of the DIMM, one thumb on each side.

5. Press the DIMM into the socket. When the DIMM is properly seated, the ejector tabs automatically snap into the vertical position.

note It sometimes takes a surprising amount of force to get the module fully seated in the socket. Some sockets are just really tight fits, so you have to press really hard to get the module all the way in.

FIGURE 8.16

Slide the memory module into the channels at both ends of the memory socket.

Note that it's very easy to think that you've inserted a memory module fully, when in fact it's not quite seated properly. How can you tell? Check out the ejector tabs. If the module isn't fully seated in the socket, the ejector tabs will not be perfectly vertical, as shown in Figure 8.17. The ejector tab should look like the one shown in Figure 8.18.

FIGURE 8.17

Incorrect: If the ejector tab isn't vertical, the DIMM isn't seated.

FIGURE 8.18

Correct: A vertical ejector tab tells you the DIMM is fully seated in the socket.

Installing an Expansion Card

Expansion cards are circuit boards that provide extra functionality such as networking, video, and sound. You install them by inserting them into bus slots on your motherboard. Again, however, you can't install any type of card into any type of slot. The various interface types—PCI, AGP, and the various flavors of PCI Express—all use different slot configurations. That's good news for you as a system builder because it means you can't insert a card into the wrong slot and you can't insert a card into the correct slot with the wrong orientation.

As with memory modules, system designers ensure foolproof expansion card connections by using two configuration parameters:

- **Length**—The various slot types all use different lengths. For example, a PCI slot is larger than a PCI Express x4 slot, but smaller than a PCI Express x16 slot. This ensures that you can't install a card in the wrong type of slot. For example, Figure 8.19 shows a PCI card next to a PCI Express x1 slot. As you can see, the PCI card is much too long to fit into the slot.

FIGURE 8.19

The length of an expansion card's connectors must match the length of the motherboard slot, unlike the PCI card and PCI Express x1 slot shown here.

■ **Slot ridges**—Each slot type has one or more ridges that correspond to notches in the expansion card's connector area. This ensures that you can't install a card with the incorrect orientation. For example, Figure 8.20 shows a PCI Express x16 card next to a PCI Express x16 slot. As you can see, the notches in the card match up perfectly with the ridges in the slot.

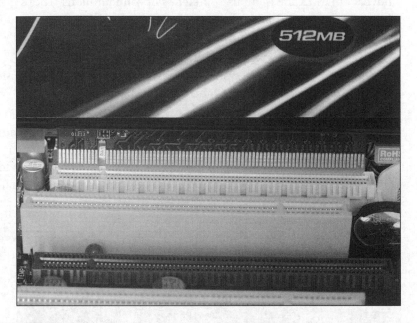

FIGURE 8.20

The notches in an expansion card's connectors must match the ridges in the motherboard slot, as shown here with a PCI Express x16 card and slot.

Note that PCI Express provides certain exceptions to all this. That is, smaller PCI Express cards always fit into larger PCI Express slots. For example, a PCI Express x1 card fits into any other PCI Express slot (x4, x8, or x16). Figure 8.21 shows a PCI Express x1 card next to a PCI Express x16 slot. The card's notches match the slot's first two ridges, so you can successfully insert the card, even though it's the "wrong" length.

You always install an expansion card after you've mounted the motherboard to the case because the card's metal bracket must mate up with the slot opening in the back of the case. This enables the card's ports or jacks to stick out of the back of the case so you can access them.

FIGURE 8.21

You can always insert smaller PCI Express cards into larger PCI Express slots, such as the x1 card into the x16 slot shown here.

In days of yore (the 1990s), all case slot covers were attached using a screw. Now, like case side panels, manufacturers have been experimenting with various tool-free slot covers—latches, levers, and so on—so there's no longer a universal way to either remove a slot cover or attach an expansion card to the slot. You'll need to consult your case manual to see how things work.

With that in mind, here are the generic steps to follow to install an expansion card:

1. Make sure the computer is turned off and the power cable is disconnected.

2. Remove the computer's side panel.

3. Touch something metal to ground yourself.

tip When the screw is out, the slot cover should come out easily; it might even fall out on its own, so it's a good idea to hold onto the slot cover with your free hand to ensure that it doesn't fall onto the motherboard and damage a component. If the slot cover won't budge, it's probably being held in place by the slot cover above it (or, less often, the slot cover below it). Loosen—but don't remove—the screw on the other slot cover. This should give you enough slack to remove the cover for the empty slot. When that slot cover is out, you can tighten the screw on the other slot cover.

4. Locate the slot you want to use (see Figure 8.22).

5. Remove the slot cover. If the slot cover is held in place with a screw, use a Phillips screwdriver to remove the screw and then place the screw in a handy place.

Slot Cover — PCI Slot

FIGURE 8.22

An empty PCI slot with an increasingly old-fashioned screw-on slot cover.

6. Place the expansion card so that its bracket is flush with the open slot cover, and slowly slide the card toward the slot.

7. When the card's connectors are touching the slot and are perfectly aligned with the slot opening, place your thumbs on the edge of the card and press the card firmly into the slot (see Figure 8.23).

8. Attach the bracket to the case, as shown in Figure 8.24.

> **tip** How do you know whether the card is completely inserted into the slot? The easiest way to tell is to look at the portion of the bracket that attaches to the case. If that portion isn't flush with the case, the card isn't fully inserted.

8

FIGURE 8.23

Press the NIC firmly into the slot.

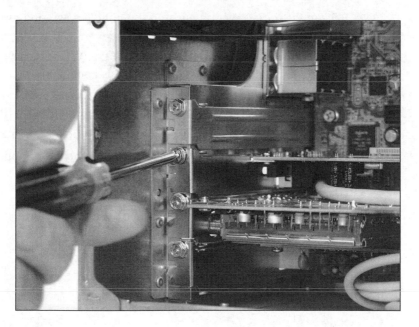

FIGURE 8.24

Screw (or whatever) the expansion card's bracket to the computer chassis.

Installing a Processor

Installing a processor into a motherboard's CPU socket is a relatively delicate operation, but it doesn't require any extraordinary skills. Almost all processor installations take one of the following forms:

caution With the plastic cover off the socket, take extra care not to touch the contacts inside the socket.

- Inserting an Intel processor into a socket 775 motherboard.
- Inserting an AMD processor into a socket AM2 motherboard.

The next two sections take you through the steps required to install both types of processor.

Installing an Intel CPU in a Socket 775 Board

Almost all Intel processors fit in motherboards that come with an LGA775 CPU socket, and the following steps show you how it's done:

1. Lift off the plastic cover that protects the processor socket. (Place the cover in the motherboard box for safekeeping, just in case you need to use it again if you store the board later.)

2. Release the socket lever by pushing the handle down and away from the socket, as shown in Figure 8.25.

3. Pivot the socket lever as far back as it will go. (When the lever is past vertical, you can just let it go so that it falls open.)

4. Lift the metal plate that sits on the socket, as shown in Figure 8.26.

5. Take the processor out of the packaging and remove the plastic cover. (Save this cover in case you need to store the processor later.)

6. On the top of the processor, locate the gold triangle that appears in one corner.

7. Holding the processor on the edges with your thumb and forefinger, orient the processor so the gold triangle is on the bottom left.

8. Orient the processor over the CPU socket as shown in Figure 8.27.

caution Only handle the processor by its side edges. Don't touch the pads on the bottom of the processor.

Press down on the socket lever...

...and gently move the arm to the side until it
clears the latch; then lift up gently on the arm.

FIGURE 8.25

Push the socket lever down and away from the socket to release it.

FIGURE 8.26

Lift the metal plate to open the socket and reveal the contacts.

FIGURE 8.27

Orient the processor over the socket so that the gold triangle is on the bottom left.

9. When you're sure the processor is lined up exactly with the edge of the socket, carefully place the processor into the socket.

10. Close the metal plate.

11. Press the socket lever down and then under the metal hook at the side of the socket, as shown in Figure 8.28. (Note that it's not unusual to have to apply a lot of force to get the lever under the hook.)

tip To help you align the processor, the socket includes two small protrusions: one on the top wall of the socket (near the upper-left corner) and one on the bottom wall (near the bottom-left corner). These correspond to notches on the top and bottom edges of the processor, so make sure these line up exactly before placing the processor into the socket.

FIGURE 8.28

Press the socket lever down and under the metal hook to secure the processor in place.

Installing an AMD CPU in a Socket AM2 Board

Most AMD processors fit in motherboards that come with an AM2 CPU socket, and the following steps show you how it's done:

1. Release the socket lever by pushing the handle down and away from the socket, as shown in Figure 8.29.

2. Pivot the socket lever to the vertical position.

3. Take the processor out of the packaging.

4. On the top of the processor, locate the gold triangle that appears in one corner.

5. Holding the processor on the edges with your thumb and forefinger, orient the processor so that the gold triangle is on the upper right.

6. Orient the processor over the CPU socket as shown in Figure 8.30.

caution Only handle the processor by its side edges. Don't touch the pins on the bottom of the processor.

Press down on the socket lever...

...and gently move the arm to the side until it
clears the latch; then lift up gently on the arm.

FIGURE 8.29

Push the socket lever down and away from the socket to release it.

FIGURE 8.30

Orient the processor over the socket so that the gold triangle is on the upper right.

7. When you're sure the processor is lined up exactly with the edge of the socket, carefully place the processor into the socket.

8. Press the socket lever down and then under the plastic hook at the side of the socket, as shown in Figure 8.31. (Note that it's not unusual to have to apply quite a bit of force to get the lever under the hook.)

FIGURE 8.31

Press the socket lever down and under the metal hook to secure the processor in place.

From Here

■ To learn more about memory module configurations, **see** "The Memory Module Configuration and Pins," **p. 71**.

■ To check out the various pin configurations of DVI-D and DVI-I connectors, **see** "Video Card Connectors," **p. 112**.

■ To learn how to remove memory modules, **see** "Pulling Out Memory Modules," **p. 232**.

■ To learn how to take out an expansion card, **see** "Removing an Internal Expansion Card," **p. 225**.

Scavenging an Old PC for Parts

How to save the old that's worth saving, whether in landscape, houses, manners, institutions, or human types, is one of our greatest problems, and the one that we bother least about.

—John Galsworthy, *Over the River*

At its simplest, building a PC means gathering all the parts you need and then putting them together in such a way that you end up with a working machine crafted with your bare hands. Note my use of the intentionally vague term *gathering*. Yes, most of the time you'll "gather" the parts for your future PC by purchasing them as described in Chapter 7, "Buying PC Parts." However, there's no law that decrees you *must* buy new components. If you have an old computer or two lying around gathering dust, there could be gold in them thar PCs. Well, okay, not gold so much as usable PC parts you can salvage and reuse in your custom-built computer.

9

Why go to the trouble? First, let me assure you that it's really not all that much trouble, as I hope you'll learn in this chapter: Taking out most components is straightforward, with the added bonus that the more parts you remove, the easier it gets to remove the remaining parts!

Second, reusing old parts is a great way to go if your PC-building budget is limited. By including a few "free" parts in your build, you can take the money you saved and apply it to purchasing higher-quality components for the rest of your PC.

Third, salvaging existing components is much faster than ordering new parts online or trudging out to your local retailer. Depending on how crammed with stuff the old PC is, you can strip the machine to its case in as little as 30 minutes. So, if you find yourself needing a particular component mid-build, you can scavenge the part in just a few minutes and then continue your build without a significant delay.

Fourth, sometimes salvaging an old part for a new PC is the best way to go. For example, if your old PC has a hard drive full of files that you want to preserve, including that drive in your build makes those files easily accessible on the new machine.

Are used parts reliable? Of course, there's no such thing as a PC component that lasts forever. Most manufacturers know more or less how long their components last, and they keep track of a value called the *mean time before failure (MTBF)* for each part. These values are often measured in tens of thousands or even hundreds of thousands of hours, so devices these days are extremely reliable. I'm talking about averages here, meaning that some devices fail after just a few hundred hours, whereas some devices can have a million hours of useful life. The point, though, is that unless your old PC is *really* old (more than, say, four or five years old), there's an excellent chance there's a lot of life left in each component (because there are 8,760 hours in a year).

→ Before continuing, you need to open the old computer's case; **see** "Opening the Computer Case," **p. 199**.

caution I should tell you right off the bat that you might come across parts that simply refuse to be salvaged. Many (okay, the vast majority of) PC manufacturers don't adhere to the "Build It. Fix It. Own It." philosophy, so they construct their machines as though no one will ever even *look* inside the case, much less try to take anything out of it. Therefore, you often find processors hidden behind seemingly impenetrable walls of plastic, hard drives attached with screws that should have been physically impossible to insert in the first place, and extra hunks of metal that seem to serve no other purpose than to make your salvage operation as frustrating as possible.

→   To learn how to clean the inside of a PC, **see**
"Cleaning the Computer," **p. 498**.

Removing an Internal Expansion Card

Perhaps the most routinely salvaged PC
part is the internal expansion card because
many cards in old PCs are still useful in a
new computer. For example, if you have a
10/100 network interface card (NIC) in the old machine and your new PC will
be part of a Fast Ethernet network, the old NIC will be just the ticket for your
custom machine. Similarly, you might want to salvage an old sound card if
your motherboard doesn't have built-in sound (or its sound capabilities are
worse than your sound card's), an internal fax/modem card, or a card that
offers extra ports for FireWire or USB connections.

→   For more information on Fast Ethernet, **see** "Getting Wired: Understanding Ethernet Networks," **p. 132**.

Whatever the card, there are two important things you need to consider before
starting the salvage operation:

- Is the card compatible with your motherboard? That is, does the card's
  slot type match any open slot on your board? For example, a video
  card that uses the AGP bus requires an AGP slot on the motherboard.

- Do you have device drivers for the
  card, particularly drivers that are
  compatible with whatever operating system you'll be installing on
  your custom PC? Check the manufacturer's website to see whether the
  appropriate drivers are available.

As I mentioned in Chapter 8, "Basic Skills
for PC Building and Upgrading," the case
slot covers on most older PCs were
attached using screws. This is likely to be
the case with your salvage PC, but it's possible that your case might have a tool-free
slot cover design. In that case, you might

tip Before beginning the
salvage operation, I
highly recommend giving the
inside of your old PC a reasonably thorough cleaning. The
more dust you remove, the easier
it will be to work with each part
and the less chance you'll have of
getting a eyeful, noseful, or
mouthful of dust as you work.

note How do you know
which driver you
need? In some cases, you can
open the case and examine the
card in place to look for a model
name or, ideally, a model number.
If the old PC still works, crank it
up and examine the devices
using, say, Windows' Device Manager utility to learn the manufacturer and the card's model name.
If you can't get the information
using these methods, you'll need
to wait until you remove the card
and can examine it more closely.

need to consult your computer manual to see how the slots operate. If the manual is long gone, and you can't find it on the Web, a bit of trial-and-error should suffice.

Here are the steps to follow to remove an internal expansion card:

1. Make sure the computer is turned off and the power cable is disconnected.

2. Remove any external cables connected to the card's ports.

3. Remove the computer's side panel.

4. Touch something metal to ground yourself.

5. Locate the expansion card you want to remove.

6. Remove any internal cables connected to card.

7. Detach whatever is holding the expansion card to the case slot cover. If the card is held in place with a screw (see Figure 9.1), use a Phillips screwdriver to remove the screw and then place the screw in a handy place.

Card to be removed

A screw holds the card to the case

FIGURE 9.1

Many older PCs use a screw to attach an expansion card to the case.

8. Take hold of the expansion card as follows (see Figure 9.2):

   ■ With the thumb and forefinger of your left hand, grasp an empty (that is, plastic only) portion in the middle of the back part of the card (the edge closest to you).

   ■ With the thumb and forefinger of your right hand, grasp an empty (plastic only) portion on the right edge of the card (the closer to the motherboard, the better).

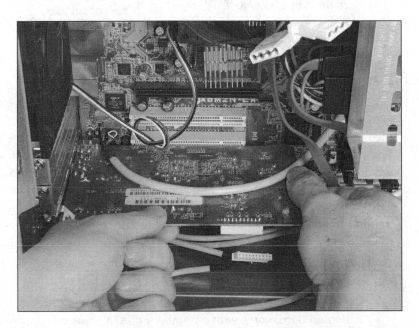

FIGURE 9.2

Grasp the expansion card with both hands, as shown here.

9. While simultaneously pulling the card toward you, jiggle the card back and forth to loosen it in the slot. (If you have trouble getting the card moving, a good first move is to slightly rotate the card counter-clockwise, which brings the card's bracket away from the slot and loosens the left side of the connectors.)

> **tip** If the expansion card won't budge, its bracket might be held in place by the slot cover above it (or, less often, the slot cover below it). Loosen—but don't remove—the screw on the other slot cover. This should give you enough slack to remove the expansion card. When the card is out, be sure to retighten the screw on the other slot cover.

10. When the card is free of the connector, slowly bring the card straight back toward you, taking care not to bump against any other cards that are in the adjacent slots.

11. Place the expansion card in an antistatic bag—also known as an *electrostatic discharge (ESD) bag*—until you're ready to use it.

> **note** Most computer components come in antistatic bags, so as you use these parts, it's a good idea to save the bags for later use. You can also purchase antistatic bags from most PC supply stores (a 10-pack of 6" × 8" bags will set you back about $5).

Taking Out a Hard Drive

Giving an old hard drive a new lease on its digital life is popular because the extra storage space can come in handy. The most common scenario is to use the old hard drive as a backup medium. Backing up to a hard drive is many times faster than using optical media, and you get the not-insignificant advantage of having your data and your backups on separate hard drives: If your main drive goes south on you, your backups aren't affected (and vice versa). Adding an old hard drive to your new system is also useful for storing important data you don't use frequently, such as downloads and device drivers.

To reuse the old hard drive on your new system, there are a couple of things to watch for:

- Is the hard drive compatible with your motherboard? Most modern motherboards come with a number of SATA connectors, as well as at least one PATA (IDE) connector that is likely to be the connector type required by your old hard drive (because PATA was the standard for many years before SATA hit the mainstream in the past couple of years). So, you'll be able to use the old hard drive in your home-built system as long as your motherboard has the proper connector.

- You need a free internal bay that's the correct size for your hard drive. Most hard drives now are 3.5 inches across, but some older drives are 5.25 inches. Make sure your new case has an open drive bay that's the correct width.

> **note** If your case has only open 5.25-inch drive bays and you have a 3.5-inch hard drive, you can solve the problem by purchasing a bracket that enables you to mount the 3.5-inch drive in the 5.25-inch bay.

Here are the steps to follow to remove a hard drive:

1. Make sure the computer is turned off and the power cable is disconnected.

2. Remove the computer's side panel.

3. Touch something metal to ground yourself.

4. Locate the hard drive you want to remove.

5. Remove the drive's power cable (see Figure 9.3).

6. Remove the drive's interface cable.

Hard drive to be removed

Interface Cable

Power Cable

FIGURE 9.3

You need to remove the power and interface cables attached to the hard drive.

7. Remove any screws or loosen any other mechanism that's holding the drive in the drive bay.

8. Slide the drive out of the drive bay.

9. Place the hard drive in an antistatic bag until you're ready to use it.

Prying Out a CPU

Not many people think about reusing an old processor in a custom-built PC. After all, with dual-core CPUs available from AMD for about $50 and from Intel for about $70, why cut corners on the machine's most important component? On the other hand, if you're salvaging a machine that's only a few years old, it might have an Intel Pentium 4 or an AMD Athlon 64, both of which are single-core processors suitable for very low-end systems. They might have a few years of life left in them if your goal is to build a system for the lowest possible cost.

It seems like only a short while ago that the insertion or removal of a processor was a task fraught with all kinds of danger. Back in the day (I'm talking here about the early '90s, so please forgive this mercifully brief detour into ancient history), you needed to exert up to 100 pounds of force to insert a CPU properly in its socket! Later so-called *low insertion force* sockets required a mere 60 pounds of force! As you can imagine, any processor that required so much force to seat properly wasn't going to come out very easily and, indeed, all those old processors required special extraction tools.

So you can be very thankful that those old socket types are long gone. Since at least the mid-'90s, all motherboard processor sockets have used a technology called *zero insertion force (ZIF)*, which makes installing a processor almost as easy as dropping a battery into a flashlight.

This is good news, indeed, because it also means that taking out any CPU is just as easy, as the following steps show:

1. Make sure the computer is turned off and the power cable is disconnected.

2. Remove the computer's side panel.

3. Touch something metal to ground yourself.

4. Locate the CPU cooler's fan, trace its power cable to its motherboard connection, and then disconnect the power cable.

5. Remove the CPU cooler:

   ■ Many Intel stock coolers are attached to the motherboard using four plastic snap-in standoffs. In most cases, you loosen these standoffs by using a flat-head screwdriver to turn each standoff 90° counterclockwise.

   ■ Most AMD stock coolers are attached to the motherboard using a metal clip. You loosen the clip by turning a lever on the side of the cooler counterclockwise (see Figure 9.4).

- Third-party coolers use a variety of attachment methods, but they're almost always a variation on the previous two themes. That is, the cooler either attaches to the motherboard directly using screws of some type or sits on the motherboard using some type of metal clip you release using a lever.

FIGURE 9.4

Remove the CPU cooler.

6. Clean the thermal grease from the bottom of the cooler and from the processor's heatsink. A soft cloth and a bit of isopropyl alcohol should do the trick.

7. Find the ZIF lever on the side of the motherboard's processor socket.

8. Press the lever down and away from the socket to release the lever, as shown in Figure 9.5; then slowly raise the lever to the upright position.

caution On some sockets, there is quite a bit of pressure on the lever, so don't just let it go after it's loose.

FIGURE 9.5

Release the ZIF lever that's holding the processor in place.

9. If the processor socket has a cover, raise the cover.

10. Using your thumb and forefinger, grasp the processor's heatsink and lift the processor out of the socket.

11. If you're not using the processor right away, prepare it for storage:

■ If you have a bit of hard foam, insert the processor pins into the foam. Otherwise, consider wrapping the processor in bubble wrap or something similar that will keep the pins from getting damaged.

■ Place the processor in an antistatic bag.

Pulling Out Memory Modules

Although memory prices remain relatively low, outfitting your custom PC with memory modules can still consume a significant portion of your build budget, particularly if you'd like to populate your machine with something north of 1GB of RAM. In many cases, it therefore makes sense to strip an old PC of its memory modules and add them to your homebrew machine for a free memory upgrade.

Of course, you can't just pop out some old modules and pop them into your new motherboard. There are compatibility issues, all of which I discussed in some detail back in Chapter 3, "The Work Area: Memory." However, there are two in particular that you need to watch out for:

→   **See** "DDR, DIMM, and More: Understanding Memory Specs," **p. 66**.

> **tip**
>
> The old memory modules should come with a sticker or other text that tells you the memory type and speed (or the memory standard, such as PC2-4200). If not, and if the old PC still works, you can usually determine the module information by using a tool that sniffs out memory module specs. One tool I use frequently is Crucial Technology's Memory Advisor (see www.crucial.com).

9

■ **The memory type**—The memory type, such as DDR, DDR2, or DDR3, of the old module must match the slot type used by your motherboard.

■ **The memory speed**—The clock speed of the old module must be at least as fast as the minimum clock speed supported by your motherboard. The old module can support a faster clock speed than your motherboard (the module will just operate at the slower speed), but it can't be slower.

Here are the steps to follow to remove a memory module:

1. Make sure the computer is turned off and the power cable is disconnected.
2. Remove the computer's side panel.
3. Touch something metal to ground yourself.
4. Locate the memory module you want to remove.
5. Press down on one of the memory socket's ejector tabs to pivot the tab away from the module.
6. Press down on the other memory socket ejector tab to pivot the tab away from the module, as shown in Figure 9.6.
7. Remove the memory module from the socket. Take care not to bump the module against any other component.
8. Repeat steps 4–7 to remove any other module you want to salvage.
9. Place the memory modules in an antistatic bag until you're ready to use them.

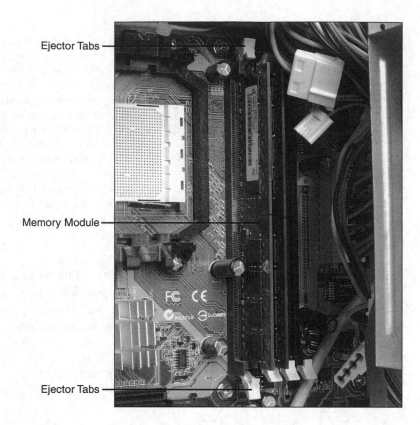

Ejector Tabs

Memory Module

Ejector Tabs

FIGURE 9.6

Press down on the ejector tabs to pivot the tabs away from the module.

Releasing the Power Supply

Of all the components in an old PC, the power supply is most often the one that's most easily repurposed for a new build. That's because what a power supply does hasn't changed all that much for many years. Yes, today's modern PSUs offer loads of power, high electrical efficiency, and extra goodies such as modular designs that let you use just the cables you need. Still, if the machine you're salvaging is no more than a few years old, its power supply ought to still be more than adequate for your build. There are just two things to watch out for:

■ Most importantly, the unit must be able to supply enough power to support your components. Check the label on the side of the unit to see how many watts it delivers. If the unit supplies anything less than 300W, you should look elsewhere.

■ Make sure the unit has power connectors that are compatible with your gear, particularly your motherboard. For example, if your board supports ATX 2.2, the power supply must have a 24-pin main connector and a 4-pin 12V connector.

→ For more about power supply connectors, **see** "Getting to Know the Power Supply," **p. 34**.

Here are the steps to follow to remove a power supply:

1. Make sure the computer is turned off and the power cable is disconnected.

2. If the power supply has its own power switch, turn off the unit.

3. Remove the computer's side panel.

4. Touch something metal to ground yourself.

5. Locate the power supply unit. Some computers hide the PSU behind a plastic cover, so you might need to remove the cover to expose the unit.

6. Disconnect all the internal power cables. The unit will likely be connected to at least some of the following components:

    Motherboard main connector

    Motherboard 12V connector

    PATA hard drive

    SATA hard drive

    Optical drive

caution If you're planning on using your new machine as a gaming or high-performance rig, forget about using a scavenged power supply. These types of computers need a lot of power delivered efficiently, so you're always better off getting a new PSU with lots of juice—at least 500W for the high-performance machine and at least 600W for the gaming PC.

caution My editor, Rick Kughen, offers up the following warning about using proprietary PSUs: "I don't know if this is still the case, but for a while, Dell was using a supposed ATX PSU with what looked like a standard ATX motherboard connector. Unfortunately, if you looked closely (and most people didn't) the pin wiring was different, meaning when the PSU was installed on a non-Dell mobo, mayhem ensued. I know a pretty prominent author who actually set his PC on fire when trying to scavenge a PSU from a Dell PC for use in one of his own custom builds."

tip To ensure you've disconnected all the power supply cables, trace each cable from the PSU to its connector.

Floppy drive

Other internal drive bay components (such as a memory card reader)

PCI Express video card

7. Using a Phillips screwdriver, remove the four external screws that hold the power supply to the case, as shown in Figure 9.7. Be sure you place the screws in a handy place for easier retrieval later.

Remove these screws.

Make sure power switch is off.

Remove these screws.

Remove these screws.

Remove these screws.

FIGURE 9.7

Most power supplies are attached to the case by four Phillips head screws.

8. Hold the power supply in one hand and the power cable in the other; then slowly remove the unit and cable from the case, taking care not to bang against any other component.

9. Place the power supply in a clean, dry spot until you're ready to use it. If you won't be using the unit for a while, place it inside a box or an antistatic bag to prevent it from getting dusty.

Removing the Motherboard

One of my favorite build challenges is to construct a so-called *FrankenPC*: a machine cobbled together exclusively using either components from old computers or whatever spare parts you have kicking around the shop. For these builds, I try to pick the best available motherboard, and if that mobo happens to be currently residing in a case I don't want to use, then I have no choice but to dive into that case and extract the board.

Removing a motherboard is the hardest of the PC salvage operations because you almost always have to practically strip the rest of the computer's innards to get to the board. This means you need to ensure that the motherboard will be useful to you in your upcoming build. This means opening the case and examining the motherboard to see whether you can find the name of the manufacturer and the board's model name or number. With this information in hand, you can Google the board and get its specs: which processors it supports, which memory types it can take, and so on.

When you're sure you want the mobo, follow these steps to extract it:

1. Make sure the computer is turned off and the power cable is disconnected.

2. Remove the computer's side panel.

3. Touch something metal to ground yourself.

4. Remove any expansion cards that are inserted into the motherboard's slots (refer to "Removing an Internal Expansion Card," earlier in this chapter).

5. If you won't be reusing the processor with this board, remove the CPU cooler and the processor (refer to "Prying Out a CPU," earlier in this chapter).

6. If any installed hard drives are in the way, remove those hard drives (refer to "Taking Out a Hard Drive," earlier in this chapter).

7. If the power supply unit is blocking the motherboard, remove the unit (refer to "Releasing the Power Supply," earlier in this chapter).

8. Disconnect all cables that are attached to the motherboard. You'll likely need to disconnect some or all of the following cables:

   Motherboard power supply (main and 12V)

   Case fans

   SATA hard drive

   PATA hard drive

9

Optical drive

Floppy drive

Front panel ports

Front panel switches

Front panel lights

> **tip** Many motherboard screws are tucked away in hard-to-reach nooks. In such cases, a 1/4-inch (or 7mm) nut driver works wonders.

9. Use a Phillips screwdriver to remove the screws that connect the motherboard to the mount points. The number of screws depends on the motherboard form factor, but most boards are mounted using nine or ten screws.

> **caution** Be very careful when removing screws from a motherboard. If your screwdriver slips, you can easily damage a circuit or other component and trash the board.

10. Slowly remove the board from the case, taking care not to bang the board against any other case components.

11. Place the motherboard in an antistatic bag until you're ready to use it.

12. If the case has a detachable I/O plate (the metal plate through which the motherboard's external ports appeared), detach the plate and save it with the motherboard for later use.

From Here

- For more about power supply connectors, **see** "Getting to Know the Power Supply," **p. 34**.

- For the lowdown on memory types, **see** "DDR, DIMM, and More: Understanding Memory Specs," **p. 66**.

- For more information on Fast Ethernet, **see** "Getting Wired: Understanding Ethernet Networks," **p. 132**.

- To salvage PC parts, you need to remove the old computer's case, **see** "Opening the Computer Case," **p. 199**.

- To learn how to install memory, **see** "Installing Memory Modules," **p. 205**.

- To learn how to install an expansion card, **see** "Installing an Expansion Card," **p. 211**.

- To learn how to clean the inside of a PC, **see** "Cleaning the Computer," **p. 498**.

PC Building and Upgrading Projects

Building a Basic Business PC

*Fortunate, indeed, is the man who takes
exactly the right measure of himself and
holds a just balance between what he
can acquire and what he can use, be it
great or be it small!*

—Peter Latham, *Collected Works*

Let's launch the project portion of the book with a look
at how to build a PC that can ably perform all basic
business tasks. Business PCs are the workhorses of the
computer world, and unless you specialize in graphics, programming, or some other field that requires major-league
computing power, you need such a PC for everyday work
tasks, whether you're self-employed, freelance, teleworking/
telecommuting, or part of a small office inside or outside the
home.

In this chapter I set out some design goals for the basic business PC; then I take you through the parts I chose to meet those goals, from the computer case right down to the memory modules. Then, with the parts assembled, I show you step-by-step how to build your own business PC.

Design Goals for a Basic Business PC

I can sum up the design goals for a basic business PC in a single word: balance. Indeed, the basic business PC should be the Goldilocks of the computer world:

- **Not too cheap, but not too expensive**—A business PC isn't the place to skimp. You want to get your work done efficiently and reliably, and those two qualities are in short supply when you head down Cheap Road. A much better direction is to buy brand-name parts that provide excellent value, meaning they combine high quality (for reliability) with mid-range performance (for efficiency).

- **Not too slow, but not a screamer**—From a performance standpoint, the basic business PC should be competent but not spectacular. As a business user, you just want the machine to stay out of your way while you get your work done, which means you definitely don't want a system that's too slow. A mid-range processor, a decent motherboard, and a couple of gigabytes of RAM mean your machine won't break any speed records but will easily handle any business task you throw at it.

- **Not too loud, but not super-quiet**—Offices are generally quiet places, so you don't want a machine that disturbs the peace by roaring away. Our goal is to keep the noise level down, but we don't need to try to make the PC whisper quiet because that would just make the machine more expensive than necessary.

- **Not ugly, but not cutting-edge stylish**—Most offices are relatively conservative places, so they're no place for a machine festooned with rakish graphics, aggressive bevel designs, and see-through side panels. The basic business PC should be buttoned-down, but it doesn't have to be a plain box, either.

- **Good at most tasks, but a master of none**—The basic business PC does email, word processing, spreadsheets, web browsing, presentations, scheduling, contact management, and perhaps some light graphics and database work. In each case, you probably use only a few features of each program. All this means the basic business PC doesn't require any specialized hardware. It doesn't need a quad-core CPU; tons of RAM; a terabyte or 10,000 RPM hard drive; or a high-end video card. Audio isn't important, so whatever's integrated into the motherboard will be fine, and most boards come with gigabit networking nowadays, so no separate network card is required.

Choosing Parts for the Basic Business PC

With the word *balance* echoing around our heads, it's time to equip the basic business PC. The next few sections keep the points from the previous section in mind and discuss the components we'll use to put together our balanced business machine.

Selecting a Case for the Basic Business PC

Our basic business PC requires a case that puts function over form, but not overly so. We still want our case to look good under our desk, but you don't want it to take up too much room. The ideal case should have good airflow so we don't have to worry about heat problems, front connectors for easy access, and a tool-free design to make the build easier.

For this build, I chose the Ultra Gladiator (see Figure 10.1), a mid-tower case that supports both ATX and microATX motherboards. This is a mid-price case—it lists for $119.99—that's actually a bit of a steal because it comes with an Ultra 500W power supply and two 120mm Ultra case fans (one in front and one in back). None of these are top-of-the-line components, but they're more than adequate for our business PC and the power supply and fans are certainly quiet enough for any office.

> **note** The next few sections discuss specific parts for this build, but there's no reason you have to use the same components in your build. Feel free to tweak the parts based on your own budget and computing needs.

FIGURE 10.1

The Ultra Gladiator: the case for our basic business PC.

Besides these extra goodies that come with the case, the Gladiator also supports the following features:

- Two USB ports, one FireWire port, one microphone connector, and one Line Out connector on the top of the case, near the front. This is my preferred location for these external ports because that's where they're most easily accessed.

- An aluminum front bezel that opens to reveal the external drive bays.

- Lots of drive bays: one 3.5-inch external (for a memory card reader or floppy drive), four 5.25-inch external (for optical or tape drives), and five 3.5-inch internal (for hard drives).

- Relatively easy side panel access: You remove two thumb screws and slide the panel off the case.

- The side panel (it comes in solid and clear versions; I got the former) is vented with a CPU duct and a VGA vent. A CPU duct is a plastic tube that's attached to a mesh-covered hole in the side panel. The tube sits over the processor and allows the CPU cooler fan to blow air directly out of the case. A VGA vent is a mesh-covered hole in the side panel that sits over the video card, allowing the card fan to blow air directly out of the case.

■ The expansion slots are tool-free: a plastic latch slides out to insert the card and then slides back in to hold the card in place.

■ Three of the internal hard drive bays are side-mounted, which means the connectors face the side panel, making connecting the drives incredibly easy and also serving to keep the drives from covering any part of the motherboard. These drive bays are also tool-less: they use plastic rails that snap onto the sides of the drive and enable you to simply slide the drive into the bay.

Choosing a Motherboard for the Basic Business PC

First and foremost, a business PC should be reliable. You don't have time for downtime, so your machine needs to just work, and that starts with the motherboard. For this build, I wanted a board that had a solid reputation for working solidly right from the first boot. This meant I had to shy away from low-end boards (those priced at $100 or less) because it's hard to find a truly reliable board at that level. On the other hand, a basic business PC is just that: basic. We don't want or need bells or even whistles because business computing requires neither. This means we can ignore high-end boards (those priced at $300 and up) that support all the latest technologies.

For high-quality, reliable motherboards, look no further than Intel, which makes mobos that just work. For a mid-range board, the Extreme Series (despite the name) is right up our alley. I ended up choosing the Intel D975XBX2 (see Figure 10.2), an ATX board that's available online in an OEM version for about $190. (The retail version is about $220, and for the extra cash you get a two-port USB adapter, rounded interface cables, and SATA cables that latch into place so they don't fall out as easily as regular SATA connectors.)

The Intel D975XBX2 offers the following features:

■ A clean and well-designed layout

■ Support for a wide variety of Intel processors, including the Intel Core 2 Extreme (this is where the name "Extreme Series" comes from), Intel Core 2 Quad, Intel Core 2 Duo, Intel Pentium Dual-Core, Intel Pentium Extreme Edition, Intel Pentium 4 Extreme Edition, Intel Pentium D, and Intel Pentium 4

note For a full list of compatible processors, go to the following page and click the Supported Processors link:

http://support.intel.com/ support/motherboards/ desktop/d975xbx2/index.htm

- Support for dual-channel DDR2 800, 667, or 533 memory modules (up to 8GB)
- Three PCI Express x16 slots (plus two PCI slots)
- Four external USB ports and one external FireWire port
- Eight internal SATA connectors
- Integrated 10/100/1000 network adapter
- Integrated Dolby 7.1 audio

FIGURE 10.2

The Intel D975XBX2: the basic business PC's motherboard.

Selecting a Power Supply for the Basic Business PC

No business PC should be a power hog, and this computer is no exception to that rule. Our PC will be a relatively simple affair with the major devices being a hard drive, DVD burner, and video card. Any good quality, mid-range 400W power supply could handle this workload without a problem. In our case (literally), the Ultra Gladiator comes with a 500W PSU, which will be more than adequate for our needs.

Picking Out a CPU for the Basic Business PC

A basic business PC doesn't need the latest-and-greatest CPU because nothing it does requires scads of power. However, what the average business PC *does* do a lot of is multitask. We business types are always running multiple programs simultaneously: our email client, our web browser, our word processor, our spreadsheet, and perhaps a folder window or two. Not only that, but these programs often make simultaneous claims on the CPU's time—while the email client checks for messages, the web browser might be downloading a file, the word processor might be printing a document, or the spreadsheet might be recalculating a model.

note If you want a bit more performance out of your CPU in this build, get the Intel Core 2 Duo E6600, instead. It will cost you about $60 or $70 more, but you get a much faster clock speed (2.4GHz).

To handle these all-too-common scenarios without bogging down our PC (and thus bogging down our work), our basic business PC requires a dual-core processor. That way, if one core is busy performing a background task, the other core is available for whatever we're working on in the foreground.

So, the obvious processor choice for the basic business PC is a member of the Intel Core 2 Duo family. The Intel D975XBX2 motherboard has a 1,066MHz front-side bus, so we need a CPU that runs at that speed. We have a few choices at this speed, and in the end I chose the Intel Core 2 Duo E6320 (see Figure 10.3). It comes with a 1.86GHz clock speed and a 4MB L2 cache.

FIGURE 10.3

The Intel Core 2 Duo E6320: the basic business PC's processor.

As a final thought on the CPU, note that I'm going to use the stock cooler Intel supplies with the retail version of the E6320 (see Figure 10.4). Intel's coolers do a good job and are reasonably quiet when not under too much strain (which they won't be, given the business tasks this PC will be performing), and you keep your processor's warranty intact. Even more important, the Ultra Gladiator's CPU duct on the side panel extends a few inches into the case, which means we can't put a tall cooler on the CPU. Most third-party coolers are quite tall, but the Intel stock cooler is just the right height.

> **note** If you get an OEM version of the E6320, or if you want a quieter CPU cooler, I suggest the CoolerMaster XDream P775. It's a low-profile cooler that will fit in your case and includes a remarkably quiet 17dBA fan.

FIGURE 10.4
The basic business PC will use Intel's stock CPU cooler.

How Much Memory Does the Basic Business PC Need?

Memory is one of the most important performance factors in any PC, which means, simply, that the more memory you add to any system, the better that system will perform. Happily, we live in a world where the enhanced performance of extra RAM can be had for a relative pittance, with 1GB memory modules selling online for $25–$50.

All this means it doesn't make any sense to hobble our basic business PC with a mere 512MB or even 1GB of RAM. No, we're going to do the right thing and load up our machine with 2GB, meaning we'll be running with 1GB per core, which should offer great performance.

We need to match our modules to our motherboard's memory speed, and the Intel D975XBX2 can use PC2 6400 (DDR2 800), PC2 5400 (DDR2 667), or PC2 4200 (DDR2 533). I opted for two 1GB PC2 6400 memory modules from OCZ (see Figure 10.5).

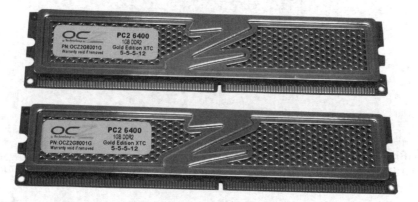

FIGURE 10.5

The basic business PC's memory: a couple of 1GB PC2 6400 modules from OCZ.

Storage Options for the Basic Business PC

The basic business PC needs a hard drive, of course, but only one (because I assume it will be backed up to a network share or to another external drive if you work from home). The hard drive should be big enough to hold the operating system and all our business applications, with enough room left over to store all our documents and data. A 500MB drive seems about right, and I like Seagate drives, so I choose the Seagate Barracuda 7200.10 (see Figure 10.6)—a 500GB SATA drive that's available in an OEM version online for just $120. It spins at 7,200 RPM; features a 16MB cache; and offers a decent 8.5 average seek time, so it won't slow down our work.

Any self-respecting business PC needs an optical drive, of course, and for this machine I chose the Sony DRU-830A, a dual-layer DVD/CD rewritable drive that supports write speeds of 18x DVD±R, 8x DVD±R DL, and 48x CD-R, plus read speeds of 16x DVD-ROM and 48x CD-ROM.

note The Sony DVD burner is being discontinued by Sony, so you might not be able to get one. No matter: get the Sony DRU-840A, instead, which offers a slightly faster 20x DVD±R write speed.

FIGURE 10.6

The basic business PC's hard drive: the Seagate Barracuda 7200.10 500GB SATA drive.

Determining the Video Needs of the Basic Business PC

Our basic business PC is solidly in the computing mainstream; thus, it ought to have top-notch 2D graphics support (to make our business applications look good and draw quickly). However, big-time 3D graphics aren't that much of a concern because we won't be using the machine for gaming or high-end graphics. Not that 3D graphics should be ignored completely. If you plan on running Windows Vista on this machine, for example, you need support for at least DirectX 9 and Pixel Shader 2.0 to take advantage of Vista's Aero Glass interface.

We don't need anything high-end here, so I opted for a mid-range solution: ATI's Radeon HD 2600XT, a solid GPU that costs about $130 and supports DirectX 10 as well as the CrossFire multi-GPU technology used by our Intel motherboard, so we can always add a second card down the road. (Not that this is likely in a business scenario, but it's nice to have the option.) I went with the HIS Hightech card, (see Figure 10.7), which is a PCI Express x16 card that offers 256MB of DDR4 graphics memory, two DVI ports (as well as a DVI-to-VGA adapter, just in case), and an S-Video port in case we need to hook up the PC to a TV.

FIGURE 10.7

The basic business PC's video card: the HIS Hightech Radeon HD 2600 XT.

Selecting Audio Equipment for the Basic Business PC

Audio isn't a major factor in our basic business PC, mostly because few business applications require sophisticated audio, but also because you don't want to be making a lot of noise in an office environment. Given that, our motherboard's integrated support for Dolby 7.1 audio is more than enough for our purposes.

Choosing Networking Hardware for the Basic Business PC

Any business PC must network, of course, and these days networking is easier than ever because it's a rare motherboard that doesn't come with a networking adapter built in. Even better, almost all motherboard-based NICs support Ethernet (10Mbps), Fast Ethernet (100Mbps), and Gigabit Ethernet (1Gbps or 1,000Mbps), so you're covered no matter to which type of network you'll be connecting. Our basic business PC is no exception, because our Intel motherboard has a 10/100/1000 NIC onboard. Therefore, no extra networking equipment is needed.

Pricing the Basic Business PC

As you've seen, our basic business PC doesn't have any big-ticket items. The most expensive component is the motherboard, which you can find online in an OEM version for under $200. We also saved quite a bit of money by going with the stock CPU cooler, the PSU and fans that came with the Gladiator case, and the motherboard's integrated audio chip and network adapter.

Table 10.1 summarizes the basic business PC's components and prices. As you can see, our total price of $835 is actually quite good, given the high-quality components in this build.

Table 10.1	Components and Prices for the Basic Business PC	
Component	**Model**	**Average Price**
Case	Ultra Gladiator	$100
Motherboard	Intel D975XBX2	$190 (OEM)
Power supply	Ultra V-Series 500W	N/A
CPU	Intel Core 2 Duo E6320	$180
CPU cooler	Intel stock cooler	N/A
Memory	OCZ PC2 6400 1GB (×2)	$70
Hard drive	Seagate Barracuda 7200.10 500GB SATA (OEM)	$120
Optical drive	Sony DRU-830A DVD/CD Rewritable Drive	$45
Video card	HIS Hightech Radeon HD 2600 XT	$130
Audio card	Motherboard integrated	N/A
Network card	Motherboard integrated	N/A
TOTAL		**$835**

Putting Together the Basic Business PC

With parts at the ready (see Figure 10.8), your tools by your side, and a stretch of free time ahead (you can build this PC in an afternoon or evening), you're ready to start the build. The rest of this chapter takes you through the steps you need to follow. Happy building!

FIGURE 10.8

The basic business PC, ready to be built.

Removing the Generic I/O Shield

The Ultra case comes with a generic I/O shield, a piece of metal designed to cover the I/O controller in the back of the motherboard while leaving openings for each of the motherboard's I/O ports. Of course, the I/O shield on the case never fits the I/O ports on the motherboard, so you always have to replace it. Fortunately, all mobos come with their own I/O shield that *does* match the board's ports.

As you see in the next section, when test-fitting the motherboard in the case to determine where to put the standoffs, it helps if the I/O shield isn't in the way. You remove the generic I/O shield by accessing the back of the case and gently pushing the edges of the I/O shield back into the case. The I/O shield should pop out without too much of a struggle.

Installing the Motherboard Standoffs

A standoff (or a *mount point*, as it's often called) is a hex-nut screw, so it actually consist of two parts: a bottom screw that enables you to insert the standoff into a hole in the side of the case and a top hex nut into which you can insert a screw. The idea is that you install eight to ten (depending on the motherboard form factor) of these stand-offs into the case, sit the motherboard on top of the standoffs, align the mother-board's holes with the hex nuts, and then attach the motherboard. This gives the board a solid footing but also separates the board from the metal case to prevent short-ing out the board.

note If you don't have any standoffs, for some reason, you can purchase a screw kit that comes with a wide variety of computer-related screws and fasteners, including standoffs.

Installing the standoffs is easiest when the motherboard is bare, so that should be your first task:

1. Find the standoffs that came with the case and put them aside.

2. Remove the case side panel.

3. Lay the case flat on its side, with the open side facing up.

4. Move all the case cables out of the way so you can clearly see the side panel that has the mounting holes. If you have trouble getting the power supply cable out of the way, consider temporarily removing the power supply, as described in Chapter 9, "Scavenging an Old PC for Parts."

→   See "Releasing the Power Supply," **p. 234**.

5. If the case comes with any prein-stalled standoffs (the Ultra Gladiator doesn't), remove them.

6. If you haven't done so already, touch something metal to ground yourself.

7. Take the motherboard out of its antistatic bag and lay the board inside the case, oriented so that the board's back-panel I/O ports are lined up and flush with the case's I/O slot.

8. Note which case holes correspond to the holes in the motherboard (see Figure 10.9). You might need to use a flashlight to ensure there's a case hole under each motherboard hole.

caution I suggest removing preinstalled standoffs because you need to ensure that you only have the correct number of standoffs inserted and that they're inserted in the correct positions. One standoff in the wrong position can cause a short circuit.

tip Rather than trying to remember which case holes correspond with each motherboard hole, you can mark the correct case holes. After you have the board lined up with the holes, stick a felt-tip pen through each hole and mark the case. (You might need to offset the board slightly to do this properly.)

Mounting Holes

FIGURE 10.9

The motherboard has 10 holes through which you attach the board to the standoffs.

9. Place the motherboard back inside its antistatic sack and set it carefully aside.

10. Screw the standoffs into the corresponding holes in the side of the case.

Just to be safe, you might want to place the motherboard into the case again to double-check that each motherboard hole corresponds to a standoff.

Getting the Motherboard Ready for Action

Although you might be tempted to install the motherboard right away, and technically you can do that, it's better to hold off for a bit and do some of the work on the board while it's out of the case. We'll be installing the processor and the memory modules, and although it isn't impossible to install these parts with the board inside the case, it's a lot easier outside.

Before getting started, be sure to touch something metal to ground yourself. Next, take the motherboard and lay it flat on your work surface. For the Intel D975XBX2, it's best to orient the board so that the I/O ports are facing away from you. This enables you to work with the processor socket without having to reach over the heatsinks or the I/O ports.

Inserting the Processor

Begin by inserting the Intel E6320 processor in the motherboard's LGA775 socket. I won't go into the details here because I showed you how to insert Intel processors back in Chapter 8.

➔   **See** "Installing an Intel CPU in a Socket 775 Board," **p. 216**.

caution Don't install the CPU cooler now. The fasteners used by the Intel stock cooler must go through the motherboard, so they won't go through properly while the board is lying on a flat surface. After the mobo is mounted, installing the cooler will be a lot easier.

Inserting the Memory Modules

With your processor all snug and cozy, it's time to populate your board with your memory modules. Where you install the modules on the D975XBX2 board depends on how many modules you're adding (see Figure 10.10):

- **One module**—Install the module in any socket.
- **Two modules**—Install identical modules in Channel A DIMM 0 and Channel B DIMM 0. This ensures a proper dual-channel configuration.
- **Three modules**—Install a set of identical modules in Channel A (DIMM 0 and DIMM 1), and install the third module in Channel B (either DIMM 0 or DIMM 1). To ensure dual-channel operation, the Channel B module must be the same speed as the Channel A modules and its size must equal the sum of the Channel A modules (this is called *dual-channel asymmetric mode.*). For example, if you have two 512MB modules in Channel A, then the Channel B module must be 1GB.
- **Four modules**—Install one set of identical modules in Channel A DIMM 0 and Channel B DIMM 0, and install a second set of identical modules in Channel A DIMM 1 and Channel B DIMM 1. This ensures a proper dual-channel configuration.

I won't go through the installation steps here because I already covered how to install memory modules in Chapter 8, "Basic Skills for PC Building and Upgrading." Figure 10.11 shows our motherboard with our two 1GB modules installed.

➔   **See** "Installing Memory Modules," **p. 205**.

DIMM 0 ———
DIMM 1 ———
DIMM 0 ———
DIMM 1 ———

——— Channel A
——— Channel B

10

FIGURE 10.10

The memory module sockets on the Intel D975XBX2.

FIGURE 10.11

Our motherboard with two 1GB memory modules in place.

Installing the Motherboard

With our motherboard populated with a processor and memory, it's just about ready to roll. The next few sections take you through the detailed installation steps for the motherboard. This is the most finicky, most time-consuming, and most important part of the build. As you'll see, getting a motherboard configured involves lots of separate steps, and lots of cable connections. It's crucial to take your time and make sure you have all the connections just so.

Inserting the Motherboard I/O Shield

Earlier you removed the case's generic I/O shield, so now it's time to insert the I/O shield that came with the motherboard. Take the motherboard's I/O shield and fit it into the case's I/O opening. Make sure you have the I/O shield oriented properly:

- The two holes for the mouse and keyboard PS/2 ports should be at the top, and the six audio ports should be at the bottom.

- The protruding ridge that runs around the I/O shield should face the back of the case.

When the I/O shield is flush with the case, firmly press the bottom of the shield until it snaps into place; then press the top of the shield until it, too, snaps into place.

Attaching the Motherboard to the Case

With the custom I/O shield in place, you're now ready to install the motherboard inside the case. Here are the steps to follow:

1. Move all the case cables out of the way so you can clearly see the side panel that has the mounting holes and the installed standoffs.

tip It's not always easy to get the I/O shield perfectly seated. If you have trouble getting a corner of the shield to snap into place, use the end of a plastic screwdriver handle to gently tap the recalcitrant corner into place.

caution Many I/O shields have small metal tabs around some of the port openings. Make sure none of these tabs are blocking the openings, or you might have trouble either inserting the motherboard or, later, attaching a connector to the port. If you see a tab that looks like it could get in the way of an opening, gently bend the tab back so that it's out of the way.

tip Notice that the motherboard PATA header lies sideways and, when the board is attached, will directly face the case's hard drive bays. This will be problematic later because you have no room to make a PATA cable connection directly after you install the optical drive. Therefore, you might want to install the PATA cable now, before you attach the motherboard.

2. If you haven't done so already, touch something metal to ground yourself.

3. Gently and carefully maneuver the motherboard into the case and lay
   it on top of the standoffs.

4. Adjust the position of the board so the board's back-panel I/O ports are
   lined up and flush with the openings in the I/O shield, as shown in
   Figure 10.12.

FIGURE 10.12

Make sure the motherboard's I/O ports are lined up and flush with the I/O shield's openings.

5. You should now see a standoff
   under each motherboard mounting
   hole. If not, it likely means that the
   I/O shield isn't fully seated. Remove
   the board, fix the I/O shield, and
   then try again.

6. Use the mounting screws supplied
   with the case to attach the board to
   each standoff. To ensure a trouble-
   free installation, I use the following
   technique:

   ■ First, insert but don't tighten
     the upper-right screw.

note Bear in mind, however, that it's normal
for the board's mounting holes to
be slightly offset from the standoffs. There's a bit of give to the I/O
shield, so you usually have to
force the board slightly to the left
(toward the I/O shield) to get the
holes and standoffs to line up
perfectly. When you have one
screw in place, the rest of the
holes should line up with the
standoffs without having to force
the board into place.

- Next, insert but don't tighten the bottom-left screw. (The bottom-left screw is often the hardest one to install because it's usually in the corner of the case. If you prefer to start with an easier target, insert the bottom middle screw, instead.)

- Make sure all the holes and standoffs are properly aligned, and then tighten the first two screws.

- Insert and tighten all the rest of the screws.

caution Don't over-tighten the motherboard screws or you risk cracking the board. Also, when tightening the screws be very careful that the screwdriver doesn't slip off the screw and damage a nearby component on the motherboard. Wherever possible, use one hand to guide and hold the screwdriver into place, and use the other hand to tighten the screw.

Installing the CPU Cooler

Now that the mobo's safely and securely attached to the case, it's a good time to add the CPU cooler to the processor. We're using the stock cooler that came with the processor, so we already know it's compatible with both the CPU and the motherboard. Even better, the stock cooler already comes with the thermal compound preapplied, so we don't need to mess with any of that.

Here are the steps to follow to install Intel's stock cooler:

1. Touch something metal to ground yourself.

2. Remove the cooler from the box, being careful not to smudge the thermal compound on the cooler's heatsink.

3. With the cooler's fan facing up, position the cooler's four fasteners over the four holes that surround the motherboard's CPU socket, as shown in Figure 10.13.

4. As you hold the cooler in place, push down on each fastener until it clicks into place. For the smoothest installation, follow a diagonal pattern. For example, if you start with the bottom-right fastener, next do the upper-left fastener.

5. Connect the cooler's power cable to the motherboard's CPU fan header, as shown in Figure 10.14.

10

FIGURE 10.13

Place the cooler's fasteners over the four holes that surround the CPU socket.

CPU fan header is located here

FIGURE 10.14

Connect the CPU cooler's power cable to the motherboard's CPU fan header.

Connecting the Motherboard Power Cables

Our next order of business is to connect the power cables that supply juice to the motherboard. A bit unusually, our Intel board has three power headers:

> **tip** Most of the pins on a power cable connector are square, but a few are rounded on one side. These rounded pins have corresponding rounded holes on the header. To install a power cable connector with the correct orientation, match up the rounded pins with the rounded holes.

- A 24-pin main power header, into which you plug the power supply's 24-pin connector, as pointed out in Figure 10.15. (Note that this header is backward-compatible with 20-pin connectors. This means that if your power supply has only a 20-pin connector, you can safely plug it into the 24-pin header.)

> **note** If you happen to have a power supply unit that offers only a 4-pin 12V connector, you're not out of luck. The Intel board offers a 4-pin–to–8-pin adapter that you can use. Nice!

- An 8-pin 12V connector. Our power supply actually has two separate 4-pin 12V connectors, so you first need to snap these two together. When that's done, you can plug the combined connector into the motherboard, as shown in Figure 10.15.

- A 4-pin Molex connector. Intel says you need to use this connector only if your power supply has just a 20-pin main connector and you're using a PCI Express x16 video card that consumes up to 75W of power. Our power supply supports the full 24-pin connection, so we won't use this connector.

Connecting the Front-Panel IEEE-1394 Cable

Our Ultra case offers the convenience of a front panel IEEE-1394 (FireWire) port, which is a nice (although now fairly common) touch. For this port to work, you must connect its cable (the connector is usually labeled 1394) to the IEEE-1394 header on the motherboard, as shown in Figure 10.16.

8-Pin 12V
Connection

24-Pin Main Connection

FIGURE 10.15

Connect the power supply's 24-pin and 8-pin connectors to the corresponding headers on the motherboard.

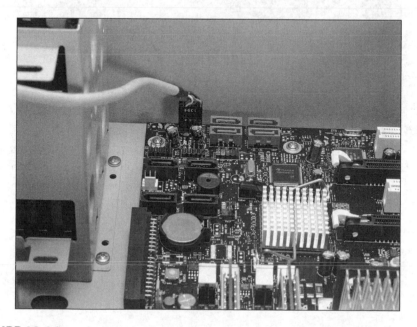

FIGURE 10.16

Connect the cable that runs from the IEEE-1394 front-panel port to the IEEE-1394 header on the motherboard.

Connecting the Front-Panel USB Cable

The Ultra case also offers a couple of front-panel USB 2.0 ports. You need to connect the USB 2.0 ports' cable (the connector is usually labeled USB) to one of the motherboard's two USB headers, as shown in Figure 10.17.

FIGURE 10.17

Connect the cable that runs from the USB 2.0 front-panel ports to one of the USB headers on the motherboard.

Connecting the Front-Panel Audio Cables

The rest of the Ultra case's front-panel ports consist of Line Out (audio output) and Mic In (microphone input) audio ports. You need to connect the audio ports' cable (the connector is usually labeled Audio) to the motherboard's Audio header, as shown in Figure 10.18.

FIGURE 10.18
Connect the cable that runs from the front-panel audio ports to the Audio header on the motherboard.

Connecting the Power Switch, Reset Switch, and LEDs

The next item on our build to-do list is to tackle the mess of wires snaking out from the front of the case, just above the front fan. These wires correspond to the following front panel features:

- **Power switch**—This is the button you press to turn the system on and off. Its lead consists of two wires, one white and one blue, and the connector is labeled POWER SW.

- **Reset switch**—This is the button you press to reboot a running system. Its lead consists of two wires, one green and one black, and the connector is labeled RESET SW.

- **Power LED**—This LED lights up when the system is powered up. It consists of two wires with two separate connectors: the white wire is the negative (ground) lead and its connector is labeled POWER LED -; the green wire is the positive (signal) lead and its connector is labeled POWER LED +.

■ **Hard drive LED**—This LED lights up when the hard drive is active. It consists of two wires with a single connector: the white wire is the negative (ground) lead, the red wire is the positive (signal) lead, and the connector is labeled H.D.D. LED.

> **note** The Ultra case has a fifth set of wires, a red-and-black pair with a connector labeled SPEAKER that's connected to the case's external speaker. However, the Intel motherboard has its own internal speaker, which means it doesn't offer a header for the external speaker, so you won't use these wires in this build.

Connecting all these wires is a bit tricky, but the good news is that you won't destroy anything if you get the connections wrong the first time around. For one thing, the connectors for both the power switch and the reset switch can be attached in either orientation (they'll work fine either way); for another, if you get the LED connectors backward, it just means that the LEDs won't work.

For the connections themselves, you use the motherboard's front-panel header, a collection of eight pins beside the USB headers. The pins themselves are color-coded, as shown in Figure 10.19.

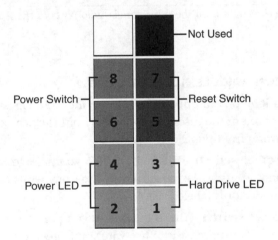

FIGURE 10.19

The pin assignments and color codes used on the motherboard's front-panel header.

Give the pin assignments shown in Figure 10.19, here's how you connect the front-panel wires:

■ **Power switch**—Connect this to pins 6 and 8 (red) in any orientation.

■ **Reset switch**—Connect this to pins 5 and 7 (purple) in any orientation.

■ **Power LED**—Connect the POWER LED - connector to pin 4 (green), and connect the POWER LED + connector to pin 2 (green).

■ **Hard drive LED**—Connect this to pins 1 and 3 (orange), with the white wire on pin 3 (ground) and the red wire on pin 1 (signal).

Figure 10.20 shows the wires connected to the front-panel header on the motherboard.

FIGURE 10.20

Connect the front-panel wires to the motherboard's front-panel header.

Connecting the Case Fan Power Cables

At long last, the motherboard's connections are almost complete. Your final chore is to connect the power leads for the two case fans to the motherboard's case fan headers. Here's what you do:

■ **Rear fan**—Connect the rear fan's power lead to the Rear Fan header, which is located between the Northbridge and the back-panel audio ports, as shown in Figure 10.21.

■ **Front fan**—Connect the front fan's power lead to the Front Fan header, which is located between the two pairs of black SATA headers, as shown in Figure 10.22.

FIGURE 10.21
Connect the rear fan's power lead to the motherboard's Rear Fan header.

FIGURE 10.23
Connect the front fan's power lead to the motherboard's Front Fan header.

Installing the Hard Drive

The Ultra case offers a simple tool-free system for attaching internal components such as hard drives and optical drives to the chassis. The hard drive bays are located immediately behind the front fan, and out-of-the-box the top drive bay holds a plastic caddy to which are attached seven pairs of plastic rails. The four pairs on top of the caddy are for optical drives and other 5.25-inch devices, and the three pairs on the bottom of the caddy are for hard drives and other 3.5-inch devices. Each bottom pair consists of a left and a right rail (marked *L* and *R*, respectively). Figure 10.23 shows the caddy and a hard drive rail pair (left and right).

FIGURE 10.23

You use pairs of plastic rails to attach drives to the Ultra's drive bays.

Each rail has a set of two or more protrusions that are spaced a standard distance apart so they line up perfectly with the holes in the side of a drive. Here's how you use this rail system to install a hard drive:

1. Touch something metal to ground yourself.

2. Orient the hard drive so the connectors are facing you and the drive label is facing up.

3. Snap a left rail into the holes on the left side of the hard drive.

4. Snap a right rail into the holes on the right side of the hard drive. Figure 10.24 shows a hard drive fitted with rails.

5. With the hard drive connectors facing out, slide the hard drive into a drive bay until the rails click into place.

FIGURE 10.24

A hard drive with left and right rails attached.

6. Run a SATA cable from the hard drive's interface connection to a SATA header on the motherboard. If you have the retail version of the Intel motherboard, it comes with SATA cables that have a lock mechanism on one connector. Insert the locking connector to the motherboard SATA header and the regular connector to the hard drive.

7. Connect a SATA power cable from the power supply to the hard drive's power connector. Figure 10.25 shows a connected hard drive.

FIGURE 10.25

The hard drive is ready for action.

Installing the Optical Drive

You add the optical drive to your system by inserting it into one of the Ultra's 5.25-inch external drive bays. You use the same rail system, but for an optical drive you use the larger rails that sit on top of the caddy, and those rails are the same for both sides of the drive (that is, there are no left and right rails). Here are the steps to follow:

1. Touch something metal to ground yourself.

2. Orient the optical drive so the connectors are facing you and the drive label is facing up.

3. Snap a rail into the holes on the left side of the optical drive.

4. Snap a rail into the holes on the right side of the optical drive.

5. Place the case in the upright position.

6. Lift the front of the case, grasp the opening on the underside of the bezel, and pull the bezel away from the case to detach it.

7. The Ultra's top 3.5-inch external drive bay is open, so with the optical drive's connectors facing the inside of the case, slide the drive into a drive bay until the rails click into place.

8. Open the door in the front of the bezel.

9. Remove the plastic drive bay cover. To do this, push one of the plastic tabs on the back of the cover toward the edge of the bezel while at the same time pushing the edge

note Most optical drives give you a choice of fronts, usually beige or black. If your optical drive currently has a beige front, switch to the black, which will look better with the black bezel of the Ultra case. See the drive's manual to learn how to exchange fronts.

caution Don't pull the bezel too far away from the case because you might yank out one or more of the front-panel wires.

note Unfortunately, making the motherboard connection is problematic because the PATA header lies sideways and directly faces the case's hard drive bays. This means you have no room to make the connection directly. However, there's a technique you can use to finagle the PATA cable connector into the header. First, turn the connector so it's at right angles to the cable and the protrusion is on the outside (facing away from the cable). Bring the connector toward the PATA header at about a 45° angle. When the leading edge of the connector is just inside the header, turn the connector counterclockwise until it's directly facing the header. (This is similar to angling a tall object around a corner.) Now press the connector until it's firmly seated in the header.

10

of the cover in from the front. Repeat for the other side of the cover. Figure 10.26 shows the inserted optical drive and the bezel with the bay cover removed.

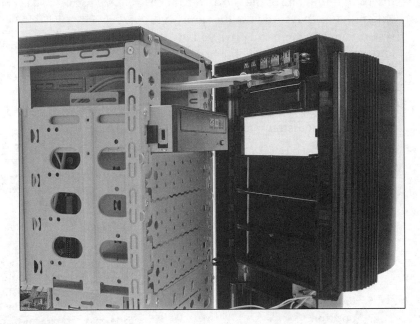

FIGURE 10.26

The optical drive in the drive bay with the plastic bay cover removed from the bezel.

10. Close the bezel door, make sure the front panel wires aren't bunched up on the outside of the case, and then snap the bezel back into place.

11. Run a PATA cable from the optical drive's interface connection to the motherboard's PATA (IDE) header.

12. Connect a 4-pin Molex power cable from the power supply to the optical drive's power connector. Figure 10.27 shows the optical drive connections.

Inserting the Video Card

The last chore in the build is to insert the video card into one of the motherboard's PCI Express x16 slots. I won't go into all the details here because I gave you specific instructions on inserting an expansion card in Chapter 8.

→   **See** "Installing an Expansion Card," **p. 211**.

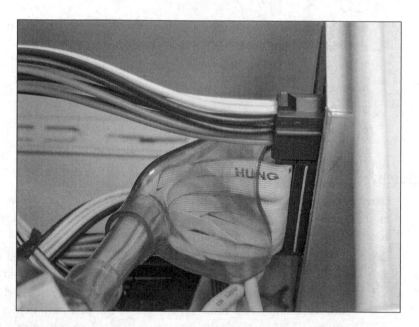

FIGURE 10.27
The optical drive's interface and power connections.

However, note that the Ultra Gladiator case uses a tool-free design for attaching expansion cards to the chassis. Here's how you use this feature to install our build's video card:

1. Touch something metal to ground yourself.

2. Place the case in an upright position (if it isn't already).

3. Locate the bus slot you want to use. For this build, you should probably use the topmost PCI Express x16 slot.

4. Locate the slot cover that corresponds to the slot you selected in step 3. If you're using the topmost PCI Express x16 slot, the corresponding slot cover is the second one from the top.

5. Each slot cover has a plastic tab to the left of the slot (looking at the slot from inside the case). Flip up that tab to loosen it.

> **note** The Intel D975XBX2 also comes with a USB 2.0 adapter, which gives you two extra USB 2.0 slots in the back of the computer. Everyone can use more USB slots, so go ahead and install the adapter. Because the adapter doesn't require a bus slot, be sure to install it using one of the case slot openings that doesn't correspond with a bus slot (such as the topmost slot opening). After you insert the adapter, connect its cable to one of the motherboard's USB headers.

10

6. Holding the loosened tab as high as it will go, slide the tab away from the slot cover.

7. Remove the slot cover by pushing from the back of the case.

8. Insert the card into the slot.

9. Slide the plastic tab toward the slot cover.

10. Turn the tab down to lock the card in place.

Final Steps

Okay, your basic business PC is just about ready for its debut. Before the big moment, however, there are a few tasks you should perform and a few things you need to check. Here's the list:

- **Route and tie off the cables**—A well-built PC doesn't just have cables all over the place. Instead, the cables should be routed as far away from the motherboard as possible and as close to the sides of the case as possible. This makes the inside of the case look neater and improves airflow throughout the case. Use Velcro cable ties if need be to keep unruly cables out of the way.

- **Double-check connections**—Go through all the connections and ensure that they're properly seated.

- **Double-check devices**—Check the hard drive, optical drive, and expansion cards to ensure that they're not loose.

- **Look for loose screws**—Ensure that there are no loose screws or other extraneous bits and pieces in the case.

- **Check the power supply input voltage**—This build's power supply has a switch to toggle the input voltage between 115V and 230V. Ensure that it's set correctly for your jurisdiction (115V in North America).

Powering Up

Now, at last, you're ready to fire up your new PC. Rather than just diving willy-nilly into the operating system install, however, there's a procedure I like to follow to ensure that the BIOS, motherboard, and processor are all working in harmony. Follow these steps:

1. Connect a monitor, keyboard, and mouse to the PC; then turn on the monitor.

2. Connect the power cable to a wall socket and then to the power supply unit.

3. If the PSU's switch is off (0), turn it on (1).

4. Press the power switch on the front of the case. Make sure the case fans and CPU fan are all working.

5. Press F2 to enter the motherboard's BIOS setup program, which is called System Setup.

> **note** If all is well with your motherboard power connections, the board's power LED (located right beside the main 24-pin power header) will light up as soon as your turn on the PSU. If the LED remains off, turn off the PSU, remove the power cable, and then check your motherboard power cable connections.

6. Make sure your devices are working properly by checking the following:

   - On the Main page, check the Processor Type to ensure that the Intel E3200 appears.
   - On the Main page, check that the Total Memory is 2048MB and that the Memory Mode is Dual Channel.
   - On the Advanced page, select Drive Configuration and make sure your hard drive and optical drive appear.

7. Just to be safe, press **F9** to load the default values for the system, and then press **Y** when System Setup asks you to confirm.

8. Press **F10** to save your changes and exit System Setup, and then press **Y** when the program asks you to confirm you want to save changes.

9. Press the power switch to shut down the PC.

10. Replace the case's side panel.

11. Connect the computer to your network by running a network cable from the back panel's network port to your switch or router.

12. Press the power switch on the front of the case.

13. Open the optical drive and insert your operating system disc. (For my build, I installed Windows Vista Business Edition.) The computer will now boot from the disc and install the OS.

14. If you install Windows, be sure to update your version—particularly by installing all available security patches—immediately.

15. When the OS is installed and running, insert the Intel Express Installer Driver CD that came with the board (see Figure 10.28). This contains all the drivers you need for the board's devices.

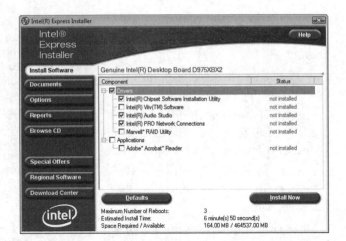

FIGURE 10.28
Run the Intel Express Installer CD to complete the installation of the motherboard.

16. Update the motherboard's BIOS, as described in Chapter 17, "Maintaining Your Computer Hardware."

→ **See** "Updating the Motherboard BIOS," **p. 507**.

17. Use Device Manager to check for device problems (see Chapter 17) and install drivers for any device Windows didn't recognize. (In this build, for example, you need to install the video card drivers. Be sure to install the drivers using the CD that comes with the card.)

→ **See** "Updating Device Drivers," **p. 519**.

Final Thoughts

This was a sweet build right from go to whoa. All told, the build took about four hours, *including* doing the photography that accompanies this chapter. Your build time should be shorter, particularly because there are no significant snags with our chosen hardware.

The initial boot went without a hitch, and System Setup reported that all devices were present and accounted for. I had Vista Business installed within 30 minutes, and another 30 minutes later I had the machine patched, the Intel motherboard's drivers installed and its BIOS updated, and the video card driver installed. The machine is now a solid and hard-working member of our office local area network (LAN).

My only quibble with the system is that the video card's fan is a bit loud. It's not a huge problem, but if I'm looking for a quieter office down the road, I might exchange the HIS card for the fanless Gigabyte card I'm going to use for the home theater PC in the next chapter.

From Here

- For the details on installing memory, **see** "Installing Memory Modules," **p. 205**.

- To learn about installing cards, **see** "Installing an Expansion Card," **p. 211**.

- To learn how to install an Intel CPU, **see** "Installing an Intel CPU in a Socket 775 Board," **p. 216**.

- If you need to temporarily remove the power supply, **see** "Releasing the Power Supply," **p. 234**.

- To learn how to use Device Manager to look for problem devices, **see** "Updating Device Drivers," **p. 519**.

- For instructions on updating the BIOS, **see** "Updating the Motherboard BIOS," **p. 507**.

Building a Home Theater PC

*To be happy at home is the ultimate
result of all ambition.*

—Samuel Johnson, *The Rambler*

I t wasn't all that long ago when your average household
had two separate entertainment and education areas
centered around screens: the TV room and the computer
room. You could play or learn in only one area at a time, and
the idea of somehow bringing these two worlds together
either never occurred to anyone or was seen as just too hard.

That has all changed in the past few years, and the agent of
that change is a newfangled type of computer: the home
theater PC (often abbreviated to HTPC, but I won't do that in
this chapter). This PC has become the hub around which a
family's entertainment—TV, movies, music, and the Web—
revolves. The home theater PC connects to the TV and the
audio system, enabling it to record shows and play back
movies and music with big-time sound.

For this project, you build a state-of-the-ever-evolving-art home theater PC, chock full of the bells, whistles, and other accoutrements that will make your handcrafted machine a true entertainment hub. I set out some design goals for the home theater PC; then I take you through the parts I chose to meet those goals, from the computer case right down to the memory modules. Then, with the parts assembled, I show you step-by-step how to build your own home theater PC.

Design Goals for a Home Theater PC

Your home theater PC will be your home's digital media hub, which means it has to be capable of working with digital media of all kinds—images, movies on disc, digital video files, music on disc, digital music files, TV signals, and recorded TV, to name the most common. It also has to be a hub—it has to connect to a myriad of devices, including a TV and an audio system. So, unlike most PCs which are generalists, the home theater PC is a specialist; thus, it requires special equipment and special design considerations:

- **Connections galore**—The home theater PC should be capable of connecting to a monitor, an analog TV, a digital TV, an analog set-top box, a digital set-top box or antenna, an analog audio system, a digital audio system, and a gaming console. That's a lot of devices, but our home theater PC will be able to handle them all.

- **Quiet, *real* quiet**—Nobody wants to hear a hard drive rumble to life during a tender movie moment, and you don't want your favorite tunes drowned out by the roar of a PC's case fans. Out of necessity, the home theater PC will reside in the same area where you and your family will be enjoying your entertainment, so this PC is a device that should be seen and not heard.

- **Just another component**—Actually, you don't even want to really *see* the home theater PC, either. That is, you might want to hide the machine inside a console or other enclosed area (assuming the case allows this; see your documentation). If the PC is exposed, you certainly don't want it to look like a computer. No one wants a massive tower hulking beside their nice, sleek LCD TV. Instead, the home theater PC should blend in with the other components in your home entertainment center.

- **Future-proof**—Because it uses specialized components, the home theater PC isn't cheap. Therefore, you want to get the most life out of it that you can, and the way to do that is to build in a bit of future-proofing. If you make the hard drive really large, include support for the latest media formats, and include connections to every possible device, this machine won't be obsolete for quite a while.

note The next few sections discuss specific parts for this build, but there's no reason you have to use the same components in your build. Feel free to tweak the parts based on your own budget and computing needs.

Choosing Parts for the Home Theater PC

Okay, it's time to equip our home theater PC. The next few sections keep the points from the previous section in mind and discuss the components we'll use to put together our digital media hub. I should point out here that, although the components I recommend here and use in the build are fairly expensive, there are plenty of ways to save money with this build. I point these out as I go along.

Selecting a Case for the Home Theater PC

The most important consideration for the home theater PC's case is the overall look. We don't want a tower or mid-tower case because they look too "computer-like," and we want no such thing in our entertainment area. Something that looks more or less like a typical audio/visual component is what we want.

On the practical side, we don't want a small form factor case because we want a bit of extra leg room for all our components. The ideal case should have good airflow so we don't have to worry about heat problems, and it should have front panel connectors for easy access.

For this build, I chose the Thermaltake Mozart, which uses the HTPC form factor and, as you can see Figure 11.1, looks great. The case supports both ATX and microATX motherboards. This is a mid-price case—you can find it online for about $100 in the version that doesn't come with the "media lab" extras— that also comes with the case fans: one 80mm intake fan in front and two 60mm exhaust fans in back.

Besides these extra goodies that come with the case, the Mozart also supports the following features:

- Two USB ports, one FireWire port, one microphone connector, and one Line Out connector on the front panel of the case for easy access.

- An aluminum front bezel that opens to reveal the external drive bays.

■ Lots of drive bays: three 5.25-inch external (for optical or tape drives) and five 3.5-inch internal (for hard drives). Unfortunately, the case doesn't include any 3.5-inch external drive bays, which would have been nice for a memory card reader. However, you can always add an external USB reader.

■ Relatively easy top panel access: You remove three thumb screws and lift the panel off the case.

note As this book was going to press, Thermaltake released an updated version of the Mozart case. Called the Mozart IP, it comes with an integrated iPod dock that enables you to sync your iPod with iTunes when the PC is on, and listen to the iPod when the PC is off. See the following page for more details:

http://www.thermaltake.com/product/Chassis/desktop/mozartIP/vf3001sns.asp

FIGURE 11.1

The Thermaltake Mozart: the case for our home theater PC.

Choosing a Motherboard for the Home Theater PC

Our home theater PC will connect to lots of devices, and those connections will mostly happen via the motherboard, so we need a board that offers many digital media ports. For that reason, I love the Gigabyte GA-MA69GM-S2H. It has ports galore, including the following:

■ VGA

■ DVI-D

■ HDMI

■ Optical S/PDIF

- Six audio ports
- S-Video (on a separate adapter)
- HDTV component Y/Pr/Pb (on a separate adapter)

Toss in four USB ports, an IEEE-1394 port, and a network port, and there's nothing we can't connect to this baby. It uses the microATX form factor (see Figure 11.2), which will help us maneuver it into the relatively tight confines of the Mozart case.

FIGURE 11.2
The Gigabyte GA-MA69GM-S2H: the home theater PC's motherboard.

The Gigabyte GA-MA69GM-S2H also offers the following features:

- A near-perfect layout in which all the connectors are in just-so positions. The only bit of weirdness is the SATA connectors, which point off to the side of the board rather than straight up.

- An AM2 processor socket that supports a wide variety of AMD processors, including the AMD Athlon 64 FX, AMD Athlon 64 X2, AMD Athlon 64, and AMD Sempron.

- Support for dual-channel DDR2 800, 667, or 533 memory modules (up to 16GB!).

- One PCI Express x16 slot and one PCI Express x4 slot (plus two PCI slots).

- Four internal SATA connectors, plus two SATA cables with the locking connectors.

> **note** For a full list of compatible processors, see the following page:
>
> www.gigabyte-usa.com/Support/Motherboard/CPUSupport_Model.aspx?ProductID=2547

- Three internal USB headers and two internal IEEE-1394 headers.
- Integrated Radeon X1250 video card.
- Integrated Dolby 7.1 audio.
- Integrated 10/100/1000 network adapter.
- A TV adapter that includes an S-Video port and HDTV component (Y/Pr/Pb) ports (red, green, and blue connectors).

This is a pretty impressive list of features for a microATX board, but that doesn't translate into an impressive price. You can find the GA-MA69GM-S2H online for around $80, which to my mind is one of the outstanding bargains in today's motherboard market.

Selecting a Power Supply for the Home Theater PC

We have two main concerns when it comes to the power supply for our home theater PC: noise and cable management. On the noise front, one of our main design goals for this machine is a quiet operation, so the power supply will be a major factor here. Most PSUs are far too loud for our purposes. In the past I've used Seasonic power supplies (www.seasonic.com) because they have a great reputation as quiet performers. However, for this PC I'm going to try the Antec NeoHE 430, which claims a noise level of a mere 19dBA (just a notch above silent) with the fan running at 1,000RPM. This is the same noise level as the legendary Seasonic S12-430, so I have high hopes.

The NeoHE 430 also comes with modular cables, which will enable us to use only the cables we need. This will ease the congestion inside the Mozart case and greatly improve airflow.

The NeoHE (see Figure 11.3) is a 430W PSU, which is enough power for our needs; it sells online for about $70.

Picking a CPU for the Home Theater PC

How much a home theater PC stresses a processor depends on what the PC is doing. If it's just playing music or a movie, the processor barely notices. (The exception here is when you're watching high-definition video, as I describe a bit later; see "Determining the Video Needs of the Home Theater PC.") However, if the PC is *recording* anything, particularly video, the CPU starts sweating noticeably. Therefore, a lower-end Sempron or Athlon 64 just isn't going to be good enough. For this build, I'm going to go for it a bit and choose the AMD Athlon 64 X2 6400+, a dual-core CPU that, as I write this, is AMD's fastest processor at 3.2GHz.

FIGURE 11.3

The Antec NeoHE 430: the home theater PC's power supply.

I elected to purchase the Athlon 64 X2 6400+ without a stock cooler, which saves about $10 (you can find the processor online without a cooler for around $160). I'm a little concerned about heat in this project. As you see a bit later, the video card I'll be using has a passive cooling system which, while silent, also generates a lot of heat. Add the slow fans the Mozart case uses (one 80mm and two 60mm), and there's the possibility of heat build-up in the case, which could affect the CPU. Fortunately, the Athlon 64 X2 6400+ isn't known as a massive heat source, but we want to protect it. A third-party cooler offers better protection; plus we can also then choose a quieter fan than the one we'd get on the stock cooler.

The Mozart case doesn't offer much room over the processor, so that severely limits our choice of a third-party cooler because most coolers are quite tall. We need a low-profile cooler, so I chose the SilverStone Nitogon NT06-Lite (about $50 online), which is socket AM2 compatible and should fit inside the case without much trouble. It also requires a separate fan, so I got the Thermaltake Silent Cat (about $10), a 120mm fan that's rated at just 16dBA at 1,600RPM. Figure 11.4 shows our CPU system for this build.

caution Remember that by not using the stock cooler, you void the processor's warranty.

FIGURE 11.4

The AMD Athlon 64 X2 6400+: the home theater PC's processor and its cooling components.

How Much Memory Does the Home Theater PC Need?

Memory is one of the most important performance factors in any PC, which means, simply, that the more memory you add to any system, the better that system performs. Happily, we live in a world where the enhanced performance of extra RAM can be had for a relative pittance, with 1GB memory modules selling online for $25–$50.

All this means that it doesn't make any sense to hobble our home theater PC with a mere 512MB or even 1GB of RAM. No, we're going to do the right thing and load up our machine with 2GB, so we'll be running with 1GB per core, which should offer great performance.

We need to match our modules to our motherboard's memory speed, and the Gigabyte GA-MA69GM-S2H can use PC2 6400 (DDR2 800), PC2 5400 (DDR2 667), or PC2 4200 (DDR2 533). I opted for two 1GB PC2 6400 memory modules from Corsair (see Figure 11.5).

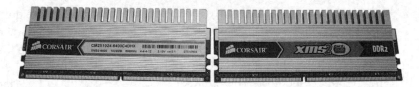

FIGURE 11.5

The home theater PC's memory: a couple of 1GB PC2 6400 modules from Corsair.

Storage Options for the Home Theater PC

For our home theater PC's hard drive, we need to somehow blend a lot of storage space (for all the digital content we'll be recording) and quiet performance. That's a tall order, but it's one that's neatly filled by a great drive: the Western Digital Caviar SE16 (see Figure 11.6). This 750GB SATA drive is available in an OEM version online for about $160. It spins at 7,200 RPM; features a 16MB cache; and offers a decent 8.9 average seek time, so it won't get in the way of our entertainment. The drive puts out between 28dBA and 33dBA, depending on how hard it's working, so although it won't be a silent drive (for that you need to get into solid-state drives that lack moving parts), it won't be a major noisemaker, either.

> **tip** During the build, I discovered that the hard drive's power and interface connectors come awfully close to one of the installed expansion cards. One way to work around this problem is to get right-angled SATA cables, in which the cable is attached to the connector at a right angle, helping it fit into tight spots. You'll need a SATA interface cable and an adapter for the SATA power cable.

FIGURE 11.6

The home theater PC's hard drive: the Western Digital Caviar SE16 750GB SATA drive.

Any self-respecting home theater PC needs an optical drive, of course. If you'll be ripping audio CDs and DVDs, you need the fastest readers you can find, which usually means 48x CD-ROM and 16x DVD-ROM. You can find such drives online for $25–$50, and any brand-name drive—Lite-On, Sony, Pioneer, or Philips—will do you good.

However, for this home theater PC, I want
to do something special. As you know,
there's a war going on for supremacy in
the next-generation high-definition video
format, with Blu-ray and HD DVD duking
it out. As I write this, it's still not clear
which format will win this war, but the
content is already out there, and I want to
watch high-def movies on my digital TV.
So what to do? The short-term answer is to
not pick either side. How do you do that? By

note As this book was
going to press,
Toshiba announced that it was
surrendering the HD disc war and
leaving the field to Sony and Blu-
ray. This should mean that Blu-ray
players and discs will get cheaper
in the medium term as manufacturers and publishers rally around
the Blu-ray banner.

getting an optical drive that supports *both* standards! LG makes an excellent
drive called the Super Blue Multi GGC-H20L that can read both Blu-ray and
HD DVD discs (see Figure 11.7). This SATA drive is also a decent dual-layer
DVD/CD rewritable drive that supports write speeds of 16x DVD±R, 4x DVD±R
DL, and 40x CD-R, plus read speeds of 16x DVD-ROM and 48x CD-ROM. Now
the bad news: this bleeding-edge bit of technology will set you back about
$300! Sorry about that.

FIGURE 11.7

The home theater PC's optical drive: the LG Super Blue Multi GGC-H20L.

Determining the Video Needs of the Home Theater PC

You saw earlier that the Gigabyte motherboard comes with a Radeon XT1250
GPU integrated into the Northbridge. This is a powerful integrated chip that
even supports high-def video decoding, a must for our home theater PC.
However, there's a downside to this decoding support: the chip relies on the
processor to handle much of the workload, so our AMD CPU will have to work

hard when all we're doing is watching HD content. A hard-working CPU means more heat (although our Nitrogon cooler should handle that easily enough) and, more importantly, more noise (the faster the CPU fan has to spin, the more noise it makes).

Noise is our enemy in this build, so even though it will add to the overall cost of the build, I decided to get a separate video card. You might be thinking that this doesn't make much sense given that one of the major sources of noise in modern PCs is the video card, with its noisy fan. However, it's possible to get fanless video cards that use a heatsink instead of a fan. This generates more heat inside the chassis, but the blissfully silent operation of the video card is worth it.

For this build, I chose the Gigabyte Radeon HD 2600 XT, which is a fanless PCI Express x16 card that offers 256MB of DDR3 graphics memory, two DVI ports (as well as two DVI-to-VGA adapters, just in case), and an S-Video port. The card also comes with an HDTV adapter that connects to the card's S-Video port and offers HDTV component (Y/Pr/Pb) ports (as well as another S-Video port). As you can see in Figure 11.8, the card is fanless, with heat dissipated by a large heatsink that covers the card.

FIGURE 11.8

The home theater PC's video card: the Gigabyte Radeon HD 2600 XT.

Any self-respecting home theater PC must be able to record TV, of course, and for that we need a TV tuner. For this build, I used the Hauppauge WinTV HVR-1800, a PCI Express x1 card that will fit in our motherboard's x4 slot. I chose the HVR-1800 because it has two TV tuners—a 125-channel analog NTSC tuner and a digital HD ATSC tuner—which gives us maximum flexibility. It also has an FM tuner and built-in MPEG-2 decoding, all for about $100 online.

Selecting Audio Equipment for the Home Theater PC

For the home theater PC, audio is every bit as important as video, so we want top-of-the-line sound. The Gigabyte motherboard comes with 7.1 surround sound built in, but that's not going to be good enough for us. For one thing, the onboard chip doesn't produce the highest-quality sound. For another, the chip will offload much of its processing work to the CPU, which, as I mentioned earlier, will lead to more heat and more noise.

For this build, I opted for Creative Labs' Sound Blaster X-Fi Fatal1ty sound card, a 7.1-channel card with 24-bit digital audio and a 192KHz sample rate. You can get just the card for about $140, but I selected the Platinum package that comes with a breakout box that slips into an external drive bay and provides easy access to a wide variety of connectors.

Choosing Networking Hardware for the Home Theater PC

Ideally, your home theater PC should be on your home network so you can easily share your media with the rest of the house. Fortunately, almost all motherboard-based network interface cards (NICs) support Ethernet (10Mbps), Fast Ethernet (100Mbps), and Gigabit Ethernet (1Gbps or 1,000Mbps), so you're covered no matter to which type of wired network you'll be connecting. Our home theater PC is no exception because our Gigabyte motherboard has a 10/100/1000 NIC onboard.

However, there's a good chance your home theater PC won't be able to make a wired connection to your network because your family room (or den or whatever) might be a ways from your router. If that's the case, you'll need to make a wireless connection to the network. For this build, I chose to add an ASUS WL-130N wireless NIC, which supports 802.11n (Draft 2.0) for maximum bandwidth.

Pricing the Home Theater PC

As you've seen, our home theater PC is loaded with incredible technology that will make this machine the envy of any neighborhood. Unfortunately, all that technology comes at a heavy cost to the bank account. As you can see in Table 11.1, our total price is $1,515, which is up there.

Table 11.1   Components and Prices for the Home Theater PC

Component	Model	Average Price
Case	Thermaltake Mozart	$100
Motherboard	Gigabyte GA-MA69GM-S2H	$80
Power supply	Antec NeoHE 430	$70
CPU	AMD Athlon 64 X2 6400+	$160
CPU cooler	Nitrogon NT06-Lite	$50
CPU cooler fan	Thermaltake Silent Cat 120mm	$10
Memory	Corsair XMS2 PC2 6400 1GB (×2)	$110
Hard drive	Western Digital Caviar SE16 750GB SATA	$160
Optical drive	LG Super Blue Multi GGC H20L	$300
Video card	Gigabyte Radeon HD 2600 XT	$120
TV tuner	Hauppauge WinTV HVR-1800 PCI	$100
Audio card	Sound Blaster X-Fi Fatal1ty Platinum	$165
Network card	Motherboard integrated	N/A
Wireless NIC	ASUS WL-130N	$90
TOTAL		**$1,515**

If that's more than you want to spend, I mentioned in the previous sections that there are ways to trim the costs on this project: go with the stock AMD cooler; use a regular CD/DVD rewritable drive; and stick with the Gigabyte board's integrated video and audio. If you do all that as shown in Table 11.2, the price comes down by $600 to a more reasonable $915. This PC will be a bit noisier, will run a bit hotter, and won't support the latest video formats, but it still has plenty of juice to make a great digital media hub for your home.

Table 11.2   Components and Prices for a More Cost-Conscious Home Theater PC

Component	Model	Average Price
Case	Thermaltake Mozart	$100
Motherboard	Gigabyte GA-MA69GM-S2H	$80
Power supply	Antec NeoHE 430	$70
CPU	AMD Athlon 64 X2 6400+	$170
CPU cooler	AMD stock cooler	N/A
CPU cooler fan	AMD stock fan	N/A
Memory	Corsair XMS2 PC2 6400 1GB (×2)	$110
Hard drive	Western Digital Caviar SE16 750GB SATA	$160
Optical drive	Any brand-name optical drive	$35
Video card	Motherboard integrated	N/A
TV tuner	Hauppauge WinTV HVR-1800 PCI	$100
Audio card	Motherboard integrated	N/A
Network card	Motherboard integrated	N/A
Wireless NIC	ASUS WL-130N	$90
TOTAL		**$915**

Putting Together the Home Theater PC

With the home theater PC parts ready to go (see Figure 11.9), your tools by your side, and a stretch of free time ahead (you can build this PC in an afternoon or evening), you're ready to start the build. The rest of this chapter takes you through the steps you need to follow. Happy building!

Getting the Case Ready

The Mozart case requires a bit of prep work before we can move on to more productive tasks. First, remove the top panel (which is the equivalent of a side panel in a tower case) by removing the three thumbscrews that attach it to the back of the case.

FIGURE 11.9

The home theater PC, ready to build.

For easier access to the interior of the case, I suggest removing the two cross-bars, shown in Figure 11.10:

- The left (if you're facing the front of the case) crossbar attaches via a screw in the back. Remove the screw, tilt up the crossbar, and then remove it.

- The second crossbar is attached via a screw to the case that holds the 3.5-inch external drive bays. Remove the screw, tilt up the crossbar, and then remove it.

Place the screws and crossbars in a safe place until you're ready to reattach them at the end of the build.

Figure 11.10 also points out the case's secondary hard drive (3.5-inch) bay. (The main hard drive bay is under the longer of the two crossbars you just removed.) To install anything in the 5.25-inch external drive bay, you must first remove this secondary 3.5-inch bay. However, that bay is very difficult to remove after you've installed the motherboard, so it's best to take it out now by removing the three screws that attach it to the case. We won't be needing the secondary hard drive bay in this build, so you can put it aside. (As an added bonus, losing this bay will also give you more room to work and improve airflow through the case.)

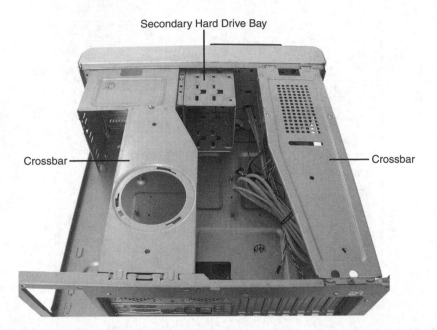

Secondary Hard Drive Bay

Crossbar

Crossbar

FIGURE 11.10

To get easier access to the inside of the Mozart case, remove the two crossbars.

The Mozart case also case comes with a generic I/O shield, a piece of metal designed to cover the I/O controller in the back of the motherboard, while leaving openings for each of the motherboard's I/O ports. Of course, the I/O shield on the case never fits the I/O ports on the motherboard, so you always have to replace it. Fortunately, all mobos come with their own I/O shields that *do* match the board's ports.

As you see in the next section, when test-fitting the motherboard in the case to determine where to put the standoffs, it helps if the I/O shield isn't in the way. You remove the generic I/O shield as follows:

1. Look inside the case and locate the screw that attaches the generic I/O shield to the case.

2. Remove the screw.

3. Gently push the edges of the I/O shield back into the case. I actually found the I/O shield to be wedged in quite tightly, so I used the tip of a flat-head screwdriver to push the edges of the shield into the case.

Finally, examine the floor of the case; in the approximate middle of the floor you'll see a gold hex-nut–like object screwed into the floor. I haven't the faintest idea what that thing is or why it's there. In any case, it's in the way, so get a pair of pliers and remove it.

note If you don't have any standoffs for some reason, you can purchase a screw kit that comes with a variety of computer-related screws and fasteners, including standoffs.

Installing the Motherboard Standoffs

A *standoff* (or a *mount point*, as it's often called) is a hex-nut screw, so it actually consist of two parts: a bottom screw that enables you to insert the standoff into a hole in the side of the case and a top hex nut into which you can insert a screw. The idea is that you install from eight to ten (depending on the motherboard form factor) of these standoffs into the case, sit the motherboard on top of the standoffs, align the motherboard's holes with the hex nuts, and then attach the motherboard. This gives the board a solid footing but also separates the board from the metal case to prevent shorting out the board.

Installing the standoffs is easiest when the motherboard is bare, so that should be your first task:

1. Find the standoffs that came with the case and put them aside.

2. Move all the case cables out of the way so you can clearly see the floor and its mounting holes.

3. If the case comes with any preinstalled standoffs (the Mozart doesn't, other than the standoff-like doohickey you removed in the previous section), remove them.

4. If you haven't done so already, touch something metal to ground yourself.

5. Take the motherboard out of its antistatic bag and lay the board inside the case, oriented so that the board's back-panel I/O ports are lined up and flush with the case's I/O slot.

6. Note which case holes correspond to the holes in the motherboard (see Figure 11.11). You might need to use a flashlight to ensure that there's a case hole under each motherboard hole.

caution I suggest removing preinstalled standoffs because you want to ensure that you only have the correct number of standoffs inserted and that they're inserted in the correct positions. One standoff in the wrong position can cause a short circuit.

tip Rather than trying to remember which case holes correspond with each motherboard hole, you can mark the correct case holes. After you have the board lined up with the holes, stick a felt-tip pen through each hole and mark the case. (You might need to offset the board slightly to do this properly.)

Mounting Holes

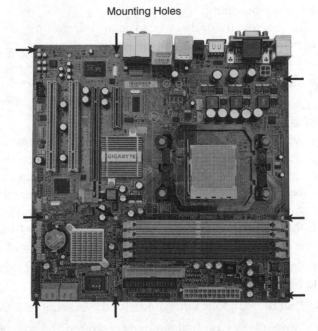

FIGURE 11.11

The motherboard has nine holes through which you attach the board to the standoffs.

7. Place the motherboard carefully aside.

8. Screw the standoffs into the corresponding holes in the floor of the case.

Just to be safe, you might want to place the motherboard into the case once again to double-check that each motherboard hole corresponds to a standoff.

Getting the Motherboard Ready for Action

Although you might be tempted to install the motherboard right away, and technically you can do that, it's better to hold off for a bit and do some of the work on the board while it's out of the case. We'll be installing the CPU cooler back plate, the processor, and the memory modules. The back plate must be installed now, and although it isn't impossible to install the processor and memory modules with the board inside the case, it's a lot easier outside.

Before getting started, be sure to touch something metal to ground yourself. Now take the motherboard and lay it flat on your work surface. For the Gigabyte GA-MA69GM-S2H, it's best to orient the board so that the I/O ports are facing away from you, which gives you easiest access to the processor socket and memory sockets.

Installing the CPU Cooler Back Plate

Let's begin with the back plate for the Nitrogon CPU cooler. This cooler is compatible with the motherboard's AM2 CPU socket, but it requires a bit of work to install because it doesn't use the board's standard retention plate. Instead, you have to remove the standard retention plate and then install a back plate under the board. The back plate exposes the screws to which you'll later attach the cooler itself (see "Installing the CPU Cooler," later in this chapter).

Here are the steps to follow to install the cooler's back plate:

1. Touch something metal to ground yourself.

2. Use a flat-head screwdriver to lift up the plastic locking mechanism that holds each of the four retention plate pins in place, as shown in Figure 11.12.

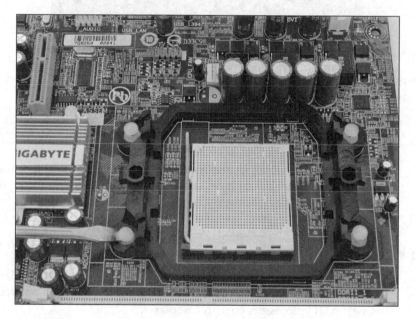

FIGURE 11.12

Lift up the locking mechanism for each retention plate pin.

3. Under the motherboard, carefully poke each retention plate pin through the board, and then lift off the retention plate and, under the motherboard, the plastic back plate.

4. Under the motherboard, place the cooler's back plate, felt side down, over the holes that were used by the stock retention plate, as shown in Figure 11.13.

FIGURE 11.13

Place the cooler's back plate under the motherboard.

5. Run the four long screws through the holes in the back plate that correspond to the four holes in the motherboard.

6. On the top of the motherboard, place a washer on each of the four long screws protruding through from the bottom of the board; then fasten a standoff to each screw, as shown in Figure 11.14.

Inserting the Processor

Now it's time to install the AMD Athlon 64 X2 6400+ processor in the motherboard's AM2 socket. I won't go into the details here because I showed you how to insert AMD processors back in Chapter 8.

→   **See** "Installing an AMD CPU in a Socket AM2 Board," **p. 219**.

FIGURE 11.14

For each protruding screw, add a washer and a standoff to fasten the back plate to the motherboard.

Inserting the Memory Modules

Our final bit of mobo prep work is to populate the board with the memory modules. Where you install the modules on the Gigabyte GA-MA69GM-S2H board depends on how many modules you're adding (see Figure 11.15):

- **One module**—Install the module in any socket.

- **Two modules**—Install identical modules in DIMM 1 and DIMM 2. This ensures a proper dual-channel configuration.

- **Three modules**—Install the modules in DIMM 1, DIMM 2, and DIMM 3. Unfortunately, our motherboard doesn't support dual-channel mode with three modules.

- **Four modules**—Install one set of identical modules in DIMM 1 and DIMM 2 (the yellow sockets) and a second set of identical modules in DIMM 3 and DIMM 4 (the red sockets). This ensures a proper dual-channel configuration.

note In Figure 11.15, I've labeled the module sockets DIMM 1, DIMM 2, and so on. The actual labels on the board itself are DDRII_1, DDRII_2, and so on.

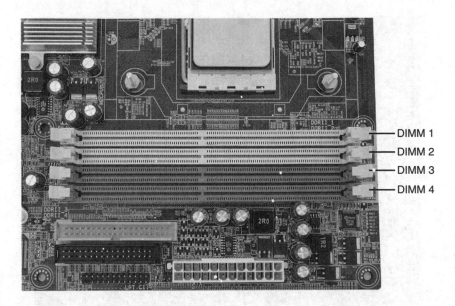

FIGURE 11.15
The memory module sockets on the Gigabyte GA-MA69GM-S2H.

I won't go through the installation steps here because I already covered how to install memory modules in Chapter 8, "Basic Skills for PC Building and Upgrading." Figure 11.16 shows our motherboard with our two 1GB modules installed.

→ **See** "Installing Memory Modules," **p. 205**.

Installing the Motherboard

With your motherboard populated with a processor, cooler back plate, and memory, it's just about ready to roll. The next few sections take you through the detailed installation steps for the motherboard. This is the most finicky, most time-consuming, and most important part of the build. As you'll see, getting a motherboard configured involves several separate steps and lots of cable connections. It's crucial to take your time and make sure you have all the connections just so.

FIGURE 11.16
Our motherboard with two 1GB memory modules in place.

11

Inserting the Motherboard I/O Shield

Earlier you removed the case's generic I/O shield, so now it's time to insert the I/O shield that came with the motherboard. Take the motherboard's I/O shield and fit it into the case's I/O opening. Make sure you have the I/O shield oriented properly:

- If you're looking at the back of the case, the two holes for the mouse and keyboard PS/2 ports should be toward the left (that is, toward the power supply bay), while the six audio ports should be toward the right.

- The protruding ridge that runs around the I/O shield should face the back of the case.

When the I/O shield is flush with the case, firmly press the bottom of the shield until it snaps into place; then press the top of the shield until it, too, snaps into place.

tip It's not always easy to get the I/O shield perfectly seated. If you have trouble getting a corner of the shield to snap into place, use the end of a plastic screwdriver handle to gently tap the recalcitrant corner into place.

Attaching the Motherboard to the Case

With the custom I/O shield in place, you're now ready to install the motherboard inside the case. Here are the steps to follow:

1. Move all the case cables out of the way so you can clearly see the case floor where you installed the standoffs.

2. If you haven't done so already, touch something metal to ground yourself.

3. Gently and carefully maneuver the motherboard into the case and lay it on top of the standoffs.

4. Adjust the position of the board so the board's back-panel I/O ports are lined up and flush with the openings in the I/O shield, as shown in Figure 11.17.

FIGURE 11.17

Make sure the motherboard's I/O ports are lined up and flush with the I/O shield's openings.

5. You should now see a standoff under each motherboard mounting hole. If not, it likely means that the I/O shield isn't fully seated. Remove the board, fix the I/O shield, and then try again.

6. Use the mounting screws supplied with the case to attach the board to each standoff. To ensure a trouble-free installation, I use the following technique:

   - First, insert but don't tighten the upper-right screw.
   - Next, insert but don't tighten the bottom-left screw.

- Make sure all the holes and standoffs are properly aligned, and then tighten the first two screws.
- Insert and tighten all the rest of the screws.

Installing the CPU Cooler

Here are the steps to follow to install the Nitrogon cooler:

1. Remove the cooler from the box and turn it right side up so the cooling fins are on top.

2. Attach the Thermaltake Silent Cat fan to the top of the CPU cooler. For easiest installation later, orient the fan so the power cable is on the side of the cooler where the three heat pipes emerge.

3. Turn the cooler upside down so the heatsink and original retention brackets face up.

4. Remove the protective film that covers the heatsink.

5. Remove the plastic film that covers the two retention brackets on either side of the heatsink, remove the two screws that attach each bracket, and then remove the retention brackets. Keep the screws handy.

6. Take out the roughly V-shaped AM2 retention brackets, and locate the same-shaped plastic coating (this is insulation for the bracket). For each bracket, orient the bracket so the recessed screw holes face up; then apply a plastic coating on the top surface of the bracket.

note Bear in mind, however, that it's normal for the board's mounting holes to be slightly offset from the standoffs. There's a bit of give to the I/O shield, so you usually have to force the board slightly to the left (toward the I/O shield) to get the holes and standoffs to line up perfectly.

caution Be sure you use the correct screws! Most cases come with a variety of screws, and not all of them fit the standoffs. Test-fit the screws until you find the correct kind.

tip The screws that come with the Silent Cat are a bit too long and can damage the cooling fins if you use them on their own. Instead, for each screw, attach a hex nut and slide a washer onto the screw (the hex nuts and washers are supplied with the fan). These act as spacers so the screws attach to the cooler without a hitch.

tip In my experience with these plastic insulation films, it's best to lay the film down on a flat surface with the sticky side facing up. Then place the bracket over the coating, line them up as best you can, and then lay the bracket down on the coating.

11

7. Use the screws from step 3 to attach each AM2 retention bracket to the cooler, as shown in Figure 11.18. Be sure to position each bracket with the recessed screw holes facing up, which enables the screws to sit flush with the bracket surface.

FIGURE 11.18

Place the cooler's fasteners over the four holes that surround the CPU socket.

8. Spread a thin but even coating of thermal compound over the cooler's heatsink.

9. Turn the cooler over so the fan is facing up; then maneuver the four holes of the AM2 retention brackets over the four back plate screws extending up from the motherboard. Orient the cooler so the side where the heat pipes emerge is toward the board's I/O panel, as shown in Figure 11.19.

10. Use the cooler's thumb screws to hand-tighten the cooler to the back plate screws.

11. Examine how the heatsink is positioned over the processor: they should be lined up evenly and there should be no gaps between them.

12. Tighten the thumb screws.

> **note** It doesn't look like it in Figure 11.19, but the cooler *does* clear the cooling fins of the memory modules, but only by a hair. Whew!

FIGURE 11.19

Drop the cooler's retention brackets onto the four screws that protrude up through the motherboard from the cooler's back plate.

13. Connect the fan's power cable to the motherboard's CPU fan header, as shown in Figure 11.20. (The fan uses a 3-pin connector, but it fits the motherboard's 4-pin fan header.)

Installing the Power Supply

Okay, now let's get the power supply onboard:

1. Orient the power supply unit so the back (the side with the power cable connector, on/off switch, and fan) is toward the back of the case and the power cable connector is toward the I/O shield.

2. Maneuver the power supply into the case's power supply bay.

3. Make sure the power supply is flush with the back of the case.

4. Attach the unit to the case with four screws, as shown in Figure 11.21.

> **tip** The Mozart case offers a very tight power supply bay—so tight in fact that you can't simply slide the power supply unit into the bay. Instead, first angle the top, leading edge of the unit under the metal ridge that forms the top of the power supply bay. You should then be able to pivot the rest of the unit into the bay without much trouble.

CPU fan header is located here.

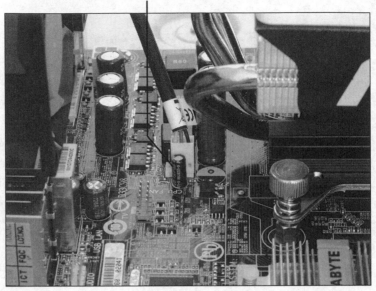

FIGURE 11.20
Connect the CPU cooler's power cable to the motherboard's CPU fan header.

FIGURE 11.21
Use four screws to attach the power supply unit to the case as shown here.

Connecting the Motherboard Power Cables

Our next order of business is to connect the power cables that supply juice to the motherboard. Our Gigabyte board has two standard power headers:

> **tip** Most of the pins on a power cable connector are square, but a few are rounded on one side. These rounded pins have corresponding rounded holes on the header. To install a power cable connector with the correct orientation, match up the rounded pins with the rounded holes.

- A 24-pin main power header, into which you plug the power supply's 24-pin connector, as pointed out in Figure 11.22. (Note that this header is backward-compatible with 20-pin connectors. Thus, if your power supply has only a 20-pin connector, you can safely plug it into the 24-pin header.)

- A 4-pin 12V header, into which you plug the power supply's 4-pin connector, as pointed out in Figure 11.22.

4-Pin 12V
Connection

24-Pin Main
Connection

FIGURE 11.22

Connect the power supply's 24-pin and 4-pin connectors to the corresponding headers on the motherboard.

Connecting the Front-Panel IEEE-1394 and USB Cables

Our Mozart case offers the convenience of a front-panel IEEE-1394 (FireWire) port. For this port to work, you must connect its cable (the connector is labeled 1394) to one of the motherboard's two internal IEEE-1394 headers, as shown in Figure 11.23.

The case also offers a couple of front-panel USB 2.0 ports. You need to connect the USB 2.0 ports' cable (the connector is labeled USB) to one of the motherboard's three internal USB headers, as shown in Figure 11.23.

tip This is a good time to route as much of the main power cable as you can around the side of the 5.25-inch external drive bay (in the open area where the secondary 3.5-inch drive bay used to be). Getting as much of the cable out of the way now will make it easier to install the Sound Blaster breakout box and the optical drive later.

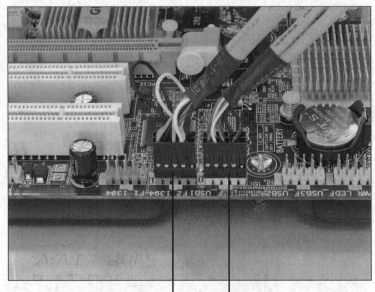

IEEE-1394 Connector
USB Connector

FIGURE 11.23

Connect the cable that runs from the IEEE-1394 front-panel port to a IEEE-1394 header, and connect the cable that runs from the USB 2.0 front-panel ports to a USB header.

Connecting the Front-Panel Audio Cables

The rest of the Mozart case's front-panel ports consist of Line Out (audio output) and Mic In (microphone input) audio ports. Note that the audio ports' cable has two connectors, one for standard audio (labeled AC '97) and one for high-definition audio (labeled HD AUDIO). Our Gigabyte motherboard supports HD audio, so we need to connect the HD AUDIO connector to the motherboard's Audio header (labeled F_AUDIO), as shown in Figure 11.24.

FIGURE 11.24

Connect the front-panel audio ports' HD AUDIO connector to the Audio header on the motherboard.

Connecting the Power Switch, Reset Switch, and LEDs

The next item on our build to-do list is to tackle the mess of wires snaking out from the front of the case, beside the front fan. These wires correspond to the following front panel features:

- **Power LED**—This LED lights up when the system is powered up. It consists of two wires with a single connector: the white wire is the negative (ground) lead, and the blue wire is the positive (signal) lead; the connector is labeled POWER LED.

- **Hard drive LED**—This LED lights up when the hard drive is active. It consists of two wires with a single connector: the white wire is the negative (ground) lead, and the red wire is the positive (signal) lead; the connector is labeled H.D.D. LED.

- **Power switch**—This is the button you press to turn the system on and off. Its lead consists of two wires, one white and one blue, and the connector is labeled POWER SW.

- **Reset switch**—This is the button you press to reboot a running system. Its lead consists of two wires, one green and one black, and the connector is labeled RESET SW.

- **Speaker**—This is the case's internal speaker. It consists of two wires with a single connector: the black wire is the negative (ground) lead, and the red wire is the positive (signal) lead; the connector is labeled SPEAKER.

note The back of the Mozart case has a chassis intrusion switch, which alerts the motherboard if someone opens the case. You can connect this lead to the motherboard's Chassis Intrusion header (it's beside the 24-pin main power header), but these devices have always struck me as overly paranoid. I removed the chassis intrusion switch from my case to avoid having an extra wire floating around.

Connecting all these wires is a bit tricky, but the good news is that you won't destroy anything if you get the connections wrong the first time. For one thing, the connectors for both the power switch and the reset switch can be attached in either orientation (they'll work fine either way); for another, if you get the LED connectors backward, it just means the LEDs won't work.

For the connections themselves, you use the motherboard's front-panel header, a collection of 16 pins beside the USB headers. Figure 11.25 shows the pin assignments. (Note that the pins numbers are ones I made up myself; they don't correspond to actual pin numbers used on the board.)

Give the pin assignments shown in Figure 11.25, here's how you attach the front-panel connectors:

- **POWER LED**—Connect this to the Power LED header—pins 1, 2, and 3—where the blue (supply) wire is on pin 1.

- **H.D.D. LED**—Connect this to the hard drive LED header—pins 4 and 6—with the red wire (supply) on pin 4.

- **RESET SW**—Connect this to reset switch header—pins 8 and 10—in any orientation.

- **POWER SW**—Connect this to the power switch header—pins 9 and 11—in any orientation.
- **SPEAKER**—Connect this to the speaker header—pins 12 to 15—with the red wire (supply) on pin 12.

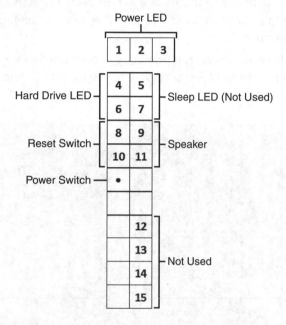

FIGURE 11.25

The pin assignments used on the motherboard's front-panel header.

Figure 11.26 shows the wires connected to the front-panel header on the motherboard.

Connecting the Case Fan Power Cables

At long last, the motherboard's connections are almost complete. Your final chore is to connect the power leads for the three case fans. For the Mozart case, the fans don't use motherboard connectors. Instead, they use standard 4-pin Molex connectors. Fortunately, the Neo HE 430 power supply comes with several 4-pin Molex connectors, so this won't be a problem.

Here are the steps to follow to attach the case fan leads:

1. Find a power supply cable that has three of the 4-pin Molex connectors.

2. Attach the cable's six-pin connector to the back of the power supply unit.

3. Attach one of the power cable's 4-pin Molex connectors to one of the rear fans. Note that each fan comes with both a male and a female connector. The power cable's Molex connector is male, so you must attach it to the fan's female connector.

4. Take the first fan (the fan you connected in step 3) and attach its male 4-pin Molex connector to the other rear fan's female 4-pin Molex connector.

5. Take the second fan (the fan you connected in step 4) and attach its male 4-pin Molex connector to the front fan's female 4-pin Molex connector.

FIGURE 11.26

Connect the front-panel wires to the motherboard's front-panel header.

Installing the 5.25-inch Drives

The next item on the build agenda is to install our two 5.25-inch drives. Ideally, we'd like to install the optical drive in the middle bay because the Mozart case has a slot in the drive bay door through which the drive tray can slide in and out. Unfortunately, that's not possible because if you try to insert the optical drive into the middle bay, it bumps up against the motherboard's 24-pin power connector.

So, instead, we need to install the optical drive in the top bay and the break-out box in the middle bay.

Installing the Optical Drive

Here are the steps to follow to install the LG Super Blue Multi optical drive:

1. Remove the four screws that hold the top drive bay cover in place. Keep the screws in a handy place.

2. On the front of the case, open the drive bay door.

3. Remove the drive bay cover by sliding it out of the bay toward the front of the case.

4. Touch something metal to ground yourself.

5. With the optical drive's connectors facing the inside of the case, slide the drive into the drive bay. Be sure to line up the drive's four front holes (two on each side) with the case holes that held the drive bay cover in place.

6. Attach the drive to the case using the screws from step 1. If you have four extra screws, you can use them to attach the back of the drive to the case using the drive's four rear holes.

7. Run a SATA cable from the optical drive's interface connection to one of the motherboard's SATA headers.

8. Take out one of the power supply's SATA power cables. Attach the 6-pin connector to the back of the power supply and attach a SATA connector to the optical drive's SATA power header.

Installing Sound Blaster Breakout Box

Follow these steps to install the breakout box:

1. Remove the four screws that hold the middle 5.25-inch external drive bay cover in place. Keep the screws in a handy place.

2. On the front of the case, open the drive bay door.

3. Remove the drive bay cover by sliding it out of the bay toward the front of the case.

4. Touch something metal to ground yourself.

5. With the breakout box's connectors facing back, slide the box into the drive bay. Be sure to line up the drive's four front holes (two on each side) with the case holes that held the drive bay cover in place.

6. Attach the box to the case using the screws from step 1. If you have four extra screws, you can use them to attach the back of the box to the case using the box's four rear holes.

7. Attach the power cable that came with the breakout box to the 4-pin connector on the back of the box's circuit board.

8. Attach a 4-pin Molex power cable from the power supply to the breakout box's power connector.

9. Take out the interface cable that came with the breakout box. Attach the cable to the header on the back of the box's circuit board. (The other end gets attached to a similar header on the sound card, which we'll get to a bit later.)

> **note** The Mozart case comes with an aluminum H bar that is at first attached to the back of the front panel's drive bay door. If we'd been able to place the optical drive in the middle bay, we could have used this bar to access the optical drive without opening the drive bay door. That's not the case, unfortunately, so you need to remove the H bar to allow the door to close properly now that the breakout box is installed.

FIGURE 11.27
The optical drive's interface and power connections.

Installing the Expansion Cards

The next task in the build is to insert three of the expansion cards:

- **TV tuner**—Install this card in the motherboard's PCI Express x4 slot.
- **Video card**—Install this card in the motherboard's PCI Express x16 slot.
- **Wireless networking card**—Install this card in the motherboard's second PCI slot (the one next to the PCIe x16 slot).

I won't go into all the details here because I gave you specific instructions on inserting an expansion card in Chapter 8.

→   See "Installing an Expansion Card," **p. 211**.

Here are the basic steps:

1. Touch something metal to ground yourself.
2. Push up and remove the slot cover that corresponds to the PCI Express x4 slot.
3. Insert the TV tuner card into the slot and attach it to the case with a screw.
4. Push up and remove the slot cover that corresponds to the PCI Express x16 slot.
5. Insert the video card into the slot and attach it to the case with a screw.
6. Push up and remove the slot cover that corresponds to the second PCI slot.
7. Insert the wireless networking card into the slot and attach it to the case with a screw.

Figure 11.28 shows the case with the three expansion cards installed.

Installing the Sound Card

Next, we need to install the Sound Blaster X-Fi Fatal1ty sound card. The sound card uses the motherboard's remaining PCI slot. I won't go into all the details here because I gave you specific instructions on inserting an expansion card in Chapter 8.

→   See "Installing an Expansion Card," **p. 211**.

FIGURE 11.28

The TV tuner card, video card, and wireless networking card installed.

Here are the basic steps:

1. Touch something metal to ground yourself.
2. Push up and remove the slot cover that corresponds to the first PCI slot.
3. Insert the sound card into the slot and attach it to the case with a screw.
4. Attach the breakout box interface cable to the header on the sound card. Figure 11.29 shows the sound card with the interface cable connected.

Installing the Hard Drive

Our final task is to install the hard drive. In the Mozart case, you use the primary 3.5-inch drive bay, which is under the longer of the two crossbars you removed from the case earlier.

FIGURE 11.29
The sound card with the breakout box interface cable attached.

Here are the steps to follow to install the hard drive:

1. Touch something metal to ground yourself.

2. Slide the hard drive into the bottom drive bay. Make sure the drive's headers are toward the back, and make sure the four holes in the sides of the drive are aligned with the four holes in the sides of the drive bay.

3. Attach the hard drive to the drive bay with four screws. Figure 11.30 shows the hard drive installed in the crossbar.

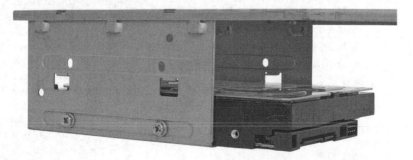

FIGURE 11.30
You install the hard drive using the drive bays attached to the longer of the two crossbars.

4. Reattach the cross bar to the case.

5. Run a SATA cable from the hard drive's interface connection to a SATA header on the motherboard.

6. Take out one of the power supply's SATA power cables. Attach the 6-pin connector to the back of the power supply and attach a SATA connector to the hard drive's SATA power header.

> **tip** You'll likely find that the hard drive's headers are a bit too close to the Sound Blaster audio card. You might need to use those right-angled connectors I mentioned earlier. Alternatively, consider switching the audio card and the wireless LAN card to give yourself more room.

Final Steps

Okay, your home theater PC is just about ready for the show to begin. Before the big moment, however, there are a few tasks you should perform and a few things you need to check. Here's the list:

- **Route and tie off the cables**—A well-built PC doesn't just have cables all over the place. Instead, the cables should be routed as far away from the motherboard as possible and as close to the sides of the case as possible. This makes the inside of the case look neater and improves airflow throughout the case. Use Velcro cable ties if need be to keep unruly cables out of the way.

- **Double-check connections**—Go through all the connections and make sure they're properly seated.

- **Double-check devices**—Check the optical drive, breakout box, hard drive, and expansion cards to ensure that they're not loose.

- **Look for loose screws**—Make sure there are no loose screws or other extraneous bits and pieces in the case.

> **note** Why not use the same SATA cable that we used earlier for the LG optical drive? Because the two SATA power connectors on each of the power supply's SATA power cables are fairly close together. However, our hard drive and the LG optical drive are quite far apart, so you can't use a single SATA power cable for both devices. Bummer. Still, it's probably a good idea to give the optical driver its own power rail to ensure it always gets a steady and smooth dose of power. Plus, if you decide to add a second hard drive to this system later, you'll have an extra SATA power connector standing by.

11

Powering Up

Now, at last, you're ready to fire up your new PC. Rather than just diving willy-nilly into the operating system install, however, there's a procedure I like to follow to ensure the BIOS, motherboard, and processor are all working in harmony. Follow these steps:

note Why didn't we reattach the smaller of the two crossbars? Because it no longer fits! The combined height of the CPU cooler and fan is almost as tall as the case itself. That's good because it means the processor's cooling system fits inside the case. The problem is that the crossbar that would normally sit over the processor has flaps on both sides that hang down about an inch, and these flaps bump up against the CPU fan.

1. Connect the monitor, keyboard, and mouse to the PC, and turn on the monitor.

2. Connect the power cable to a wall socket and then to the power supply unit.

3. If the PSU's switch is off (0), turn it on (1).

4. Press the power switch on the front of the case. Make sure the case fans and CPU fan are all working.

5. Press **Delete** to enter the motherboard's BIOS setup program, which is called the CMOS Setup Utility.

6. Make sure your devices are working properly by checking the following:

   ■ Select Standard CMOS Features, and then check that the date and time are correct, that your hard drive and optical drive appear, and that the Extended Memory is 2046MB.

   ■ Select Advanced BIOS Features, select First Boot Device, select CDROM, and press **Enter**. This ensures that the system boots from the optical drive so you can install your operating system.

   ■ Select PC Health Status and note the Current System Temperature. This value should always be well under 60°, and it's something you should check from time to time.

7. Press **F10** to save your changes and exit CMOS Setup Utility. The program asks you to confirm that you want to save changes.

8. Press **Y** and then press Enter.

9. Press the power switch to shut down the PC.

10. Replace the case's top panel.

11. Connect the computer to your network by running a network cable from the back panel's network port to your switch or router.

11

12. Press the power switch on the front of the case.

13. Open the optical drive and insert your operating system disc. (For my build, I installed Windows Vista Home Premium.) The computer will now boot from the disc and install the OS.

14. If you install Windows, be sure to update your version—particularly by installing all available security patches—immediately.

> **note** If you built your system with a video card and an audio card, you don't need to install the ATI Chipset driver (for the onboard graphics) or the Realtek High Definition Audio driver (for the onboard audio). You only need to install the Realtek LAN driver. Select the Click the Install Button to Install the Drivers Individually option, and then click Install in the Realtek LAN Driver section.

15. When the OS is installed and running, insert the motherboard's Gigabyte Utility CD for your OS—there's one disc for Vista and another for Windows XP and 2000 (see Figure 11.31). This contains all the drivers you need for the board's devices.

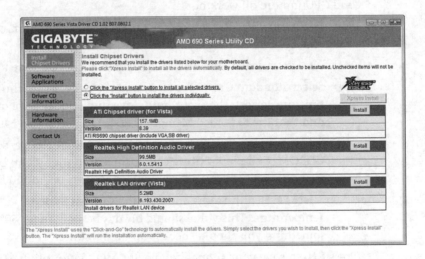

FIGURE 11.31
Run the Gigabyte Express Installer CD to complete the installation of the motherboard.

16. Update the motherboard's BIOS, as described in Chapter 17, "Maintaining Your Computer Hardware."

→ **See** "Updating the Motherboard BIOS," **p. 507**.

17. Use Device Manager to check for device problems (see Chapter 17) and install drivers for any device that Windows didn't recognize. For this build, you need to use the discs that came with the video card, sound card, TV tuner, and wireless LAN card to install the drivers for these devices.

➔   **See** "Updating Device Drivers," **p. 519**.

Final Thoughts

This was a pretty smooth build, although we did run into a few snags along the way:

- The LG optical drive wouldn't fit in the middle 5.25-inch drive bay because the motherboard's 24-pin power connector was in the way.

- The case's front drive bay door wouldn't close properly after the break-out box was installed because of the H bar attached to the back of the door. We needed to remove the H bar.

- The connectors for the hard drive are awfully close to the sound card, in most cases probably too close to install the hard drive cable properly. You probably found that you needed to switch the sound card and the wireless LAN card.

- The shorter of the two case crossbars wouldn't fit back on the case because its flaps bump into the CPU fan. We can easily live without it, though.

All told, the build took about six hours, *including* doing the photography that accompanies this chapter. Your build time should be shorter, but this was a longer build than normal because we had so many devices to install.

The initial boot went without a hitch, and the CMOS Setup Utility reported that all devices were present and accounted for. I had Vista Home Premium installed within 30 minutes, and another hour later I had the machine patched; the Gigabyte motherboard's drivers installed and its BIOS updated; and the drivers for the video card, sound card, TV tuner, and wireless LAN card installed.

I'm also happy to report that this system is *really* quiet. If you get up close to the machine, you can hear the CPU fan, but you don't hear much from the machine at all when you're 10 feet away, which is the typical home theater distance. Nice!

11

From Here

- For the details on installing memory, **see** "Installing Memory Modules," **p. 205**.

- To learn about installing cards, **see** "Installing an Expansion Card," **p. 211**.

- To learn how to use Device Manager to look for problem devices, **see** "Updating Device Drivers," **p. 519**.

- For instructions on updating the BIOS, **see** "Updating the Motherboard BIOS," **p. 507**.

- For the specifics on installing an AMD processor, **see** "Installing an AMD CPU in a Socket AM2 Board," **p. 219**.

11

Building a High-Performance PC

*Speed, it seems to me, provides the one
genuinely modern pleasure.*

—Aldous Huxley

an a computer be *too* fast? If you laughed when you read that question, I don't blame you one bit. After all, we've all spent the vast majority of our computing careers cursing at machines that are too *slow*. Wouldn't it be nice if, for once, our programs opened in just a few seconds instead of a few tens of seconds? Wouldn't it be great if our documents saved in the blink of an eye? Wouldn't it just make your day for windows to redraw without delay, for spreadsheets to recalculate lickety-split, and for database queries to not require grab-a-cup-of-coffee wait times?

Of course it would, and meeting all those everyday computing challenges is what this project is all about. Our goal here is to build a high-performance PC that will simply do everything faster, whether you're a wordsmith, a spreadsheet jockey, a database maven, or a graphics pro.

In this chapter I set out some design goals for the high-performance PC; then I take you through the parts I chose to meet those goals, from the computer case right down to the memory modules. Then, with the parts assembled, I show you step-by-step how to build your own high-performance PC.

Design Goals for a High-Performance PC

The biggest assumption I'm going to make when planning the high-performance PC is that you're a lot like me. I use my main computer a lot, and although I use it mostly for writing, I also use it for a wide variety of other activities, including website design, spreadsheet modeling, database management, processing photographs, ripping music CDs, and of course the usual day-to-day tasks involving email and the Web.

In short, there isn't one activity that requires a huge amount of computing horsepower. Instead, I want a fast PC because it will help me to perform *all* my daily tasks faster, which will make me more efficient and more productive. And because I'm almost always working on several things at once, I want a fast PC that will help me multitask easily and smoothly, so that I can always have everything I need open and available. So my design goals for this project are driven by this overarching idea of needing a system that does a wide variety of things very quickly, not one or two things extremely fast:

- **Don't break the bank**—When it comes to PC performance, the basic principle is simple: The more you pay, the faster things get. That's why the top processors cost over $1,000 and the top video cards cost over $300. So, it would be easy to put together a PC that uses nothing but the highest of the high-end components. Such a PC would positively scream, but then again so would you when your next credit card bill arrived! I don't have $4,000 or $5,000 to throw at a homebrew PC, and this build assumes you don't either. So my first goal is to keep costs in line. This won't be a cheap PC by any means (my budget is $2,000), but you can't get high-performance without spending at least a few dollars.

- **As fast as possible**—This project is all about speed, of course, so my second goal for this build is a PC that's as fast as possible given the constraints of a not-unlimited budget. This means I'll look for places to save money (for example, integrated Gigabit Ethernet) and spend those savings on more important components (particularly the motherboard and hard drive). I'll look for components that are wickedly fast, but that are a notch or two below the top end, so they don't cost an arm and a leg (see my choice of CPU, for example).

- **Keep it simple**—Your average dragster isn't loaded down with extra components, so your high-performance PC shouldn't be, either. So my third goal here is to build a machine that has only the minimum components required for average daily computer use. Unlike the home theater PC we built in the previous chapter, our high-performance PC won't be stocked with relatively exotic components such as TV tuner and sound card breakout box. We're keepin' it simple on this build.

- **Room to expand**—Having said all that, who know what "average daily computer use" might mean six months from now? So my final goal here is to end up with a system that has lots of room to expand whenever the need might arise.

Choosing Parts for the High-Performance PC

With these design goals rattling around in our heads, it's time to break out the brass tacks and start choosing components to match those goals. The next few sections take you through the components we'll use to put together our high-performance machine.

Selecting a Case for the High-Performance PC

There's something very attractive about small computers: they are portable, can fit into small spaces, and often just have a certain cuteness about them. Unfortunately, building a computer using a small case can often be problematic because the interior can get crowded in a hurry. So purely from a system builder's perspective, there's nothing like the luxurious spaciousness you get in a full tower case. And, too, there's something appropriate about matching big performance with a big case. Besides size, our ideal case should have good airflow so we don't have to worry about heat problems, lots of front connectors for easy access, and a tool-free design to make the build easier.

For this build, I chose the CoolerMaster Cosmos case, a full-tower case I consider to be the Cadillac of big cases. Notice I said "Cadillac" and not, say, Ferrari or Lamborghini. That is, you can easily pay $400, $500, and even more (a lot more) for a case, but the Cosmos can be yours for less than $200. That's still a lot for a case, in my book, but believe me the Cosmos is

note The next few sections discuss specific parts for this build, but there's no reason you have to use the same components in your build. Feel free to tweak the parts based on your own budget and computing needs.

12

worth every penny. For starters, the darn thing is just so nice to look at, with its brushed steel finish, reflective black bezel door, and the unique touch of a couple of curvy handles up top (see Figure 12.1).

FIGURE 12.1

The CoolerMaster Cosmos: the case for our high-performance PC.

Besides its good looks, the Cosmos case is plenty functional, too. Here's a summary of the major features:

- Four (count 'em) USB ports, one FireWire port, one eSATA port (very nice!), one microphone connector, and one Line Out connector on the top of the case, near the front. This is my preferred location for these external ports because that's where they're most easily accessed.

- Loads of drive bays: one 3.5-inch external (for a memory card reader or floppy drive), four 5.25-inch external (for optical or tape drives), and six 3.5-inch internal (for hard drives).

- Super-easy side panel access: You lift a latch on the back of the case, the side panel slides open at the top, and you just lift it off. Very slick.

- Both side panels are lined with foam rubber that should act as excellent sound insulation.

12

- The expansion slots are blissfully tool-free: a thumb screw holds each slot cover in place.

- The external drive bays are very easy to work with. They have a simple mechanism that automatically locks each 5.25-inch drive into place as you insert it. (3.5-inch devices must be attached to a bracket.) To release a drive, you just push a button. It's almost *too* easy!

- Each hard drive bay is side-mounted for easy access and has its own bracket that attaches using a thumb screw and slides in and out of the bay. You use special screws to attach the hard drive to the bracket. In a nice touch, the drive rests on silicone grommets, not metal, which reduces noise.

- Four (!) 120mm fans: an intake fan on the bottom of the case, two exhaust fans on the top of the case, and a third exhaust fan in the back of the case. Airflow is not going to be a problem with this case! Fortunately, each of the fans puts out just 17dBA at 1,200 RPM, so they won't make tons of noise.

- The case doesn't include an air duct for the video card exhaust fan, but it does include a plastic VGA vent, which serves to draw cool air from the intake fan to the video card area.

- A bottom-mounted power supply bay. This location makes it easier to keep the CPU cool (because in most cases the PSU sits just above the CPU), but it also means a long stretch to the motherboard's 12V power header, which will sit near the top of the case.

- A couple of dust filters, one at the front and one under the power supply bay.

12

Choosing a Motherboard for the High-Performance PC

For our high-performance PC's motherboard, we want a top-notch product that will give us excellent performance and reduce overall build costs by including features that save us purchasing extra parts.

My choice for this build is the ASUS P5K3 Deluxe, an ATX board that's available online for about $220 (see Figure 12.2).

FIGURE 12.2

The ASUS P5K3 Deluxe: the high-performance PC's motherboard.

The ASUS P5K3 Deluxe offers the following features:

- Support for a wide variety of Intel processors, including the Intel Core 2 Extreme, Intel Core 2 Quad, Intel Core 2 Duo, Intel Pentium Extreme Edition, Intel Pentium 4 Extreme Edition, Intel Pentium D, and Intel Pentium 4

- A front side bus that supports 1333MHz, 1066MHz, and 800MHz

- Support for dual-channel DDR3 1333, 1066, or 800 memory modules (up to 8GB)

- Two PCI Express x16 slots (which support ATI's Crossfire multi-GPU technology), two PCI Express x1 slots, and three PCI slots

- Six external USB ports, one external IEEE-1394 port, and two external eSATA ports

- Six internal SATA connectors

- Integrated 10/100/1000 network adapter

- Integrated 802.11g wireless network adapter

- Integrated Dolby 7.1 audio, plus coaxial and optical S/PDIF audio ports

- Large heat pipes to keep the Northbridge and Southbridge chipsets cool

> **note** One quirk of the P5K3 is that its rear panel connectors don't include a PS/2 port for a mouse! So you need to use a USB mouse with this build.

12

Selecting a Power Supply for the High-Performance PC

We have two main concerns when it comes to the power supply for our high-performance PC: power (duh) and cable management. On the power front, although we won't be loading this PC with tons of devices, we will be using a couple of video cards, an optical drive, and a memory card reader. Plus, we want to reserve the option to expand later. Therefore, we need a power supply with lots of watts to spare. I also prefer power supplies that use modular cables, which will enable us to use only the cables we need. This will keep things neat and tidy inside the Cosmos case and greatly improve airflow.

My choice for this build is the Neo HE 500, a modular PSU that can handle up to 500W, which is more than enough power for our needs (see Figure 12.3). It sells online for about $90. (As an added bonus, the NEO HE 500 is nice and quiet, with a noise level of a mere 19dBA with the fan running at 1,000RPM.)

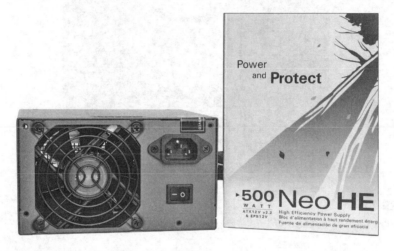

FIGURE 12.3

The Antec Neo HE 500: the high-performance PC's power supply.

Picking Out a CPU for the High-Performance PC

Choosing a processor for the high-performance PC is when we really need to keep our eye on the budget. We need an Intel CPU for our motherboard, but with Intel's high-end CPUs hovering around $1,000, going for broke here would have two meanings. Fortunately, there's a lot of performance out there if you're willing to climb down a notch or three from the CPU nosebleed section.

In other words, we're trying to maximize the bang-for-the-buck ratio, and for my money (literally, in this case) you need look no further than the Intel Core 2 Quad Q6600 (see Figure 12.4)—a four-core processor with a clock speed of 2.4GHz, an 8MB L2 cache, and support for the 1,066MHz bus. You can find the retail version for around $280. However, we'll be using a third-party CPU cooler in this build, so I chose the OEM version of the Q6600, which brought the price down to $255.

FIGURE 12.4

The Intel Core 2 Quad Q6600: the high-performance PC's processor.

The Cosmos case requires a unique processor cooling solution because the case has no CPU duct to take the air blown from the cooler's fan. If you put the stock Intel cooler on the processor, it would just blow the air into the solid steel side of the case, which doesn't do much good. However, the case's exhaust fans are nicely positioned to give us a hand here:

- The rear exhaust fan is right beside the I/O slots.
- The two top exhaust fans are right above the motherboard with nothing between the board and the fans. (In this case, the power supply is mounted on the bottom.)

So, we need a cooler with a fan that will send its air toward either the rear exhaust fan or the top exhaust fans. In other words, the cooler fan must send its air *parallel* to the motherboard, rather than straight up from the processor. The perfect solution here is the Thermaltake CL-P0401, shown in Figure 12.5. The fan sits between the cooling fins and therefore blows air off to the side. It's also quiet and adds a mere $60 to the cost of the build.

caution Remember that using a third-party CPU cooler voids the processor's warranty.

FIGURE 12.5

The Thermaltake CL-P0401: the high-performance PC's CPU cooler.

12

How Much Memory Does the High-Performance PC Need?

Memory is one of the most important performance factors in any PC, which means, simply, that the more memory you add to any system, the better that system will perform. Happily, we live in a world where the enhanced perform-ance of extra RAM can be had for a relative pittance, with 1GB memory mod-ules selling online for $25–$50.

Of course, I went and ignored all that by choosing a motherboard that requires DDR3 memory modules, which is a much more expensive proposi-tion. Why go the DDR3 route? First, on its own DDR3 usually (although not always) has a slight performance edge on DDR2. (DDR3's relatively slow laten-cies hamper its overall performance.) What tipped the scale for me was our motherboard's support for Super Memspeed, an ASUS technology that really cranks up DDR3 and gives it a decided performance edge over DDR2.

So, how much memory do we need? You might think I'm going to fill up the board's memory modules, but that's not the case. First, remember from Chapter 3, "The Work Area: Memory," that 32-bit Windows won't let you use much more than 3GB of RAM no matter how much is installed.

> **See** "Windows and RAM: The 4GB Conundrum," **p. 73**.

caution One of the P5K3's memory sockets is *really* close to the heat pipes that circle the CPU socket area. We won't be using that memory socket in this build, but if you decide to use four memory modules on this board, be sure to get modules that don't have a wide heat spreader. A fat spreader would end up touching or being blocked by the heat pipes.

Okay, so we install three 1GB sticks of DDR3 RAM. Well, unfortunately, this is also problematic because of a quirk of the motherboard: Whichever of the two memory channels has the least amount of memory determines the overall size of the memory bus. For example, if you use just two 1GB modules in a dual-channel configuration, you get a 2GB bus size. However, if you add a third 1GB module in the other channel, the board reduces the memory bus size to 1GB.

So, 4GB doesn't work because the extra 1GB is wasted, and 3GB doesn't work because it means reducing the memory bus to 1GB, which defeats the purpose of a dual-channel configuration.

Therefore, somewhat surprisingly, our high-performance PC will have just 2GB of DDR3 memory. I've seen reports online that DDR3-1333 modules perform poorly on the P5K3 board, so I opted for two 1GB sticks of DDR3-1066 (PC3 8500) RAM from OCZ, which sell as a package for about $240 (see Figure 12.6).

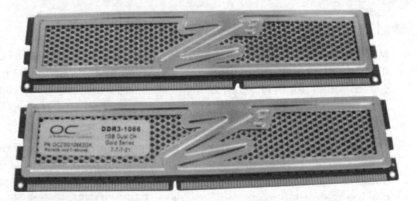

FIGURE 12.6

The high-performance PC's memory: a couple of 1GB PC3 8500 modules from OCZ.

Storage Options for the High-Performance PC

We want our high-performance PC's hard drive to be blazing fast. I briefly considered getting the Western Digital Raptor WD1500, a 10,000 RPM drive that's currently the speed champ (outside of the world of SCSI hard drives). However, the

tip One way to make an incredibly fast hard drive is to combine two Raptors in a RAID 0 array. I don't do that in this build, but I do in Chapter 13, "Building a Killer Gaming PC."

Raptor's relatively small capacity of 150GB just isn't large enough for my needs right now, much less into the future.

The hard drive that's currently generating all the buzz is the Barracuda 7200.11, Seagate's entry into the 1TB club. The reviews of this drive have uniformly said the same thing: this is the fastest 7,200 RPM drive available, hands down. And, heck, I just love the idea of a machine with a terabyte of storage on a single drive! So, the Barracuda 7200.11 will be the high-performance PC's hard drive (see Figure 12.7). You can find one online for about $270, a mere 27¢ per gigabyte!

FIGURE 12.7

The high-performance PC's hard drive: the Seagate Barracuda 7200.11 1TB SATA drive.

We want our high-performance PC to have a high-performance optical drive, too. My choice is the Samsung SH-S203B, a dual-layer DVD/CD rewritable drive that uses the blazingly fast SATA interface (see Figure 12.8). It supports write speeds of 20x DVD±R, 12x DVD±R DL, 8x DVD+RW, 6x DVD-RW, 48x CD-R, 32x CD-RW, plus read speeds of 16x DVD-ROM and 48x CD-ROM, all for a very reasonable price of about $40.

For day-to-day computing these days, you really need a memory card reader, particularly one that supports all the major formats. For this build I chose the AFT Pro-28U, a $35 internal/external reader that supports 28 formats (see Figure 12.9).

note The memory card reader requires an internal USB connection. However, the P5K3 motherboard offers only two USB headers, and we're going to use them both for the Cosmos case's four front-panel USB connectors. Therefore, I'm going to add a USB 2.0 PCI card to this build. I chose a Bytecc card that offers four external ports and one internal port, which is the one the memory card reader will use.

FIGURE 12.8
The high-performance PC's optical drive: the Samsung SH-S203B.

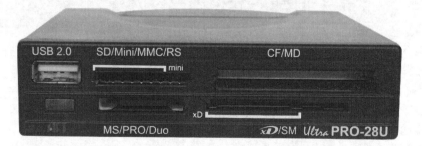

FIGURE 12.9
The high-performance PC's memory card reader: the AFT Pro-28U.

Determining the Video Needs of the High-Performance PC

Is video important for our high-performance PC? On the one hand, the answer depends on what you do with your computer. If you're a graphics pro or want to watch high-def content on your machine, then you need some solid video components. If you just write memos and emails and surf the Web all day, then something more basic might be in order.

On the other hand, the video component of a PC isn't determined solely in terms of the video performance. Many power users now regularly use at least two monitors because it's convenient to have your work on one screen and something else (such as your email) on another. To support a dual-monitor setup, you either need two video cards, or a single video card that has dual-monitor support built in. I prefer the latter, and plenty of cards out there offer multiple-monitor support.

That's all good, but for this build I want to take things up a notch. I normally use two monitors with my office PC, but I have a third monitor on my desk, which normally gets used with my testing machines. This means the monitor is often idle, so why not put it to work the rest of the time? How? By giving my main computer a *third* monitor. Nice!

Okay, so just how do you go about doing that? By adding a second video card to the system and linking them together using a multi-GPU technology such as SLI or Crossfire. The latter is what the ASUS motherboard supports, so that's the way I'm going to go with this build. I chose the HIS Radeon HD 2600 XT, a PCI Express x16 card that offers 256MB of DDR4 graphics memory, two DVI ports (as well as DVI-to-VGA and DVI-to-HDMI adapters), and an S-Video port. The card runs about $140, which isn't too bad. Figure 12.10 shows the two cards I'll be using for this build.

Selecting Audio Equipment for the High-Performance PC

Unless you're a sound pro of some description, audio isn't a major factor in your high-performance PC, mostly because few day-to-day applications require audio that's more sophisticated than what's integrated into the motherboard. Most boards come with the Realtek audio chip integrated, and that chip produces only so-so sound. As an added bonus for this build, the ASUS P5K3 board comes with a high-definition, 7.1-channel audio chip made by Analog Devices that produces sound that's as good as it gets on the integrated front.

FIGURE 12.10

The high-performance PC's video system: two HIS Radeon HD 2600 XT cards.

Choosing Networking Hardware for the High-Performance PC

Any high-performance PC must network, of course, and these days networking is easier than ever because it's a rare motherboard that doesn't come with a networking adapter built in. Even better, almost all motherboard-based network interface cards (NICs) support Ethernet (10Mbps), Fast Ethernet (100Mbps), and Gigabit Ethernet (1Gbps or 1,000Mbps), so you're covered no matter which type of network you'll be connecting to. Our high-performance PC is no exception because our ASUS motherboard has a 10/100/1000 NIC onboard.

Even better, the motherboard also comes with an integrated wireless NIC, which supports 802.11g. Support for 802.11n (Draft 2.0) would have been nice, but we'll just put that on the list of things to add to the machine down the road.

The bottom line: no extra networking equipment is needed for this build.

Pricing the High-Performance PC

For this build, I tried as best as I could to balance price and performance. It's not always easy, and tradeoffs sometimes have to be made, but overall I think we've got a good thing going here. Table 12.1 summarizes the high-performance PC's components and prices. As you can see, our total price of $1,700 is well under my $2,000 budget, so that's a good thing.

Table 12.1	Components and Prices for the High-Performance PC	
Component	**Model**	**Average Price**
Case	CoolerMaster Cosmos	$190
Motherboard	ASUS P5K3 Deluxe	$220
Power supply	Antec Neo HE 500	$90
CPU	Intel Core 2 Quad Q6600	$255
CPU cooler	Thermaltake CL-P0401	$60
Memory	OCZ DDR-1066 PC3 8500 1GB (×2)	$250
Hard drive	Seagate Barracuda 7200.11 1TB SATA	$270
Optical drive	Samsung SH-S203B DVD/CD Rewritable Drive	$40
Card reader	AFT Pro-28U	$35
USB 2.0 card	Bytecc 5-port USB 2.0 PCI Card	$10
Video card	HIS Radeon HD 2600 XT (×2)	$280
Audio card	Motherboard integrated	N/A
Network card	Motherboard integrated	N/A
TOTAL		**$1,700**

Putting Together the High-Performance PC

I don't know about you, but I'm really excited about this build! We've got a really solid collection of parts (see Figure 12.11), and I think the result is going to be one mean computing machine. And the good news is that by keeping the machine relatively simple at this point, we have fewer components to install. Add the ease of use and spaciousness of the Cosmos case, and I'm expecting a fairly quick build (you can easily build this PC in an afternoon or evening). The rest of this chapter takes you through the steps you need to follow.

FIGURE 12.11

The high-performance PC, ready to be built.

Getting the Case Ready

The Cosmos case requires a bit of prep work before we can move on to more productive tasks:

- **Remove the two side panels**—You need both panels off for this build. In each case, you release the panel by flipping up a plastic latch on the back of the case. Tilt the panel back a bit from the case, and then lift it off.

- **Remove the VGA vent**—This is the large plastic crossbar that runs from the hard drive bays to the back of the case. Press the latch on the left side of the vent, and then pivot the vent out of the case.

- **Remove the generic I/O shield**—As you see in the next section, when test-fitting the motherboard in the case to determine where to put the standoffs, it helps if the I/O shield isn't in the way. Gently push the edges of the I/O shield back into the case until it's loose and you can remove it.

Installing the Motherboard Standoffs

A standoff (or a *mount point*, as it's often called) is a hex-nut screw, which means it actually consist of two parts: a bottom screw that enables you to insert the stand-off into a hole in the side of the case and a top hex nut into which you can insert a

screw. The idea is that you install from eight to ten (depending on the motherboard form factor) of these standoffs into the case, sit the motherboard on top of the standoffs, align the motherboard's holes with the hex nuts, and then attach the motherboard. This gives the board a solid footing but also separates the board from the metal case to prevent shorting out the board.

Installing the standoffs is easiest when the motherboard is bare, so that should be your first task:

1. Find the standoffs that came with the case and put them aside.

2. Lay the case flat on its side, with the open side facing up.

3. Move all the case cables out of the way so you can clearly see the side panel that has the mounting holes.

4. Remove the piece of paper that covers the mounting panel.

5. If you haven't done so already, touch something metal to ground yourself.

6. Take the motherboard out of its antistatic bag and lay the board inside the case, oriented so the board's back-panel I/O ports are lined up and flush with the case's I/O slot.

7. Note which case holes correspond to the holes in the motherboard (see Figure 12.12). You might need to use a flashlight to ensure that there's a case hole under each motherboard hole.

8. Place the motherboard carefully aside.

9. Screw the standoffs into the corresponding holes in the side of the case.

Just to be safe, you might want to place the motherboard into the case again to double-check that each motherboard hole corresponds to a standoff.

12

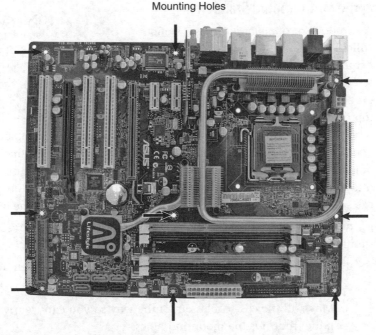

Mounting Holes

FIGURE 12.12

The motherboard has nine holes through which you attach the board to the standoffs.

Getting the Motherboard Ready for Action

Although you might be tempted to install the motherboard right away—and technically you can do that—it's better to hold off for a bit and do some of the work on the board while it's out of the case. We'll be installing the processor and the memory modules, and although it isn't impossible to install these parts with the board inside the case, it's a lot easier outside.

Before getting started, be sure to touch something metal to ground yourself. Now take the motherboard and lay it flat on your work surface. For the ASUS P5K3, it's best to orient the board so the I/O ports are facing away from you. This enables you to work with the processor socket without having to go over the heatsinks or the I/O ports.

Inserting the Processor

Begin by inserting the Intel Q6600 processor in the motherboard's LGA775 socket. I won't go into the details here because I showed you how to insert Intel processors back in Chapter 8.

→ **See** "Installing an Intel CPU in a Socket 775 Board," **p. 216**.

Inserting the Memory Modules

With your processor all snug and cozy, it's time to populate your board with your memory modules. Where you install the modules on the ASUS P5K3 board depends on how many modules you're adding (see Figure 12.13):

■ **One module**—Install the module in either socket A2 or in socket B2 (the black sockets).

■ **Two modules**—Install identical modules in sockets A2 and B2 (the black sockets). This ensures a proper dual-channel configuration.

■ **Three modules**—Install a set of identical modules in sockets A2 and B2 (the black sockets) and the third module in either socket A1 or socket B1. As I mentioned before, I don't recommend this configuration because the size of the memory channel is determined by the third memory stick. For example, if you have two 1GB modules A2 and B2 and a 1GB module in A1 or B1, the memory bandwidth will be only 1GB.

■ **Four modules**—Install one set of identical modules in sockets A2 and B2 (the black sockets), and install a second set of identical modules in sockets A1 and B1 (the orange sockets). This ensures a proper dual-channel configuration.

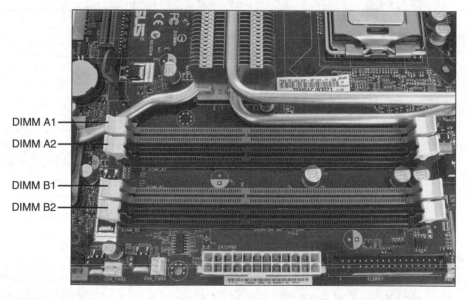

DIMM A1
DIMM A2
DIMM B1
DIMM B2

FIGURE 12.13

The memory module sockets on the ASUS P5K3.

I won't go through the installation steps here because I already covered how to install memory modules in Chapter 8, "Basic Skills for PC Building and Upgrading." Figure 12.14 shows our motherboard with our two 1GB modules installed.

➔   **See** "Installing Memory Modules," **p. 205**.

FIGURE 12.14
Our motherboard with two 1GB memory modules in place.

Installing the Motherboard

With your motherboard populated with a processor and memory, it's just about ready to roll. The next few sections take you through the detailed installation steps for the motherboard. This is the most finicky, most time-consuming, and most important part of the build. As you'll see, getting a motherboard configured involves a lot of separate steps and a lot of cable connections. It's crucial to take your time and make sure you have all the connections just so.

Inserting the Motherboard I/O Shield

Earlier you removed the case's generic I/O shield, so now it's time to insert the I/O shield that came with the motherboard. Take the motherboard's I/O shield and fit it into the case's I/O opening. Be sure you have the I/O shield oriented properly:

- The hole for the keyboard PS/2 port should be at the top, while the six audio ports and the hole for the wireless NIC's antenna post should be at the bottom.

- The protruding ridge that runs around the I/O shield should face the back of the case.

When the I/O shield is flush with the case, firmly press the bottom of the shield until it snaps into place; then press the top of the shield until it, too, snaps into place.

tip It's not always easy to get the I/O shield perfectly seated. If you have trouble getting a corner of the shield to snap into place, use the end of a plastic screwdriver handle to gently tap the recalcitrant corner into place.

caution On the I/O shield, the two openings for the motherboard's network ports each have two small prongs that extend down from the top of the opening. Be sure to bend these prongs back so they're parallel with the motherboard.

Attaching the Motherboard to the Case

With the custom I/O shield in place, you're now ready to install the motherboard inside the case. Here are the steps to follow:

1. Move all the case cables out of the way so you can clearly see the side panel that has the mounting holes and the installed standoffs.

2. If you haven't done so already, touch something metal to ground yourself.

3. Gently and carefully maneuver the motherboard into the case and lay it on top of the standoffs.

4. Adjust the position of the board so the board's back-panel I/O ports are lined up and flush with the openings in the I/O shield, as shown in Figure 12.15.

5. You should now see a standoff under each motherboard mounting hole. If not, it likely means the I/O shield isn't fully seated. Remove the board, fix the I/O shield, and then try again.

note Bear in mind, however, that it's normal for the board's mounting holes to be slightly offset from the standoffs. There's a bit of give to the I/O shield, so you usually have to force the board slightly to the left (toward the I/O shield) to get the holes and standoffs to line up perfectly.

12

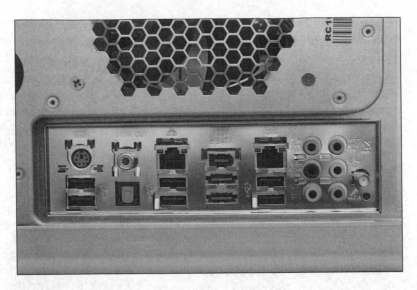

FIGURE 12.15

Make sure the motherboard's I/O ports are lined up and flush with the I/O shield's openings.

6. Use the mounting screws supplied with the case to attach the board to each standoff. To ensure a trouble-free installation, I use the following technique:

- First, insert but don't tighten the upper-right screw.

- Next, insert but don't tighten the bottom-left screw. (The bottom-left screw is often the hardest one to install because it's usually in the corner of the case. If you prefer to start with an easier target, insert the bottom middle screw, instead.)

- Make sure all the holes and standoffs are properly aligned, and then tighten the first two screws.

- Insert and tighten the rest of the screws.

Installing the Power Supply

Okay, now let's get the power supply onboard:

1. Orient the power supply unit so the back (the side with the power cable connector, on/off switch, and fan) is toward the back of the case, with the power cable connector and on/off switch on the left (as you face the back of the case).

2. Maneuver the power supply into the power supply bay on the bottom of the case.

3. Make sure the power supply is flush with the back of the case.

4. Attach the unit to the case with four screws, as shown in Figure 12.16.

Insert mounting screws here.

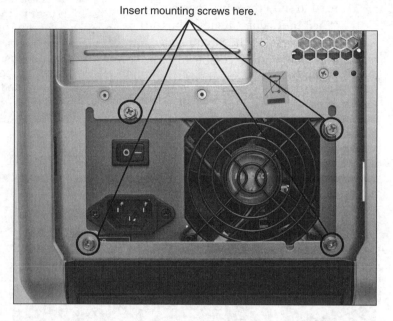

FIGURE 11.16

Use four screws to attach the power supply unit to the case as shown here.

Connecting the Motherboard Power Cables

Our next order of business is to connect the power cables that supply juice to the motherboard. Our ASUS board has two power headers:

- A 24-pin main power header, into which you plug the power supply's 24-pin connector, as pointed out in Figure 12.17.

tip Most of the pins on a power cable connector are square, but a few are rounded on one side. These rounded pins have corresponding rounded holes on the header. To install a power cable connector with the correct orientation, match up the rounded pins with the rounded holes.

12

■ An 8-pin 12V header. Our power
supply actually has two separate
4-pin 12V connectors, so you first
need to snap these two together.
When that's done, remove the cap
that covers half the 8-pin header
and then plug the combined connector into the motherboard, as
shown in Figure 12.17.

note As I proceeded in the
build, I noticed the
12V rail was constantly in the way.
The problem is that the power
supply is a long way from the 12V
header, so the 12V rail just barely
reached. To avoid constantly moving the 12V rail, I disconnected it
and then reconnected it at the
end of the build.

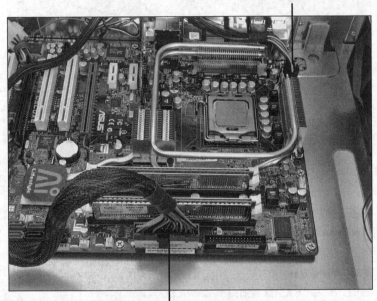

8-Pin 12V Connection

24-Pin Main Connection

FIGURE 12.17

*Connect the power supply's 24-pin and 8-pin connectors to the corresponding headers on the
motherboard.*

Installing the CPU Cooler

Now that the mobo's safely and securely attached to the case, it's a good time
to add the CPU cooler to the processor. Here are the steps to follow to install
the Thermaltake cooler:

1. Our motherboard uses an LGA775 CPU socket, so find the cooler's two pairs of LGA775 push-pin brackets and use the screws provided to attach to the bottom of the cooler.

2. Apply a thin, even layer of thermal compound to the cooler's heatsink. (Place a bead of thermal compound about the size of a BB in the middle of the heatsink, and then use a piece of plastic or stiff cardboard to spread the compound so that it covers the entire heatsink.)

3. Orient the CPU cooler so the back (the side where the wires come out) is facing the top of the case. (The back is the direction the air will flow, so we need to direct that air toward the case's top exhaust fans. Alternatively, you could also orient the back toward the case's rear exhaust fan.)

4. Position the cooler's four push-pin fasteners over the four holes that surround the motherboard's CPU socket, as shown in Figure 12.18.

Push-Pin Fasteners

FIGURE 12.18

Place the cooler's fasteners over the four holes that surround the CPU socket.

5. As you hold the cooler in place, push down on each fastener until it clicks into place. For the smoothest installation, follow a diagonal pattern and press down two fasteners at a time. For example, first push

down the bottom-right and upper-left fasteners at the same time; then push down the bottom-left and upper-right fasteners at the same time.

6. Connect the fan's power cable to the motherboard's CPU fan header, as shown in Figure 12.19. (The fan uses a 3-pin connector, but it fits the motherboard's 4-pin fan header.)

CPU fan header is located here.

FIGURE 12.19

Connect the CPU cooler's power cable to the motherboard's CPU fan header.

Connecting the Front-Panel IEEE-1394 and USB Cables

Our Cosmos case offers the convenience of a front-panel IEEE-1394 (FireWire) port. For this port to work, you must connect its cable (the connector is labeled 1394) to one of the motherboard's internal IEEE-1394 headers, as shown in Figure 12.20.

The case also offers a whopping *four* front-panel USB 2.0 ports. You need to connect the USB 2.0 ports' two cables (on both the connector is labeled USB) to the motherboard's two internal USB headers, as shown in Figure 12.20.

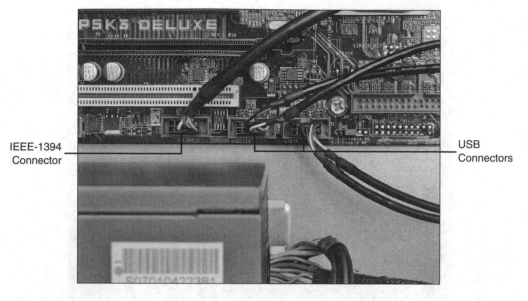

FIGURE 12.20
Connect the cable that runs from the IEEE-1394 front-panel port to a IEEE-1394 header and the cables that run from the USB 2.0 front-panel ports to the USB headers.

Connecting the Front-Panel eSATA Cable

One nice perk we get with the Cosmos case is a front-panel eSATA port, which will be convenient for connecting an external SATA drive for backups or whatever. For this port to work, you must connect its red SATA cable to one of the motherboard's black SATA headers, as shown in Figure 12.21.

note Why a black SATA header and not one of the red ones? The ASUS board reserves the red SATA headers for boot devices, so unless you think you might want to boot from an external SATA drive, you should use a black SATA header for the eSATA port.

Connecting the Front-Panel Audio Cables

The rest of the Cosmos case's front-panel ports consist of Line Out (audio output) and Mic In (microphone input) audio ports. Note that the audio ports' cable has two connectors, one for standard audio (labeled AC '97) and one for high-definition audio (labeled HD AUDIO). Our Gigabyte motherboard supports HD audio, so you need to connect the HD AUDIO connector to the motherboard's audio header (labeled AAFP), as shown in Figure 12.22.

FIGURE 12.21

Connect the cable that runs from the eSATA front-panel port to a black SATA header on the motherboard.

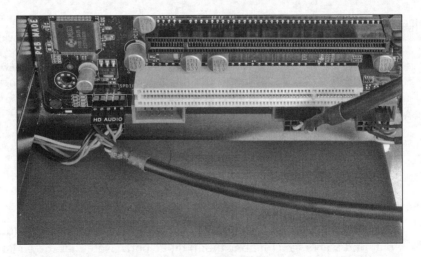

FIGURE 12.22

Connect the cable that runs from the front-panel audio ports to the Audio header on the motherboard.

Connecting the Power Switch, Reset Switch, and LEDs

The next item on our build to-do list is to tackle the rest of the wires snaking out from the case's front panel. These wires correspond to the following front-panel features:

- **Power switch**—This is the button you press to turn the system on and off. Its lead consists of two wires, one white and one blue, and the connector is labeled POWER SW.

- **Reset switch**—This is the button you press to reboot a running system. Its lead consists of two gray wires, and the connector is labeled RESET SW.

- **Power LED**—This LED lights up when the system is powered up. It consists of two wires with a single connector: the white wire is the negative (ground) lead, and the green wire is the positive (signal) lead; the connector is labeled POWER LED.

- **Hard drive LED**—This LED lights up when the hard drive is active. It consists of two wires with a single connector: the white wire is the negative (ground) lead, and the gray wire is the positive (signal) lead; the connector is labeled H.D.D. LED.

Connecting all these wires is a bit tricky, but the good news is that you won't destroy anything if you get the connections wrong the first time around. For one thing, the connectors for both the power switch and the reset switch can be attached in either orientation (they'll work fine either way); for another, if you get the LED connectors backward, it just means the LEDs won't work.

For the connections themselves, you use the motherboard's front-panel header, a collection of seven pins beside the USB headers. Figure 12.23 shows the pin assignments. (Note that the pins numbers are ones I made up myself; they don't correspond to actual pin numbers used on the board.).

Given the pin assignments shown in Figure 12.23, here's how you connect the front-panel wires:

- **Power switch**—Connect this to pins 3 and 4 in any orientation.

- **Reset switch**—Connect this to pins 5 and 6 in any orientation.

- **Hard drive LED**—Connect this to pins 1 and 2, with the white wire on pin 2 (ground) and the gray wire on pin 1 (signal).

note Having a two-pin case connector and a three-pin motherboard connector for the power LED is becoming increasingly common. One solution is to buy a three-pin female to two-pin male power LED adapter. You can buy one (it's just $2.99) from Directron.com: www.directron.com/3pinled.html.

12

■ **Power LED**—Here we hit a bit of a snag. The case power LED wire uses a single two-pin connector, but the motherboard expects a three-pin connector (where the middle "pin" isn't used). So, unfortunately, we can't connect the power LED wire.

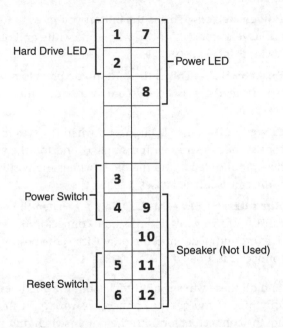

FIGURE 12.23

The pin assignments used on the motherboard's front panel header.

Figure 12.24 shows the wires connected to the front-panel header on the motherboard.

Connecting the Case Fan Power Cables

At long last, the motherboard's connections are almost complete. Your final chore is to connect the power leads for the four case fans to the motherboard's case fan headers. First, disconnect the 4-pin Molex adapters that are connected to each fan lead. We want to connect the fans directly to the motherboard, not to the power supply. With the motherboard connections, we can monitor fan speed using the system BIOS program.

FIGURE 12.24

Connect the front-panel wires to the motherboard's front-panel header.

Here's what you do:

- **Rear fan**—Connect this fan's power lead to the header labeled CHA_FAN1, which is located behind the rear-panel audio connectors.

- **Bottom fan**—Connect this fan's power lead to the header labeled CHA_FAN4, which is located on the front side of the board (that is, the side of the board opposite the rear-panel connectors), just above the headers for the power and reset switches.

- **Top fans**—Connect these fans' power leads to the headers labeled CHA_FAN2 and CHA_FAN3, which are located on the front side of the board, just above the SATA headers.

Figure 12.25 shows the connections.

12

Case Fan Headers

FIGURE 12.25

Remove the Molex adapters and then connect all four fans to the motherboard.

Installing the Hard Drive

The Cosmos case offers six internal hard drive bays, each of which has a metal bracket that slides in and out of the bay. You remove the brackets, attach the hard drive, and then reinsert the bracket.

Here are the steps to follow to install a hard drive:

1. Remove the thumb screw from the hard drive bay you want to use.

2. Pull the bracket out of the drive bay.

3. Lay the hard drive inside the bracket as follows:

   - The interface and power connectors should face toward the back (open) end of the bracket.

   - The hard drive label should be facing up (that is, the underside of the hard drive—the side where the circuit board appears—should sit on the rubber grommets inside the bracket).

tip In the collection of screws that come with the Cosmos case, you'll find some flat-topped screws that are designed for connecting the hard drive to the bracket. The flat tops ensure the screws won't get in the way when you insert the bracket back into the drive bay. You can see the screws (the tops, anyway) in Figure 12.26.

4. Align the four holes on the underside of the hard drive with the four holes on the bracket, and then use screws to attach the hard drive to the bracket. Figure 12.26 shows the hard drive attached to the bracket.

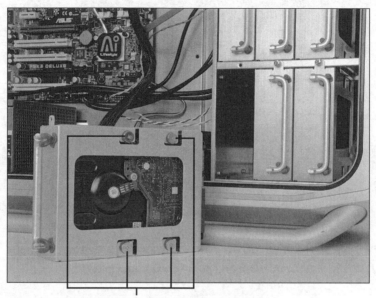

Use the flat-head screws included with the Cosmos case to connect the hard drive to the bracket.

FIGURE 12.26

Each drive bay contains a bracket to which you attach the hard drive.

5. Slide the bracket/hard drive into the drive bay.

6. Use the thumb screw to attach the bracket to the chassis.

7. Move to the other side of the case (you removed the side panel earlier); you should see the hard drive's headers. Run a SATA cable from the hard drive's interface connection to a red SATA header on the motherboard.

8. Connect a SATA power cable from the power supply to the hard drive's power connector. Figure 12.27 shows a connected hard drive.

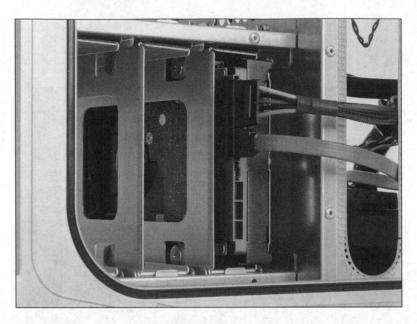

FIGURE 12.27
The hard drive with SATA interface and power cables attached.

Installing the Optical Drive

You add the optical drive to your system by inserting it into one of the Cosmos case's 5.25-inch external drive bays. The Cosmos case uses an easy tool-free system that enables you to install any drive in just a few seconds. Here are the steps to follow:

1. Touch something metal to ground yourself.
2. Open the bezel door in the front of the case.
3. Remove the plastic grill that covers the top drive bay.
4. With the optical drive's connectors facing the inside of the case, slide the drive into a drive bay until the front face is lined up with the case bezel.
5. Press the button on the side of the drive bay to lock the drive into place.
6. Close the bezel door.

> **note** Most optical drives give you a choice of fronts, usually beige or black. If your optical drive currently has a beige front, switch to the black, which will look better with the black bezel of the Cosmos case. See the drive's manual to learn how to exchange fronts.

12

7. Run a SATA cable from the optical drive's interface connection to one of the motherboard's red SATA headers.

8. Connect a SATA power cable from the power supply to the optical drive's power connector. Figure 12.28 shows the optical drive connections.

FIGURE 12.28

The optical drive's interface and power connections.

Installing the Card Reader

Our memory card reader also uses a 5.25-inch external drive bay. However, because the reader is a 3.5-inch device, we need to use the bottom drive bay, which includes brackets that enable a 3.5-inch drive to fit. Here are the steps to follow:

1. Touch something metal to ground yourself.

2. Open the bezel door in the front of the case.

3. Remove the plastic grill that covers the bottom drive bay.

4. Remove the inner part of the plastic grill to allow access to the memory card's slots.

5. Remove the four screws that hold the two brackets in place, and then remove the brackets.

6. Attach one bracket to each side of the memory card reader. (The brackets have holes marked L and R. A bracket's L holes line up with the holes on the left side of the reader, and a bracket's R holes line up with the holes on the right side of the reader.)

7. With the card reader's connectors facing back, slide the reader/bracket assembly into a drive bay until the front face is lined up with the case bezel.

8. Press the button on the side of the drive bay to lock the drive into place.

9. Attach the plastic grill to the front of the drive bay. Figure 12.29 shows the front of the case with the card reader inserted.

FIGURE 12.29

The memory card reader inserted into the case.

10. Close the bezel door.

11. Connect the reader's external USB cable (yes, the *external* cable) to the back of the reader.

12. Locate the motherboard PCI slot you want to use for the USB 2.0 card. To avoid having the card too close to either of the video cards, I suggest

the second PCI slot (the one labeled PCI2 on the board).

13. Remove the thumb screw that holds the cover of the PCI slot; then remove the slot cover.

14. Insert the USB 2.0 expansion card and attach it to the chassis using the thumb screw.

15. Connect the card reader's USB cable to the USB card's internal port, as shown in Figure 12.30.

tip

Before you install any expansion cards, this is an excellent time to connect the power supply's 8-pin 12V rail to the motherboard's 12V header. You can run the cable right along the motherboard, to the left of the expansion card sockets. Each expansion card has a notch in the bottom (beside the connectors) that will fit nicely over the rail.

FIGURE 12.30
Connect the card reader's USB cable to the expansion card's internal USB port.

Inserting the Video Cards

The last chore in the build is to insert our two video cards into the motherboard's PCI Express x16 slots. I won't go into all the details here because I gave you specific instructions on inserting an expansion card in Chapter 8.

→   **See** "Installing an Expansion Card," **p. 211**.

However, we want to create a multi-GPU setup with Crossfire, so here are the steps to follow to set this up:

1. Touch something metal to ground yourself.

2. Locate the two motherboard PCI Express x16 slots you'll be using.

3. For both slots, remove the thumb screw that holds the cover of the PCI slot and then remove the slot cover.

4. For each video card, insert the card into a slot and attach it to the chassis using the thumb screw.

5. Connect the Crossfire bridges. To do this, first examine the front edge of each video card (the edge away from the bus connector) and you'll see two connectors about a quarter of an inch apart; these are the Crossfire connectors. For each Crossfire bridge, attach one end of the bridge to the Crossfire connector on one of the cards, and the other end of the bridge to the corresponding Crossfire connector on the other card. Figure 12.31 shows the video cards with the Crossfire bridges in place.

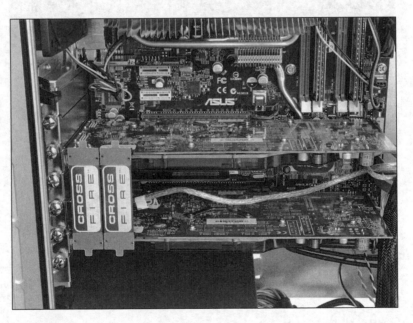

FIGURE 12.31

Insert the video cards in the PCIe x16 slots, and then connect them using the Crossfire bridges.

Final Steps

Okay, your high-performance PC is just about ready for its debut. Before the big moment, however, there are a few tasks you should perform and a few things you need to check. Here's the list:

- **Route and tie off the cables**—A well-built PC doesn't just have cables all over the place. Instead, the cables should be routed as far away from the motherboard as possible and as close to the sides of the case as possible. This makes the inside of the case look neater and improves airflow throughout the case. Use Velcro cable ties if need be to keep unruly cables out of the way.

- **Double-check connections**—Go through all the connections and make sure they're properly seated.

- **Double-check devices**—Check the hard drive, optical drive, and expansion cards to ensure that they're not loose.

- **Look for loose screws**—Make sure there are no loose screws or other extraneous bits and pieces in the case.

- **Attach the VGA vent**—The left side of the vent has small posts on the top and bottom, and these fit into slots on the left side of the case. You then pivot the vent to the right side of the case until it snaps into place.

Powering Up

Now, at last, you're ready to fire up your new PC. Rather than just diving willy-nilly into the operating system install, however, there's a procedure I like to follow to make sure the BIOS, motherboard, and processor are all working in harmony. Follow these steps:

1. Connect a monitor, keyboard, and mouse to the PC, and turn on the monitor.

2. Connect the power cable to a wall socket and then to the power supply unit.

3. If the PSU's switch is off (0), turn it on (1).

4. Press the power switch on the front of the case. Make sure the case fans and CPU fan are all working.

5. Press Delete to enter the motherboard's BIOS configuration program, which is called BIOS Setup Utility.

12

6. Make sure your devices are working properly by checking the following:

   - In the Main screen, check the date and time and set them to the correct values, if necessary.

   - In the Main screen, check the SATA headers to make sure you see two devices listed: one is the hard drive and the other is the optical drive.

> **note** If all is well with your motherboard power connections, the board's power LED (located beside the main 24-pin power header) will light up as soon as you turn on the PSU. If the LED remains off, turn off the PSU, remove the power cable, and then check your motherboard power cable connections.

   - In the Main screen, select System Information and check the Processor section to ensure that the Intel Core 2 Quad appears. Also, check that the System Memory section shows 2048MB available.

   - In the Boot screen, select Boot Device Priority, select 1st Boot Device, highlight CDROM, and press Enter.

7. Press F10 to save your changes and exit System Setup. The program asks you to confirm that you want to save changes.

8. Press Enter.

9. Press the power switch to shut down the PC.

10. Replace the case's side panel.

11. Connect the computer to your network by running a network cable from the back panel's network port to your switch or router.

12. Press the power switch on the front panel.

13. Open the optical drive and insert your operating system disc. (For my build, I installed Windows Vista Ultimate Edition.) The computer will now boot from the disc and install the OS.

14. If you install Windows, be sure to update your version—particularly by installing all available security patches—immediately.

15. When the OS is installed and running, insert the Intel P35 Chipset Support DVD that came with the board and run the install program. This contains all the drivers you need for the board's devices. In the initial window (see Figure 12.32), click ASUS InstAll - Drivers Installation Wizard.

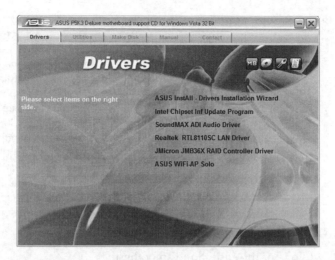

FIGURE 12.32

You see this window when you run the install program on the board's Intel P35 Chipset Support DVD.

16. In the ASUS InstAll window, shown in Figure 12.33, deactivate the check boxes for the drivers you don't want installed. (For our build, you don't need RAID support, so deactivate the JMicron JMB36X RAID Controller Driver check box.)

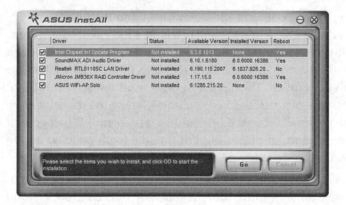

FIGURE 12.33

Use the ASUS InstAll window to install the drivers for your motherboard devices.

17. Update the motherboard's BIOS, as described in Chapter 17.

➔   **See** "Updating the Motherboard BIOS," **p. 507**.

18. Use Device Manager to check for device problems (see Chapter 17) and install drivers for any device that Windows didn't recognize. (In this build, for example, you need to install the video card drivers. Be sure to install the drivers using the CD that comes with the card.)

→   See "Updating Device Drivers," **p. 519**.

> **note** With our dual-GPU setup, you can easily run high-end games on this machine, including the latest DirectX 10 games. If you plan on running any DirectX 10 application, however, be sure to install Windows Vista update KB936710, which fixes a multi-GPU bug related to DirectX 10. You can find out more about this bug and download the update at http://support.microsoft.com/kb/936710.

Final Thoughts

This was one of the easiest and smoothest builds I've ever done. The main reason was the Cosmos case, which is so easy to work with and just has *tons* of room inside. If I have a quibble, it's that having the power supply on the bottom of the case isn't great because it's an awful long way to the motherboard's 12V connector, and the power supply's 12V rail just *barely* made it.

All told, the build took about five hours, *including* doing the photography that accompanies this chapter. Your build time should be shorter, particularly because there are no significant snags with our chosen hardware.

The initial boot went without a hitch, and the BIOS Setup Utility reported that all devices were present and accounted for. I had Vista Ultimate installed within 30 minutes, and another hour later I had the machine patched, the motherboard's drivers installed and its BIOS updated, and the video card driver installed. The biggest surprise was how quiet this PC runs: despite the presence of seven (!) fans, you barely know the machine is on. (Not having the power LED hooked up could be a problem!) It helped that we picked quiet components, of course, but I'm sure the foam padding on the sides of the Cosmos case really makes the difference.

I'm going to take a few days to break the machine in (watch for short-term device failures, make sure the machine runs as expected, and so on), and then I'm going to transfer all my files and programs and make this my main machine. Can't wait!

12

From Here

- For the details on installing memory, **see** "Installing Memory Modules," **p. 205**.

- To learn about installing cards, **see** "Installing an Expansion Card," **p. 211**.

- If you need to temporarily remove the power supply, **see** "Releasing the Power Supply," **p. 234**.

- To learn how to use Device Manager to look for problem devices, **see** "Updating Device Drivers," **p. 519**.

- For instructions on updating the BIOS, **see** "Updating the Motherboard BIOS," **p. 507**.

- For the specifics on installing an Intel processor, **see** "Installing an Intel CPU in a Socket 775 Board," **p. 216**.

Building a Killer Gaming PC

'Tis not for money they contend, but for glory.

—Herodutus, *History*

Gaming is more popular than ever, and the reason for this is simple: PC games aren't just for kids anymore. In fact, gaming is becoming an increasingly *adult* pastime. For example, in a 2007 survey of people who described themselves as the heads of their households, two out three also said that they play computer games. According to the Entertainment Software Association, the average age of a game player is 33 and 92% of game buyers are over the age of 18. Even more surprisingly, 24% of Americans over the age of 50 played games in 2007 (compared to just 9% who did so back in 1999).

It's certainly true that some of these people are just playing Solitaire, but I think you'd be surprised how many adults relax after a hard day by playing rig-rocking games such as *Crysis*, *Bioshock*, or *Call of Duty*.

Of course, you need some heavy-duty hardware to get the most out of these games, and that's what we're after here in this chapter: a killer gaming PC. In this chapter I set out some design goals for the killer gaming PC; then I take you through the parts I chose to meet those goals, from the computer case right down to the memory modules. Then, with the parts assembled, I show you step-by-step how to build your own killer gaming PC.

Design Goals for a Killer Gaming PC

Let me begin by explaining what I mean by *killer*. Really, it comes down to two things. First, of course, is gaming performance: we want hardware that will not only play the latest games, but will also play them *well*. Second is great looks: we want hardware that looks like it belongs in a local area network (LAN) party, from a cool-looking case to lots of LEDs inside to provide some wow factor.

So, my design goals for this project are driven by these two aspects of the *killer* PC, inner strength and outer beauty:

- **Video, video, video**—Getting a high-end computer game to run smoothly with a high frame rate on a large screen takes video horsepower, and lots of it. So the most important component in this build will be the video card (or, more accurately, the video *cards*).

- **Go gaming-specific**—The popularity of gaming has had an interesting side effect in the world of computer components: we're now seeing lots of parts that have been manufactured and tuned with gaming in mind. This is crucial for components such as the case and motherboard (and, of course, the video cards), so we'll go with gaming hardware wherever it makes sense.

- **Gaming-only components**—I'm assuming that you'll be using the computer mostly for playing games, although I certainly expect you'll do more garden-variety tasks with it as well. One of the key elements of a gaming rig is that it's not loaded down with extra gear that doesn't support the overall goal of creating an awesome gaming experience. This build will be no exception, and you'll see that we won't use any parts that aren't game-related in some way.

- **Don't break the bank**—Creating a PC gaming machine that uses only the highest of the high-end components would easily set you back between $4,000 and $5,000! Heck, a pair of NVIDIA GeForce 8800 Ultra video cards (as I write this, the 8800 Ultra is the fastest video card on the market) could run you as much as $1,600 all by themselves!

That's almost as much as our entire high-performance PC from Chapter 12, "Building a High-Performance PC." Now it's certainly possible that you have money to burn, and if so then by all means go for a top-end rig. However, my assumption in this chapter is that you're operating under a budget, so this killer gaming PC won't be the ultimate gaming PC. However, you'll see that we're going to spend far less than you would on an ultimate machine (my ceiling is $2,000), but our killer PC's performance will be only a bit less.

Choosing Parts for the Killer Gaming PC

With these design goals in mind, it's time to put the pedal to the metal and start choosing components to match those goals. The next few sections take you through the components we'll use to put together our killer gaming machine.

Selecting a Case for the Killer Gaming PC

When putting together a gaming PC, you need to give careful thought to the chassis that will hold everything together. In particular, you need to think about two things: interior room and layout, and airflow.

The interior of the case is important because most gaming-specific mobos almost always use the ATX form factor, so you need a case with enough elbow room to hold these large boards. But how much room you have inside is crucial for another very important reason: high-end video cards are often quite long. The 8800 Ultras, for example, are a whopping 10.5 inches from stem to stern! The video cards we'll be using are just 9 inches long, which is far less of a problem, but we still want a spacious interior.

The airflow of a case is vital because a gaming PC pushes it components to the max—and that generates heat, mostly from the video cards, but also from the hard drives and the processor. To keep everything from melting, we need lots of air flowing through the case.

So, for this build I chose the Antec Nine Hundred, a mid-tower case designed with gaming in mind. It's not the cheapest case around, but at about $120, it's not a ridiculous price either, and at least you get a good-looking exterior, as you can see in Figure 13.1.

note The next few sections discuss specific parts for this build, but there's no reason you have to use the same components in your build. Feel free to tweak the parts based on your own budget and computing needs.

13

FIGURE 13.1

The Antec Nine Hundred: the case for our killer gaming PC.

Besides its good looks, the Antec case is plenty functional, too. Here's a summary of the major features:

- Four installed fans: two 120mm intake fans in the front of the case, a 120mm exhaust fan in the back of the case, and a massive 200mm exhaust fan in the top of the case. You can also install two more 120mm exhaust fans: one in the side panel and one on the wall of the 3.5-inch drive bays. Airflow is not going to be a problem with this case! If I have a concern, it's that these fans will make a bit of noise: the 120mm fans put out 25 dBA at 1,200RPM, while the 200mm fan puts out 24 dBA at 600 RPM. As compensation, the 120mm fans have LED lights, so this machine will glow quite nicely in the dark!

- Two USB ports, one FireWire port, one microphone connector, and one Line Out connector on the top of the case, near the front. This is my preferred location for these external ports because that's where they're most easily accessed.

- Loads of drive bays: three 5.25-inch external (for optical or tape drives), one 3.5-inch external (for a memory card reader or floppy drive; this is actually one of the 5.25-inch bays with an adapter), and six 3.5-inch internal (for hard drives).

13

■ Each drive bay is front-mounted for easy access.

■ A bottom-mounted power supply bay. This location makes it easier to keep the CPU cool (because in most cases the PSU sits just above the CPU), but it also means a long stretch to the motherboard's 12V power header, which will sit near the top of the case.

Choosing a Motherboard for the Killer Gaming PC

For our killer gaming PC's motherboard, we want a top-notch gaming board that will give us excellent performance and reduce overall build costs by including features that save us purchasing extra parts.

My choice for this build is the ASUS Strike Extreme, an ATX board that's available online for about $300 (see Figure 13.2).

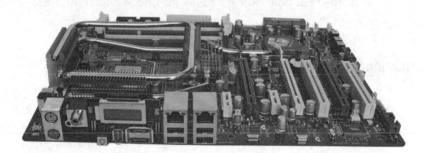

FIGURE 13.2

The ASUS Striker Extreme: the killer gaming PC's motherboard.

The Striker Extreme is part of ASUS's Republic of Gamer line of components, so it was built with hardcore gaming in mind. It offers the following features:

■ Support for a wide variety of Intel processors, including the Intel Core 2 Extreme, Intel Core 2 Quad, Intel Core 2 Duo, Intel Pentium Extreme Edition, Intel Pentium 4 Extreme Edition, Intel Pentium D, Intel Pentium 4, and Intel Celeron D.

■ A front-side bus that supports 1333MHz, 1066MHz, and 800MHz.

■ Support for dual-channel DDR2 1333, 1066, or 800 memory modules (up to 8GB).

■ Three PCI Express x16 slots (two of which support NVIDIA's SLI multi-GPU technology), two PCI Express x1 slots, and two PCI slots.

■ Four external USB ports, one external IEEE-1394 port, and two external eSATA ports.

13

- Six internal SATA connectors.
- Two integrated 10/100/1000 network adapters.
- Integrated coaxial and optical S/PDIF audio ports.
- High-definition 7.1 audio in a separate PCI Express x1 card.
- A rear-panel LCD poster that displays boot-time messages.
- A rear-panel LED switch that toggles the motherboard's built-in LEDs on and off. The switch also toggles lights that illuminate the back-panel ports, which makes it easy to see where you connect things when operating in a dark environment (such as your typical LAN party).
- On-board power and reset switches. Advanced builders use these switches to power up and reset the motherboard while it's still outside a computer case.
- Large heat pipes to keep the Northbridge and Southbridge chipsets cool.

Determining the Video Needs of the Killer Gaming PC

Now we come to the real meat of the matter for a killer gaming PC: video. Your typical high-end game requires a pretty powerful GPU just to get started. If you want sharp, detailed scenes; smooth action; no stuttering or delays; and similar game-related heavy lifting, then you're talking about an amazing amount of video muscle.

Fortunately, the graphics industry has responded with chips that in some cases have more transistors than even the most powerful Intel processors! So, there are plenty of even mid-range GPUs around that can bring you gaming joy. However, for our killer gaming rig we need to look closer to the high end—and the high end these days is populated solely by NVIDIA GPUs, particularly those in the 8800 series.

As I mentioned earlier, the highest of the high end is the NVIDIA GeForce 8800 Ultra, a monster of a card with a monster of a price: between $700 and $800, and those are the *discounted* prices! We'll be needing two cards for this build, so the idea of spending between $1,400 and $1,600 just for the video portion of the show is alarming, to say the least.

Fortunately, NVIDIA has helped us out a great deal. In late 2007, NVIDIA released the GeForce 8800 GT with a slightly slower clock speed (600MHz instead of the Ultra's 612MHz), a smaller memory path (256 bits instead of 384 bits), and less graphics memory (512MB versus 768MB). However, the 8800 GT uses a 65nm fabrication process compared to the Ultra's 90nm, which boosts performance while reducing power consumption. As a result, the overall performance of the 8800GT is only slightly less than that of the 8800 Ultra. Now for the *really* good news: you can find these cards online for about $250, a substantial savings over the 8800 Ultra and a terrific price/performance bargain.

To crank things up a notch on the video front, we'll be using two 8800 GTs, connected via SLI, NVIDIA's multi-GPU technology which the Striker Extreme motherboard supports. For this build, I chose two PNY GeForce 8800 GT boards (see Figure 13.3). Each is a PCI Express x16 card that offers 512MB of DDR3 graphics memory, two DVI ports (as well as DVI-to-VGA and DVI-to-HDMI adapters), and an S-Video port. The card runs about $140, which isn't too bad. Figure 13.3 shows the two cards I'll be using for this build.

FIGURE 13.3
The killer gaming PC's video system: two PNY GeForce 8800 GT cards.

Storage Options for the Killer Gaming PC

Besides the video, the second most important performance component for the killer gaming PC is the hard drive. When we're in mid-battle (or whatever), we don't want our game to sputter while it waits to load data from the hard drive. To avoid that, we'll need the fastest hard drive available, and currently that title falls to the Western Digital Raptor 1500WD (a 150GB drive that spins at 10,000RPM, which enables it

caution The disadvantage of a striped RAID 0 array is that all the PC's data is split between the two hard drives. That is, no one drive contains a complete set of your computer's data. This means that if one hard drive dies, you lose *all* your data! Therefore, when you use a striped RAID 0 configuration, you *must* make regular backups of all your data to another drives.

13

to achieve average seek times of just 4.6ms, which is blazingly fast).

That's a great start, but I want more. To make the hard drive system even faster, I'm going to add a second Raptor (see Figure 13.4) and combine the two drives into a single 150GB drive using a technology called redundant array of inexpensive disks (RAID). Specifically, I'm going to use RAID 0, which combines the two drives in a *striped* array where the data is split between the two drives. The advantage of a RAID 0 configuration is that the system can read or write from the two drives at the same time, which boosts overall performance.

We want our killer gaming PC to have a killer optical drive, too. My choice is the Samsung SH-S203B, a dual-layer DVD/CD rewritable drive that uses the blazingly fast SATA interface (see Figure 13.5). It supports write speeds of 20x DVD±R, 12x DVD±R DL, 8x DVD+RW, 6x DVD-RW, 48x CD-R, and 32x CD-RW, plus read speeds of 16x DVD-ROM and 48x CD-ROM.

> **caution** The other drawback of a RAID array (of any kind) is that you must install the motherboard's RAID drivers when you install Windows. However, the Windows Setup program knows how to load these drivers only from a floppy disk! Of course, we're not going to put such antiquated technology in our slick gaming PC. Later in this chapter (see "Configuring the RAID Array"), I'll show you how to build a custom Windows installation disc that includes the RAID drivers, enabling you to bypass the floppy option completely. On the other hand, creating a custom Windows install disc requires access to another computer that has a CD or DVD burner, as well as software that can burn an ISO file. If you don't have any of these, you need to either go the floppy drive route or forget about RAID.

FIGURE 13.4

The killer gaming PC's hard drives: two 10,000RPM Western Digital Raptor 1500WD drives that we'll configure as a RAID 0 striped set.

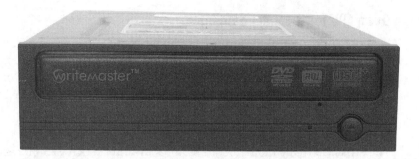

FIGURE 13.5

The killer gaming PC's optical drive: the Samsung SH-S203B.

Selecting a Power Supply for the Killer Gaming PC

We have just one concern when it comes to the power supply for our killer gaming PC: power. Although we won't be loading this PC with tons of devices, we will be using a couple of video cards (which need 110W each), two 10,000RPM hard drives, and an optical drive. All this means we need a power supply with lots of watts to spare.

My choice for this build is the Apevia Iceberg, a PSU that supports SLI and can handle up to 680W, which is more than enough power for our needs (see Figure 13.6). It sells online for about $120. In the How Cool Is *That* department, the Iceberg comes with a clear case, three-color internal LEDs, and fluorescent green sleeves and connectors.

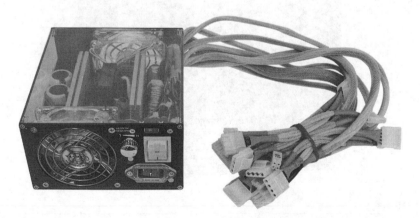

FIGURE 13.6

The Apevia Iceberg: the killer gaming PC's power supply.

13

Picking Out a CPU for the Killer Gaming PC

It might come as a slight surprise to you, but the processor is not a vital component in our killer gaming PC. That's because the real action will be going on inside the GPUs, which will handle almost all the processing while we're gaming. Not that the CPU doesn't have a role in our PC—quite the contrary. We'll be using this machine for other chores such as web surfing and playing music, so the processor will occasionally have *something* to do!

The Striker Extreme motherboard requires an Intel socket 775 processor, and because it also supports a 1,333MHz front-side bus, we can look for a processor that also operates at that speed. My choice is the Intel Core 2 Duo E6750, a dual-core processor with a clock speed of 2.66GHz, a 4MB L2 cache, and support for the 1,333MHz bus (see Figure 13.7). You can find the retail version for around $190. However, we'll be using a third-party CPU cooler in this build, so try to get the OEM version of the E6750, which should save you some cash (usually at the expense of a shorter warranty; check the fine print to know what you're getting).

FIGURE 13.7

The Intel Core 2 Due E6750: the killer gaming PC's processor.

13

The Antec case has a side panel grill to which you can attach an exhaust fan. Because that fan would sit right over the CPU, you could use the Intel stock cooler. However, we want to make sure our case is well ventilated, so I decided to get a third-party cooler, which will not only improve the cooler, but also be quieter.

I decided against installing the side-panel exhaust fan because our case already has four fans on the go. Instead, we want to take advantage of the fact that the Antec case has that giant 200mm exhaust fan on top of the case, right above the motherboard with nothing between the board and the fans. (Remember, in this case the power supply is mounted on the bottom.) So, we need a cooler with a fan that will send its air toward the top exhaust fans. In other words, the cooler fan must send its air *parallel* to the motherboard, rather than straight up from the processor. The perfect solution here is the Zalman CNPS9500, shown in Figure 13.8. The fan sits on the side of the cooling fins, so after it's mounted it blows air straight up. It's also nice and quiet, has a blue LED that adds to our build's bling factor, and adds a mere $50 to the cost of the build.

FIGURE 13.8

The Zalman CNPS9500: the killer gaming PC's CPU cooler.

13

How Much Memory Does the Killer Gaming PC Need?

Memory is one of the most important performance factors in any PC, which means, simply, that the more memory you add to any system, the better that system will perform. For our killer gaming PC, we need high-performance memory to ensure that RAM isn't a bottle neck on this system. For that reason, I went with a relatively high-end solution: two 1GB modules of PC2 6400 (DDR2 800) from Corsair's powerful Dominator series (see Figure 13.9). If you don't want to spend that much (the two sticks cost about $250), 2GB of any brand-name PC2 6400 RAM will do.

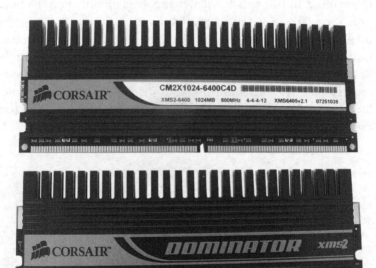

FIGURE 13.9

The killer gaming PC's memory: a couple of 1GB PC2 6400 modules from Corsair's Dominator family.

Selecting Audio Equipment for the Killer Gaming PC

Video is the most important aspect of gaming, of course, but there's also a major audio component, as well. You want to hear those explosions and tire screeches and whatever splats an alien makes when it meets its match. Fortunately, we've got great audio built right in to the Striker Extreme motherboard: coaxial and optical S/PDIF audio ports on the rear panel and a separate card that offers high-definition 7.1-channel audio. Even better, although most boards come with the Realtek audio chip integrated (which produces only so-so sound), the Striker Extreme board comes with an audio chip made by Analog Devices that produces sound almost as good as dedicated boards that cost big bucks.

note The audio card that ships with the Asus mobo also contains the header for the front panel audio jacks, which is another good reason to install the card.

Choosing Networking Hardware for the Killer Gaming PC

Any killer gaming PC must network, of course, and these days networking is easier than ever because it's a rare motherboard that doesn't come with a networking adapter built in. Even better, almost all motherboard-based network interface cards (NICs) support Ethernet (10Mbps), Fast Ethernet (100Mbps), and Gigabit Ethernet (1Gbps or 1,000Mbps), so you're covered no matter to which type of network you'll be connecting. Our killer gaming PC is no exception because our ASUS motherboard has a 10/100/1000 NIC onboard.

Pricing the Killer Gaming PC

For this build, I tried to use top-shelf components for those areas that most affect gaming performance; then I balanced those with lesser components for those areas that only tangentially affect gaming. Table 13.1 summarizes the killer gaming PC's components and prices. As you can see, our total price of $1,900 is nicely under my $2,000 ceiling.

Table 13.1   Components and Prices for the Killer Gaming PC

Component	Model	Average Price
Case	Antec Nine Hundred	$120
Motherboard	ASUS Striker Extreme	$300
Power supply	Ultra V-Series 500W	$90
CPU	Intel Core 2 Due E6750	$190
CPU cooler	Zalman CNPS9500	$50
Memory	Corsair Dominator PC2 6400 1 GB (×2)	$250
Hard drive	Western Digital Raptor WD1500 ×2	$360
Optical drive	Sony DRU-830A DVD/CD Rewritable Drive	$40
Video card	NVIDIA GeForce 8800 GT ×2	$500
Audio card	Motherboard integrated	N/A
Network card	Motherboard integrated	N/A
TOTAL		**$1,900**

13

Putting Together the Killer Gaming PC

My trigger finger is getting itchy just thinking about this awesome build! We've got a great collection of parts (see Figure 13.10), and I think the result is going to be a machine worthy of the *killer* adjective. And the good news is that by keeping the machine relatively simple at this point, you have fewer components to install, so you can easily build this PC in an afternoon or evening. The rest of this chapter takes you through the steps you need to follow.

FIGURE 13.10

The killer gaming PC's parts, ready to be built.

Getting the Case Ready

The Antec case requires a bit of prep work before we can move on to more productive tasks:

- **Remove the two side panels**—You need both panels off for this build. In each case, you release the panel by removing the thumb screws and then sliding the panels off.

- **Remove the generic I/O shield**—As you see in the next section, when test-fitting the motherboard in the case to determine where to put the standoffs, it helps if the I/O shield isn't in the way. Gently push the edges of the I/O shield back into the case until it's loose and you can remove it.

■ **Remove the 3.5-inch drive bay fan mount**—This fan mount sticks out of the drive bay wall into the interior of the case (see Figure 13.11). We won't need this fan mount in this build, and it will just cramp our style when working with the motherboard, so it's best to remove it now. Here are the steps to follow:

FIGURE 13.11

Get rid of the drive bay fan mount to give yourself more room to operate inside the case.

1. Remove the eight (yes, *eight!*) thumb screws that attach the upper of the two hard drive cages to the chassis.

2. Slide the hard drive cage out of the chassis.

3. On one side of the cage is the power cable and speed controller for the fan that's attached to the front of the cage. Use a flat-head screwdriver to carefully lift up the plastic lip that holds the cables in place on the fan mount; then slide the cables out from under the lip.

4. The fan mount is attached to the cage by four plastic clips. On one side of the fan mount, push the clips in to release them, and then repeat on the other side.

> **note** Although those are ostensibly thumb screws that attach the hard drive cage, I found them quite tight and had to resort to a Philips screwdriver to loosen them.

13

Installing the Motherboard Standoffs

A standoff (or a *mount point*, as it's often called) is a hex-nut screw, which means it actually consist of two parts: a bottom screw that enables you to insert the standoff into a hole in the side of the case and a top hex nut into which you can insert a screw. The idea is that you install from eight to ten (depending on the motherboard form factor) of these standoffs into the case, sit the motherboard on top of the standoffs, align the motherboard's holes with the hex nuts, and then attach the motherboard. This gives the board a solid footing but also separates the board from the metal case to prevent shorting out the board.

Installing the standoffs is easiest when the motherboard is bare, so that should be your first task:

1. Find the standoffs that came with the case and put them aside.

2. Lay the case flat on its side, with the open side facing up.

3. Move all the case cables out of the way so you can clearly see the side panel that has the mounting holes.

4. If you haven't done so already, touch something metal to ground yourself.

5. Remove the preinstalled standoffs.

6. Take the motherboard out of its antistatic bag and lay the board inside the case, oriented so that the board's back-panel I/O ports are lined up and flush with the case's I/O slot.

7. Note which case holes correspond to the holes in the motherboard (see Figure 13.12). You may need to use a flashlight to make sure there's a case hole under each motherboard hole.

tip You could insert the hard drive cage back into the case at this point, but you'll be using this cage later to install one of the hard drives, so you can save yourself some work by leaving the cage off to the side for now.

caution I suggest removing preinstalled standoffs because you want to ensure that you only have the correct number of standoffs inserted and that they're inserted in the correct positions. One standoff in the wrong position can cause a short circuit.

tip Rather than trying to remember which case holes correspond with each motherboard hole, you can mark the correct case holes. After you have the board lined up with the holes, stick a felt-tip pen through each hole and mark the case. (You might need to offset the board slightly to do this properly.)

13

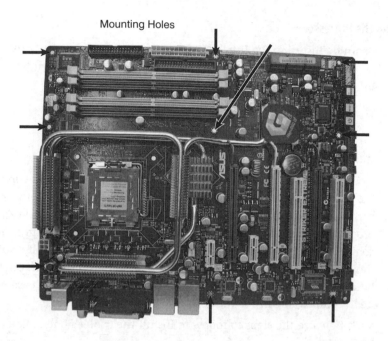

Mounting Holes

FIGURE 13.12

The motherboard has nine holes through which you attach the board to the standoffs.

8. Place the motherboard carefully aside.

9. Screw the standoffs into the corresponding holes in the side of the case.

Just to be safe, you might want to place the motherboard into the case once again to double-check that each motherboard hole corresponds to a standoff.

Getting the Motherboard Ready for Action

Although you might be tempted to install the motherboard right away, and technically you can do that, it's better to hold off for a bit and do some of the work on the board while it's out of the case. We'll be installing the processor and the memory modules, and although it isn't impossible to install these parts with the board inside the case, it's a lot easier outside.

Before getting started, be sure to touch something metal to ground yourself. Now take the motherboard and lay it flat on your work surface. For the ASUS Striker Extreme, it's best to orient the board so that the I/O ports are facing away from you. This enables you to work with the processor socket without having to go over the heat sinks or the I/O ports.

13

Inserting the Processor

Begin by inserting the Intel E6750 processor in the motherboard's LGA775 socket. I won't go into the details here because I showed you how to insert Intel processors back in Chapter 8.

→   **See** "Installing an Intel CPU in a Socket 775 Board," **p. 216**.

Installing the CPU Cooler

Now it's time to install the Zalman CPU cooler. This cooler is compatible with the motherboard's LGA775 CPU socket, but it requires a bit of work to install because you have to install a back plate under the board and a support bracket for the cooler itself. Note, too, that we're also going to install the cooler itself while the motherboard is out of the case. I usually wait until the motherboard is installed in the case before adding the cooler, but the clip that holds the cooler in place is tricky to install even outside the case and would be nearly impossible inside the case.

First, here are the steps to follow to install the cooler's back plate and support bracket:

1. Touch something metal to ground yourself.

2. Under the motherboard, align the four nuts in the cooler's back plate with the four holes that surround the CPU socket. The nuts should be facing the motherboard, as shown in Figure 13.13.

3. On top of the motherboard, align the four holes on the cooler's support bracket with the four holes that surround the CPU socket. Also, be sure to orient the bracket's lever slot as shown in Figure 13.14 (this allows you to fully open the CPU socket's lever, should the need arise.)

4. Using a Philips screwdriver, attach the support bracket to the back plate using the four screws supplied with the cooler, as shown in Figure 13.14.

FIGURE 13.13

Place the cooler's back plate under the motherboard.

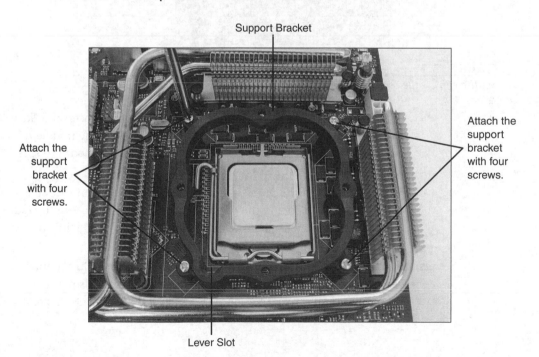

Support Bracket

Attach the support bracket with four screws.

Attach the support bracket with four screws.

Lever Slot

FIGURE 13.14

Attach the cooler's support bracket to the back plate.

Now that the back plate and support bracket are in place, we can add the cooler itself. Here are the steps to follow to install the Zalman cooler:

1. Our motherboard uses an LGA775 CPU socket, so find the cooler's S-type clip (it's the one with two holes, not four).

2. Place the large hole in the middle of the clip over the round protrusion on the plate that sits above the cooler's heatsink. Orient the clip so that it's perpendicular to the cooler's heat pipes, as shown in Figure 13.15.

FIGURE 13.15

Set the clip on the cooler.

3. Apply a thin, even layer of thermal compound to the processor. (Place a bead of thermal compound about the size of a BB in the middle of the heatsink, and then use a piece of plastic or stiff cardboard to spread the compound so that it covers the entire heatsink.)

4. Place the cooler on the processor, oriented so that the front (the side where the fan is) is facing the expansion cards slots, as shown in Figure 13.16. Make sure the cooler's heatsink is perfectly aligned with the processor.

5. Using a Philips screwdriver, begin attaching one of the clip's mounting screws. However, don't attach the screw all the way at this point, because that will make it too hard to attach the other screw. Instead, just insert the screw enough so that it catches.

13

FIGURE 13.16

To ensure that air from the cooler flows to the top of the case, orient the cooler with the fan facing the expansion slots.

6. Use your screwdriver to push the screw on the opposite side of the clip down into the bracket hole, and then turn until the screw catches.

7. Alternate tightening each screw until they're fully seated.

8. Take out the fan's power cable (it's inside the cooler's fins) and attach it to the motherboard's CPU fan header, as shown in Figure 13.17. (The fan uses a three-pin connector, but it fits the motherboard's four-pin fan header.)

note It takes quite a bit of pressure to get that second screw into the hole, so don't worry about using lots of force here. This is why we're inserting the cooler now—because getting these screws attached in the cramped confines of the case would be pretty tough.

caution While you're wrestling with the mounting screws, keep your eye on the cooler's heatsink to ensure is stays aligned with the processor.

13

CPU fan header is located here.

FIGURE 13.17

Connect the CPU cooler's fan wire to the motherboard's CPU fan header.

Inserting the Memory Modules

With your processor in its rightful place, it's time to populate your board with your memory modules. Where you install the modules on the ASUS Striker Extreme board depends on how many modules you're adding (see Figure 13.18):

- **One module**—Install the module in either socket A2 or in socket B2 (the white sockets).

- **Two modules**—Install identical modules either in sockets A2 and B2 (the white sockets) or sockets A1 and B1 (the blue sockets). This ensures a proper dual-channel configuration.

note The Zalman cooler comes with a fan speed controller that enables you to dial back the fan when you're not blowing away nasty things. To install it, remove the fan's power cable from the motherboard's CPU fan header and plug it into the three-pin male connector on the power wire that comes with the fan speed controller. Then plug the controller's three-pin female connector into the motherboard's CPU fan header. Finally, attach the six-pin connector to the controller itself.

■ **Three modules**—Install a set of identical modules in sockets A2 and B2 (the white sockets) and the third module in either socket A1 or socket B1. To ensure dual-channel operation, the size of the A1/B1 module must equal the sum of the A2 and B2 modules (this is called *dual-channel asymmetric mode*). For example, if you have two 512MB modules in A2 and B2, the A/1/B1 module must be 1GB.

■ **Four modules**—Install one set of identical modules in sockets A2 and B2 (the white sockets) and a second set of identical modules in sockets A1 and B1 (the blue sockets). This ensures a proper dual-channel configuration.

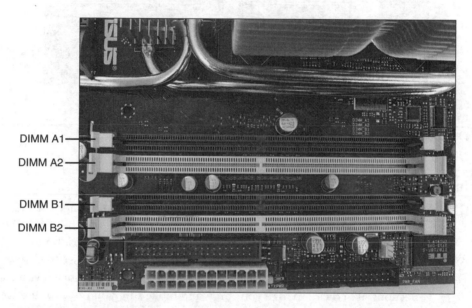

DIMM A1
DIMM A2
DIMM B1
DIMM B2

FIGURE 13.18

The memory module sockets on the ASUS Striker Extreme.

I won't go through the installation steps here because I already covered how to install memory modules in Chapter 8, "Basic Skills for PC Building and Upgrading." Figure 13.19 shows our motherboard with our two 1GB modules installed.

→   **See** "Installing Memory Modules," **p. 205.**

13

FIGURE 13.19

Our motherboard with two 1GB memory modules in place.

Installing the Motherboard

With your motherboard populated with a processor and memory, it's just about ready to roll. The next few sections take you through the detailed installation steps for the motherboard. This is the most finicky, most time-consuming, and most important part of the build. As you'll see, getting a motherboard configured involves lots of separate steps, and lots of cable connections. It's crucial to take your time and make sure you have all the connections just so.

Inserting the Motherboard I/O Shield

Earlier you removed the case's generic I/O shield, so now it's time to insert the I/O shield that came with the motherboard. Take the motherboard's I/O shield and fit it into the case's I/O opening. Make sure you have the I/O shield oriented properly:

- The hole for the keyboard PS/2 port should be at the top, and the six audio ports and the hole for the

tip One other thing you can do while you have the motherboard out of the case is remove the cap that covers half the eight-pin power header at the top of the board (I point out this header later in Figure 13.35). It's a bit tricky to pull out this cap after the board is installed (as I found out the hard way in this build!), so you'll be doing yourself a small favor by popping it out now.

wireless NIC's antenna post should be at the bottom.

- The protruding ridge that runs around the I/O shield should face the back of the case.

When the I/O shield is flush with the case, firmly press the bottom of the shield until it snaps into place; then press the top of the shield until it, too, snaps into place.

Attaching the Motherboard to the Case

With the custom I/O shield in place, you're now ready to install the motherboard inside the case. Here are the steps to follow:

1. Move all the case cables out of the way so that you can clearly see the side panel that has the mounting holes and the installed standoffs.

2. If you haven't done so already, touch something metal to ground yourself.

3. Gently and carefully maneuver the motherboard into the case and lay it on top of the standoffs.

4. Adjust the position of the board so the board's back-panel I/O ports are lined up and flush with the openings in the I/O shield, as shown in Figure 13.20.

5. You should now see a standoff under each motherboard mounting hole. If not, it likely means that the I/O shield isn't fully seated. Remove the board, fix the I/O shield, and then try again.

tip It's not always easy to get the I/O shield perfectly seated. If you have trouble getting a corner of the shield to snap into place, use the end of a plastic screwdriver handle to gently tap the recalcitrant corner into place.

caution On the I/O shield, the two openings for the motherboard's network ports each have two small prongs that extend down from the top of the opening. Be sure to bend these prongs back so they're parallel with the motherboard.

note Bear in mind, however, that it's normal for the board's mounting holes to be slightly offset from the standoffs. There's a bit of give to the I/O shield, so you usually have to force the board slightly to the left (toward the I/O shield) to get the holes and standoffs to line up perfectly.

13

FIGURE 13.20

Make sure the motherboard's I/O ports are lined up and flush with the I/O shield's openings.

6. Use the mounting screws supplied with the case to attach the board to each standoff. To ensure a trouble-free installation, I use the following technique:

   - First, insert but don't tighten the upper-right screw.

   - Next, insert but don't tighten the bottom-left screw. (The bottom-left screw is often the hardest one to install because it's usually in the corner of the case. If you prefer to start with an easier target, insert the bottom middle screw, instead.)

   - Make sure all the holes and standoffs are properly aligned, and then tighten the first two screws.

   - Insert and tighten all the rest of the screws.

> **tip** With the CPU cooler in place, the upper-left motherboard screw is *really* hard to get to. I ended up using a pair of long needle-nose pliers to drop the screw into the hole, and then used my longest Philips screwdriver to carefully straighten and tighten the screw.

> **note** Are you wondering why we're not connecting the wires for the front panel audio jacks? That's because the Striker Extreme motherboard doesn't come with a front-panel audio header! At least not on the board itself. Instead, the header's on the sound card that comes with the board, so we'll wait until we install that card before connecting the front-panel audio wires (see "Inserting the Sound Card," later in this chapter).

13

Connecting the EL I/O

One of my favorite features of the Striker Extreme board is also one of its unique features. The rear panel comes with an LED switch that, when pressed, turns on the motherboard's built-in LEDs (shown earlier in Figure 13.20). That's pretty good, but the real value of the LED switch is that it also activates a feature that ASUS calls electroluminescent (EL) I/O. This is a series of lights that, rather amazingly, are built in to the I/O shield itself! So when the LED switch is on, the name of each back-panel port lights up, so you can easily see which port is which when you're trying to attach something in low-light conditions. This applies to the underside of any desk, but it also shows the gaming soul of the Striker Extreme board because most LAN parties keep their lights turned low for effect.

> **tip** As I mentioned earlier, the upper-left corner of the motherboard is pretty cramped with the CPU cooler in place. This means that getting the tiny EL I/O connector in place is a tricky bit of business, and might even be impossible if you have large hands. What I did was grab the connector between the thumb and forefinger of my right hand, with the connector in its proper orientation (the two little protrusions on the side of the connector should be facing away from the I/O shield). With my left hand I shone a flashlight through the top fan's grill so that I could see where the header was. Yes, it took a few tries.

The EL I/O sticks out of the top of the I/O shield, just above the mouse port hole. The wire attached to the EL 1/O connects to a header in the upper-left corner of the board, just above the PS/2 connectors, as shown in Figure 13.21.

Connecting the Front-Panel IEEE-1394 and USB Cables

Our Antec case offers the convenience of a front-panel IEEE-1394 (FireWire) port. For this port to work, you must connect its cable (the connector is labeled 1394) to one of the motherboard's internal IEEE-1394 header, as shown in Figure 13.22.

The case also offers two front-panel USB 2.0 ports. You need to connect the USB 2.0 port's cable (the connector is labeled USB) to one of the motherboard's three internal USB headers, as shown in Figure 13.22.

13

FIGURE 13.21

Connect the EL I/O wire to the header shown here.

FIGURE 13.22

Connect the cable that runs from the IEEE-1394 front-panel port to a IEEE-1394 header, and the cable that runs from the USB 2.0 front-panel ports to a USB header.

Connecting the Power Switch, Reset Switch, and LEDs

The next item on our build to-do list is to tackle the rest of the wires snaking out from the case's front panel. These wires correspond to the following front-panel features:

> **note** One surprising feature of the Antec Nine Hundred case is that it has no Power LED that lights up when the system power is on. Instead, the two front fans have onboard LEDs which are lit when the power is on, so these act as de facto power LEDs.

- **Power switch**—This is the button you press to turn the system on and off. Its lead consists of two wires, one white and one blue, and the connector is labeled POWER SW.

- **Reset switch**—This is the button you press to reboot a running system. Its lead consists of two gray wires and the connector is labeled RESET SW.

- **Hard drive LED**—This LED lights up when the hard drive is active. It consists of two wires with a single connector: the white wire is the negative (ground) lead, and the gray wire is the positive (signal) lead; the connector is labeled H.D.D. LED.

Connecting all these wires is a bit tricky, but the good news is that you won't destroy anything if you get the connections wrong the first time around. For one thing, the connectors for both the power switch and the reset switch can be attached in either orientation (they'll work fine either way); for another, if you get the LED connector backward, it just means that the LED won't work.

For the connections themselves, you use the motherboard's front-panel header, a collection of pins in the bottom-right corner of the board. Figure 13.27 shows the pin assignments. (Note that the pins numbers are ones I made up myself; they don't correspond to actual pin numbers used on the board.)

Give the pin assignments shown in Figure 13.23, here's how you connect the front-panel wires:

- **Power switch**—Connect this to pins 3 and 4 in any orientation.
- **Reset switch**—Connect this to pins 5 and 6 in any orientation.
- **Hard drive LED**—Connect this to pins 1 and 2, with the white wire on pin 2 (ground) and the blue wire on pin 1 (signal).

Figure 13.24 shows the wires connected to the front-panel header on the motherboard.

13

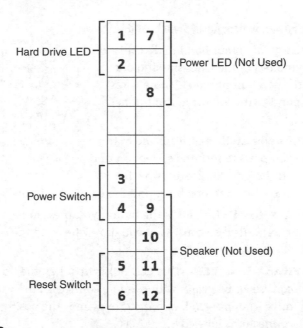

FIGURE 13.23

The pin assignments used on the motherboard's front-panel header.

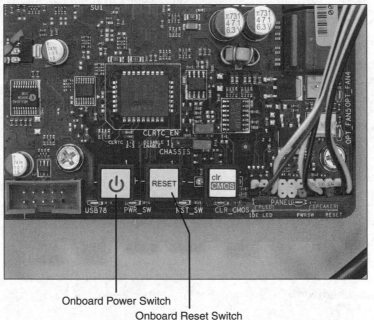

FIGURE 13.24

Connect the front-panel wires to the motherboard's front-panel header.

Installing the Hard Drive

The Antec case offers six internal hard drive bays, which are enclosed in two cages that sit at the front of the case, below the external drive bays. Each cage has a fan mounted on the front and three drive bays. You remove a cage, attach the hard drive, and then reinsert the cage. For better airflow over our Raptor drives, we'll install one in each cage, so that each drive has a dedicated intake fan.

Here are the steps to follow to install the hard drives:

1. Remove the eight thumb screws that attach the upper of the two hard drive cages to the chassis.

2. Slide the hard drive cage out of the chassis.

3. Slide the hard drive into the middle bay as follows:

   ■ The interface and power connectors should face toward the back (open) end of the bracket.

   ■ The hard drive label should be facing up (that is, the underside of the hard drive—the side where the circuit board appears—should sit on the "shelf" of the drive bay).

4. Align the two holes on each side of the hard drive with the holes on the side of the cage; then use screws to attach the hard drive to the cage. Use the long screws and the washers that come with the Antec case. Figure 13.25 shows the hard drive attached to the cage.

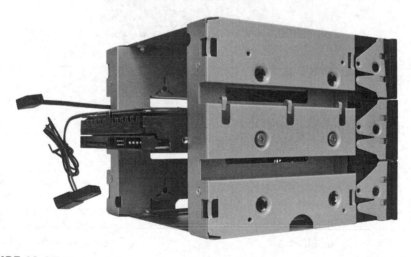

FIGURE 13.25

Attach the hard drive to the middle bay of the hard drive cage.

5. Slide the cage back into the case.

6. Use the thumb screws to attach the cage to the chassis.

7. Repeat steps 1–6 to attach the second hard drive to the lower of the two hard drive cages.

8. For each drive, run a SATA cable from the hard drive's interface connection to a SATA header on the motherboard. Figure 13.26 shows the connected hard drives.

FIGURE 13.26

The hard drives with SATA interface cables attached.

Installing the Optical Drive

You add the optical drive to your system by inserting it into one of the Antec case's 5.25-inch external drive bays. Here are the steps to follow:

1. Touch something metal to ground yourself.

2. Remove the two screws that hold the plastic grill that covers the top drive bay, and then them remove the grill.

> **note** Most optical drives give you a choice of fronts, usually beige or black. If your optical drive currently has a beige front, switch to the black, which will look better with the black bezel of the Antec case. See the drive's manual to learn how to exchange fronts.

13

3. With the optical drive's connectors facing the inside of the case, slide the drive into a drive bay until the front face is lined up with the case bezel.

4. Use the screws that came with the optical drive to attach it to the case.

5. Run a SATA cable from the optical drive's interface connection to one of the motherboard's SATA headers. Figure 13.27 shows the optical drive connections.

FIGURE 13.27

The optical drive's interface connection.

Inserting the Sound Card

Next, we need to install the sound card that came with the Striker Extreme board. This is a PCI Express x1 card; I therefore suggest using the top PCIe x1 slot so that the card's connectors appear right beside the rest of the back panel connectors. I won't go into all the details here because I gave you specific instructions on inserting an expansion card in Chapter 8.

→   See "Installing an Expansion Card," **p. 211**.

Here are the basic steps:

1. Touch something metal to ground yourself.
2. Push up and remove the slot cover that corresponds to the first PCI slot.
3. Insert the sound card into the slot and attach it to the case with a screw.

With the sound card in place, you can now connect the cable for the Antec case's front panel Line Out (audio output) and Mic In (microphone input) audio ports. Note that the audio ports' cable has two connectors, one for standard audio (labeled AC '97) and one for high-definition audio (labeled HD AUDIO). The sound card supports HD audio, so you need to connect the HD AUDIO connector to the card's audio header (labeled AAFP), as shown in Figure 13.28.

FIGURE 13.28

Connect the cable that runs from the front-panel audio ports to the audio header on the sound card.

Inserting the Video Cards

The last chore in the build is to insert our two video cards into the motherboard's blue PCI Express x16 slots. I won't go into all the details here because I gave you specific instructions on inserting an expansion card in Chapter 8.

→   **See** "Installing an Expansion Card," **p. 211**.

However, we want to create a multi-GPU setup with SLI, so here are the steps to follow to set this up:

1. Touch something metal to ground yourself.

2. Locate the two blue motherboard PCI Express x16 slots you'll be using.

3. For both slots, remove the thumb screw that holds the cover of the PCI slot; then remove the slot cover.

4. For each video card, insert the card into a slot and attach it to the chassis using the thumb screw.

5. Connect the SLI bridge. To do this, first examine the front edge of each video card (the edge away from the bus connector) and you'll see a connector; this is the SLI connector. Attach one end of the SLI bridge to the SLI connector on one of the cards, and then other end of the bridge to the SLI connector on the other card. Figure 13.29 shows the video cards with the SLI bridge in place.

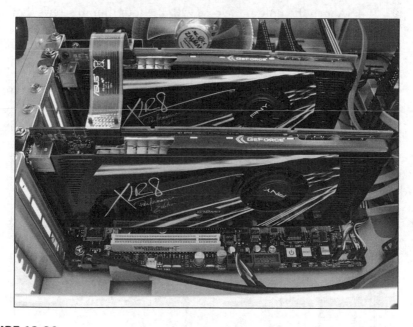

FIGURE 13.29

Insert the video cards in the blue PCIe x16 slots and then connect them using the SLI bridge.

13

Installing the Power Supply and Power Cables

Okay, now let's get the power supply onboard:

1. Orient the power supply unit so that the back (the side with the power cable connector, on/off switch, and fan) is toward the back of the case, with the power cable connector and on/off switch on the right (as you face the back of the case).

2. Maneuver the power supply into the power supply bay on the bottom of the case.

3. Make sure the power supply is flush with the back of the case.

4. Attach the unit to the case with the four thumb screws that come with the Apevia power supply, as shown in Figure 13.30.

> **note** Yes, we actually installed the PSU upside down! This is necessary because we want the transparent side of the unit to face the inside of the case, which will enable the unit's LEDs to light up the case interior. When the unit is right-side up, the LEDs shine down, so clearly Apevia assumed the PSU would be installed in the top of the case rather than the bottom.

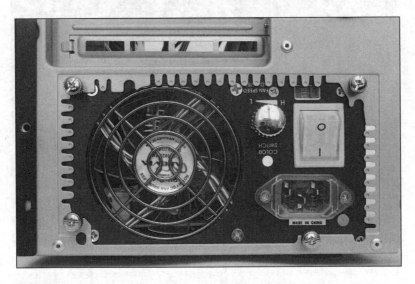

FIGURE 13.30

Use four thumb screws to attach the power supply unit to the case as shown here.

With the power supply onboard, we can now connect the power cables that supply juice to the motherboard. Our ASUS board has two power headers:

- A 24-pin main power header, into which you plug the power supply's 24-pin connector (it's actually two connectors, one 20-pin and one 4-pin), as pointed out in Figure 13.30.

- An 8-pin 12V header. Our power supply actually has two separate 4-pin 12V connectors, so you first need to snap these two together. After that's done, remove the cap that covers half the 8-pin header (if you didn't do this earlier) and then plug the combined connector into the motherboard, as shown in Figure 13.31.

8-Pin 12V
Connection

24-Pin Main
Connection

FIGURE 13.31

Connect the power supply's 24-pin and 8-pin connectors to the corresponding headers on the motherboard.

Your next chore is to connect the power leads for the four case fans. The fans come with 4-pin Molex connectors, so you must attach each connector to a 4-pin Molex connector on a power supply peripheral rail (happily, each of the PSU's peripheral rails has four connectors—just enough for the four fans—so you have to use only one rail).

Finally, you need to get power to the rest of the devices:

> **note** In Figure 13.31, note that I had to use a cable tie to keep the 12V motherboard power rail away from the CPU cooler's fins. This rail only barely reaches the header because the PSU is way down at the bottom of the case. Note that if you don't care about the PSU's LED, you can give yourself a bit more slack in the motherboard power rails by removing the PSU and installing it with the transparent side upside down.

1. Connect a six-pin power supply rail to the power connector on each video card, as shown in Figure 13.32.

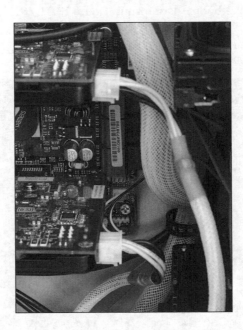

FIGURE 13.32

Supply power to the video cards by attaching the PSU's two 6-pin connectors.

2. Connect a SATA power cable from the power supply to the optical drive's power connector.

3. Locate a SATA power cable from the power supply, and use its two connectors to attach to each hard drive's power connector.

Final Steps

Okay, your killer gaming PC is just about ready for its debut. Before the big moment, however, there are a few tasks you should perform and a few things you need to check. Here's the list:

- **Route and tie off the cables**—A well-built PC doesn't just have cables all over the place. Instead, the cables should be routed as far away from the motherboard as possible and as close to the sides of the case as possible. This makes the inside of the case look neater and improves airflow throughout the case. Use cable ties if need be to keep unruly cables out of the way.

- **Double-check connections**—Go through all the connections and make sure they're properly seated.

- **Double-check devices**—Check the hard drive, optical drive, and expansion cards to ensure that they're not loose.

- **Look for loose screws**—Make sure there are no loose screws or other extraneous bits and pieces in the case.

Powering Up

Now, at last, you're ready to fire up your new PC. Rather than just diving willy-nilly into the operating system install, however, there's a procedure I like to follow to make sure the BIOS, motherboard, and processor are all working in harmony. Follow these steps:

1. Connect a monitor, keyboard, and mouse to the PC, and then turn on the monitor.

2. Connect the power cable to a wall socket and then to the power supply unit.

3. If the PSU's switch is off (0), turn it on (1).

4. Press the power switch on the front of the case. Make sure the case fans and CPU fan are all working.

5. Press Delete to enter the motherboard's BIOS configuration program, which is called CMOS Setup Utility.

note If all is well with your motherboard power connections, the board's power LED (located right beside the main 24-pin power header) will light up as soon as you turn on the PSU. If the LED remains off, turn off the PSU, remove the power cable, and then check your motherboard power cable connections.

13

6. Make sure your devices are working properly by checking the following:

   - On the Main screen, check the date and time and set them to the correct values, if necessary.

   - On the Main screen, check the SATA headers to ensure you see three devices listed: the two hard drives and the optical drive. Make note of the SATA header numbers used by the hard drives.

   - On the Main screen, check that the Installed Memory section shows 2048MB.

   - On the Boot screen, select Boot Device Priority, select 1st Boot Device, highlight CDROM, and press Enter.

7. Press F10 to save your changes and exit System Setup. The program asks you to confirm that you want to save changes.

8. Press Enter and then shut down your computer for now.

Configuring the RAID Array

Now let's get the RAID 0 array set up. Before getting to the specifics, you need to use another computer to create a disk with the RAID drivers for whatever operating system you'll be installing.

If you added a floppy drive to your gaming PC, you can put the drivers on a floppy. Here are the steps to follow:

1. Insert a blank floppy disk.

2. Insert the Striker Extreme DVD and run the Setup program on the disc.

3. Select the Make Disk tab.

4. Click the link for the RAID driver you want. For example, if you're going to install Windows Vista on your gaming PC, click NVIDIA Vista 32bit SATA RAID Driver. The program adds the drivers to the disk.

If you don't have a floppy drive (and who does these days?), then you have to jump through a lot more hoops. Basically, you need to create a custom Windows installation disc that includes the NVIDIA RAID drivers. You can do this using a nifty freeware program called nLite, which you can download from http://www.nliteos.com/.

note For this to work, you need an original disc for the version of Windows you'll be installing on your gaming PC, access to another computer that has a CD or DVD burner, and a program that can burn an ISO file to a disc. Note that many burners come with disc-burning software. For example, the Samsung drive that we used in this build comes with Nero, which is probably the most popular disc-burning software.

Before getting to nLite, you first need to copy the RAID drivers from the ASUS disc:

1. Insert the Striker Extreme DVD, but don't run the Setup program on the disc.

2. Open the DVD in Explorer and navigate to the one of the following folders:

   - **If you'll be installing Windows XP on your gaming PC**—Open the folder `\Drivers\Chipset\32bit\Xp\Ide\WinXP`.

   - **If you'll be installing Windows Vista on your gaming PC**—Open the folder `\Drivers\Chipset\Vista_32bit\Ide\Win2K`.

3. Copy the `sataraid` folder.

4. Paste the `sataraid` folder somewhere on your hard disk.

Now you're ready to create your custom Windows installation disc:

1. Start the nLite program. (If you're running nLite on Vista, you need to select Start, All Programs, nLite; right-click the nLite program icon; click Run As Administrator; and then enter your User Account Control credentials.)

2. In the initial nLite window, click Next.

3. Insert your Windows install disc.

4. Click Browse and then choose the drive where you inserted the Windows install disc. nLite prompts you to select a folder where the Windows files will be copied.

5. Select the folder you want to use. nLite copies the files from the Windows install disc to the folder.

6. Click Next.

7. Click Next. The Task Selection window appears, as shown in Figure 13.33.

8. In the Integrate section, click Drivers to activate it.

9. Click the Bootable ISO option to select it.

10. Select any other options you want to add to the disc. (For example, click Unattended to specify a username and product key.)

11. Click Next. The Drivers window appears.

12. Click Insert and then click Single Driver.

13. Navigate to the `sataraid` folder you copied earlier, click the `nvraid.inf` file, and then click Open. You now see the Storage Device Textmode Driver dialog box, as shown in Figure 13.34.

13

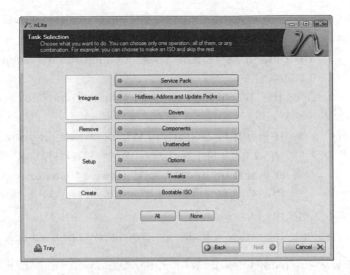

FIGURE 13.33
You use nLite to create a new Windows install disc that includes the NVIDIA RAID drivers.

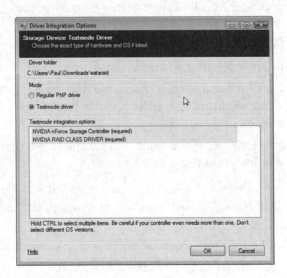

FIGURE 13.34
In this dialog box you should see the NVIDIA drivers listed.

14. Make sure that Textmode Driver is selected, and then click OK.

15. Click Next.

16. Fill in your other installation options, and then click Next. nLite asks if you want to start the process.

17. Click Yes. nLite combines all the files it needs for the custom Windows installation disc.

18. Click Next. The Bootable ISO window appears.

19. Click Make ISO, choose a folder in which to store the ISO file, and then click Save. nLite creates the ISO file.

20. Click Next.

21. Click Finish.

Insert a blank CD (for Windows XP) or DVD (for Windows Vista) in your burner and use your favorite disc-burning software to burn the ISO file to the blank disc.

Now you can configure the striped RAID 0 array on your new PC:

1. Restart your gaming PC and press Delete to enter the CMOS Setup Utility.

2. Select Advanced.

3. Select Onboard Device Configuration.

4. Select Serial-ATA Configuration.

5. Select RAID Enabled, press Enter, select Enabled, and then press Enter.

6. Select a SATA header used by one of the hard drives, press Enter, select Enabled, and then press Enter.

7. Select the SATA header used by the other hard drive, press Enter, select Enabled, and then press Enter.

8. Press F10 to save your changes and exit System Setup. The program asks you to confirm that you want to save changes.

9. Press Enter.

10. When the PC reboots, wait until you see the message Press F10 to enter RAID setup utility...; then press F10. The MediaShield Utility appears.

11. Select RAID Mode, press Enter, select Striping, and then press Enter.

12. Select the first hard drive and then press the right arrow key to add it to the array.

13. Select the second hard drive and then press the right arrow key to add it to the array.

14. Press **F7**. The utility asks if it can clear the disk data.

15. Press **Y**. The Array List appears.

13

16. Press **B** to configure the array as the boot device.

17. Press **Ctrl+X** to exit the utility.

Installing the Operating System

Okay, you're ready to install the operating system. If you see DISK BOOT FAILURE on your screen, don't worry about that. Here are the steps to follow:

> **note** If you're using a custom Windows installation disc, you don't need to do anything extra during the install. If you're using a floppy disk with the RAID drivers, wait until you see the Press F6 if you need to install a third-party SCSI or RAID driver message at the bottom of the screen. Press F6 and follow the instructions.

1. Replace the case's side panels, if you haven't done so already.

2. Connect the computer to your network by running a network cable from the back panel's network port to your switch or router.

3. Open the optical drive and insert your operating system disc. (For my build, I installed Windows Vista Home Premium.)

4. Press Enter. The computer will now boot from the disc and begin the OS install.

5. If you install Windows, be sure to update your version—particularly by installing all available security patches—immediately.

6. When the OS is installed and running, insert the NVIDIA nForce 680i SLI Support DVD that came with the board, run the install program, and then click the drivers you want to install (see Figure 13.35).

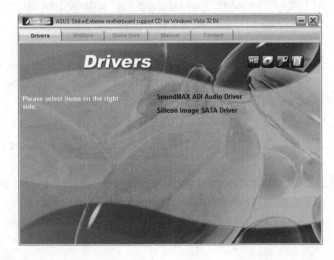

FIGURE 13.35

Install the motherboard drivers from the DVD that came with the board.

7. Update the motherboard's BIOS, as described in Chapter 17, "Maintaining Your Computer Hardware."

→   **See** "Updating the Motherboard BIOS," **p. 507**.

8. Use Device Manager to check for device problems (see Chapter 17) and install drivers for any device that Windows didn't recognize. (In this build, for example, you need to install the video card drivers. Be sure to install the drivers using the CD that comes with the card.)

→   **See** "Updating Device Drivers," **p. 519**.

9. After you install the video drivers in Windows Vista, you see the message shown in Figure 13.36. Click the message to display the NVIDIA Control Panel View Selection dialog box.

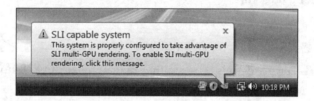

FIGURE 13.36

Click this message to enable SLI on your gaming PC.

10. Click Advanced Settings, and then click OK. The NVIDIA Control Panel appears.

11. Select the Enable SLI Technology option, and then click Apply.

Final Thoughts

This was a pretty smooth build, and there were no significant snags. As with the high-performance PC and its Cosmos case, I wasn't happy about having the power supply on the bottom of the Antec case because the 12V rail for the motherboard power supply has to climb over the video cards, required a cable tie to keep it away from the CPU cooler's fins, and with all

note Our killer gaming PC can easily run high-end games, including the latest DirectX 10 games. If you plan on running any DirectX 10 application, however, be sure to install Windows Vista update KB936710, which fixes a multi-GPU bug related to DirectX 10. You can find out more about this bug and download the update at http://support.microsoft.com/kb/936710.

After you've done that, you should then download another hotfix that fixes some virtual address space usage problems, particularly with the GeForce cards we used in this build. You can find out more about this hotfix and download it at http://support.microsoft.com/kb/940105.

13

that just *barely* made the connection. Having the PSU on the bottom of the case is better overall because it stabilizes the case and provides better airflow. However, PSU manufacturers are going to have to start making longer rails to accommodate this.

All told, the build took about six hours, *including* doing the photography that accompanies this chapter. Your build time should be shorter, particularly because there are no significant snags with our chosen hardware.

The initial boot went without a hitch, and the CMOS Setup Utility reported that all devices were present and accounted for. It took a while to configure the RAID array and create a custom Windows installation disc, but I had Vista Home Premium installed within an hour, and in another hour later I had the machine patched, the motherboard's drivers installed and its BIOS updated, and the video card driver installed. I was playing a rousing game of *Bioshock* not long after that!

From Here

- For the details on installing memory, **see** "Installing Memory Modules," **p. 205**.

- To learn about installing cards, **see** "Installing an Expansion Card," **p. 211**.

- If you need to temporarily remove the power supply, **see** "Releasing the Power Supply," **p. 234**.

- To learn how to use Device Manager to look for problem devices, **see** "Updating Device Drivers," **p. 519**.

- For instructions on updating the BIOS, **see** "Updating the Motherboard BIOS," **p. 507**.

- For the specifics on installing an Intel processor, **see** "Installing an Intel CPU in a Socket 775 Board," **p. 216**.

Building a Budget PC

Frugality is the mother of virtue.
—Justinian, *Corpus Juris*

I f you built (or just read along with) the previous two projects, you saw that their price tags were a bit on the high side: $1,700 for the high-performance PC (Chapter 13) and $1,900 for the killer gaming PC (Chapter 14). Those aren't cheap PCs, but in both cases I made significant compromises to keep the prices down! With top-shelf components throughout, these machines would have had our credit cards smoking thanks to price tags in the $4,000–$5,000 range.

One of the key things about a PC that many system builders forget is that no matter what hardware you use, the machine will eventually become obsolete. Yes, you can future-proof a machine to a certain extent by giving yourself room to expand, by buying high-quality parts, and by picking parts at or near the high end. However, all you're doing is delaying the inevitable.

With that in mind, there's a school of thought among some PC builders that it's better to put together an inexpensive machine every 6–12 months, rather than build one expensive PC every 2–3 years. With this strategy, you get fresh hardware fairly often, and you get the joy of building your own PC more frequently. Of course, this approach assumes you're looking to build just a general-purpose computer rather than one designed for a specific purpose, such as a home theater PC or a gaming rig.

With that assumption in mind, this chapter shows you how to build a PC when you're on a tight budget. I set out some design goals for the budget PC; then I take you through the parts I chose to meet those goals, from the computer case right down to the memory modules. Then, with the parts assembled, I show you step-by-step how to build your budget PC.

Design Goals for a Budget PC

This is a budget PC, so we need start with a budget, which I'm going to set at $400. That total is high enough that we won't have to resort to shoddy parts but low enough to be affordable to many. Within the constraints of that budget, we can set the following goals:

- **Thrifty, not cheap**—The key to building a solid budget PC is to avoid the lowest-of-the-low when it comes to parts. Generally speaking, you get what you pay for when it comes to computer components, so a PC built from the cheapest parts would end up exactly that: cheaply made. I guarantee you the machine would either not work or work poorly, and neither is acceptable in this build. Our goal, instead, is to look for good bargains on well-made, brand-name components.

- **A solid performer**—The budget PC needs to be a all-purpose machine, which means it needs to do email; web surfing; some light gaming; and business-oriented tasks such as word processing, spreadsheets, scheduling, and contact management. Nothing here is going to push the machine to its limits or require specialized hardware. This PC doesn't need a quad-core CPU; tons of RAM; a terabyte or 10,000 RPM hard drive; or high-end video and audio cards. All this bodes well for our budget.

- **No instant obsolescence**—Even though we're not spending a lot of money on this PC, and even though we're operating under the assumption that we'll build a replacement for it before too long, we *don't* want this machine to force us into building a replacement in just a few months. We need to select components that are good enough that this PC will perform well for as long as we want it to (at least a year).

■ **Get good value for the money—** The secret to reaching our design goals while staying within budget will be to get the most bang for the few bucks we're going to spend. That means not only buying brand-name parts for their high quality, but also looking for those components that provide excellent value for the money, whether it's extra features or extra performance.

> **note** The next few sections discuss specific parts for this build, but there's no reason you have to use the same components in your build. Feel free to tweak the parts based on your own budget and computing needs.

Choosing Parts for the Budget PC

Okay, our budget is set in stone, as is our determination to build a solid, reliable PC within the constraints of that budget. The next few sections keep the points from the previous section in mind and discuss the components that we'll use to put together our budget machine.

Selecting a Case for the Budget PC

In some of my early PC-building projects, I figured I could save money by skimping on the case. After all, it's just a case, right? Surely what's inside the case is more important, and the money saved on the case can be better spent on those internal components.

Boy, was I wrong! Building a PC using a cheap case is almost always an exercise in frustration, with much hair-pulling and gnashing of teeth. Nothing fits right; parts are hard to remove; and when you finally do remove them, they don't go back on the same way and you get lacerations all over your body from the sharp edges. Take my hard-won advice: although you can buy cases for $50 or less, don't do it.

Of course, we've got a budget to consider, so we can't go overboard right off the bat. Our budget PC requires a case that puts function over form, but not overly so. We still want our case to look good under our desk but not take up too much room. The ideal case should have good airflow so we don't have to worry about heat problems, front connectors for easy access, and a design that makes the build easier.

For this build, I chose the Antec Sonata III, a terrific mid-tower case that supports both ATX and microATX motherboards (see Figure 14.1). You can find this case online for about $115, which makes it a mid-priced case. However, that's actually a pretty good deal because the case comes with an Antec 500W power supply and a 120mm Antec case fan (the rear exhaust fan). None of these are top-of-the-line components, but they're more than adequate for our budget PC.

FIGURE 14.1

The Antec Sonata III: the case for our budget PC.

Besides these extra goodies that come with the case, the Sonata III also supports the following features:

- Two USB ports, one eSATA port, one microphone connector, and one Line Out connector in the front of the case.

- An aluminum front bezel that opens to reveal the external drive bays.

- Lots of drive bays: two 3.5-inch external (for a memory card reader or floppy drive), three 5.25-inch external (for optical or tape drives), and four 3.5-inch internal (for hard drives).

- Relatively easy side panel access: You remove two thumb screws and slide the panel off the case.

- The expansion slots are tool-free: A plastic latch slides out to insert the card and then slides back in to hold the card in place.

- Each hard drive bay is side-mounted for easy access and has its own bracket that attaches using side rails and slides in and out of the bay. You use special screws to attach the hard drive to the bracket. In a nice touch, the drive rests on silicone grommets, not metal, which reduces noise.

- A dust filter, which is removable for washing.

One thing our Antec case lacks is a front intake fan. Many people report that the case cools quite well with just the default rear exhaust fan, but you should never be overly thrifty when it comes to keeping your components cool. For a mere $10, I added an Antec Tri-Cool 120mm case fan to this build. Like the rear fan that comes with the case, this fan has a three-way switch that lets you set the fan speed. On the lowest speed, the fan still pushes through a decent 39 CFM, while keeping the noise down to 25 dBA. (The middle speed pushes 56 CFM at 28 dBA, while the high speed pushes 79 CFM at 30 dBA.)

Choosing a Motherboard for the Budget PC

For our budget PC's motherboard, we want a product from a big-name manufacturer, for sure, but we also want decent integrated features so we don't have to spend extra cash on things like expansion cards. That's a tall order, but there are some sub-$100 boards out there that meet these criteria if you look around and do your homework.

For this build, I went with an ASUS board (there's your big name) called the M2A-VM HDMI (see Figure 14.2). It's a microATX board that's available online for just $75.

FIGURE 14.2

The ASUS M2A-VM HDMI: the budget PC's motherboard.

Despite the low price, the ASUS M2A-VM HDMI offers a pretty good set of features:

- A clean and well-designed layout
- An AM2 processor socket that supports a wide variety of AMD processors, including the AMD Athlon 64 FX, AMD Athlon 64 X2, AMD Athlon 64, and AMD Sempron
- Support for dual-channel DDR2 800, 667, or 533 memory modules (up to 8GB)
- One PCI Express x16 slot, one PCI Express x1 slot, and two PCI slots
- Four external USB ports and three internal USB headers
- One external IEEE-1394 (FireWire) port
- Four internal SATA connectors
- Integrated Radeon X1250 video card, with DVI-D and VGA ports and support for dual monitors
- Integrated high-definition 8-channel audio
- Integrated 10/100/1000 network adapter
- A PCI Express x16 card that provides HDMI support (including HDMI, S-video, and composite video ports) and S/PDIF digital audio output

Selecting a Power Supply for the Budget PC

Our budget PC will be a relatively simple affair with the major devices being a hard drive, a DVD burner, and the motherboard's HDMI card. Any mid-range 400W power supply could handle this workload without a problem, so the Antec case's 500W PSU will be more than adequate for our needs.

Picking Out a CPU for the Budget PC

In a budget PC, the processor is where we can save big bucks because you don't need to spend $200 or $300 to get decent performance these days. At the lowest end of the processors are the single-core CPUs such as the AMD Sempron. However, single-core chips are on their way out, and with AMD you can move up to dual-core by spending just a few more dollars. In fact, for a mere $60, you can get the Athlon 64 X2 4000+ (see Figure 14.3), a dual-core CPU that runs at 2.1GHz, supports our motherboard's 2000MHz HyperTransport bus, and offers a 1MB L2 cache.

14

FIGURE 14.3

The Athlon 64 X2 4000+: the budget PC's processor.

As a final thought on the CPU, note that I'm going to use the stock cooler that AMD supplies with the retail version of the Athlon 64 X2 4000+. AMD's coolers do a decent job and are reasonably quiet when not under too much strain (which they won't be given the tasks this budget PC will be performing).

How Much Memory Does the Budget PC Need?

Memory is one of the most important performance factors in any PC, which means, simply, that the more memory you add to any system, the better that system will perform. Happily, we live in a world where the enhanced performance of extra RAM can be had for a relative pittance, with 1GB memory modules selling online for $25–$30.

All this means that it doesn't make any sense to hobble our budget PC with a mere 512MB or even 1GB of RAM. No, we're going to do the right thing and load up our machine with 2GB, so we'll be running with 1GB per core, which should offer great performance.

We need to match our modules to our motherboard's memory speed, and the ASUS M2A-VM HDMI can use PC2 6400 (DDR2 800), PC2 5400 (DDR2 667), or PC2 4200 (DDR2 533). I opted for two 1GB PC2 6400 memory modules from Corsair (see Figure 14.5), which set me back about $60.

14

FIGURE 14.4
The budget PC will use AMD's stock CPU cooler.

FIGURE 14.5
The budget PC's memory: a couple of 1GB PC2 6400 modules from Corsair.

14

Storage Options for the Budget PC

The budget PC needs a hard drive, of course, but we don't want one that's too big because we'll break our budget. We need just enough room to install an operating system, a few applications, and our data. With that in mind, I opted for the Western Digital Caviar SE WD1600AAJS, a 160GB drive that ought to be plenty big enough (see Figure 14.6). It's a SATA drive that's available in an OEM version online for just $50. It spins at 7,200 RPM; features an 8MB cache; and offers a very respectable 8.9 average seek time, so it won't slow us down.

FIGURE 14.6

The budget PC's hard drive: the Western Digital Caviar SE WD1600AAJS 160GB SATA drive.

Our budget PC needs an optical drive, of course, and for this machine I chose the Lite-On DH-20A4P, a dual-layer DVD/CD rewritable drive that supports write speeds of 20x DVD±R, 8x DVD+Rw, 6x DVD-RW, 8x DVD±R DL, 48x CD-R, 32x CD-RW, plus read speeds of 16x DVD-ROM and 48x CD-ROM, all for a mere $30 or so.

Determining the Video Needs of the Budget PC

The ASUS M2A-VM HDMI motherboard comes with a Radeon X1250 GPU integrated. This is an excellent GPU that provides very high-quality graphics. It requires 256MB of system memory, but that's not a huge problem because we've supplied our budget PC with a generous 2GB of RAM. The Radeon chip supports DVI-D resolutions up to 2560×1600, RGB resolutions up to 2048×1536, and dual monitors. Combine these impressive stats with the HDMI

14

PCIe card supplied with the motherboard, and we can ask for no more from an integrated video system. Therefore, we won't be adding a separate video card to the budget PC.

Selecting Audio Equipment for the Budget PC

When trying to save money on a PC build, one of the first components to go is the separate audio card because good ones are expensive and cheap ones are often no better than what's integrated into the motherboard. This build is no exception. Our motherboard has integrated 8-channel high-def audio, although the Realtek chip isn't the greatest one around. The HDMI card that comes with the board offers S/PDIF digital audio output, so sticking with the board's audio is a no-brainer for this project.

Choosing Networking Hardware for the Budget PC

Even a budget PC must network, of course, and these days networking is easier than ever because it's a rare motherboard that doesn't come with a networking adapter built in. Even better, almost all motherboard-based NICs support Ethernet (10Mbps), Fast Ethernet (100Mbps), and Gigabit Ethernet (1Gbps or 1,000Mbps), so you're covered no matter what type of network you'll be connecting to. Our budget PC is no exception because our ASUS motherboard has a 10/100/1000 NIC onboard. Therefore, no extra networking equipment is needed.

Pricing the Budget PC

As you've seen, our budget PC doesn't have any big-ticket items. The most expensive component is the case, although as I mentioned before you need a decent case with *any* build—even one on a budget. We also saved quite a bit of money by going with the stock CPU cooler, the PSU and fan that came with the Antec case, the motherboard's integrated video and audio chips, and the integrated NIC.

Table 14.1 summarizes the budget PC's components and prices. As you can see, our total price of $400 is right on our budget.

Table 14.1   Components and Prices for the Budget PC

Component	Model	Average Price
Case	Antec Sonata III	$115
Case fan	Antec Tri-Cool 120mm	$10
Motherboard	ASUS M2A-VM HDMI	$75

Table 14.1   Continued

Component	Model	Average Price
Power supply	Comes with the case	N/A
CPU	AMD Athlon 64 X2 4000+	$60
CPU cooler	AMD stock cooler	N/A
Memory	Corsair XMS2 PC2 6400 1 GB (×2)	$60
Hard drive	Western Digital Caviar SE WD1600AAJS 160GB	$50
Optical drive	Lite-On DH-20A4P DVD/CD Rewritable Drive	$30
Video card	Motherboard integrated	N/A
Audio card	Motherboard integrated	N/A
Network card	Motherboard integrated	N/A
TOTAL		**$400**

Putting Together the Budget PC

With parts at the ready (see Figure 14.7), your tools by your side, and a stretch of free time ahead (you can build this PC in an afternoon or evening), you're ready to start the build. The rest of this chapter takes you through the steps you need to follow. Happy building!

FIGURE 14.7
The budget PC, ready for the build.

Getting the Case Ready

The Antec case requires a bit of prep work before we can move on to more productive tasks:

- **Remove the side panel**—Remove the two thumb screws that attach the side panel to the back of the case. Slide the side panel's plastic handle toward the front of the case, swing the panel toward you, and then remove it.

- **Liberate the screws, standoffs, and other case hardware**— These bits and pieces are in a bag, and that bag is inside a box that comes behind the internal 3.5-inch drive bays, which consists of four removable metal trays. Remove the bottom two trays (for each tray, squeeze the metal clips toward each other until they release and then slide out the tray), remove the box, and then reinsert the drive trays.

- **Remove the generic I/O shield**—As you see in the next section, when test-fitting the motherboard in the case to determine where to put the standoffs, it helps if the I/O shield isn't in the way. Gently push the edges of the I/O shield back into the case until it's loose and you can remove it.

Installing the Motherboard Standoffs

A standoff (or a *mount point*, as it's often called) is a hex-nut screw, which means it actually consist of two parts: a bottom screw that enables you to insert the standoff into a hole in the side of the case and a top hex nut into which you can insert a screw. The idea is that you install from eight to ten (depending on the motherboard form factor) of these standoffs into the case, sit the motherboard on top of the standoffs, align the motherboard's holes with the hex nuts, and then attach the motherboard. This gives the board a solid footing but also separates the board from the metal case to prevent shorting out the board.

Installing the standoffs is easiest when the motherboard is bare, so that should be your first task:

1. Find the standoffs that came with the case and put them aside.

2. Lay the case flat on its side, with the open side facing up.

3. Move all the case cables out of the way so you can clearly see the side panel that has the mounting holes. If you have trouble getting the power supply cable out of the way, consider temporarily removing the

power supply, as described in Chapter 9, "Scavenging an Old PC for Parts."

→   **See** "Releasing the Power Supply," **p. 234**.

4. Remove the preinstalled standoffs.

5. If you haven't done so already, touch something metal to ground yourself.

6. Take the motherboard out of its anti-static bag and lay the board inside the case, oriented so the board's back-panel I/O ports are lined up and flush with the case's I/O slot.

7. Note which case holes correspond to the holes in the motherboard (see Figure 14.8). You might need to use a flashlight to ensure that there's a case hole under each motherboard hole.

> **caution** I suggest removing preinstalled standoffs because you want to make sure that you only have the correct number of standoffs inserted and that they're inserted in the correct positions. One standoff in the wrong position can cause a short circuit.

> **tip** Rather than trying to remember which case holes correspond with each motherboard hole, you can mark the correct case holes. After you have the board lined up with the holes, stick a felt-tip pen through each hole and mark the case. (You might need to offset the board slightly to do this properly.)

Mounting Holes

FIGURE 14.8

The motherboard has ten holes through which you attach the board to the standoffs.

14

426 PART II   PC Building and Upgrading Projects

8. Place the motherboard carefully aside.

9. Screw the standoffs into the corresponding holes in the side of the case.

Just to be safe, you might want to place the motherboard into the case once again to double-check that each motherboard hole corresponds to a standoff.

Getting the Motherboard Ready for Action

Although you might be tempted to install the motherboard right away, and technically you can do that, it's better to hold off for a bit and do some of the work on the board while it's out of the case. We'll be installing the processor and the memory modules, and although it isn't impossible to install these parts with the board inside the case, it's a lot easier outside.

Before getting started, be sure to touch something metal to ground yourself. Now take the motherboard and lay it flat on your work surface. For the ASUS, it's best to orient the board so the I/O ports are facing away from you. This enables you to work with the processor socket without having to go over the heatsinks or the I/O ports.

Inserting the Processor

Begin by installing the AMD Athlon 64 X2 4000+ processor in the motherboard's AM2 socket. I won't go into the details here because I showed you how to insert AMD processors back in Chapter 8.

→   **See** "Installing an AMD CPU in a Socket AM2 Board," **p. 219**.

Installing the CPU Cooler

Now it's time to install the AMD stock cooler. We're using the stock cooler that came with the processor, so we already know it's compatible with both the CPU and the motherboard (and the AMD warranty on the processor remains in effect). Even better, the stock cooler already comes with the thermal compound preapplied, so we don't need to mess with any of that. I usually wait until the motherboard is installed in the case before adding the cooler, but the clip that holds the cooler in place is tricky to install even outside the case, and would be nearly impossible inside the case.

1. If the plastic lever on the cooler's clip is perpendicular to the clip, pivot the lever counterclockwise so it stands straight up.

2. Remove the plastic that covers the cooler's heatsink. Take care not to smudge the thermal grease on the underside of the heatsink.

14

3. Orient the cooler over the CPU socket so the plastic lever that sticks up from the clip is on the same side of the CPU socket as the Northbridge (see Figure 14.9).

FIGURE 14.9

Orient the cooler over the CPU socket as shown here.

4. On the side opposite the lever, maneuver the square hole in the clip over the rectangular protrusion in the plastic bracket that surrounds the CPU socket, as shown in Figure 14.10.

5. On the same side as the lever, press down on the clip and maneuver the square hole in the clip over the rectangular protrusion in the plastic bracket.

6. Make sure the cooler's heatsink is lined up perfectly with the processor.

7. Pivot the lever clockwise until it snaps into place, as shown in Figure 14.11.

8. Connect the cooler's power cable to the motherboard's CPU fan header (labeled CPU_FAN), as shown in Figure 14.12.

FIGURE 14.10

Slip one end of the clip onto the bracket.

FIGURE 14.11

Pivot the lever clockwise to secure the cooler.

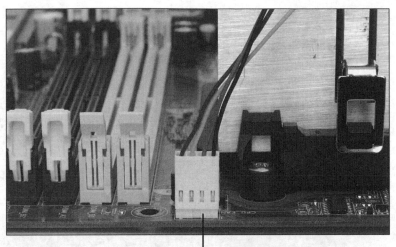

CPU fan header is located here.

FIGURE 14.12

Connect the CPU cooler's power cable to the motherboard's CPU fan header.

Inserting the Memory Modules

Now it's time to populate your board with your memory modules. Where you install the modules on the ASUS M2A-VM HDMI board depends on how many modules you're adding (see Figure 14.13):

- **One module**—Install the module in either socket A1 or in socket B1 (the yellow sockets).

- **Two modules**—Install identical modules in sockets A1 and B1 (the yellow sockets). This ensures a proper dual-channel configuration.

- **Three modules**—Install a set of identical modules in sockets A1 and B1 (the yellow sockets) and the third module in either socket A2 or socket B2. I don't recommend this configuration because the size of the memory channel is determined by the third memory stick. For example, if you have two 1GB modules A1 and B1, and a 1GB module in A2 or B2, then the memory bandwidth will be only 1GB.

- **Four modules**—Install one set of identical modules in sockets A1 and B1 (the yellow sockets) and a second set of identical modules in sockets A2 and B2 (the black sockets). This ensures a proper dual-channel configuration.

14

FIGURE 14.13

The memory module sockets on the ASUS M2A-VM HDMI.

I won't go through the installation steps here since I already covered how to install memory modules in Chapter 8, "Basic Skills for PC Building and Upgrading." Figure 14.14 shows our motherboard with our two 1GB modules installed.

➜   **See** "Installing Memory Modules," **p. 205.**

Installing the Motherboard

With your motherboard populated with a processor, cooler, and memory, it's just about ready to roll. The next few sections take you through the detailed installation steps for the motherboard. This is the most finicky, most time-consuming, and most important part of the build. As you'll see, getting a motherboard configured involves lots of separate steps and lots of cable connections. It's crucial to take your time and make sure you've got all the connections just so.

FIGURE 14.14

Our motherboard with two 1GB memory modules in place.

Inserting the Motherboard I/O Shield

Earlier you removed the case's generic I/O shield, so now it's time to insert the I/O shield that came with the motherboard. Take the motherboard's I/O shield and fit it into the case's I/O opening. Make sure you have the I/O shield oriented properly:

- The two holes for the mouse and keyboard PS/2 ports should be at the top, while the three audio ports should be at the bottom.

- The protruding ridge that runs around the I/O shield should face the back of the case.

When the I/O shield is flush with the case, firmly press the bottom of the shield until it snaps into place; then press the top of the shield until it, too, snaps into place.

tip It's not always easy to get the I/O shield perfectly seated. If you have trouble getting a corner of the shield to snap into place, use the end of a plastic screwdriver handle to gently tap the recalcitrant corner into place.

14

Attaching the Motherboard to the Case

With the custom I/O shield in place, you're now ready to install the motherboard inside the case. Here are the steps to follow:

1. Move all the case cables out of the way so you can clearly see the side panel that has the mounting holes and the installed standoffs.

2. If you haven't done so already, touch something metal to ground yourself.

3. Gently and carefully maneuver the motherboard into the case and lay it on top of the standoffs.

4. Adjust the position of the board so the board's back-panel I/O ports are lined up and flush with the openings in the I/O shield, as shown in Figure 14.15.

FIGURE 14.15

Make sure the motherboard's I/O ports are lined up and flush with the I/O shield's openings.

5. You should now see a standoff under each motherboard mounting hole. If not, it likely means the I/O shield isn't fully seated. Remove the board, fix the I/O shield, and then try again.

6. Use the mounting screws supplied with the case to attach the board to each standoff. To ensure a trouble-free installation, I use the following technique:

> **note** Bear in mind, however, that it's normal for the board's mounting holes to be slightly offset from the standoffs. There's a bit of give to the I/O shield, so you usually have to force the board slightly to the left (toward the I/O shield) to get the holes and standoffs to line up perfectly.

- First insert but don't tighten the upper-right screw.

- Next insert but don't tighten the bottom-left screw. (The bottom-left screw is often the hardest one to install because it's usually in the corner of the case. If you prefer to start with an easier target, insert the bottom-middle screw, instead.)

- Make sure all the holes and standoffs are properly aligned, and then tighten the first two screws.

- Insert and tighten all the rest of the screws.

Connecting the Front-Panel USB and eSATA Cables

Our Antec case offers the convenience of two front-panel USB 2.0 ports. You need to connect the USB 2.0 ports' cable (the connector is labeled USB) to one of the motherboard's internal USB headers.

One nice perk we get with the Antec case is a front-panel eSATA port, which will be super-convenient for connecting an external SATA drive for backups or whatever. For this port to work, you must connect its black SATA cable to one of the motherboard's SATA headers.

Figure 14.16 shows the USB and eSATA cable connections.

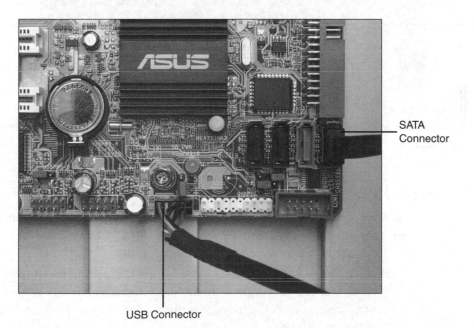

FIGURE 14.16

Connect the cable that runs from the USB 2.0 front-panel port to a USB headers, and connect the cable that runs from the eSATA front-panel port to a SATA header.

Connecting the Front-Panel Audio Cables

The rest of the Antec case's front-panel ports consist of Line Out (audio output) and Mic In (microphone input) audio ports. Note that the audio ports' cable has two connectors, one for standard audio (labeled AC '97) and one for high-definition audio (labeled HDA). Our ASUS motherboard supports HD audio, so you need to connect the HDA connector to the motherboard's audio header (labeled AAFP), as shown in Figure 14.17.

FIGURE 14.17

Connect the cable that runs from the front-panel audio ports to the AAFP audio header on the motherboard.

Connecting the Power Switch, Reset Switch, and LEDs

The next item on our build to-do list is to tackle the mess of wires snaking out from the front of the case, just below the external drive bays. These wires correspond to the following front panel features:

■ **Hard drive LED**—This LED lights up when the hard drive is active. It consists of two wires with a single connector: the blue wire is the negative (ground) lead, the red wire is the positive (signal) lead, and the connector is labeled H.D.D. LED.

- **Power switch**—This is the button you press to turn the system on and off. Its lead consists of two wires, one white and one green, and the connector is labeled POWER SW.

- **Reset switch**—This is the button you press to reboot a running system. Its lead consists of two wires, one white and one blue, and the connector is labeled RESET SW.

- **Power LED**—This LED lights up when the system is powered up. It consists of two wires with a single connector: the blue wire is the negative (ground) lead, and the green wire is the positive (signal) lead; the connector is labeled POWER LED.

- **Speaker**—This is the lead for the case's external speaker. It consists of an orange and black pair of wires with a connector labeled SPEAKER.

Connecting all these wires is a bit tricky, but the good news is that the ASUS motherboard comes with a special connector that can greatly simplify things. It's called the Q Connector and contains the 12 pins that are required by the five front-panel connectors. Each pin is labeled, so you can easily see where each front-panel connector goes. After you've attached all five leads, you then attach the Q Connector itself to the motherboard's front-panel header.

Figure 14.18 shows the pin assignments on the Q Connector.

Given the pin assignments shown in Figure 14.18, here's how you connect the front-panel wires:

- **Hard drive LED**—Connect this with the red wire on IDE LED + and the blue wire on IDE LED –.

- **Power switch**—Connect this with the green wire on PWR and the white wire on Ground (Power).

- **Reset switch**—Connect this with the blue wire on Reset and the white wire on Ground (Reset).

- **Power LED**—Connect this with the green wire on PLED + and the blue wire on PLED –.

- **Speaker**—Connect this with the orange wire on +5V and the black wire on Speaker.

Figure 14.19 shows the wires connected to the Q Connector and points out the motherboard's front-panel header to which you attach the Q Connector.

14

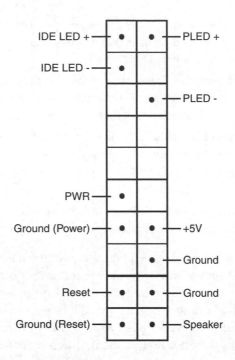

FIGURE 14.18

The pin assignments used on the Q Connector.

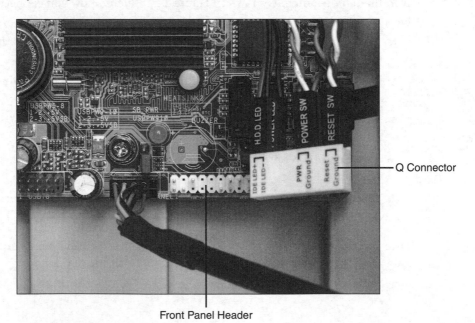

Front Panel Header

FIGURE 14.19

Connect the front-panel wires to the Q Connector, and connect the Q Connector to the motherboard's front-panel header.

Installing the Hard Drive

The Antec case offers four internal hard drive bays, each of which has a metal bracket that slides in and out of the bay. You remove the brackets, attach the hard drive, and then reinsert the bracket.

Here are the steps to follow to install a hard drive:

1. Pull the bracket out of the drive bay you want to use.

2. Lay the hard drive inside the bracket as follows:

   ■ The interface and power connectors should face toward the back (open) end of the bracket.

   ■ The hard drive label should be facing up (that is, the underside of the hard drive—the side where the circuit board appears—should sit on the silicone grommets inside the bracket).

3. Align the four holes on the underside of the hard drive with the four holes on the bracket, and then use screws to attach the hard drive to the bracket. Figure 14.20 shows the hard drive attached to the bracket, and it also shows one of the screws you need to use to make the attachment.

> **note** There's actually no reason you couldn't orient the drive with the interface and power connectors facing the opposite way (that is, toward the inside of the case). If you do this, however, be sure to connect the SATA interface and power cables to the drive before inserting the bracket back into the drive bay.

FIGURE 14.20

Each drive bay contains a bracket to which you attach the hard drive.

4. Slide the bracket/hard drive into the drive bay until it clicks into place.

5. Run a SATA cable from the hard drive's interface connection to a SATA header on the motherboard, as shown in Figure 14.21.

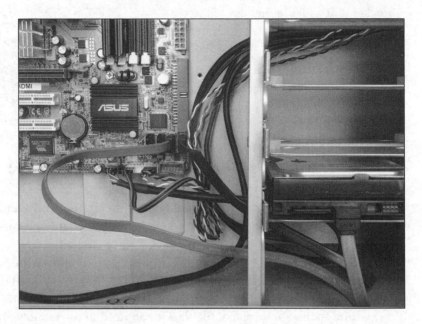

FIGURE 14.21

The hard drive with a SATA interface cable attached.

Installing the Optical Drive

You add the optical drive to your system by inserting it into one of the Antec case's 5.25-inch external drive bays. Here are the steps to follow:

1. Touch something metal to ground yourself.

2. Open the bezel door in the front of the case.

3. Remove the plastic cover for the top drive bay.

4. Remove the two purple rails that are attached to the inside of the drive bay cover.

5. Use screws to attach the rails to the sides of the optical drive, as shown in Figure 14.22.

note Most optical drives give you a choice of fronts, usually beige or black. If your optical drive currently has a beige front, switch to the black, which will look better with the black bezel of the Antec case. See the drive's manual to learn how to exchange fronts.

Insert two screws on each side of the
bracket to secure the drive to the bracket.

FIGURE 14.22

Attach a purple rail to each side of the optical drive.

6. With the optical drive's connectors facing the inside of the case, slide
   the drive into a drive bay until it clicks into place. The front face of the
   optical drive should be lined up with the case bezel.

7. Close the bezel door.

8. Run a SATA interface cable from the optical drive's interface connection
   to one of the motherboard's SATA headers, as shown in Figure 14.23.

Inserting the HDMI Card

Finally, we need to install the HDMI card that came with the ASUS board. This
is a PCI Express x16 card, so it will fill our board's single x16 slot. I won't go
into all the details here because I gave you specific instructions on inserting
an expansion card in Chapter 8.

→   **See** "Installing an Expansion Card," **p. 211**.

Here are the basic steps:

1. Touch something metal to ground yourself.

2. Remove the screw and the slot cover that corresponds to the PCIe x16
   slot.

3. Insert the HDMI card into the slot and attach it to the case with the
   screw.

4. Connect the HDMI card's S/PDIF digital audio cable to the motherboard's S/PDIF Out digital audio header, as shown in Figure 14.24.

14

FIGURE 14.23

The optical drive's SATA interface connection.

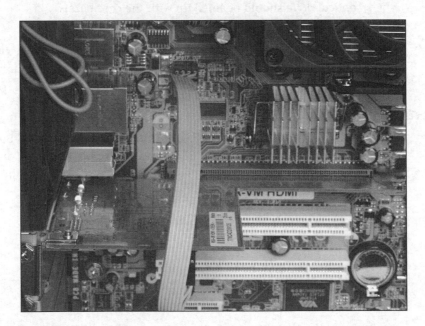

FIGURE 14.24

Connect the HDMI card's digital audio cable to the digital audio header on the motherboard.

Installing the Case Intake Fan

To ensure good airflow through the case, we should add to the case's default exhaust fan an intake fan. Our Antec TriCool 120mm fan attaches to the fan mount, which is on the outside wall of the 3.5-inch drive bays. (By *outside*, I mean that part of the wall that faces the motherboard.)

Here are the steps to follow:

1. Orient the fan so the Antec label faces the inside of the case.

2. Align the fan with the mount's four holes.

3. Use the long screws that came with the Antec case to attach the fan to the mount, as shown in Figure 14.25.

Insert two screws here to secure the fan to the case.

Insert two screws here to secure the fan to the case.

FIGURE 14.25

Attach the intake fan to the fan mount on the wall of the 3.5-inch drive bays.

Connecting the Power Cables

Our next order of business is to connect the power cables that supply juice to the motherboard and peripherals.

14

First, note that our ASUS board has two power headers:

- A 24-pin main power header, into which you plug the power supply's 24-pin connector, as pointed out in Figure 14.26.

- A 4-pin 12V header, into which you plug the power supply's 4-pin connector, as pointed out in Figure 14.26.

tip Most of the pins on a power cable connector are square, but a few are rounded on one side. These rounded pins have corresponding rounded holes on the header. To install a power cable connector with the correct orientation, match up the rounded pins with the rounded holes.

4-Pin 12V Connection

24-Pin Main Connection

FIGURE 14.26

Connect the power supply's 24-pin and 4-pin connectors to the corresponding headers on the motherboard.

Your next chore is to connect the power leads for the two case fans. The rear exhaust fan (the one that came with the Antec case) only has a 4-pin Molex connector, so you must connect it to a 4-pin Molex connector on a power supply peripheral rail. The front intake fan that we added earlier comes with both a 4-pin Molex connector and a 3-pin motherboard connector. Attach the Molex connector to a 4-pin Molex connector on a power supply peripheral rail, and attach the 3-pin connector to the motherboard fan header labeled CHA_FAN1, which is located in the upper-right corner of the board.

Finally, you need to get power to the drives:

1. Connect a SATA power cable from the power supply to the optical drive's power connector.

2. Connect a SATA power cable from the power supply to the hard drive's power connector.

Final Steps

Okay, your budget PC is just about done. However, there are a few tasks you should perform and a few things you need to check. Here's the list:

- **Route and tie off the cables**—A well-built PC doesn't just have cables all over the place. Instead, the cables should be routed as far away from the motherboard as possible, and as close to the sides of the case as possible. This makes the inside of the case look neater and improves airflow throughout the case. Use cable ties if need be to keep unruly cables out of the way.

- **Double-check connections**—Go through all the connections and make sure they're properly seated.

- **Double-check devices**—Check the hard drive, optical drive, and expansion cards to ensure that they're not loose.

- **Look for loose screws**—Make sure there are no loose screws or other extraneous bits and pieces in the case.

Powering Up

Now, at last, you're ready to fire up your new PC. Rather than just diving willy-nilly into the operating system install, however, there's a procedure I like to follow to ensure the BIOS, motherboard, and processor are all working in harmony. Follow these steps:

1. Connect a monitor, keyboard, and mouse to the PC, and then turn on the monitor.

2. Connect the power cable to a wall socket and then to the power supply unit.

3. If the PSU's switch is off (0), turn it on (1).

14

4. Open the bezel door and press the power switch on the front of the case. Make sure the case fans and CPU fan are all working.

5. Press Delete to enter the motherboard's BIOS configuration program, which is called CMOS Setup Utility.

6. Make sure your devices are working properly by checking the following:

> **note** If all is well with your motherboard power connections, the board's power LED (located right beside the main 24-pin power header) will light up as soon as your turn on the PSU. If the LED remains off, turn off the PSU, remove the power cable, and then check your motherboard power cable connections.

■ In the Main screen, check the date and time and set them to the correct values, if necessary.

■ In the Main screen, check the SATA headers to make sure you see two devices listed: one is the hard drive and the other is the optical drive.

■ In the Main screen, check that the Installed Memory section shows 2048MB.

■ In the Boot screen, select Boot Device Priority, select 1st Boot Device, highlight CDROM, and press Enter.

7. Press F10 to save your changes and exit CMOS Setup. The program asks you to confirm that you want to save changes:

■ In the Main screen, select System Information and check the Processor section to make sure the Intel Core 2 Quad appears. Also, check that the System Memory section shows 2048MB available.

■ In the Boot screen, select Boot Device Priority, select 1st Boot Device, highlight CDROM, and press Enter.

8. Press F10 to save your changes and exit System Setup. The program asks you to confirm you want to save changes.

9. Press Enter and then press the power switch to shut down the PC.

10. Replace the case's side panel.

11. Connect the computer to your network by running a network cable from the back panel's network port to your switch or router.

12. Press the power switch on the front panel.

13. Open the optical drive and insert your operating system disc. (For my build, I installed Ubuntu, a really nice—and, appropriately for a

14

budget PC, free—Linux distribution.) The computer will now boot from the disc and install the OS.

14. If you install Windows, be sure to update your version—particularly by installing all available security patches—immediately. Also, use Device Manager to check for device problems (see Chapter 17) and install drivers for any device Windows didn't recognize.

→   **See** "Updating Device Drivers," **p. 519**.

15. Update the motherboard's BIOS, as described in Chapter 17.

→   **See** "Updating the Motherboard BIOS," **p. 507**.

When the OS is installed and running, insert the ASUS 690G Chipset Support DVD that came with the board and run the install program. This contains all the drivers you need for the board's devices.

If you decide to install Linux as I did, you need to follow these steps to start the program that installs the Linux drivers:

1. Insert the disc and navigate to the /LinuxDrivers/Chipset directory.

2. Copy the file in that directory to the desktop. (In my version, the file is called ati-driver-installer-8.35.5-x86.x86_64.run.)

3. Start a Terminal session and change to your user account's Desktop directory (that is, enter cd /home/*user*/Desktop/, where *user* is your username).

4. Make the .run file executable by running the command chmod a+x *file*, where *file* is the name of the .run file. Here's an example:

   chmod a+x ati-driver-installer-8.35.5-x86.x86_64.run

5. Enter the command sudo ./ati-driver-installer-8.35.5-x86.x86_64.run, and enter your password if prompted. If the install program runs, skip the rest of these steps. Otherwise, you'll see a message similar to this:

   ```
   Detected version of X does not have a matching 'x130' directory
   You may override the detected version using the following syntax:
       X_VERSION=<xdir> ./ati-driver-installer-<ver>-<arch>.run
       ➥[--install]

   The following values may be used for <xdir>:
       x430          XFree86 4.3.x
       x430_64a      XFree86 4.3.x 64-bit
   ```

14

```
x680          X.Org 6.8.x
x680_64a      X.Org 6.8.x 64-bit
x690          X.Org 6.9.x
x690_64a      X.Org 6.9.x 64-bit
x700          X.Org 7.0.x
x700_64a      X.Org 7.0.x 64-bit
x710          X.Org 7.1.x
x710_64a      X.Org 7.1.x 64-bit
```

6. Determine which version you need to install (for example, I'm running Ubuntu 7.10, so I need x710).

7. Start a super-user shell by running the command sudo -i.

8. Enter the command X_VERSION=*xdir* ./*file*, where *xdir* is the version number from step 6 and *file* is the name of the .run file. Here's an example:

   ```
   X_VERSION=x710 ./ati-driver-installer-8.35.5-x86.x86_64.run
   ```

   You should now see the installer, as shown in Figure 14.27.

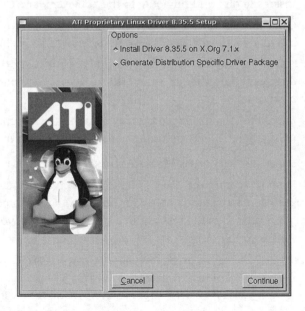

FIGURE 14.27
Run the Linux Driver Installer to install the chipset drivers.

Final Thoughts

This build was a real pleasure from start to finish. The Antec case was great to work with: roomy and well laid-out, with excellent fit-and-finish. Everything installed without a hitch, and the build went real quick because we didn't have to install a power supply, video card, sound card, or networking card. All told, the build took about three hours, *including* doing the photography that accompanies this chapter, which is very fast. Your build time should be even shorter.

> **tip** If you decide to install Ubuntu and are new to the world of Linux, I suggest picking up a copy of *Ubuntu Linux Unleashed, 2008 Edition*, by Andrew Hudson and Paul Hudson, published by Sams.

The initial boot went without any problems, and CMOS Setup reported that all devices were present and accounted for. I had Ubuntu installed within 25 minutes, and another half hour later I had the machine patched, the ASUS motherboard's drivers installed, and its BIOS updated.

From Here

- For the details on installing memory, **see** "Installing Memory Modules," **p. 205**.
- To learn about installing cards, **see** "Installing an Expansion Card," **p. 211**.
- If you need to temporarily remove the power supply, **see** "Releasing the Power Supply," **p. 234**.
- To learn how to use Device Manager to look for problem devices, **see** "Updating Device Drivers," **p. 519**.
- For instructions on updating the BIOS, **see** "Updating the Motherboard BIOS," **p. 507**.
- For the specifics on installing an AMD processor, **see** "Installing an AMD CPU in a Socket AM2 Board," **p. 219**.

14

This Old PC: Renovating a Computer

Could you and I with Him conspire

To grasp this Sorry Scheme of Things entire,

Would not we shatter it to bits—and then

Remold it nearer to the Heart's Desire!

—Edward Fitzgerald, *The Rubaiyat of Omar Khayyam*

We live in a world of rapid and relentless obsolescence: a car is worth a fraction of the selling price as soon as you drive it off the lot; our cell phones come and go like streetcars; a computer is practically obsolete after the first boot. Faced with this inevitable decay, most people chuck the old and ring in the new: The lease is up? Great, let's start a new one! My cell phone's dead? No problem, I'll get another! Our computer is yesterday's technology? Let's get today's, instead!

If there's a problem with this disposable lifestyle, it's that it tends to be awfully hard on the planet because new things require new resources and old things have to rot *somewhere*. Plus, it's expensive to always be constantly replacing our gadgets. Finally, although buying new things can be exhilarating, the thrill wears off soon after each new gadget is up and running.

Many people are saying "Enough!" to all this. They'd rather save the planet's resources, avoid contributing to landfills, save a few bucks, and take on a project that's satisfying and interesting. They want, in short, not to toss their old technology, but to *upgrade* it to make it better and give it a longer life. You might have a tough time upgrading a cell phone, but a PC is upgradeable and then some. It might be some extra RAM, a new video card, a bigger hard drive, a faster processor, some quieter fans, or even all of the above. However far you're willing to go, it doesn't take much effort or cash to give an old computer a new lease on life, as you see in this chapter.

Getting Started: Researching the Upgrade

Like building a new PC, a proper upgrade doesn't proceed willy-nilly. You need to get your bearings and get a sense both of what needs to be done and, perhaps more importantly, what *can* be done. To do that, I always begin an upgrade by doing five things:

- Look inside the computer to check out the existing hardware.
- Access the system's BIOS configuration program to gather information about the machine.
- If the computer is currently running Windows XP or Vista, launch the Device Manager and System Information utilities, which provide oodles of information about the system.
- If the computer was built by a mainstream manufacturer, look for the system manual online.
- Use online utilities to gather information about specific components.

I talk about each of these techniques in the next few sections.

Looking Inside the Computer

Before you begin your PC renovations, it's best to take stock of what you're dealing with so that you can better tell what needs to be replaced and what you can replace it with. So, the first thing I always do is go under the hood and see what I've got to work with inside the computer.

In this chapter, I take a Dell computer I bought nearly five years ago and see if I can spruce it up. To begin, I removed the side panel of the Dell. Figure 15.1 shows what I saw: lots of dust!

FIGURE 15.1

The Dell's innards revealed: what a mess!

So, my first chore was to tidy things up a bit:

- I cleaned the inside to get rid of the dust.

→ **See** "Cleaning the Computer," **p. 498**.

- I disconnected the interface and power cables and stuffed them out of the way so that I could take a good look at things.
- I moved the processor's airflow shroud out of the way.

Figure 15.2 shows the results.

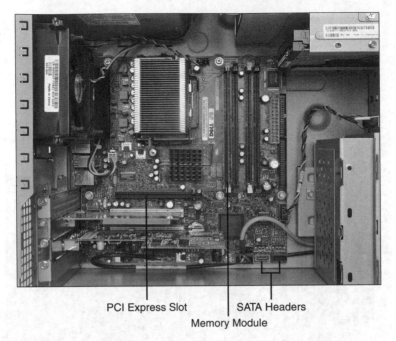

PCI Express Slot   SATA Headers
Memory Module

FIGURE 15.2

The Dell actually cleans up too not bad.

I immediately saw three things that made me very confident that I could upgrade this computer significantly:

- The memory sockets contain just a single module. This gives us lots of room to improve the memory by adding at least one other module. Also, I pulled out the existing module and the sticker on the side of the DIMM told me it contained 512MB of RAM, which is low (and explains much of Vista's poor performance because 512MB is Vista's minimum). The sticker also told me that the RAM is PC2-3200 (DDR2-400), so fingers crossed that the motherboard supports a faster RAM speed. We'll also have to find out whether this motherboard supports dual-channel mode; if it does, we can kick things up an extra notch.

- The motherboard includes a single PCI Express slot. The current video card is a PCI card, so we'll be able to upgrade the card to PCIe for much improved performance (which will, again, make Vista very pleased).

- The motherboard has a couple of SATA headers. This existing hard drive is PATA (which I know because its interface cable was connected to the motherboard's PATA header), so a move from PATA to SATA bodes well for the hard drive upgrade.

On the downside, that processor cooler looks pretty firmly ensconced, and I see no obvious way to remove it. After I research which processors are compatible with this machine's chipset, I'll have a better idea of whether tackling that cooler is worth it.

Accessing the System BIOS Configuration Program

Although you can glean some specific information by physically examining the inside of the PC (such as the memory data that I got from the DIMM), we're going to need a lot more data if we hope to perform a successful and useful upgrade. A great source for this extra data is the motherboard's BIOS configuration program, which you access at system startup. For the Dell machine (I had to press F2 after power-up but before Windows started loading), the BIOS utility told me the following:

note Snags such as the head-scratching CPU cooler are pretty routine when you're working with PCs built by mainstream manufacturers. They all have unique ways of organizing, orienting, and attaching components, and some of those ways aren't meant to be fiddled with by the likes of you and I.

note If you're not sure which key to press to access the BIOS setup program on your old PC, look for a message such as Press F2 to Enter BIOS Setup soon after the computer starts up. If you don't see such a message, the most common access keys are F2, Delete, F1, F10, and Esc.

- The processor type and speed: Intel Pentium 4 processor running at 2.8GHz
- The chipset used by the motherboard: Intel 915G Express
- The make and model of the computer: Dell Dimension 4700

The BIOS utility also confirmed that the system did indeed have a single 512MB DDR2-400MHz memory module.

Knowing the motherboard's chipset is crucial because that will give us some idea of what the board is capable of. A quick Google search for "Intel 915G Express" brought up the Intel product page for this chipset as the first result (see Figure 15.3). This page is a gold mine of information for our upgrade (see Figure 15.4): supported processors, CPU socket, bus slot types, memory, hard drive interfaces, and more. (I'll get into some of these details when I discuss specific upgrades a bit later.)

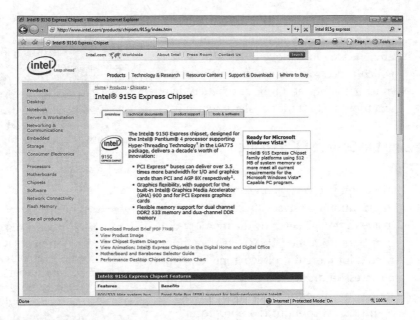

FIGURE 15.3

The Intel product page for the 915G Express chipset.

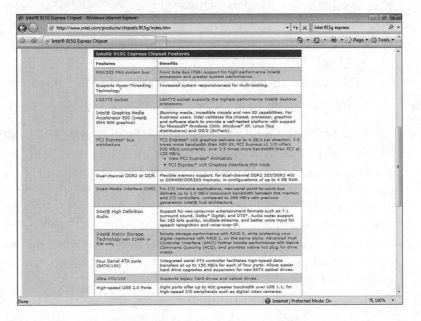

FIGURE 15.4

The 915G Express chipset's product page gives detailed information on the features and capabilities of the chipset.

Running the Device Manager and System Information Utilities

If you can't access the system's BIOS program for some reason, but you can boot into Windows, then you can still find out a lot of information using various Windows tools. For the purposes of most upgrade projects, two tools supply you with most of the data you need: Device Manager and the promisingly named System Information.

To run Device Manager, use one of the following techniques, depending on your version of Windows:

- **Windows Vista**—Click Start, type `device` in the Search box, and then click Device Manager in the search results. Enter your User Account Control credentials to continue.

- **Windows XP**—Select Start, Run; type `devmgmt.msc`; and then click OK.

In the Device Manager window, the following branches contain information pertinent to upgrading your PC (see Figure 15.5):

- **Disk drives**—This branch tells you the hard drive that's installed, albeit a bit cryptically. In Figure 15.5, you see `WDC WD800JB-00JJC0 ATA Device`. This tells you that the drive was manufactured by Western Digital and its model number is WD800JB.

- **Display adapters**—This branch tells you the video devices that are installed. In Figure 15.5, you can see that this old PC has both an integrated video adapter (the Intel 82615G) and a separate video card (the Radeon 9250).

- **Processors**—This branch tells you the type and speed of the PC's processor.

- **System devices**—This branch gives you a hint about the chipset in the Processor to I/O Controller item, which in Figure 15.5 shows Intel 915G/P/GV/PL/910GE/GL.

> **note** Why does Windows show two items in the Processors branch? Normally, Windows shows one item in that branch for each core or processor, but the Pentium 4 is a single-core CPU, right? Well, sort of. The later Pentium 4 processors use a technology called *hyper-threading* that enables the CPU to execute instructions using two nearly simultaneous processes, or *threads*. It's still a single-core, but hyper-threading makes it appear as though the Pentium 4 has two cores, so that's why Windows thinks the Pentium 4 is a dual-core CPU.

FIGURE 15.5
Device Manager contains lots of data about your PC's hardware.

To run System Information, use one of the following techniques, depending on your version of Windows:

- **Windows Vista**—Click Start, type `system` in the Search box, and then click System Information in the search results.
- **Windows XP**—Select Start, Run; type `msinfo32`; and then click OK.

In the System Information window (see Figure 15.6), the System Summary shows various bits of useful data, particularly the System Manufacturer, System Model, Processor, BIOS Version/Date, and Total Physical Memory.

Searching for the System Manual Online

If you purchased your old PC from a system manufacturer, particularly a larger company such as Dell or HP, chances are you can find the computer's original manual online. (I'm assuming, of course, that the manual that came with the computer is long lost.) Even better, you can sometimes find more in-depth documentation for a machine. Dell, for example, usually offers a "service manual" that shows the motherboard's components, power supply watts (important if you'll be adding more components to your old PC), BIOS settings, and instructions for removing and installing parts.

FIGURE 15.6

System Information gives you some good basic information about your system.

To look for the manual online, you have a couple of ways to proceed:

- Head for the manufacturer's site, find the Support section, look up your old PC's make and model number, and then look for a link named Manual or Documentation.

- Head for Google and run a search on the manufacturer's name, the PC's make and model, and the word *manual*.

In my case, I Googled "Dell Dimension 4700 manual" and was rewarded with a direct link to the Dell Dimension 4700 Series Service Manual as the first result. Figure 15.7 shows the first page of the manual.

This service manual is a gold mine of useful information for the upgrader. For example, clicking the System Board Components link takes me to a really useful map of the PC's motherboard, as shown in Figure 15.8.

note The manual is useful only if it applies to the specifications of your computer. Manufacturers often update a model's specs, so they update the manual to reflect those changes. Make sure the manual you find applies to your computer and not to some later iteration. If it doesn't, either keep searching for the correct version of the manual, or contact the manufacturer to see if one is available.

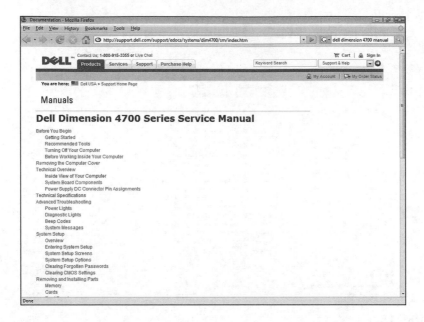

FIGURE 15.7

The service manual for my Dell Dimension 4700.

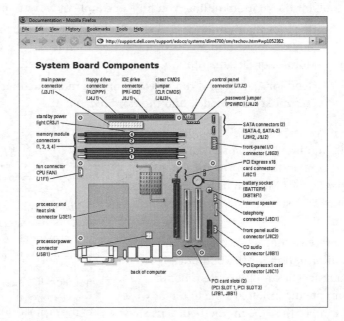

FIGURE 15.8

The service manual includes a useful map of the motherboard's components.

Even better, clicking the Technical Specifications link takes me to a page chock full of great data about the machine and its capabilities (see Figure 15.9). I'll be making good use of this data in the sections to come.

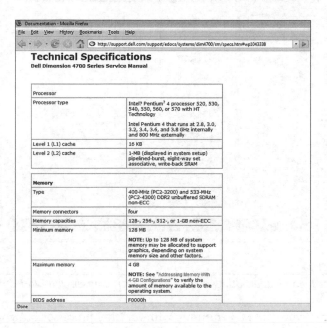

FIGURE 15.9
The service manual's Technical Specifications page contains tons of great information on the machine's components and capabilities.

Using Third-Party Tools to Research Components

If you want to find out even more about your old PC before getting your hands dirty with the upgrade, there are tons of tools available, and I'll tell you about a few of them in this section.

For starters, if your old PC is running with an Intel chipset but you're not sure which one, or if you don't know anything about the chipset, you can use the Intel Chipset Identification Utility, which is available here:

http://www.intel.com/support/chipsets/inf/sb/CS-009266.htm

Download the utility and save it to your hard disk. To run it, right-click `chiputil.exe` and then click Run As Administrator. (If you're using Vista, you'll need to enter your UAC credentials at this point.) The utility examines your system and then reports the chipset identity, as shown in Figure 15.10.

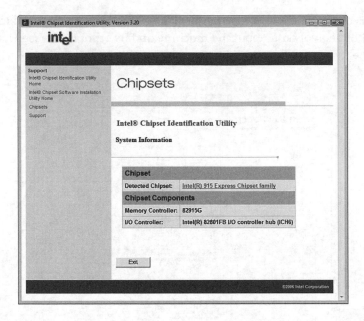

FIGURE 15.10

Intel's Chipset Identification Utility can tell you which chipset your old PC is using.

Also, if your old PC is running with an Intel processor but you're not sure which one, or if you don't know anything about the processor, you can use the Intel Processor Identification Utility, which is available here:

http://www.intel.com/support/processors/tools/piu/

Download the utility, install it, and then run the program. The utility examines your system and then reports the processor identity, as shown in Figure 15.11.

These utilities won't work if your old PC is using non-Intel hardware. In that case, you need to turn to one of the other hardware detection tools that are available. One utility I like is HWiNFO32, a shareware product (it's $15 if you register it, or you can use it free for 14 days) that's available here:

http://www.hwinfo.com/

Download and install the program, and then run it. (In Vista, you need to right-click the executable program, click Run As Administrator, and then enter your User Account Control [UAC] credentials.) Figure 15.12 shows the output of the Motherboard section of the program.

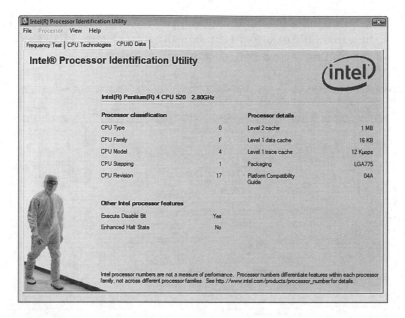

FIGURE 15.11

Intel's Chipset Identification Utility can tell you which chipset your old PC is using.

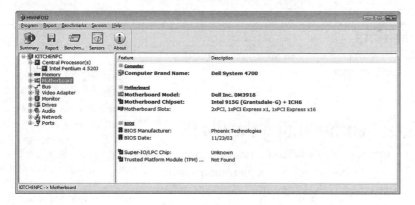

FIGURE 15.12

HWiNFO32 is a nice shareware program for determining your old PC's hardware information.

A good tool for checking out your system's memory is the System Scanner Tool made available online by Crucial, a memory manufacturer. This tool not only gives you the details about the installed memory modules, but also tells you about the memory system itself, including which types of memory you can install. Go to www.crucial.com and click the Scan My System link. (In

Windows XP, the scan runs online; if you're running Vista, you need to download a small file before you can start the scan.) Figure 15.13 shows the results of the scan on my old Dell machine.

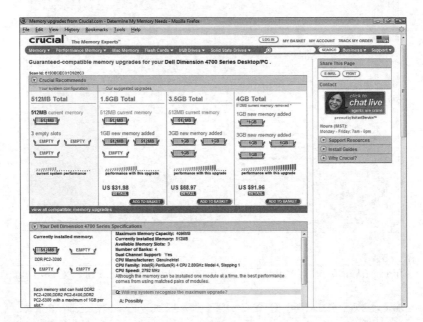

FIGURE 15.13

Crucial's System Scanner Tool gives you the goods on your old PCs memory.

Before: Benchmarking the Old PC

When you're working on an upgrade project, it's best if you track your progress by measuring the computer's current performance and then seeing the effect that each upgrade has on how the machine runs.

There are lots of benchmarking tools out there, but I prefer to keep things simple and use the benchmarking tool built right in to Windows Vista. It's called Performance Information and Tools, and it rates your system on various aspects of performance: graphics, memory, processor, and storage. It uses five metrics:

> **caution** Third-party hardware scanning tools aren't always perfect, so they sometimes can lead you astray. For example, the Crucial System Scanner Tool reports that my Dell can run DDR2-400 (PC2-3200) and DDR2-533 (PC2-4300) memory, which is confirmed by my chipset research and the computer's manual. However, Crucial also claims that this PC can run DDR2-800 (PC2-6400) memory. Ever hopeful, I popped a couple of DDR2-800 modules into the system, rebooted, and brought up the BIOS Setup utility. Sure enough, my 800MHz modules were running at only 533MHz.

- **Processor**—This metric determines how quickly the system can process data. The Processor metric measures calculations per second processed.

- **Memory (RAM)**—This metric determines how quickly the system can move large objects through memory. The Memory metric measures memory operations per second.

- **Graphics**—This metric determines the computer's capability to run a desktop like the one created by Windows Vista and its Aero interface. The Graphics metric expresses frames per second.

- **Gaming Graphics**—This metric determines the computer's capability to render 3D graphics, particularly those used in gaming. The Gaming Graphics metric expresses effective frames per second.

- **Primary Hard Disk**—This metric determines how quickly the computer can write to and read from the hard disk. The Storage metric measures megabytes per second.

Each of these metrics is given a score, and your computer is given an overall base score that's called the Windows Experience Index base score.

To launch this tool, click Start, type `performance` in the Search box, and then click Performance Information and Tools in the results. As you can see in Figure 15.14, Vista supplies a subscore for each of the five categories and calculates an overall base score. You can get a new rating (for example, if you change performance-related hardware) by clicking the Update My Score link.

Interpreting the ratings is a bit of a black art, but I can tell you the following:

- In general, the higher the rating, the better the performance.

- The lowest possible value is 1.0.

- There doesn't seem to be a highest possible value, but I've never seen a value higher than 5.9. The killer gaming PC from Chapter 13 achieved this score in all categories except the Processor, where it scored 5.5.

- The base score takes a weakest-link-in-the-chain approach. That is, you could have nothing but 5.9 scores for everything else, but if you get 1.0 just because your computer can't do gaming graphics, your base score will be 1.0.

Taking a closer look at Figure 15.14, you can see why this PC runs Vista so slowly:

- The Gaming Graphics component gets the lowest possible score of 1.0.

- The Graphics component garners only 1.9, which is still quite low.

- The Memory (RAM) component manages only a 2.9.

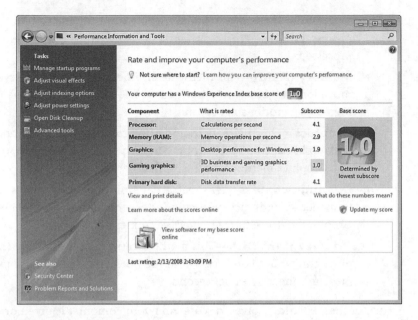

FIGURE 15.14
Vista calculates a Windows Experience Index based on five categories.

On the other hand, the scores of 4.1 generated by the Processor and Primary Hard Disk components aren't terrible, but I think we can do a lot better with only a small investment of time and money.

Making the Old PC Run Faster

Although there are many ways to upgrade an old PC—put in quieter fans, replace the power supply, and update the motherboard's BIOS and all the device drivers, to name a few—I'm going to concentrate my efforts where I'm sure most people would want to spend the upgrade time and money: making an old PC run a bit faster. There's nothing like an extra dose of horsepower to make a machine a more useful member of your PC family. Better performance gives you the ability to run more programs, upgrade to the latest operating system, or just provide a better hand-me-down machine for the kids to use.

I realized my old Dell needed *something* when I installed Windows Vista Home Premium on it. Although Vista installed without a hitch, it runs excruciatingly slowly. It's really quite painful. I needed a Vista Home Premium PC on my testing network, so either this machine needed to be fixed up to run Vista at least passably well, or I was going to have to build myself one that would.

The Chipset Is All

In the first few chapters of the book, I often mentioned that when you're buying certain components, you need to match those parts with the capabilities of your motherboard. It would have been a bit more accurate to say that you need to match those parts with the capabilities of your motherboard's *chipset*. That's because it's the chipset that defines many of the features of the motherboard, in particular the memory type and speed it supports, the processors it can take, the bus slots types the board can offer, and the data interfaces the board supports.

In other words, when it comes to upgrading a PC, the four main components related to improving performance—memory, processor, video card, and hard drive—all depend on the PC's chipset. This is why it's crucial to find out the chipset of your old PC, because once you have that information in hand, you know how far you can go to upgrade the PC.

In the next few sections, I'll show you how to use chipset data to forge an upgrade path for an old PC.

Adding More Memory

Upgrading an old PC almost always starts with adding more memory. These days, memory modules are so cheap, that there's no real reason to hobble a system with a mere 512MB (like my old Dell) or even 1GB. You can get 2GB packs for under $50, and that's money worth spending to give your computer an extra couple of years of useful life.

note In this chapter I'm ignoring a fifth component related to improving performance: the motherboard itself. It's certainly possible to clear off the board in your old PC, remove it from the system, and then replace it with another board that offers better performance. (Or, I should say, replace it with another board that has a *chipset* that offers better performance.) However, my feeling is that if you're going to go that far, then you ought to just build yourself a new PC. Plus, at some point you get the PC equivalent of grandpa's ax, which is still going strong after 50 years because the handle has been replaced five times and the head has been replaced four times!

caution It's a good idea to research your old computer's power supply, as well. Older computers have PSUs that can handle only a limited number of watts, and you can run into all kinds of trouble if the power needs of your new components exceed what the power supply can handle. Use the eXtreme Power Supply Calculator (http://www.extreme.outervision.com/psucalculator.jsp) to see how many watts your upgraded system requires, and consider swapping out your old PSU for a better one if needed.

When upgrading, you want to not only add more memory, but also add *faster* memory, if possible. Examine your chipset data to see the fastest memory speed your board supports. For example, based on my research, the Dell can run DDR2-400 (PC2-3200), which is the speed of the current module—but it can also run DDR2-533 (PC2-4300), which should provide a nice speed boost. I'm going to take out the existing 512MB DDR2-400 module and replace it with two 1GB DDR2-533 modules.

When I restarted Windows Vista and ran the Performance Information and Tools, Vista had detected the new hardware and offered a Refresh Now button. I clicked that and entered my UAC credentials to start the test. Figure 15.15 shows the updated results. As you can see, the Memory (RM) component now sports a score of 4.7, which is a huge leap from the original score of 2.9.

FIGURE 15.15
The updated Windows Experience Index after adding 2GB of DDR2-533 RAM to the old Dell.

Upgrading the Video Card

Windows Vista requires a fair amount of video horsepower to take full advantage of the Aero interface, live previews, and other graphical goodies. Even many business applications require strong graphics, and of course, if you want to do any halfway decent gaming, a decent video system is a must.

An upgraded PC doesn't require top-of-the-line components, but there's still plenty of room for improvement on most old systems:

- If your system uses integrated graphics, a move to a separate video card should be your first consideration. (Many newer chipsets have strong integrated graphics chips, but most older chipsets don't.)

- If your old PC already has a separate PCI video card, you can boost graphics performance considerably by yanking out the old card and replacing it with a PCI Express card, if your motherboard comes with the appropriate bus slot.

- As far as the GPU goes, you don't want to break the bank here, so something in the low-but-not-too-low end should suffice. That means choosing either something in the ATI Radeon HD 2000 family or the NVIDIA GeForce 7 series.

- Finally, consider the amount of graphics memory on your new card. 128MB or less isn't really enough these days, so consider 256MB the minimum.

My old Dell has a free PCI Express x16 slot, so I replaced the existing PCI card with a PNY GeForce 7300GT, a PCIe x16 card with 256MB of GDDR2 memory. I restarted, installed the driver (which required another reboot), and then reran the Performance Information and Tools test. As you can see in Figure 15.16, the new video card has made a stunning difference: the Graphics component jumped from a weak 1.9 to a strong 4.4, and the Gaming Graphics component leaped from a bottom-of-the-barrel 1.0 to the same 4.4 score. Nice!

Beefing Up the Hard Drive

Windows and your programs constantly read data from and write data to the hard drive, so a slow drive can be a real bottleneck on an otherwise decent system. Reasonably quick seek, read, and write rates are important, of course, but I think the choice of interface is even more important. If your old PC is using the PATA interface for its hard disk chores, then your system just isn't a fast as a good be. For an immediate speed boost, you should invest in a SATA drive—as long as your motherboard has at least one SATA header.

In yet another example of where your chipset research comes in handy, you need to know not only that your board supports SATA, but also what *speed* the interface runs at: is it SATA/300 or the older and slower SATA/150? In my case, my old Dell supports only SATA/150, so that limits my hard drive upgrade options. Fortunately, I had an 80GB Seagate SATA/150 drive lying around, so I added it to the system, installed Windows Vista on the new drive, and then migrated the settings over using Vista's Windows Easy Transfer program.

FIGURE 15.16

The updated Windows Experience Index after adding the PNY GeForce 7300GT video card.

With all that done, I checked the Performance Information and Tools rating once again. As you can see in Figure 15.17, the new hard drive made a significant difference: the Primary Hard Disk score when from a decent 4.1 to a very good 5.1, our first 5-plus score of the upgrade.

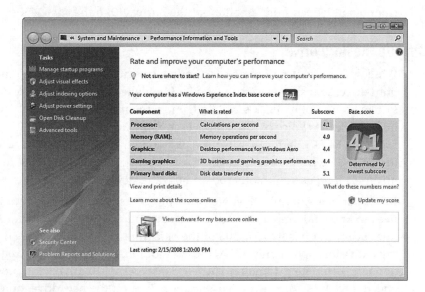

FIGURE 15.17

The updated Windows Experience Index after adding the Seagate 80GB SATA/150 hard drive.

Dropping in a Faster CPU

The final piece of the performance puzzle in this upgrade is the processor. For an upgrade to be worthwhile, you need to move to a new processor that offers some or all of the following:

- A larger L2 cache
- A faster clock speed
- A faster bus speed
- More cores

Of these, the last three are dependent on the system's chipset, which will support only certain processors. So, again, you need to turn to your chipset research to see which processors it supports and the speed of the system bus. On my Dell upgrade project, for example, I discovered that the chipset supports only the Intel Pentium 4 processor, models 520 (2.8GHz click speed), 530 (3.0GHz), 540 (3.2GHz), 550 (3.4GHz), 560 (3.6GHz), and 570 (3.8GHz), all of which use the 800MHz bus and a 1MB L2 cache. None of these are dual core.

In other words, the only thing I can upgrade on the processor side is the clock speed. If you search around a bit, you can still find online retailers selling the 3.6GHz and 3.8GHz Pentium 4, but they'll set you back between $400 and $700! That's just nuts (in Chapter 14 we built an entire computer for less than that). Finally, I found a 3.4GHz Pentium 4 550 on eBay for $90. I hesitated at first because that's too much to spend for what in the end will be only a minor performance boost, but I went for it anyway just for the sake of completeness on this project.

I removed the Dell's heatsink (the service manual showed me the way here), lifted out the old CPU, popped in the new one, and restored the heatsink. I rebooted and checked the Performance Information and Tools rating for the final time. As you can see in Figure 15.18, the new CPU bumped the Processor component from the original 4.1 to 4.4.

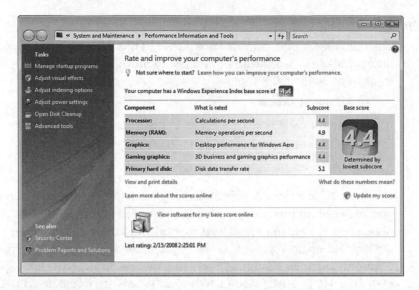

FIGURE 15.18

The updated Windows Experience Index after adding the Pentium 4 3.4GHz processor.

After: Benchmarking the Upgraded PC

The upgrade is complete, so let's take a step back and see how far we've come. To summarize, here are the specs I started out with:

Category	Component	Score
Memory	512MB DDR2 400 (PC2 3200)	2.9
Video card	ATI Radeon 9250 PCI with 256MB GDDR RAM	1.9 1.0 (Gaming)
Hard drive	Western Digital 80GB IDE	4.1
Processor	Intel Pentium 4 processor running at 2.8GHz	4.1

Here are the specs I ended up with:

Category	Component	Score
Memory	2GB DDR2-533 (PC2-4200)	4.7
Video card	PNY GeForce 7300GT PCIe with 256MB GDDR2 RAM	4.4 4.4 (Gaming)
Hard drive	Seagate 80GB SATA/150	5.1
Processor	Intel Pentium 4 processor running at 3.4GHz	4.4

15

The new numbers are much more impressive and represent an upgraded machine that's not only faster overall, but also much more balanced. The original PC had decent hard drive and processor scores, a below-average memory score, and pathetic graphics scores. The upgraded machine has good (but not spectacular) scores across the board. Even more important, the upgraded machine runs Windows Vista Home Premium beautifully, and so has gone from being just this side of a boat anchor to being a solid member of my local network and test bed.

From Here

- To learn about processor specs, **see** "Clocks, Cores, and More: Understanding CPU Specs," **p. 43**.
- For more on memory specs, **see** "DDR, DIMM, and More: Understanding Memory Specs," **p. 66**.
- For information on hard drive specs, **see** "Capacity, Cache, and More: Understanding Hard Drive Specs," **p. 82**.
- To get data about video card specs, **see** "GPU, GDDR, SLI, and More: Understanding Video Card Specs," **p. 107**.
- To learn how to remove a card, **see** "Removing an Internal Expansion Card," **p. 225**.
- To learn how to remove a hard drive, **see** "Taking Out a Hard Drive," **p. 228**.
- To learn how to remove memory modules, **see** "Pulling Out Memory Modules," **p. 232**.
- To learn how to remove a processor, **see** "Prying Out a CPU," **p. 230**.
- For instructions on cleaning a PC, **see** "Cleaning the Computer," **p. 498**.

Putting Your Network Together

This book is about building PCs, as well as maintaining those PCs and repairing them should something go down for the count. In this day and age, however, it's hard to talk about computers in such splendid isolation because it's a rare PC that isn't hooked up to a network for sharing data, peripherals (such as a printer), or an Internet connection.

This assumes, of course, that you have two or more computers to connect. If the PC you built yourself is your home's second PC, then it's time you took the networking plunge. You learned about networking hardware back in Chapter 6, "Getting Connected: Networking Hardware," so now it's time to put that knowledge to good use. In this project, I show you how to connect and configure a network for both wired and wireless connections.

Configuring Your Router

You learned in Chapter 6 that you need to add a router to your network if you want to share a broadband Internet connection with the users on your network. This saves you money in the long run because it means you don't need multiple broadband modems or multiple Internet connections. It's also more convenient because you don't have to set up a particular computer to share its Internet connection with the network. After you have the router configured, you almost never have to think about it again.

Of course, getting to that state requires taking a few minutes now to configure various aspects of the router, including the broadband connection to your Internet service provider (ISP), the feature that supplies IP addresses to each network computer, and more. Also, if your router doubles as a wireless access point (AP), you need to configure the wireless network settings. This chapter takes you through these configuration tasks and other chores.

➡ If you need a bit of router background before you start, **see** "Adding the Internet into the Mix with a Router," **p. 144**.

> **note** For much more detailed information about networking hardware and configuration, see my book *Networking with Microsoft Windows Vista* (Que 2007).

Connecting the Router for Configuration

I take you through the steps for configuring and connecting your other networking hardware later in this chapter, and that includes connecting the router to the network. For now, you need to connect your router to one of your network computers so that you can configure the router.

Here are the general steps to follow:

1. Attach the router's AC cord and plug it in.
2. Turn off the router and your broadband modem.
3. Run a network cable from the broadband modem's LAN port to the WAN port on the back of the router.

> **note** Most routers include a card or sticker that tells you to insert and run the router's CD before connecting it. This is good advice for many devices that require a driver to be installed in advance, but that's not the case with a router. Therefore, you're free to ignore the note (no matter how dire the manufacturer makes the consequences sound) and go ahead and connect the router.

4. Run another network cable from one of your computers to any RJ-45 port on the back of the router.

5. Turn on the router and modem.

Displaying the Router's Setup Pages

All routers come with a built-in configuration program. This program is a series of web pages you access via a web browser on one of your network computers. (This is why you connected the router directly to a computer in step 4 of the previous section.) These pages enable you to configure many aspects of the router, including its IP address, its password, the connection settings for your broadband ISP, and much more. You learn about these and other configuration tasks later in this chapter. For now, here are two methods you can use to access the router's setup pages:

> **note** You must connect the router to a computer even if you're going to use your router solely as a wireless AP. The initial configuration requires a wired connection. After you have your wireless network set up (see "Modifying Wireless Settings," later in this chapter), you can remove the wired connection and access the router's setup pages wirelessly when you need them.

> **note** Here are the default IP addresses used by some major router manufacturers:
>
> Belkin: 192.168.2.1
>
> D-Link: 192.168.0.1
>
> Linksys: 192.168.1.1
>
> Netgear: 192.168.1.1

- **Entering the router's IP address**—On the computer connected to the router, start Internet Explorer, use the Address bar to type the router address, and then press Enter. See your device documentation for the correct address, but in most cases the address is either http://192.168.1.1 or http://192.168.0.1.

- **Using Vista's Network Window**—On the computer connected to the router, select Start, Network. Vista displays the Network window, which contains a list of devices on your network. If your router supports Universal Plug and Play (UPnP), you should see an icon for the router. Right-click the router icon and then click View Device Webpage (see Figure 16.1).

> **tip** If you're not sure which username and password to use, try **admin** for both. If that doesn't work, leave the username blank and try either **admin** or **password** for the password. If you still can't get in, see whether your device is listed in the Default Password List maintained at http://www.phenoelit.us.org/dpl/dpl.html.

Either way, you then usually see a login screen like the one shown in Figure 16.2. Type the router's default username and password. Note that in most cases you only need to enter the password; again, see the device documentation for the logon details.

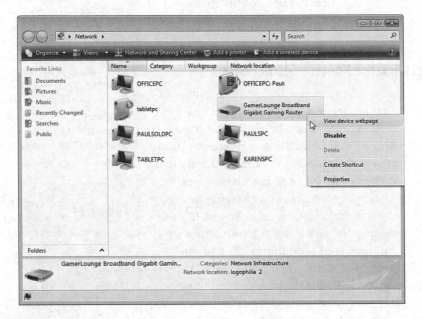

FIGURE 16.1

If your router supports UPnP, you should see an icon for it in the Network window.

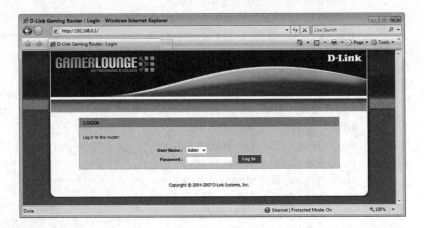

FIGURE 16.2

You must log on to the router to access its setup pages.

When you log in, the router's setup pages appear. Figure 16.3 shows a sample setup page.

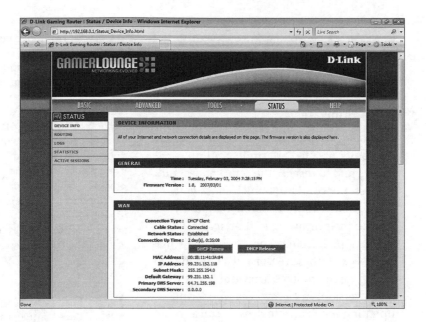

FIGURE 16.3

A typical router setup page.

Changing the Router's IP Address

In the previous section, you might find that you can't access the router's setup page. First, check whether the router is turned on and whether the computer you are using has a wired connection that runs from the computer's network interface card (NIC) to an RJ-45 port on the router.

If you still can't access the router, your broadband modem might be the culprit. Some broadband providers are using "smart" modems that include routing features. That's fine, but these modems almost always have a static IP address, and that address is usually either http://192.168.1.1 or http://192.168.0.1, which might conflict with your router's IP address.

If you have connection problems after adding the router, the likely culprit is an IP address conflict. Disconnect or turn off the broadband modem and access the router's setup pages as described in the previous

> **caution** After you change the IP address, the router's setup program might not change the IP address in Internet Explorer's Address bar, so Internet Explorer might display an error message. In that case, modify the IP address manually and press Enter to access the router's new location.

section. (This should work now.) See your router's documentation to learn how to change the router's IP address (to, say, http://192.168.1.2 or http://192.168.0.2).

Updating the Firmware

The *router firmware* is the internal program the router uses to perform its routing chores and to display the setup pages and process any configuration changes you make. Router manufacturers frequently update their firmware to fix bugs, to improve performance, and to add new features. For all these reasons, it's a good idea to update the router's firmware to get the latest version. In case you're wondering, updating the firmware doesn't cause you to lose any of your settings.

Here's the general procedure for finding out and downloading the latest firmware version:

1. Use Internet Explorer to navigate to the router manufacturer's website.

2. Navigate to the Support page.

3. Navigate to the Downloads page.

4. Use the interface to navigate to the download page for your router.

5. You should now see a list of firmware downloads. Examine the version numbers and compare them to your router's current firmware version.

6. If the latest version is later than the current version on your router, click the download link and save the firmware upgrade file on your computer.

tip The router's setup pages usually show you the current firmware version. However, if your router supports UPnP, you can usually get the router's firmware version through Windows Vista. Select Start, Network to open the Network window; then right-click the router's icon and click Properties. In the property sheet that appears, click the Network Device tab. The current firmware version usually appears as the Model Number value in the Device Details group.

tip Most product support pages require the name and model number of the router. You can usually find this information on the underside of the router.

tip A good place to save the firmware upgrade file is the Downloads folder, which is a subfolder of your main Windows Vista user account folder.

caution Most router manufacturers require that you upgrade the firmware using a wired link to the router. Using a wireless link can damage the router.

When you have the firmware file safely stored on your computer, use the router's setup pages to update the firmware. See the router's manual to learn how to do this with your router.

Setting Up Your Broadband Connection

The main point of adding a router to your network is to share a broadband Internet connection with the network computers, which means users don't have to worry about either setting up a connection or logging on to the Internet. With the broadband modem connected to the router's WAN port, the router takes over the duties of initiating and managing the Internet connection. Before it can do that, however, you need to configure the router with the Internet connection settings provided to you by your broadband provider (see your router documentation for the specific steps required).

Your broadband connection will almost certainly fall under one of the following types:

- **Dynamic (DHCP)**—With this connection type, your ISP provides the router with its external IP address automatically. Some ISPs require that you configure the router with a specific name and also that you specify a hostname (also called a system name or an account name) and a domain name. This is the most common type of broadband connection, particularly with cable providers.

- **Static**—With this type of connection, your ISP gives you an IP address that never changes, and you must configure the router to use this as its external IP address. Your ISP will in most cases also provide you with a subnet mask, a gateway, an IP address, and one or more *domain name server (DNS)* addresses. This type of broadband connection is rare these days.

- **PPPoE**—With this connection type, your ISP provides you with a username and password that you use to log on. Some ISPs also require that you configure the router with a specific name and also that you specify a hostname and a domain name. This type of broadband connection is most commonly used with *Digital Subscriber Line (DSL)* providers.

- **PPTP**—With this type of connection, your ISP usually provides you with a static IP address, a subnet mask, a gateway IP address, a username, and a password. This broadband connection type is mostly used by DSL providers in European countries.

- **Telstra BigPond**—With this connection type, your ISP provides you with a user name and password. This broadband connection type is used by Australian DSL providers.

Enabling UPnP

Most newer routers support UPnP, a technology designed to make networking devices easier to manage and configure. Traditionally, devices are controlled by a *device driver*, a small software program that serves as an intermediary between hardware devices and the operating system. Device drivers encode software instructions into signals that the device understands, and conversely, the drivers interpret device signals and report them to the operating system. However, device drivers are difficult to code and need to be upgraded as operating systems and hardware architectures change.

UPnP is designed to overcome the limitations of device drivers by eliminating them altogether. In their place, UPnP devices are controlled by software protocols, particularly *Transmission Control Protocol/Internet Protocol (TCP/IP)*, the protocols used to transmit and receive information over the Internet, including email and *File Transfer Protocol (FTP)*; *User Datagram Protocol (UDP)*, a protocol used for sending short bits of data called *datagrams* (a form of packet); and *Hypertext Transfer Protocol (HTTP)*, the protocol used to transmit and receive information on the World Wide Web. This allows any UPnP-enabled device to run in any network environment and under any operating system.

For small networks, the main advantage of UPnP is that it allows software programs to automatically read and configure a router's settings. For example, you saw earlier that Windows Vista can recognize the presence of a router and display an icon for that router in the Network window, but it can also glean the router's IP address and use that address to open the router's setup page (via the View Device Webpage command). All of this is made possible by UPnP.

Similarly, software sometimes needs to configure the router. For example, a program might need to modify the router's firewall to allow data through a particular port and have that data go directly to a particular computer on the network. For example, Windows Home Server has a remote-access feature that enables you to access computers on your network via the Internet, which requires forwarding data from two different ports to the Windows Home Server computer. So that you don't have to set this up yourself, Windows Home Server comes with a feature that configures the router automatically. Again, all of this is accomplished via UPnP.

So, UPnP is a valuable and useful technology, particularly on small networks. Most routers that support UPnP come with the technology enabled, but some have UPnP disabled by default. See your router manual to learn how to check and, if necessary, enable UPnP.

Enabling the DHCP Server

Most small networks allocate IP addresses to computers and devices dynamically. That is, instead of going to the trouble of configuring each network node with a static IP address, you can use a Dynamic Host Configuration Protocol (DHCP) server to automatically assign an IP address from a range of addresses each time a device starts up.

> **caution** When you configure the range of IP addresses the DHCP server can assign, be sure not to include the router's static IP address in that range. For example, if your router's IP address is 192.168.1.1, the DHCP server's range of IP addresses should begin at 192.168.1.2 or higher.

In your small network, the best choice for dynamic IP addressing is the router because almost all routers come with a built-in DHCP server. When configuring your router, you need to enable the DHCP server, specify the range of addresses from which the server will allocate the IP addresses, and optionally specify the length of the *DHCP lease*, the amount of time each client can use an IP address. Delve into your router manual to learn how to go about all this on your device.

Modifying Wireless Settings

If your router includes a wireless access point (AP), you need to configure a few settings before making wireless connections to the AP. On most routers, you can configure the following settings (see your documentation for the details):

- **Network name**—This is the name of your wireless network, which is often called the *service set identifier (SSID)*. All routers come with a default SSID, usually some variation on the manufacturer's name, such as linksys or belkin54g. Changing the SSID to something memorable will help you to identify your network in Vista's list of available wireless networks, and it will avoid confusion with other nearby wireless networks that still use the default name.

- **Wireless encryption**—Wireless hackers usually look for leaking wireless signals so they can piggyback on the Internet access. They might just be freeloading on your connection, but they might also have darker aims, such as using your Internet connection to send spam or download pornography. However, some wardriving hackers are interested more in your data. They come equipped with packet sniffers that can pick up and read your network packets. Typically, these crackers are looking for sensitive data such as passwords and credit card numbers. Therefore, it's absolutely crucial that you enable encryption for wireless data so that an outside user who picks up your network packets can't decipher them. Older wireless networks use a security protocol called Wired Equivalent Privacy (WEP) that protects wireless communications with (usually) a 26-character security key. That sounds impregnable, but unfortunately there were serious weaknesses in the WEP encryption scheme, and now software exists that can crack any WEP key in minutes, if not seconds. In newer wireless networks, WEP has been superseded by Wi-Fi Protected Access (WPA), which is vastly more secure than WEP. WPA uses most of the IEEE 802.11i wireless security standard, and WPA2 implements the full standard. WPA2 Personal requires a simple pass phrase for access (so it's suitable for homes and small offices), and WPA2 Enterprise requires a dedicated authentication server. Be sure to use the strongest encryption your equipment supports.

caution When previously authorized devices attempt to connect to a nonbroadcasting network, they include the network's SSID as part of the probe requests they send out to see whether the network is within range. The SSID is sent in unencrypted text, so it would be easy for a snoop with the right software (easily obtained from the Internet) to learn the SSID. If the SSID is not broadcasting to try to hide a network that is unsecure or uses an easily breakable encryption protocol, such as WEP, hiding the SSID in this way actually makes the network less secure. However, from the previous item, you should now have WPA or WPA2 encryption enabled. So in your case, disabling SSID broadcasting either keeps your security the same or improves it: if a cracker detects your nonbroadcasting SSID, you're no worse off; if the snoop doesn't have the necessary software to detect your nonbroadcasting SSID, he won't see your network, so you're more secure.

- **SSID broadcasting**—This setting determines whether your router broadcasts the SSID, which makes the wireless network visible in Windows Vista's list of available networks. It's best to enable SSID broadcasting when you first make your connections to the wireless network. However, Windows Vista can remember the networks you've connected to in the past, so you can later disable SSID broadcasting as a security measure.

- **Wireless mode**—This tells the router which Wi-Fi standard (802.11a, 802.11b, 802.11g, or 802.11b) to implement. If your router supports more than one standard, you can configure the router to use multiple standards (for example, both 802.11b and 802.11g; this is often called *mixed mode*) or just a single standard. For example, if all your wireless devices use 802.11g, you should configure the router to use only that standard.

- **Wireless channel**—This setting determines the *radio frequency (RF)* band that the wireless AP uses to transmit and receive signals. For successful wireless networking connections, all your networking devices must use the same channel.

Checking the Router Status

All routers come with a status page that provides you with the router's current settings in various categories, including the following:

- The router's current firmware version and serial number
- The router's *Media Access Control (MAC)* address and internal IP address
- Whether features such as the DHCP server, *network address translation (NAT)*, and the firewall are enabled or disabled
- The wireless network settings (SSID, mode, channel, and so on)
- Internet connection settings such as the external MAC address, the external IP address, and the addresses for your ISP's gateway and DNS servers

See your router manual to learn how to access the status page.

Connecting the Broadband Modem

A *broadband modem* is a high-speed modem used for *Asymmetric Digital Subscriber Line (ADSL)*, cable, or satellite Internet access. In almost all cases, the ISP provides you with a broadband modem that's compatible with its service. With your router configured, getting the broadband modem connected is the next step in putting your network together.

Begin by connecting and plugging in the modem's power adapter. Make sure the modem is turned off. If the modem doesn't come with a power switch, unplug the power adapter for now.

Attaching the Internet Connection Cable

Next, attach the cable that provides the ISP's Internet connection. For example, if you have an ADSL broadband modem, run a phone line from the nearest wall jack to appropriate port on the back of the modem, which is usually labeled ADSL or DSL, as shown in Figure 16.4.

> **note** Many ADSL providers require that you install a phone filter device to protect your telephones. Each phone filter comes with two RJ-11 (phone) jacks, usually labeled Line and Phone. Run a phone cable from the wall jack to the Line port on the phone filter, and run a second phone cable from the Phone port on the filter to your telephone. You need to do this for each telephone in your home or office.

FIGURE 16.4

For an ADSL broadband modem, plug a phone cable into the DSL (or ADSL) port on the back of the modem.

Similarly, if you have a cable broadband modem, connect a TV cable to the cable connector on the back of the modem, which is usually labeled Cable, as shown in Figure 16.5.

FIGURE 16.5

For a cable broadband modem, plug a TV cable into the Cable connector on the back of the modem.

Registering the Modem

How you proceed from here depends on the ISP. Nowadays, many ISPs insist that you register the broadband modem by accessing a page on the ISP's website and sometimes entering a code or the serial number of the modem. Read the instructions

> **caution** Use either the Ethernet port or the USB port, but not both. Connecting both ports to your computer can damage the modem.

that come with your ISP's Internet kit to determine whether you must first register your broadband modem online.

If you don't need to register, skip to the next section. If you do need to register, you must first connect the modem directly to a computer (instead of to your router, as described in the next section). Most broadband modems give you two ways to do this (see Figure 16.6):

■ **Ethernet**—All broadband modems have an RJ-45 port on the back that is labeled Ethernet, LAN, or 10BASE-T. Run an Ethernet cable from this port to the RJ-45 port on your computer's NIC.

■ **USB**—Most newer broadband modems also come with a USB port on the back. If you're working with a computer that doesn't yet have a NIC, or if the NIC already has a cable attached, you can use USB instead. Run a USB cable from the USB port on the modem to a free USB port on your computer. You also need to install the broadband modem's USB device driver, which should be on a CD your ISP provided.

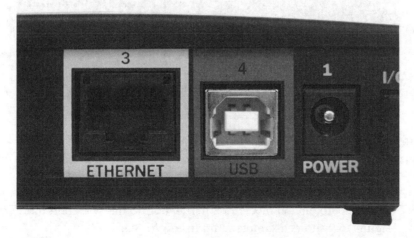

FIGURE 16.6

Almost all newer broadband modems come with both an Ethernet (RJ-45) and a USB port.

Turn on the broadband modem and wait until it makes a connection with the line. All broadband modems have an LED on the front that lights up to indicate a good connection. Look for an LED labeled Online, DSL, or something similar, and wait until you see a solid (that is, not blinking) light on that LED. You can now use a web browser to access the ISP's site (depending on the ISP, you may need to log on first) and register your modem.

Connecting the Router

You're now ready to set up your broadband modem so that its Internet connection can be shared with each computer and device on your network. You do that by connecting the broadband modem to your router.

If you had to register your broadband modem as described in the previous section, turn off the modem and disconnect the Ethernet or USB cable from your computer.

Examine the back of your router and locate the port that it uses for the Internet connection. Some routers label this port WAN (see Figure 16.7), whereas others use Internet (see Figure 16.8). Some routers don't label the Internet port at all, but instead place the port off to the side so it's clearly separate from the router's RJ-45 ports.

FIGURE 16.7

Some routers use the label WAN to indicate the port used for the Internet connection.

With the broadband modem and the router turned off, run an Ethernet cable from the broadband modem's Ethernet port to the WAN port on the router. Figure 16.9 shows a sample setup (using ADSL).

FIGURE 16.8

On other routers the Internet connection port is labeled Internet.

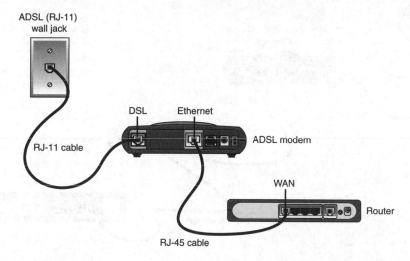

FIGURE 16.9

Connect the broadband modem's Ethernet port to the router's WAN or Internet port.

You're now ready to turn on your devices. Begin by turning on the broadband modem and waiting until it has a solid connection with the line. Then turn on your router. Because you already configured your ISP's Internet settings (refer to "Configuring Your Router," earlier in this chapter), the router will automatically connect to the ISP. The front of the router

tip On my network, I keep the broadband modem and the router side-by-side on a desk so I can easily see the LEDs on the front of both devices (particularly the LED on the broadband modem that indicates a good Internet connection). If you do this, purchase a 1-foot Ethernet cable to connect to the two devices.

should have an LED labeled WAN or Internet that turns solid when the Internet connection has been made.

Connecting the Switch

If your network setup includes a switch, the next step in your network configuration involves adding the switch. After plugging in the switch's power adapter, all that's required is to run an Ethernet cable from any RJ-45 port on the router to any RJ-45 port on the switch, as shown in Figure 16.10.

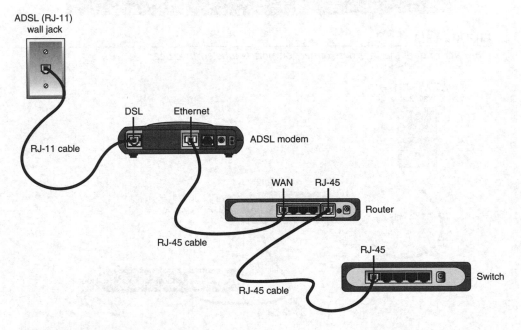

FIGURE 16.10

If your network includes a switch, run an Ethernet cable from an RJ-45 port on the router to an RJ-45 port on the switch.

Laying the Network Cable

Your final hardware-related network configuration chore is to lay the Ethernet cable for those computers and devices that will use a wired connection to the network. To do this, for each wired computer or device you run an Ethernet cable of the appropriate length from any RJ-45 port on your network's router or switch, to the RJ-45 port on the computer's or device's NIC.

You can prevent some cable problems and simplify your troubleshooting down the road by taking a few precautions and "ounce of prevention" measures in advance:

- First and foremost, always buy the highest-quality cable you can find. With network cabling, you get what you pay for.

- Make sure the cable you use is appropriate for the Ethernet standard your network uses. If you're running Fast Ethernet, you need Cat 5 cable; if you're running Gigabit Ethernet, you need Cat 5e or, even better, Cat 6 cable.

- Try to use a different-color cable for each computer or device. This makes it easy to know which computer or device is plugged into which port on the router or switch, and it simplifies the task of tracing a cable's path (for example, to see whether the cable is lying close to a source of electromagnetic radiation). If all your cables are the same color, consider adding your own labels for things such as the source and destination of the cable.

- To avoid electromagnetic interference, don't run cable near electronic devices, power lines, air conditioners, fluorescent lights, motors, and other electromagnetic sources.

- Try to avoid running cable in parallel with phone lines because the ringer signal can disrupt network data.

- To avoid the cable being stepped on accidentally, don't run it under carpet.

- To avoid people tripping over a cable (and possible damaging the cable connector, the NIC port, or the person doing the tripping!), avoid high-traffic areas when laying the cable.

- If you plan to run cable outdoors, either use special outdoor Ethernet cable or use conduit or another casing material to prevent moisture damage.

- Don't use excessive force to pull or push a cable into place. Rough handling can cause pinching or even breakage.

Changing the Computer and Workgroup Name

At this point, you pretty much have a working network: The data line is connected to the broadband modem, the modem is connected to the router, the router is connected to the switch (if you have one), and all your wired devices are connected to the switch (or router). What's left? Just a couple of things:

- For both wired and wireless clients, the machines will be able to access the network and your network chores will be easier if each computer has a unique name and every computer uses the same workgroup name. This section shows you how to modify the computer and workgroup names in Windows Vista.

- For your wireless clients, you need to know how to connect them to your wireless network. That's the topic of the next section.

Here are the steps to follow to change the computer name and workgroup name in Vista:

1. Click Start, right-click Computer, and then click Properties. (You can also press Windows Logo+Pause/Break.) The System window appears.

2. In the Computer Name, Domain, and Workgroup Settings section, click the Change Settings link. The User Account Control dialog box appears.

3. Enter your UAC credentials to continue. The System Properties dialog box appears with the Computer Name tab displayed.

4. Click Change. The Computer Name/Domain Changes dialog box appears, as shown in Figure 16.11.

5. Use the Computer Name text box to modify the name of the computer, if necessary.

note The default workgroup name in Windows Vista is Workgroup. If your network uses exclusively Vista machines, you probably won't have to change any workgroup names. However, it's a good idea to check the workgroup name for each computer.

tip Another way to open the System Properties dialog box with the Computer Name tab displayed is to press Windows Logo+R (or select Start, All Programs, Accessories, Run), type `systempropertiescomputername` (you can also type `control sysdm.cpl,,1`), click OK, and then enter your UAC credentials.

note Computer names can be a maximum of 64 characters and should include only letters, numbers, or hyphens (-).

note You need to change the computer name only if the current name conflicts with another computer on the network or if you want to use a more descriptive name. (The computer names appear in Vista's Network window, so descriptive names help you differentiate your computers.)

FIGURE 16.11

Use the Computer Name/Domain Changes dialog box to change your computer and workgroup names.

6. Select the Workgroup option.

7. Use the Workgroup text box to type the common workgroup name; you can enter a maximum of 15 characters.

8. Click OK. A dialog box welcoming you to the new workgroup appears.

9. Click OK. Windows Vista tells you that you must restart the computer to put the changes into effect.

10. Click OK to return to the System Properties dialog box.

11. Click Close. Vista prompts you to restart your computer.

12. Click Restart Now. Vista restarts you computer.

Making Wireless Network Connections

You learned earlier how to configure the wireless settings on your router's wireless AP. With that chore complete and with a wireless NIC installed, you're ready to access your wireless network. Note, however, that although connections to wired networks are automatic, Vista doesn't establish the initial connection to a wireless network automatically. This is mostly a security concern because a password or security key protects most wireless networks.

However, it's also usually the case (particularly in dense, urban neighborhoods) that Vista might detect multiple wireless networks within range, so it's up to you to specify which of those networks is your own. Fortunately, you can configure Vista to remember a wireless network's settings and automatically connect to your network the next time you log on to Vista. So, in most cases, you need to run through the connection procedure only once.

> **note** It's perfectly okay for one computer to have both a wired and a wireless connection for your network. In fact, as long as your computer has both an Ethernet and a wireless NIC, having both connections running simultaneously is a good idea because it gives you connection redundancy: If one connection goes down, you still have the other connection to perform your network chores.

Connecting to a Wireless Network

Here are the steps to follow to connect to your wireless network:

1. Select Start, Connect To. Vista opens the Connect to a Network dialog box, which displays a list of the available wireless networks, as shown in Figure 16.12. Each network displays three pieces of information:

   ■ The left column displays the network name (the SSID).

   ■ The middle column tells you whether the network requires a password or security key (Security-enabled network) or not (Unsecured network). After you connect to a wireless network, this column displays Connected for that network.

   ■ The signal strength, as indicated by the five bars to the right; the more green bars you see, the stronger the signal. Note that the networks are in descending order of signal strength.

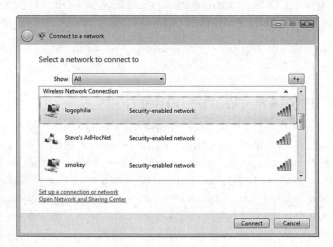

FIGURE 16.12

The Connect to a Network window displays a list of the wireless networks that are in range.

2. Select your network.

3. Click Connect. If the network you want to use is unsecured—as your network may be, and as are most public hot spots—Vista connects to the network immediately (so skip to step 6). However, most private wireless networks are (or should be) secured against unauthorized access. In this case, Windows Vista prompts you to enter the required security key or password.

4. Type the security key or password. Note that Vista displays dots in place of each character, as shown in Figure 16.13. This is a security feature just in case someone is looking over your shoulder.

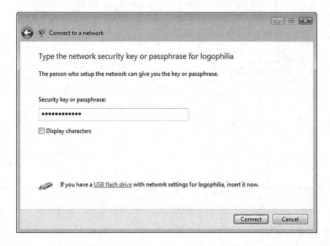

FIGURE 16.13

To access a secured wireless network, you must enter a security key or password.

5. Click Connect. Vista attempts to connect to the wireless network. If the connection went through, you see a dialog box named Successfully Connected to *Network*, where *Network* is the name of the network.

6. This dialog box gives you two options (both activated by default; see Figure 16.14):

    ■ **Save This Network**—When activated, this check box tells Vista to save the network in the Manage Wireless Networks

note If your network's security key is long or complex, you might not be sure whether you entered the security key correctly. Because the prospect of something peeking over your shoulder isn't much of an issue in most home or small office networks, it's okay to activate the Display Characters check box to tell Vista to display the actual security key characters rather than dots.

16

window. You must leave this check box activated if you want to connect to the network in the future without having to reenter the security key.

■ **Start This Connection Automatically**—When activated, this check box tells Vista to connect to the network automatically the next time you log on to Vista. If you always want to connect to the network manually, deactivate this option. Note that if you deactivate the Save This Network check box, Vista deactivates and disables the Start This Connection Automatically check box.

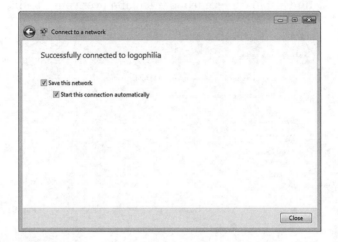

FIGURE 16.14

After a successful connection, Vista prompts you to save the wireless network.

7. Click Close. Vista prompts you to choose the location of your network.

8. Click Home or click Work (as the case may be; they both set up your network as a private network). The User Account Control dialog box appears.

9. Enter your UAC credentials to continue.

10. Click Close.

Disconnecting from a Wireless Network

If you no longer need to use your current wireless connection, follow these steps to disconnect it:

tip A faster way to disconnect is to right-click the Network icon in the taskbar's notification area, select Disconnect From, and then select your current connection.

1. Select Start, Connect To. Vista displays the Connect to a Network dialog box.

2. Select your current connection. (This is the network that displays Connected in the middle column.)

3. Click Disconnect. Vista asks you to confirm.

4. Click Disconnect. Vista disconnects from the network.

5. Click Close.

From Here

- For some information on Ethernet, **see** "Getting Wired: Understanding Ethernet Networks," **p. 132**.

- To learn more about switches, **see** "A Connection Point for Your Network: The Switch," **p. 142**.

- If you need a bit of router background before you start, **see** "Adding the Internet into the Mix with a Router," **p. 144**.

- For some information on wireless networking, **see** "Going Wireless: Understanding Wi-Fi Networks," **p. 154**.

- To learn the basic steps for inserting an Ethernet or wireless expansion card, **see** "Installing an Expansion Card," **p. 211**.

Maintaining Your Computer Hardware

A man builds a fine house; and now he has a master, and a task for life: he is to furnish, watch, show it, and keep it in repair, the rest of his days.

—Ralph Waldo Emerson, *Society and Solitude*

Now that you've cobbled together a new computer (or refurbished an old one) with the sweat of your own brow, you can just sit back and play with your PC, right? Well, sure, why not? For now at least. You see a new computer is something like a new garden, which at first looks great and is nice and neat and tidy. After a while, however, the maintenance chores start: removing the weeds, splitting overly large plants, moving plants to more suitable locations, dead-heading flowers, and on and on. It's the same thing with a PC. No, there are no dead flowers to pinch off, but there are plenty of other maintenance tasks to take care of: cleaning the computer inside and out; updating the BIOS, firmware, and device drivers; making backups; checking and defragmenting the hard drive; and on and on. This is the unglamorous side of computing (not that there's much of a glamorous side, but you get my point), but these chores are necessary if you want your PC to last until at least you're ready to build another one!

Cleaning the Computer

One of the things I've noticed about building PCs is that every new computer I construct always strikes me as a beautiful piece of machinery. Objectively I know that some of my creations are just plain black (or whatever) boxes, but subjectively they're all works of computing art. Why should that be so? Because of a very simple but very powerful phenomenon that's common to all do-it-yourselfers, and that you've probably already noticed yourself: If you build something with your own hands, that creation is always beautiful in your eyes. That shouldn't be surprising because, after all, you planned the PC, you researched and bought the parts, and you put everything together carefully and patiently. That machine has got a lot of *you* in it!

So, yes, your home-built PC is a beautiful hunk of technology, no doubt about it. However, in the long run it's only as good-looking as it is clean and, most unfortunately, computers never stay clean for very long. Screens get fingerprints on them; keyboards collect crumbs and other particles; mice get grimy; and, unless you've got some kind of heavy-duty air purifier on the job, all computer parts are world-class dust magnets.

To keep your computer looking sharp, you should give it a thorough cleaning every so often (how often depends on your own cleanliness standards and outside factors such as how dusty your room is).

Dust: Your PC's Worst Nightmare

As you've seen, your PC has interior fans that serve to flow air through the system and keep it cool. There's usually at least one intake fan that brings in cool air from the outside of the case and at least one exhaust fan that blows out hot air from inside the case. Unfortunately, in most environments the intake fan brings in lots of junk along with the outside air: mostly dust, but also human hair, pet hair, carpet fibers, and whatever else might be hanging around at ground level. Most of this grime takes up residence inside the case, which can be very bad for your computer's health:

- Dust collects on electrical connections, which can make those connections unreliable.

- A component that's covered in dust will retain more heat, which could cause it to perform erratically or even to fail because of overheating.

- The excess heat that dusty components generate causes your overall system to run hotter. This can make your system louder (because the fans have to work harder to cool the system) and can shorten the lifespan of crucial components such as the processor.

Dust, clearly, is a bad thing, but how should you deal with it? There are two ways to tackle the dust problem:

caution If you use canned air, be sure to always keep the can upright to avoid spraying liquid over your components!

- **Compressed gas or air**—This is a can of air or a gas such as carbon dioxide under pressure, and you use it to blow away dust and other debris. I'm not a huge fan of this method because all it tends to do is blow the dust back into the air where it will simply settle elsewhere. However, it's often useful for getting to dust in areas where a vacuum (discussed next) can't reach.

tip Ideally, the vacuum's hose and attachments won't have any metal parts that could damage a PC's components. If you're looking to buy a vacuum, get one with all-plastic accessories.

- **Vacuum**—Be sure to use an attachment that has soft bristles to avoid damaging any of the sensitive electronics inside your PC. If you want to take things up a notch, get a computer vacuum, which has attachments specifically designed for cleaning computers, as shown in Figure 17.1. If you want to go the whole hog, get an electronics vacuum that has an antistatic feature (and a hefty price tag, too).

FIGURE 17.1

A vacuum designed to work with computers and other electronic components.

Cleaning the Screen, Keyboard, and Mouse

The most frequent object of your cleaning duties will be the screen (because you look at it all day) and the mouse and keyboard (because you handle them all day). Here are the basic cleaning steps for these components:

1. Turn off and unplug the PC and the monitor, and remove any other cables attached to the PC.

2. Use a soft, dry, clean cloth to wipe any excess dust from the screen, keyboard, and mouse. If these components are still dirty (fingerprints, smudges, and so on), continue with the remaining steps.

3. Take a soft, clean cloth and dampen it with water. Be sure to merely dampen the cloth because you don't want there to be any excess water that might drip off the cloth.

4. Use the damp cloth to wipe the screen, keyboard, and mouse.

5. Using a soft brush attachment, vacuum your keyboard to suck up any dust or other particles that have settled in between (and even below) the keys. (If you can't get a particular piece of debris out from under a key, you can usually pop off the key, vacuum up the offending particle, and then reattach the key.)

Cleaning the Front and Back of the PC

The exterior of the PC collects a ton of dust over time, which not only looks ugly, but also can harm your computer, as I described earlier. Here are the basic steps you should follow to clean the exterior (I cover the power supply separately in the next section):

1. If you haven't done so already, turn off and unplug the PC and the monitor, and remove any other cables attached to the PC.

2. On the front of the PC, check for and, if necessary, vacuum any dust accumulating around the optical drive. If your vacuum has a micro-crevice attachment (see Figure 17.2), use it to suck up the dust in the crevices around the drive.

FIGURE 17.2

Vacuum the dust around the optical drive, ideally with a micro-crevice attachment.

3. Vacuum any dust accumulating around the floppy drive, if your PC has one.

4. Dust always builds up around the case's front intake fan (see Figure 17.3), so give that area of the case a good vacuum.

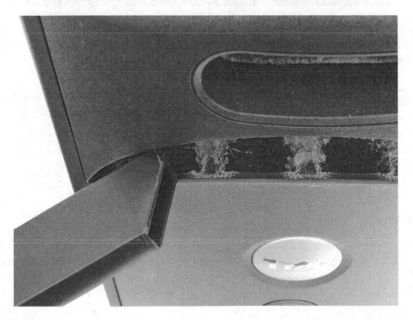

FIGURE 17.3

Vacuum the dust around the opening to the case's front intake fan.

5. Use a soft brush attachment to vacuum any dust accumulating around the ports that are on the front of the PC.

6. On the back of the PC, use a soft brush attachment to vacuum any dust accumulating around the case's slot covers and the connectors for any devices inserted into the motherboard slots (see Figure 17.4).

FIGURE 17.4

Vacuum the dust around the slot covers and expansion card connectors with a soft brush attachment.

7. Use a soft brush attachment to vacuum any dust accumulating around (and inside) the motherboard's back panel connectors

8. The case grill that covers the exhaust fan is a prime spot for dust to collect (see Figure 17.5), so give that area a thorough vacuuming.

9. Vacuum any other stray dust that you see on rear of the computer.

Cleaning the Power Supply

Back in Chapter 1, "The Barebones: The Motherboard, Case, and Power Supply," I introduced you to the power supply and made the case that it was one of the most important components in any PC because your machine needs a strong and steady supply of power to operate efficiently and steadily.

The importance of the power supply also means you should take extra care to keep it clean, so I'll cover the cleaning of this component separately.

→   **See** "Power to the PC: The Power Supply Unit," **p. 34**.

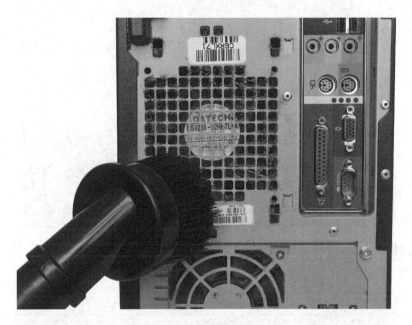

FIGURE 17.5

Vacuum the dust collecting on the exhaust fan grill.

Cleaning the power supply requires both external and internal steps, as follows:

1. If you haven't done so already, turn off and unplug the PC and the monitor and remove any other cables attached to the PC.

2. Use a soft brush attachment to vacuum any dust on the grill that covers the power supply, as shown in Figure 17.6.

3. If the back of the power supply (the part you see when you look at the back of the computer case) has a removable grill, detach the grill. (The grill is usually held in place with four screws.)

4. Use a soft brush attachment to vacuum dust from the blades of the power supply's fan.

5. Open the computer case.

6. Use a soft brush attachment to vacuum the front of the power supply, as shown in Figure 17.7.

> **tip** If the fan blades rotate as you try to vacuum them, insert a screwdriver or long, thin vacuum attachment between the grill (if it's still on) to hold the fan blades in place while you vacuum.

FIGURE 17.6

Vacuum the dust from the power supply grill.

FIGURE 17.7

Vacuum the dust from the front of the power supply inside the case.

We'll continue our cleaning duties inside the case in the next section, so leave your case open for now if you're following along.

Cleaning the Interior

It's important both aesthetically and functionally to keep dust and other grime off the outside of your PC, but cleanliness is paramount on the inside of the machine because that's where the most sensitive components are found. Here's a general cleaning procedure to follow on the inside of the PC:

1. If you haven't done so already, turn off and unplug the PC and the monitor, remove any other cables attached to the PC, and open the case.

2. It's always best to clean from the top to the bottom, so vacuum the front of the power supply, if you haven't already done so. (I'm assuming here that your case has a top-mounted power supply. If your PSU is bottom-mounted instead, clean it last.)

3. Use a soft brush attachment to vacuum the cables, the optical drive and hard drive connections, and the empty drive bays.

4. If the CPU cooler has an accessible fan, use a soft brush attachment to vacuum the fan's blades.

5. If you have a micro-crevice attachment (or some other small attachment), fit it between the CPU cooler's fan blades and vacuum any dust that has accumulated on the CPU cooler's fins, as shown in Figure 17.8.

6. If you have a small brush attachment, use it to clean the blades of the case fans, as shown in Figure 17.9.

caution While you're on a roll, you might be tempted to open the power supply case to clean inside. Don't do it! Power supplies can retain huge voltages for long periods, so by messing around inside the PSU case you risk a massive (and possible life-threatening) shock.

note It's vital to keep the CPU cooler's fins dust-free to ensure that the cooler does its job effectively. If you can't get at the fins, or if you can only vacuum up some of the dust on the cooling fins, unscrew the fan and remove it. (Note that you might also need to disconnect the fan's power lead from the motherboard's CPU fan header.) Now that you can access the fins easily, switch to a brush attachment, particularly one with relatively long bristles, and vacuum the dust from the fins.

17

FIGURE 17.8

Vacuum the dust from the CPU cooler's fins.

FIGURE 17.9

Vacuum the dust from the case fan blades.

7. Use the softest brush attachment you have to carefully vacuum the expansion cards and their motherboard slots, as shown in Figure 17.10.

FIGURE 17.10

Use a soft brush attachment to vacuum dust from the expansion cards and their slots.

8. If you see dust accumulated in the slot used by an expansion card or memory module, remove the component, vacuum the slot, and then reinsert the component.

9. Vacuum the case floor.

10. If the case has one or more air filters, remove the filters, run them through warm water to remove the dust, use a lint-free cloth to dry the filters, and then reinsert them.

> **caution** Avoid using a really powerful vacuum to clean sensitive internal parts because the strong suction on such a vacuum could loosen or damage components. Either dial back the vacuum speed (if possible) or get a vacuum designed for electronics, which uses far less suction than most ordinary vacuums.

Updating the Motherboard BIOS

It's always a good idea to keep your PC's motherboard BIOS up-to-date with the latest version. Board manufacturers are

17

always coming out with new BIOS versions that fix bugs, improve performance, and add new features, so you should check periodically for updates.

Most motherboards offer one or both of the following methods for updating the BIOS:

- Go to the motherboard's home page on the manufacturer's site, locate the latest BIOS version, download the program that updates the BIOS, and then run the program.

- Go to the motherboard's home page on the manufacturer's site, locate the latest BIOS version, download the latest version to your computer, and then use a tool in the BIOS configuration program to apply the update.

See the manual that came with your motherboard for the details. Alternatively, visit the motherboard's home page or support page and look for BIOS update instructions.

tip If the grime on any component resists the vacuum, use a small brush—I use a photographer's lens-cleaning brush, but a new paint brush or makeup brush will also do the job—to loosen the dirt and then vacuum it up. Be sure to use slow, light strokes to avoid building up static electricity, particularly if you're brushing something on the motherboard or an expansion card.

tip With the card or module out of its slot, this is a great time to clean the contacts. You can use a soft, lint-free cloth for this, or you can get contact cleaning solution specially designed for cleaning electronic contacts.

To give you a few examples of how BIOS updating works, the next five sections give you the instructions for updating the five motherboards we used in this book's PC-building projects.

Updating the BIOS for the Intel D975XBX2

Before updating any BIOS, always check your current version. With the Intel D975XBX2, you have two ways to do this:

- **System Setup**—Power up the PC and press F2 to enter System Setup, the Intel D975XBX2 BIOS configuration program. In the Main page, the BIOS Version item tells you what you need to know.

- **System Information (Windows)**—Open the System Information utility as described in Chapter 15, "This Old PC: Renovating a Computer," and then examine the BIOS Version/Date data in the System Summary branch.

→ **See** "Running the Device Manager and System Information Utilities," **p. 455**.

The Intel D975XBX2 BIOS version consists of six alphanumeric values separated by dots, as in this example:

`BX97520J.86A.2809.2007.1213.0017`

The first two values (`BX97520J.86A` in the example) identify the BIOS, and the third value (`2809` in the example) is the one you want because it identifies the actual BIOS version. (The rest of the BIOS value tells you the date and time the BIOS was released.) So, suppose the previous value is what your BIOS currently shows, and the Intel website tells you that the following is the version of the current BIOS:

`BX97520J.86A.2813.2008.0114.2256`

You can see that the current BIOS version number is 2813, which is later than your BIOS (2809), so you should upgrade.

Here are the steps to follow to update the BIOS for the Intel D975XBX2:

1. Use a web browser to navigate to the board's home page (see Figure 17.11):

   `support.intel.com/support/motherboards/desktop/d975xbx2/index.htm`

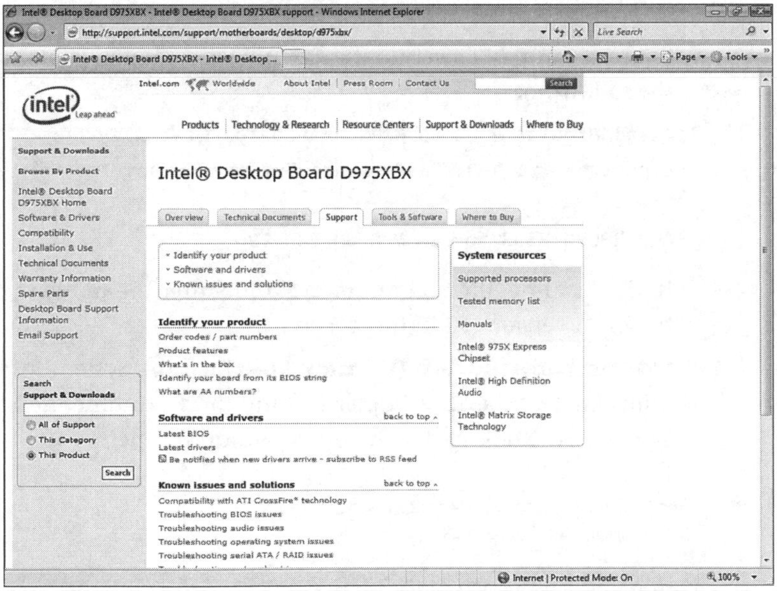

FIGURE 17.11

The home page for the Intel D975XBX2 motherboard.

2. Click the Latest BIOS link.

3. Click the link for the most recent BIOS.

4. Click the Download link for the Express BIOS file (the one with EB in the name).

5. Click the BIOS Update link.

6. If Internet Explorer blocks the download, click the Information Bar and then click Download File.

7. Click Run and then click Run again when the file is downloaded.

8. If you're running Vista, enter your User Account Control credentials to proceed. The Intel Express BIOS Update Setup program starts.

9. Click Next.

10. Click Yes.

11. Click Finish. The program updates the BIOS.

Updating the BIOS for the Gigabyte GA-MA69GM-S2H

Let's begin by checking the current BIOS version. With the Gigabyte GA-MA69GM-S2H, you have two ways to do this:

- **System Setup**—Power up the PC and immediately look for text like the following:

```
Award Modular BIOS v6.00PG, An Energy Star Ally
Copyright (C) 1994-2007, Award Software, Inc.


AMD RS690 BIOS for GA-MA69GM-S2H F2
```

In the last line, the alphanumeric value after the motherboard name is the BIOS version (F2 in this case).

- **System Information (Windows)**—Open the System Information utility as described in Chapter 15, and then examine the BIOS Version/Date data in the System Summary branch.

➔   **See** "Running the Device Manager and System Information Utilities," **p. 455.**

The Gigabyte GA-MA69GM-S2H BIOS version consists of a letter followed by a number, and the higher the number, the later the BIOS version. For example, if your

tip To pause the startup so you can read this message, press the Pause/Break key. When you're done, press Enter to resume the startup

motherboard has BIOS version F2 and Gigabyte reports that version F4 is available, you should upgrade.

Here are the steps to follow to download the latest BIOS version for the Gigabyte GA-MA69GM-S2H:

1. Use a web browser to navigate to the board's home page (see Figure 17.12):

    www.gigabyte.us/Products/Motherboard/Products_
    Overview.aspx?ProductID=2574

FIGURE 17.12

The home page for the Gigabyte GA-MA69GM-S2H motherboard.

2. Click the BIOS link.

3. Click the Download link for the most recent BIOS.

4. Click the Download link from the download location you want to use.

5. If Internet Explorer blocks the download, click the Information Bar and then click Download File.

6. Click Run and then click Run again when the file is downloaded. The WinRAR Self-Extracting Archive window appears.

7. Select a location to store the BIOS update file (you can use your hard drive or a floppy drive).

8. Click Install. The BIOS update file is extracted and then saved to the location.

You now have two ways to update the BIOS:

- **QFlash**—This is a BIOS program you can run without having to boot into Windows. Restart the PC and then press End to enter the QFlash Utility. Select Update BIOS from Drive, select the drive where the BIOS update file is stored, and then select the BIOS file you extracted.

- **@BIOS**—This is a Windows utility you can install from the Utility CD that comes with the motherboard. (Start the setup program, click Software Applications, and then click the Install button beside @BIOS.) Select Start, All Programs, Gigabyte, @BIOS. (In Windows Vista, you need to enter your UAC credentials to continue.) In the Gigabyte @BIOS Writer window (see Figure 17.13), click Update New BIOS, select the BIOS update file you extracted, and then click Open.

> **caution** Gigabyte claims that you can use a USB flash drive to store the BIOS update file, but this doesn't seem to be the case.

> **note** The BIOS update filename is ma69gms2.*ver*, where *ver* is the version number of the update. For example, if the BIOS version is F4, the filename is ma69gms2.f4

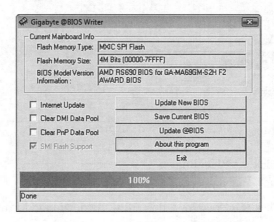

FIGURE 17.13

Use the @BIOS utility to update the BIOS from within Windows.

Updating the BIOS for the ASUS P5K3 Deluxe/WiFi-AP

First let's check the current BIOS version. With the ASUS P5K3 Deluxe/WiFi-AP, you have two ways to do this:

- **System Setup**—Power up the PC and press Delete to enter BIOS Setup Utility, the BIOS configuration program for the ASUS P5K3 Deluxe/WiFi-AP. In the Main page, select System Information and then under AMIBIOS, examine the Version number.

- **System Information** (Windows)—Open the System Information utility as described in Chapter 15 and then examine the BIOS Version/Date data in the System Summary branch.

→   **See** "Running the Device Manager and System Information Utilities," **p. 455**.

The ASUS P5K3 Deluxe/WiFi-AP BIOS version is a four-digit number, where higher numbers indicate later updates.

Here are the steps to follow to download the latest BIOS version for the ASUS P5K3 Deluxe/WiFi-AP:

1. Use a web browser to navigate to the board's home page (see Figure 17.14):

    www.asus.com/products.aspx?l1=3&l2=11&l4=0&model=1645

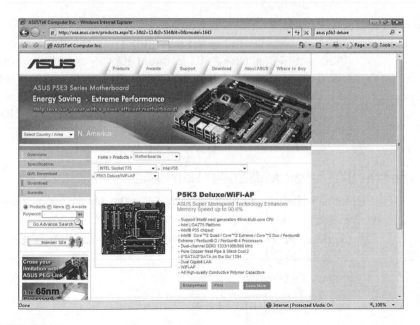

FIGURE 17.14

The home page for the ASUS P5K3 Deluxe/WiFi-AP motherboard.

2. Click Download to open the download page for the P5K3 Deluxe.

3. Click the plus sign (+) beside BIOS to display the available BIOS versions.

4. In the latest version, click the link for the download location you want to use.

> **note** The BIOS update file-name is P5K3-ASUS-Deluxe-*ver*.ROM, where *ver* is the version number of the update. For example, if the BIOS version is 1001, the filename is P5K3-ASUS-Deluxe-1001.ROM.

5. Click Save.

6. Choose a save location for the Zip file and click Save.

7. Click Open and then click Allow.

8. Extract the ROM file to your hard drive.

You now have two ways to update the BIOS:

- **EZ Flash**—This is a BIOS program you can run without having to boot into Windows. Restart the PC and then press Alt+F2 to enter the EZ Flash BIOS ROM Utility. After the utility finds the updates on your system, select the drive, select the BIN file, and then press Enter. The utility checks the file and then displays the new version number in the Update ROM section. When the utility asks whether you want to update the BIOS, select Yes.

- **ASUS Update**—This is a Windows utility you can install from the DVD that comes with the motherboard. (Start the setup program, click Utilities, and then click ASUS Update.) Select Start, All Programs, ASUS, ASUSUpdate, ASUSUpdate. (In Windows Vista, you need to enter your UAC credentials to continue.) In the ASUS Update window (see Figure 17.15), select Update BIOS From File, click Next, select the BIOS update file, and click Open.

Updating the BIOS for the ASUS Striker Extreme

First let's check the current BIOS version. With the ASUS Striker Extreme, you have two ways to do this:

- **System Setup**—Power up the PC and immediately look for text like the following:

```
Phoenix - AwardBIOS v6.00PG
Copyright (C) 1984-2007, Phoenix Technologies, LTD


ASUS StrikerExtreme ACPI BIOS Revision 1203
```

In the last line, the numeric value at the end is the BIOS version (1203 in this case).

> **tip** To pause the startup so you can read this message, press the Pause/Break key. When you're done, press Enter to resume the startup.

■ **System Information (Windows)**—Open the System Information utility as described in Chapter 15 and then examine the BIOS Version/Date data in the System Summary branch.

➜ **See** "Running the Device Manager and System Information Utilities," **p. 455**.

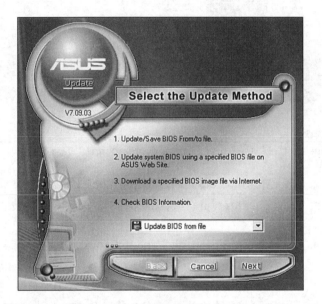

FIGURE 17.15

Use the ASUS Update utility to update the BIOS from within Windows.

The ASUS Striker Extreme BIOS version is a four-digit number, where higher numbers indicate later updates.

Here are the steps to follow to download the latest BIOS version for the ASUS Striker Extreme:

1. Use a web browser to navigate to the board's home page (see Figure 17.16):

   www.asus.com/products.aspx?l1=3&l2=11&l4=0&model=1439

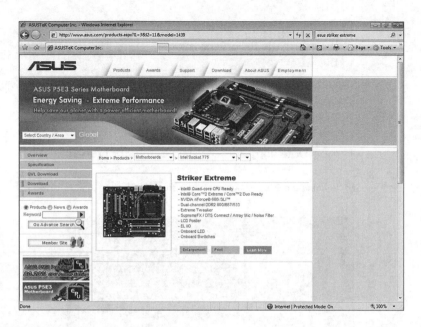

FIGURE 17.16
The home page for the ASUS Striker Extreme motherboard.

2. Click Download to open the download page for the Striker Extreme.

3. Click the plus sign (+) beside BIOS to display the available BIOS versions.

4. In the latest version, click the link for the download location you want to use.

5. Click Save.

6. Choose a save location for the Zip file and click Save.

7. Click Open and then click Allow.

8. Extract the .BIN file to your hard drive.

You now have two ways to update the BIOS:

■ **EZ Flash**—This is a BIOS program you can run without having to boot into Windows. Restart the PC and then press Alt+F2 to enter the EZ Flash BIOS ROM Utility. After the utility finds the updates on your system, select the drive, select the

> **note** The BIOS update file-name is SE*ver*.BIN, where *ver* is the version number of the update. For example, if the BIOS version is 1502, the filename is SE1502.BIN.

BIN file, and then press Enter. The utility checks the file and then displays the new version number in the Update ROM section. When the utility asks whether you want to update the BIOS, select Yes.

> **tip**
>
> To pause the startup so you can read this message, press the Pause/Break key. When you're done, press Enter to resume the startup

- **ASUS Update**—This is a Windows utility you can install from the DVD that comes with the motherboard. (Start the setup program, click Utilities, and then click ASUS Update.) Select Start, All Programs, ASUS, ASUSUpdate, ASUSUpdate. (In Windows Vista, you need to enter your UAC credentials to continue.) In the ASUS Update window (see Figure 17.15, earlier), select Update BIOS From File, click Next, select the BIOS update file, and click Open.

Updating the BIOS for the ASUS M2A-VM HDMI

First let's check the current BIOS version. With the ASUS M2A-VM HDMI, you have two ways to do this:

- **System Setup**—Power up the PC and immediately look for text like the following:

```
Phoenix - AwardBIOS v6.00PG
Copyright (C) 1984-2007, Phoenix Technologies, LTD


ASUS M2A-VM HDMI ACPI BIOS Revision 0902
```

In the last line, the numeric value at the end is the BIOS version (0902 in this case).

- **System Information (Windows)**—Open the System Information utility as described in Chapter 15 and then examine the BIOS Version/Date data in the System Summary branch.

→ **See** "Running the Device Manager and System Information Utilities," **p. 455**.

The ASUS M2A-VM HDMI BIOS version is a four-digit number, where higher numbers indicate later updates.

Here are the steps to follow to download the latest BIOS version for the ASUS M2A-VM HDMI:

1. Use a web browser to navigate to the board's home page (see Figure 17.17):

   www.asus.com/products.aspx?l1=3&l2=11&l4=0&model=1585

17

FIGURE 17.17
The home page for the ASUS M2A-VM HDMI motherboard.

2. Click Download to open the download page for the M2A-VM HDMI.

3. Click the plus sign (+) beside BIOS to display the available BIOS versions.

4. In the latest version, click the link for the download location you want to use.

5. Click Save.

6. Choose a save location for the Zip file and click Save.

7. Click Open and then click Allow.

8. Extract the .BIN file to your hard drive.

You now have two ways to update the BIOS:

■ **EZ Flash**—This is a BIOS program you can run without having to boot into Windows. Restart the PC and then press Alt+F2 to enter the EZ Flash BIOS ROM Utility. After the utility finds the updates on your

note The BIOS update file-name is M2A-VM-HDMI-*ver*.BIN, where *ver* is the version number of the update. For example, if the BIOS version is 1604, the filename is M2A-VM-HDMI-1604.BIN.

system, select the drive, select the BIN file, and then press Enter. The utility checks the file and then displays the new version number in the Update ROM section. When the utility asks whether you want to update the BIOS, select Yes.

- **ASUS Update**—This is a Windows utility you can install from the DVD that comes with the motherboard. (Start the setup program, click Utilities, and then click ASUS Update.) Select Start, All Programs, ASUS, ASUSUpdate, ASUSUpdate. (In Windows Vista, you need to enter your UAC credentials to continue.) In the ASUS Update window (see Figure 17.15, earlier), select Update BIOS From File, click Next, select the BIOS update file, and click Open.

Updating Device Drivers

For most users, device drivers exist in the nether regions of the PC world, shrouded in obscurity and the mysteries of assembly language programming. As the middlemen brokering the dialogue between the operating system and your hardware, however, these complex chunks of code perform a crucial task. After all, it's just not possible to unleash the full potential of your system unless the hardware and the operating system coexist harmoniously and optimally. To that end, you need to ensure that your operating system is using appropriate drivers for all your hardware.

The first thing you have to do is go to the manufacturer's website and find the most up-to-date driver for the device. Refer to Chapter 8, "Basic Skills for PC Building and Upgrading," for some tips on locating device drivers on manufacturer's websites.

→ See "What Software Do You Need?," **p. 192**.

After you have the latest and greatest driver, you install it using Device Manager, which I talked about in Chapter 15.

→ See "Running the Device Manager and System Information Utilities," **p. 455**.

Follow these steps to update a device driver in Windows Vista:

1. If you have a disc with the updated driver, insert it. If you downloaded the driver from the Internet, decompress the driver file, if necessary.
2. In Device Manager, click the device you want to work with.

> **note** When you look at the hardware section for your driver, bear in mind that Device Manager uses the word *adapter* for an expansion card. So a video card is a *display adapter* and a network interface card is a *network adapter*.

3. Select Action, Update Driver Software. (You can also click the Update Driver Software button in the toolbar or open the device's properties sheet, display the Driver tab, and click Update Driver.) The Update Driver Software wizard appears.

caution If the downloaded driver is contained within a compressed file (such as a Zip file), be sure to decompress the file before moving on to the next wizard step.

4. Click Browse My Computer for Driver Software.

5. In the Browse for Driver Software on Your Computer dialog box, shown in Figure 17.18, type the location of the driver files (or click Browse and use the Browse for Folder dialog box to select the location) and click Next. Windows Vista installs the driver software.

6. When the installation is complete, click Close.

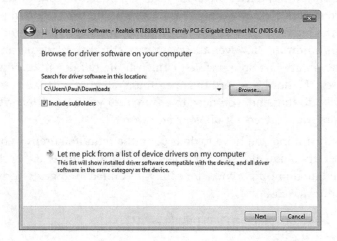

FIGURE 17.18

Let the Update Driver Software know where your downloaded device driver is located.

Creating a System Image Backup

The worst-case scenario for PC problems is a system crash that renders your hard disk or system files unusable. Your only recourse in such a case is to start from scratch with either a reformatted hard disk or a new hard disk. This usually means you have to reinstall the operating system and then reinstall and reconfigure all your applications. In other words, you're looking at the better part of a day, or—more likely—a few days, to recover your system.

However, Windows Vista has a feature that takes most of the pain out of recovering your system. It's called Complete PC Backup, and it's part of the System Recovery Options that come with the Windows Vista DVD.

note Complete PC Backup is available with Windows Vista Business, Enterprise, and Ultimate.

The safety net used by Complete PC Backup is actually a complete backup of your Windows Vista installation; this is a *system image*. It takes a long time to create a system image (at least several hours, depending on how much stuff you have), but it's worth it for the peace of mind. Here are the steps to follow to create the system image:

1. Select Start, All Programs, Accessories, System Tools, Backup Status and Configuration.

2. Select Complete PC Backup.

3. Click Create a Backup Now and enter your UAC credentials to launch the Windows Complete PC Backup Wizard.

4. The wizard asks you to specify a backup destination. You have two choices (click Next when you're ready to continue):

   ■ **On a Hard Disk**—Select this option if you want to use a disk drive on your computer. If you have multiple drives, use the list to select the one you want to use.

   ■ **On One or More DVDs**—Select this option if you want to use DVDs to hold the backup.

5. Windows Complete PC Backup automatically includes your internal hard disk in the system image, and you can't change that. However, if you also have external hard drives, you can add them to the backup by activating their check boxes. Click Next. Windows Complete PC Backup asks you to confirm your backup settings.

6. Click Start Backup. Windows Complete PC Backup creates the system image.

7. When the backup is complete, click Close.

Checking Your Hard Drive for Errors

Our hard disks store our programs and, most importantly, our precious data, so they have a special place in the computing firmament. They ought to be pampered and coddled to ensure a long and trouble-free existence, but that's rarely the case, unfortunately. Just consider everything that a modern hard disk has to put up with:

- **General wear and tear**—If your computer is running right now, its hard disk is spinning away at between 5,400 and 10,000 revolutions per minute (although the vast majority of drives run at 7,200RPM). That's right, even though you're not doing anything, the hard disk is hard at work. Because of this constant activity, most hard disks simply wear out after a few years.

- **The old bump-and-grind**—As I explained in Chapter 4, "Hard Drives and Other Storage Devices," your hard disk includes read/write heads that float on a cushion of air just above the spinning hard disk platters. A bump or jolt of sufficient intensity can send them crashing onto the surface of the disk, which could easily result in trashed data. If the heads happen to hit a particularly sensitive area, the entire hard disk could crash. Notebook computers are particularly prone to this problem.

→   See "Drive Time: How a Hard Drive Works," **p. 80**.

- **Power surges**—The current supplied to your PC is, under normal conditions, relatively constant. It's possible, however, for massive power surges to assail your computer (for example, during a lightning storm). These surges can wreak havoc on a carefully arranged hard disk.

So, what can you do about it? All versions of Windows come with a program called Check Disk that can check your hard disk for problems and repair them automatically. It might not be able to recover a totally trashed hard disk, but it can at least let you know when a hard disk might be heading for trouble.

Check Disk performs a battery of tests on a hard disk, including looking for invalid filenames, invalid file dates and times, bad sectors, and invalid compression structures. In the hard disk's file system, Check Disk also looks for the following errors:

- **Lost cluster**—This is a cluster that, according to the file system, is associated with a file, but that has no link to any entry in the file directory (it's also sometimes called an *orphaned cluster*). Program crashes, power surges, or power outages are some typical causes of lost clusters. If Check Disk comes across lost clusters, it offers to convert them to files in either the file's original folder (if Check Disk can determine the proper folder) or in a new folder named `Folder.000` in the root of the `%SystemDrive%`. (If that folder already exists, Check Disk creates a new folder named `Folder.001` instead.) In that folder, Check

Disk converts the lost clusters to files with names like `File0000.chk` and `File0001.chk`. You can look at these files (using a text editor) to see whether they contain any useful data and then try to salvage it. Most often, however, these files are unusable and most people just delete them.

> **note** Large hard disks are inherently inefficient. Formatting a disk divides the disk's magnetic medium into small storage areas called *sectors*, which usually hold up to 512 bytes of data. A large hard disk can contain tens of millions of sectors, so it would be too inefficient for the operating system to deal with individual sectors. Instead, all operating systems groups sectors into *clusters*, the size of which depends on the file system and the size of the partition. Most Windows hard drives now use the NTFS file system, which uses 4KB sectors for any drive larger than 2GB. Still, each hard disk has many thousands of clusters, so it's the job of the file system to keep track of everything. In particular, for each file on the disk, the file system maintains an entry in a *file directory*, a sort of table of contents for your files. (On an NTFS partition, this is the *Master File Table [MFT]*.)

- **Invalid cluster**—A cluster is one that falls under one of the following three categories: a file system entry with an illegal value, a file system entry that refers to a cluster number larger than the total number of clusters on the disk, a file system entry that is marked as unused but is part of a cluster chain. In this case, Check Disk asks whether you want to convert these lost file fragments to files. If you say yes, Check Disk truncates the file by replacing the invalid cluster with an EOF (end of file) marker and then converts the lost file fragments to files. These are probably the truncated portion of the file, so you can examine them and try to piece everything back together. More likely, however, you just have to trash these files.

- **Cross-linked cluster**—A cluster assigned to two different files (or twice in the same file). Check Disk offers to delete the affected files, copy the cross-linked cluster to each affected file, or ignore the cross-linked files altogether. In most cases, the safest bet is to copy the cross-linked cluster to each affected file. That way, at least one of the affected files should be usable.

- **File system cycle**—In an NTFS partition, a *cycle* is a corruption in the file system whereby a subfolder's parent folder is listed as the subfolder itself. For example, a folder named `C:\Users` should have `C:\` as its parent; if `C:\Users` is a cycle, `C:\Users`—the same folder—is listed as the parent instead. This creates a kind of loop in the file system that can cause the cycled folder to "disappear."

17

Here are the steps to follow to run Check Disk:

1. In the Computer folder (or My Computer in Windows XP), right-click the drive you want to check and then click Properties. The drive's properties sheet appears.

2. Display the Tools tab.

3. Click the Check Now button. (If you're running Windows Vista, you need to enter your User Account Control credentials to continue). The Check Disk window appears, as shown in Figure 17.19.

FIGURE 17.19

Use Check Disk to scan a hard disk partition for errors.

4. Activate one or both of the following options, if desired:

   ■ **Automatically Fix File System Errors**—If you activate this check box, Check Disk automatically repairs any file system errors that it finds. If you leave this option deactivated, Check Disk just reports on any errors it finds.

   ■ **Scan for and Attempt Recovery of Bad Sectors**—If you activate this check box, Check Disk performs a sector-by-sector surface check of the hard disk surface. If Check Disk finds a bad sector, it automatically attempts to recover any information stored in the sector and marks the sector as defective so that no information can be stored there in the future.

5. Click Start.

6. If you activated the Automatically Fix File System Errors check box and are checking a partition that has open system files, Check Disk will tell you that it can't continue because it requires exclusive access to the disk. It will then ask whether you want to schedule the scan to occur the next time you boot the computer. Click Schedule Disk Check.

7. When the scan is complete, Check Disk displays a message letting you know and provides a report on the errors it found, if any.

Defragmenting Your Hard Drive

All versions of Windows come with a utility called Disk Defragmenter that's an essential tool for tuning your hard disk. Disk Defragmenter's job is to rid your hard disk of file fragmentation. *File fragmentation* means that a file is stored on your hard disk in pieces that are scattered around the disk. This is a performance drag because, when Windows tries to open such a file, it must make several stops to collect the various chunks. If a lot of files are fragmented, it can slow even the fastest hard disk to a crawl.

Why doesn't Windows just store files contiguously? Recall that Windows Vista stores files on disk in clusters and that these clusters have a fixed size, depending on the disk's capacity. Recall, too, that Windows Vista uses a file directory to keep track of each file's whereabouts. When you delete a file, Windows Vista doesn't actually clean out the clusters associated with the file. Instead, it just marks the deleted file's clusters as unused.

When Windows is saving a new file to disk, for efficiency it just stores the first part of the file in the first available cluster, the second part in the next available cluster, and so on. Because these available clusters are almost always scattered randomly around the disk (because files are constantly being deleted), files often end up fragmented.

The good news with Windows Vista is that it configures Disk Defragmenter to run automatically—the default schedule is weekly: every Wednesday at 1:00 a.m. Therefore, you should never need to defragment your system manually. However, you might want to run a defragment before loading a particularly large software program.

Before using Disk Defragmenter, you should perform a couple of housekeeping chores:

- Delete any files from your hard disk that you don't need. Defragmenting junk files only slows down the whole process.

- Check for file system errors by running Check Disk as described earlier in this chapter (refer to "Checking Your Hard Drive for Errors").

Follow these steps to use Disk Defragmenter:

1. Select Start, All Programs, Accessories, System Tools, Disk Defragmenter. The Disk Defragmenter window appears, as shown in Figure 17.20. (Note that

note The easiest way to delete unneeded files from your system is to use Windows' Disk Cleanup tool. In the Computer folder (or My Computer in Windows XP), right-click the hard drive, click Properties, and then click Disk Cleanup.

this is the Disk Defragmenter window that comes with Vista Service Pack 1. If you're still running the original Vista release, your window will look a bit different.)

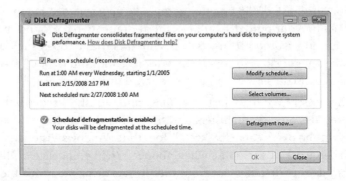

FIGURE 17.20

Use Disk Defragmenter to eliminate file fragmentation and improve hard disk performance.

2. (Vista Service Pack 1 or later) To change which disks get worked on when the program performs its weekly defragment, click Select Volumes to display the Disk Defragmenter: Advanced Options dialog box, deactivate the check box beside any disk you don't want defragmented, and then click OK to return to the Disk Defragmenter window.

> **tip** In some cases, you can defragment a drive even further by running Disk Defragmenter on the drive twice in a row. (That is, run the defragment, and when it's done immediately run a second defragment.)

3. Click Defragment Now. Windows Vista defragments your hard drives.

4. When the defragment is complete, click Close.

From Here

- For some background on read/write heads and other hard drive technologies, **see** "Drive Time: How a Hard Drive Works," **p. 80**.

- For some tips on locating device drivers on manufacturer's websites, **see** "What Software Do You Need?," **p. 192**.

- To learn how to use the Device Manager, **see** "Running the Device Manager and System Information Utilities," **p. 455**.

- To learn how to use the System Information utility, **see** "Running the Device Manager and System Information Utilities," **p. 455**.

Index

S

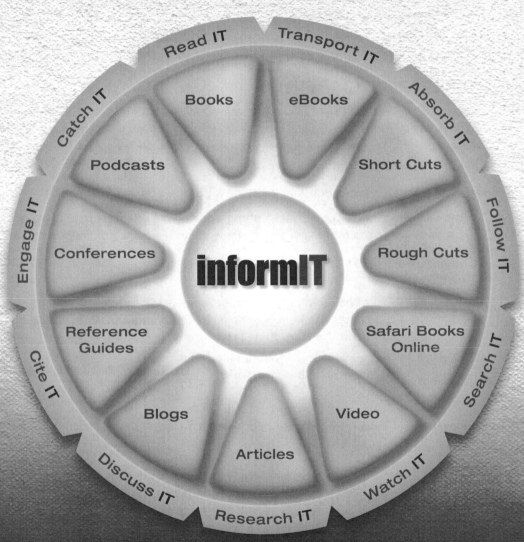

LearnIT at InformIT

Go Beyond the Book

Read IT

Transport IT

Catch IT

Absorb IT

Books

eBooks

Podcasts

Short Cuts

Engage IT

informIT

Follow IT

Conferences

Rough Cuts

Reference
Guides

Safari Books
Online

Cite IT

Search IT

Blogs

Video

Discuss IT

Watch IT

Articles

Research IT

11 WAYS TO LEARN IT at **www.informIT.com/learn**

The digital network for the publishing imprints of Pearson Education

Addison
Wesley

Cisco Press

EXAM/**CRAM**

IBM
Press

que

PRENTICE
HALL

SAMS